MACWORLD

GUIDE TO SYSTEM 7

By Lon Poole
Macworld *Quick Tips* Columnist

Foreword by Jerry Borrell

Editor-in-Chief, *Macworld* magazine

IDG BOOKS

IDG Books Worldwide, Inc.
An International Data Group Company
San Mateo, California 94402

Macworld Guide to System 7

Published by
IDG Books Worldwide, Inc.
An International Data Group Company
155 Bovet Road, Suite 730
San Mateo, CA 94402
(415) 358-1250

Library of Congress Catalog Card No.: 91-72754

ISBN 1-878058-16-9

Printed in the United States of America

10 9 8 7 6 5 4 3 2

Project Manager: Jeremy Judson, Associate Editor
Editor-in-Chief: Michael E. McCarthy
Production Manager: Lana Olson
Technical review by Dennis Cohen
Text preparation and proofreading by Shirley E. Coe
Indexing by Ty Koontz
Interior design by Peppy White and Francette Ytsma
Production by University Graphics, Palo Alto, California

Distributed in the United States by IDG Books Worldwide, Inc.
Distributed in Canada by Macmillan of Canada, a Division of Canada Publishing Corporation.
Publishing Corporation; by Woodslane Pty. Ltd. in Australia; and by Computer Bookshops in the U.K.

For information on translations and availability in other countries, contact Marc Mikulich, Foreign Rights Manager, at IDG Books Worldwide. Fax: (415) 358-1260.

For sales inquiries and special prices for bulk quantities, write to the address above or call IDG Books Worldwide at (415) 358-1250.

QUICK REFERENCE CARD

Exchanging Data with Publish and Subscribe

The Edit menu's Publish and Subscribe commands let you move information between documents and update it automatically when you change the original information. (Programs developed prior to System 7 do not have Publish and Subscribe commands.)

To publish information...

1. Select the information and choose Create Publisher.

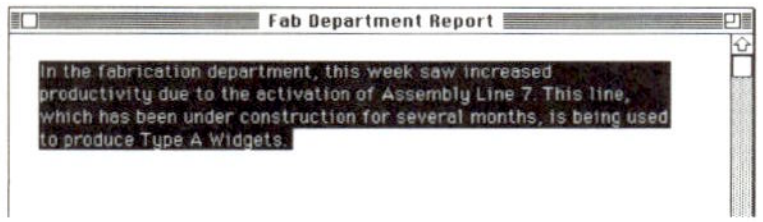

2. Name the edition and then click Publish.

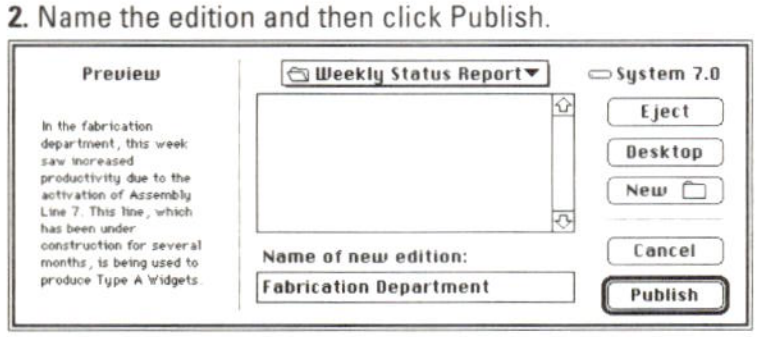

Published information is indicated by a light border

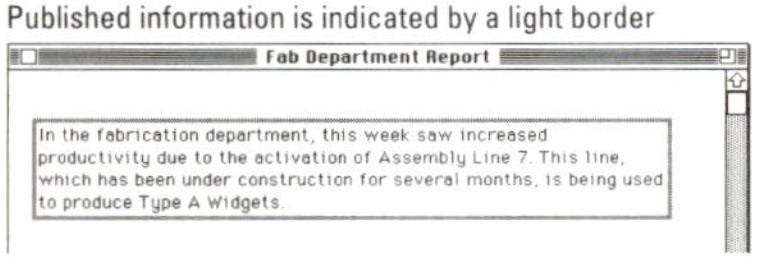

To subscribe to information...

1. Choose Subscribe To from the Edit menu.

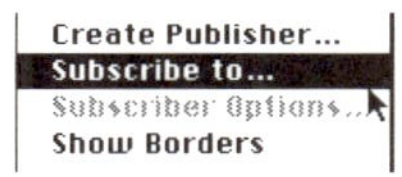

2. Locate the desired edition, and then click Subscribe.

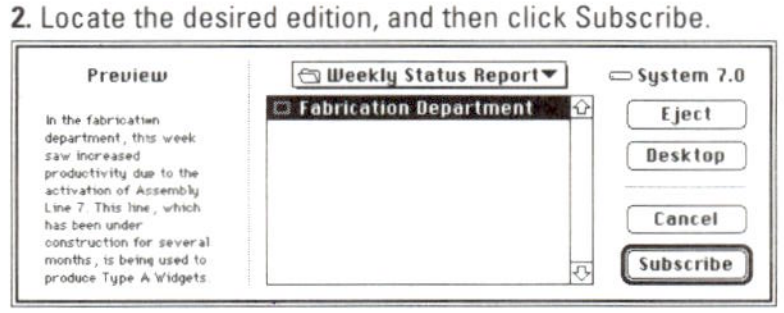

Information from an edition is indicated by a dark border.

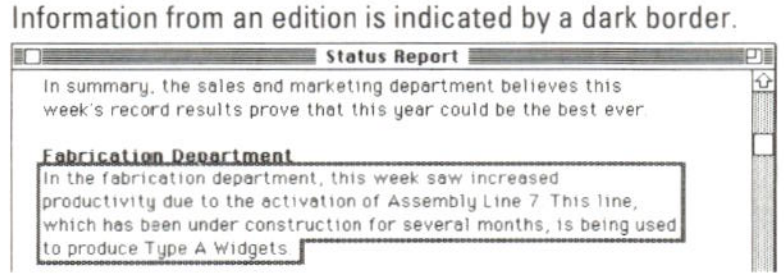

Specifying Subscriber Options for Updating

Use the Subscriber Options and Publisher Options commands to specify how and when subscribers receive the latest version of an edition. Check your program's manuals for additional options.

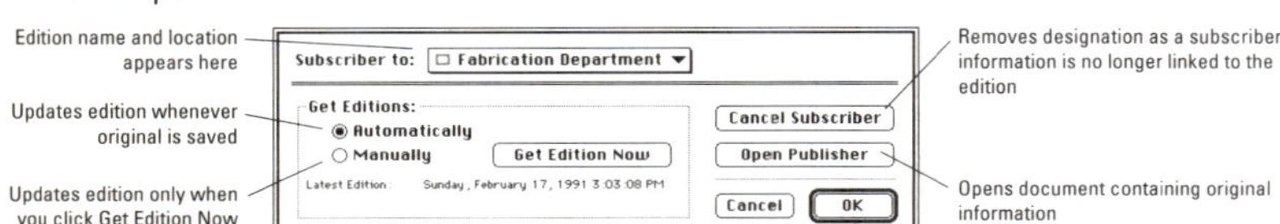

Specifying Publisher Options for Updating

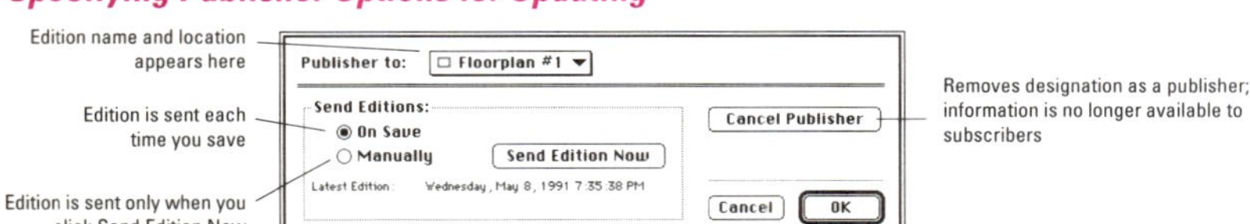

QUICK REFERENCE CARD

Sharing Folders and Hard Disks on a Network

System 7's file-sharing features allow you to share folders and entire hard disks with other Macintoshes on a network. To activate file sharing, open the Sharing Setup control panel and click the Start button in the File Sharing area. To share a folder, select the folder and choose Sharing from the Finder's File menu and then use the sharing dialog box as shown below.

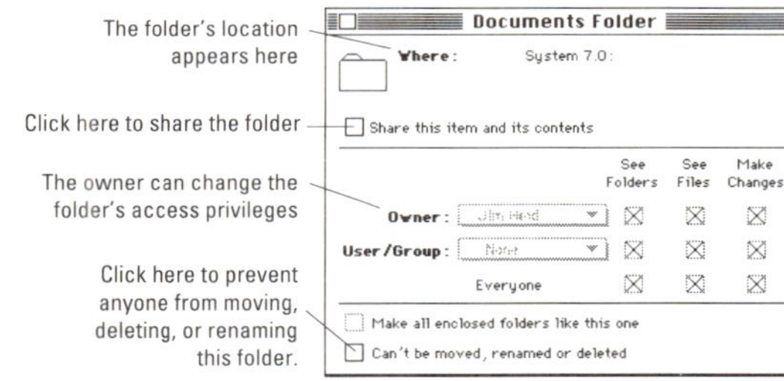

Access privileges allow you to control who can manipulate the files in a shared folder or disk. See Folders controls whether folders within the folder are visible; See Files governs whether files within the folder are visible; Make Changes denotes whether the folder's contents can be altered. You can specify access privileges for the folder's owner and for other users or groups of users.

Access Privilege Ideas

By configuring access privileges in various ways, you can be selective about who can access and modify shared folders. Four examples are shown below.

To do this...	Set privileges like this...	See Folders	See Files	Make Changes
Give everyone on the network all access privileges	Owner	☒	☒	☒
	User/Group	☒	☒	☒
	Everyone	☒	☒	☒
Keep a folder private so that only you can access it from other machines	Owner	☒	☒	☒
	User/Group	☐	☐	☐
	Everyone	☐	☐	☐
Share a folder with one person or group	Owner	☒	☒	☒
	User/Group	☒	☒	☒
	Everyone	☐	☐	☐
Keep a folder private but allow others to place files or folders in it	Owner	☒	☒	☒
	User/Group	☐	☐	☒
	Everyone	☐	☐	☒

File Sharing Icons and Access Privileges

Icon	What it means
	You can put items in this folder but you can't open the folder or access its contents
	You can't access or modify this folder
	You can use this folder normally
	You own this folder and can use it normally

ICONS IN DIRECTORY WINDOW HEADINGS

- You can't make changes to this folder.
- You can't see files within this folder.
- You can't see folders within this folder.

MACWORLD QUICK REFERENCE TO SYSTEM 7

QUICK REFERENCE CARD

Finder Shortcuts

To accomplish this...	do this...
Eject a disk and remove its icon	Drag the icon to the Trash or select the disk and choose Put Away (Command-Y).
Bypass the Trash warning dialog box	Press Option when choosing Empty Trash.
Select an icon from the keyboard	Type the first few characters of its name.
Hide the current application when switching to another application	Press Option while choosing the desired application from the application menu.
Rename an icon	Select it, press Return, and then start typing.
Quickly determine whether a file is locked or unlocked	Select the file and press Return. If no border appears around the name, the file is locked.
Organize icons by name	Choose By Name from View menu, then choose By Icon or By Small Icon. Next, press Option and choose Clean Up by Name.
Clean up everything	Press Option and choose Clean Up All.
Clean up selected items only	Press Shift and choose Clean Up Selection.
Close all disk/folder windows	Press Option while clicking a close box or choosing Close.
Copy an item from one folder to another (on the same disk) instead of moving it	Press Option while dragging the item to the destination folder.
Open an item and close its window	Press Option and double-click on the item.
Open the folder or disk window that holds the current directory window	Press Command while clicking on the window title, then choose desired folder or disk name.
Abort a program that seems to have crashed	Press Command-Option-Esc and click Force Quit.
Open a document using an application that may not have created it	Drag the document's icon to the application's icon.
Skip installing all system extensions during one startup	Hold down Shift during startup.
Zoom a directory window to fill the screen	Press Option while clicking the window's zoom box.
Copy an item to the desktop	Press Option and drag the item to the desktop.
Select the item nearest the upper-right corner of the desktop	Press Command-Shift-Up Arrow.
Change an item's icon	Copy a graphic to the Clipboard, and then select the item's icon in the Get Info window and choose Paste.

For more information on IDG Books, call 1-800-282-6657 or 415-358-1250.

MACWORLD QUICK REFERENCE TO SYSTEM 7

by Jim Heid

QUICK REFERENCE CARD

Open and Save Dialog Boxes

System 7 uses new Open and Save dialog boxes, whose components and keyboard shortcuts appear here. Programs developed prior to System 7 may not use the new components of the Save dialog box.

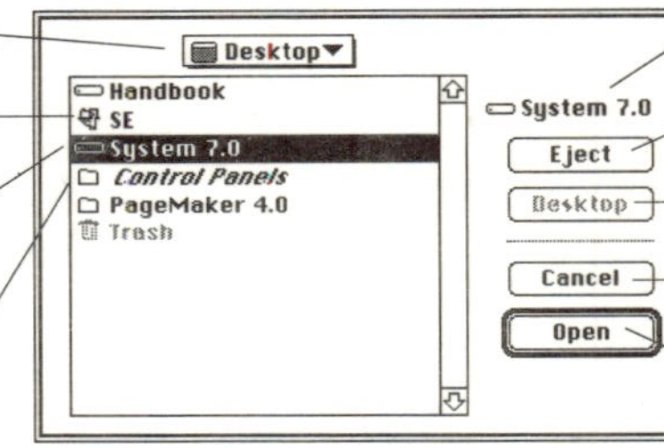

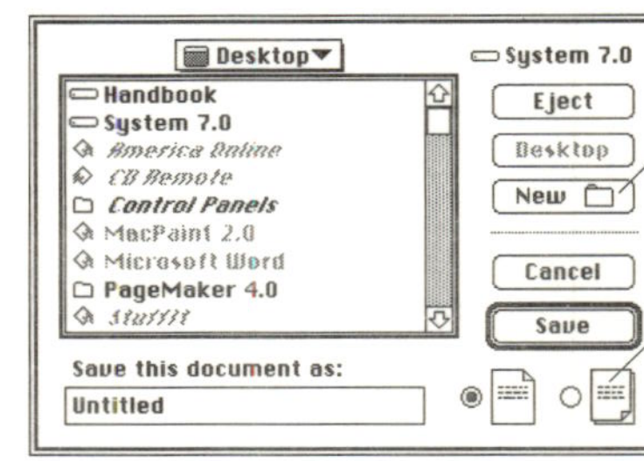

Switching Between Programs

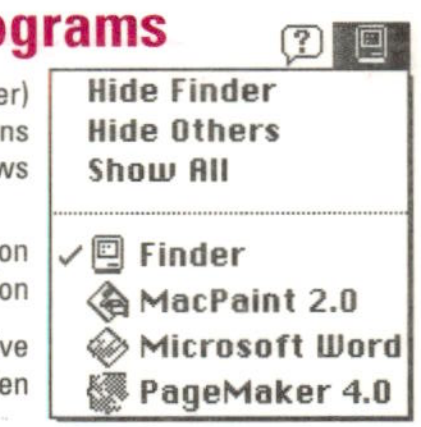

To switch to a different program, click within one of its windows, if any are visible. You can also use the application menu (at the right edge of the menu bar) to switch between programs and hide the windows of programs you aren't using.

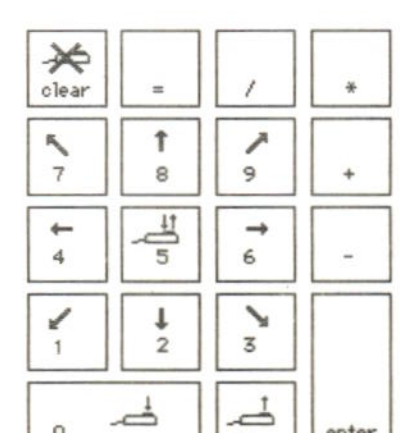

Easy Access' Mouse Keys

Mouse Keys lets you control the mouse pointer using the keypad. To activate Mouse Keys, press Command-Shift-Clear. The keypad's keys control the pointer as shown at left. To deactivate Mouse Keys, press Clear.

FINDER WINDOW SHORTCUTS

- Tab selects next icon alphabetically; Shift Tab selects previous
- Left and right arrow selects next or previous icon
- Command-right arrow expands folder outline; Command-Option-right arrow expands entire outline (Left arrow to collapse)

Acknowledgements

David Angell and Brent Heslop untied me from the log that was hurtling toward the spinning saw blade by stepping in at the last minute to research and write the initial draft of chapters 6, 8, and 9. They deserve credit for those three chapters, and I most gratefully acknowledge their contribution.

The real hero of this book is my wife. Thanks, Karin, for enduring my slavish attention to scribbling once again. You'll always be number one in my book.

(The publisher would also like to thank Bill Murphy, without whom this book would not have been possible.)

About the Author

Lon Poole, a *Macworld* magazine contributing editor, answers readers' questions every month in his column "Quick Tips." He also writes feature articles regularly, including "Installing Memory," which won a 1988 Maggie award for Best How-To Article in a Consumer Publication. His feature article "Here Comes System 7" was a finalist in the 1990 Excellence in Technology Communications competition. He helped found *Macworld* in 1983, and every issue ever published has carried at least one of his columns or articles.

In addition, Lon Poole has also authored four other Mac books, all published by Microsoft Press. They are *MacWork MacPlay* (1984), *Mac Insights* (1986), *HyperTalk* (1988), and *Big Book of Amazing Mac Facts* (1991). He also wrote the now-classic *Apple II User's Guide,* which sold over half a million copies worldwide. He has been writing books about personal computers and their practical applications since 1976 and has a BA in Computer Science from the University of California, Berkeley.

About IDG Books Worldwide

Welcome to the world of IDG Books Worldwide.

International Data Group (IDG) is the world's leading publisher of computer periodicals, with more than 150 weekly and monthly newpapers and magazines reaching 25 million readers in more than 40 countries. If you use personal computers, IDG Books is committed to publishing quality books that meet your needs. We rely on our extensive network of publications — including such leading periodicals as *Computerworld, InfoWorld, Macworld, PC World, Portable Computing, Publish, Network World, SunWorld, AmigaWorld,* and *GamePro* — to help us make informed and timely decisions in creating useful computer books that meet your needs.

Every IDG book strives to bring extra value and skill-building instruction to the reader. Our books are written by experts, with the backing of IDG periodicals, and with careful thought devoted to issues such as audience, interior design, use of icons, and illustrations. Our editorial staff is a careful mix of high-tech journalists and experienced book people. Our close contact with the makers of computer products helps ensure accuracy and thorough coverage. Our heavy use of personal computers at every step in production means we can deliver books in the most timely manner.

We are delivering books of high quality at competitive prices, on topics customers want. At IDG, we believe in quality, and we have been delivering quality for 25 years. You'll find no better book on a subject than an IDG book.

John Kilcullen
President
IDG Books Worldwide, Inc.

International Data Group's publications include: ARGENTINA'S Computerworld Argentina; ASIA'S Computerworld Hong Kong, Computerworld Southeast Asia, Computerworld Malaysia, Computerworld Singapore, Infoworld Hong Kong, Infoworld SE Asia; AUSTRALIA'S Computerworld Australia, PC World, Macworld, Lotus, Publish!; AUSTRIA'S Computerwelt Oesterreich; BRAZIL'S DataNews, PC Mundo, Automacao & Industria; BULGARIA'S Computer Magazine Bulgaria, Computerworld Bulgaria; CANADA'S ComputerData, Direct Access, Graduate CW, Macworld; CHILE'S Informatica, Computacion Personal; COLUMBIA'S Computerworld Columbia; CZECHOSLOVAKIA'S Computerworld Czechoslovakia, PC World; DENMARK'S CAD/CAM WORLD, Computerworld Danmark, PC World, Macworld, Unix World, PC LAN World, Communications World; FINLAND'S Mikro PC, Tietoviikko; FRANCE'S Le Mond Informatique, Distributique, InfoPC, Telecoms International; GERMANY'S AmigaWelt, Computerwoche, Information Management, PC Woche, PC Welt, Unix Welt, Macwelt RD; GREECE'S Computerworld, PC World, Macworld; HUNGARY'S Computerworld SZT, Mikrovilag; INDIA'S Computers & Communications; ISRAEL'S People & Computers; ITALY'S Computerworld Italia, PC World Italia; JAPAN'S Computerworld Japan, Macworld, SunWorld Journal; KOREA'S Computerworld, PC World; MEXICO'S Computerworld Mexico, PC Journal; THE NETHERLAND'S Computerworld Netherlands, PC World, AmigaWorld; NEW ZEALAND'S Computerworld New Zealand, PC World New Zealand; NIGERIA'S PC World Africa; NORWAY'S Conputerworld Norge, PC World Norge CAD/CAM, Macworld Norge; PEOPLE'S REPUBLIC OF CHINA'S China Computerworld, China Computerworld Monthly; PHILLIPPINE'S Computerworld Phillippines, PC Digest/PC World; POLAND'S Komputers Magazine, Computerworld; ROMANIA'S Infoclub; SPAIN'S CIM World, Communicaciones World, Computerworld Espana, PC World, AmigaWorld; SWEDEN'S ComputerSweden, PC/Nyhetherna, Mikrodatorn, PC World, Macworld; SWITZERLAND'S Computerworld Schweiz, Macworld; TAIWAN'S Computerworld Taiwan, PC World, Publish; THAILAND'S Computerworld; TURKEY'S Computerworld Monitor, PC World/Turkiye; UNITED KINGDOM'S Graduate Computerworld, PC Business World, ICL Today, Lotus UK, Macworld UK; UNITED STATES' AmigaWorld, A+, CIO, Computerworld, Digital News, Federal Computer Week, GamePro, InfoWorld, Lotus, Macworld, Network World, NextWorld, PC Games, PC World, Portable Office, PC Letter, Publish!, Run, SunWorld Journal; USSR'S MIR PC, Computerworld, Computer Express, Network, Manager Magazine; VENEZUELA'S Computerworld Venezuela, Micro Computerworld; YUGOSLAVIA'S Moj Mikro

The text this book is printed on recycled paper, and can be recycled.

Contents at a Glance

Table of Contents

Foreword

Do you understand the Macintosh Operating System; its system software? Do you ever wonder what impact the Mac's OS has on your computer and its software applications? Or wonder whether you are getting the most out of your Macintosh; whether you really understand all of its capabilities? Then buy this book and keep it near your computer.

Lon Poole's latest book *Macworld Guide to System 7* is your non-technical guide to the universe of Macintosh technology. A Macintosh Baedeker for everyone using the Mac's new system software; from the technically inept to the most gnarly nerd out there.

Lon was one of the founding editors of Macworld. After his last seven years of writing about the Macintosh for *Macworld*, I can confidently write that Lon knows more about the Mac than any single person outside of the engineering groups at Apple. In fact *Macworld* almost lost Lon to Apple two years ago — but that's another story. Happily he continues to write for *Macworld*, and also found time to write this book to help us all get through our confusion about Apple's latest system software.

Jerry Borrell
Editor-in-Chief, *Macworld*

Introduction

System 7 changes everything. After you install this new system software, your Apple Macintosh computer looks and feels different. On the surface it's almost as easy to use as the Macintosh you now know. But at another level System 7 makes your Macintosh more sophisticated, complicated, powerful, and fun than before. This book helps you take full advantage of System 7's power.

Whom This Book is For

This book is aimed at people who already know Macintosh basics such as choosing commands from menus, opening programs and documents, rearranging the contents of folders and disks, and copying information from one place and pasting it to another. About 95 percent of what you already know how to do transfers directly to System 7. Mastering the new system software means acquiring new skills, not learning new methods for old skills.

If you do need to learn Macintosh fundamentals, study the manual *Getting Started With Your Macintosh* or the disk *Your Tour of the Macintosh*. Both come with every Macintosh.

Macintosh veterans can also benefit from this book. If you are one, get started quickly with System 7 by reading the condensed coverage of it in the first chapter. Once you're comfortable with the new system software, pick up some tips about it by browsing Chapter 11.

How This Book is Organized

Macworld Guide to System 7 is really many books in one. First, a quick summary of System 7 contains just what you need to know to begin using System 7 immediately (Chapter 1). Second, a complete reference covers the new system software in detail (Chapters 2 – 10 and Chapter 12). Third, a tips digest lists lots of ideas for getting the most from System 7 (Chapter 11). Also included are two appendices — one (Appendix A) contains a product compatibility listing, which tells you what software and hardware will run on System 7, and the other (Appendix B) contains a glossary of terms commonly associated with System 7.

Chapter 1 concisely describes the many important new capabilities System 7 brings to the Macintosh. It also illustrates them and gives you condensed how-to instructions.

Chapter 2 shows how different System 7 looks compared to older system software. It also explains how interactive on-screen help works and how to have multiple programs open at once.

Chapter 3 details the myriad improvements in the Finder that help you organize your disks more effectively and find items in them more quickly than older Finders.

Chapter 4 covers the new special folders that organize the increasing chaos inside the System Folder. It also describes the new direct methods for installing fonts and other items in your System file.

Chapter 5 deals with changes that make desk accessories and control panels more versatile. It also tackles memory management, which gains new importance with System 7.

Chapter 6 gives you ideas for using aliases to better organize the contents of your disks and to streamline access to items you use frequently.

Chapter 7 examines Apple's TrueType font technology, which gives you smooth text at any size on screen and on any printer. It also correlates new fonts with old Macintosh fonts and PostScript fonts.

Chapter 8 explains how to share your files with other people whose computers are connected to yours, and how to share their files.

Chapter 9 explores the ability to automatically update copied material when the original material changes by using the new Publish and Subscribe commands.

Chapter 10 discusses how programs can work together. One program can use the commands and tools of other programs made by different program developers. Also covered is Apple's Data Access Language (DAL), which provides a common, simple method for getting data from a variety of large databases resident on host computers of all brands and sizes.

Chapter 11 contains a collection of tips and tricks for getting extra power, performance, and flexibility from System 7.

Chapter 12 wraps up by discussing the issues you face when you upgrade your Macintosh to System 7: equipment requirements, compatibility, networks with mixed system software versions, and where to get System 7.

Conventions Used in This Book

This book also contains COMPARISONS, WARNINGS, and TIPS to keep in mind as you learn System 7 concepts and are indicated by icons in the margins. Here is what to look for:

Comparisons explain both clear and subtle differences between System 7 and older system software.

Warnings alert you to possible problems or special exceptions you might encounter while operating System 7.

Quick Tips are how-to shortcuts that will save you time and trouble when executing an operation in System 7.

Undocumenteds include any concept or idea about System 7 not found in Apple's documentation.

Other Titles to Enhance Your Mac Knowledge

When you're through reading this book and you want to know more about Macs and what they can do, reach for the *Macworld Complete Mac Handbook*— the ultimate Mac reference that includes hardware and software from soup to nuts and powerful tips and shortcuts. The author, Jim Heid, is the "Getting Started" columnist for *Macworld* magazine where his column is the most widely read in the magazine.

For those interested in making music with the Macintosh, there's Christopher Yavelow's *Macworld Music & Sound Bible* — the only comprehensive and authoritative guide to using music, sound, digital audio, and multimedia on the Mac. Yavelow is a Macworld contributing writer and Hollywood "guru" in the music field — his clients and colleagues include David Copperfield, Jan Hammer, Quincy Jones, Herbie Hancock, Julian Lennon, Bob Moog, Steve Wozniak, and Frank Zappa.

Just getting started in the Mac world? Pick up the definitive guide to getting started with t he Mac, *Macworld Read Me First Book*. This is an anthology of subjects written by the leading Mac authors in their respective areas of expertise.

If networking's your niche, check out David Kosiur's *Macworld Networking & Communications Bible*. Whether your interests are in basic local area networks or communicatons in complex corporate MIS departments, this book's got you covered. Kosiur is the *Macworld* contributing editor for networking and network products. He is also Editor/Publisher of *Connections*, the industry authority on Macintosh network installations.

Summary

Conventional wisdom says the Macintosh is so easy to use you don't need to read books about it. In fact, discovering all the power System 7 gives your Macintosh would take months of exploring and experimenting. Reading this book shortcuts that process so you can put the full power of the new system software to work for you weeks earlier.

Macworld Guide to System 7 complements Apple's System 7 manuals. It contains lots of useful information you won't find in the manuals. It also provides a different perspective on any subjects you don't quite understand in the manuals. And because this book describes System 7 completely, you can use it instead of the reference manuals if you don't happen to have them.

To help make future editions of this book better, any feedback you could give would be especially appreciated. Please write to me, in care of IDG Books Worldwide, with questions or comments.

And now … let's get started!

7

Chapter 1

The Essence of System 7

In This Chapter

- Coloring windows and icons on a color Mac under System 7.
- The new Finder: making access and organization of information easier.
- How TrueType fonts improve the quality of on-screen text and printing devices.
- A look at file sharing under System 7.
- Multitasking: having as many programs open as will fit in your computer's memory.
- Virtual memory: increasing your Mac's memory without installing more RAM.
- A look at how balloon help makes learning new programs easier.
- Sharing information on documents dynamically by publishing and subscribing.
- IAC: giving your programs the ability to collaborate.
- A summary of System 7's data accessing capabilities.

If you want to grasp the essence of System 7 and you only have a couple of hours, read this chapter. Here you'll learn about the new features you can use as soon as you install System 7 as well as features that lay a foundation for future improvements in application programs.

As you read this chapter, you'll see three special symbols imbedded at the beginning of some paragraphs:

✔ Tells you which Macintosh models and what types of software can use the System 7 capabilities under discussion.

✘ Tells you about Macintosh models and software that can't use a particular System 7 capability.

☛ Refers you to another part of the book where you will find more information about the System 7 capability just discussed.

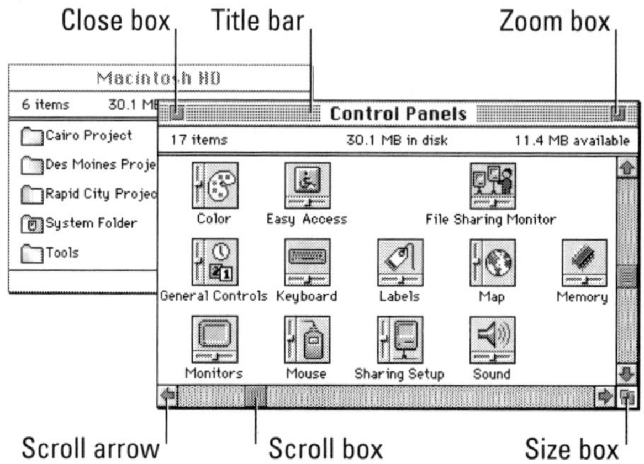

Figure 1-1
Shaded window controls

Color windows

Trendy three-dimensional shading modernizes all System 7 window frames on monitors displaying 16 colors or gray shades. Muted colors and shades of gray accent the window components under your control: title bar, close box, zoom box, size box, and scroll bars (Figure 1-1). Some of the colorized components even look like they work in three dimensions when you use them. For example, clicking the close box makes it look pressed down.

Only the active window has 3-D shading. It stands out from inactive windows behind it because System 7 displays inactive windows with gray borders and a gray title. Of course the contents of inactive windows are never dimmed so you can see the contents easily. Also, System 7 does not stray from white window backgrounds, a cornerstone of the Macintosh interface.

You choose one shading tint for all windows from nine tints listed in a pop-up menu in the Color control panel (Figure 1-2). The window tint you choose will not apply to tool palettes and special-purpose windows created by some application programs until the programs have been upgraded for System 7. You cannot create your own window-shading color using the Color control panel.

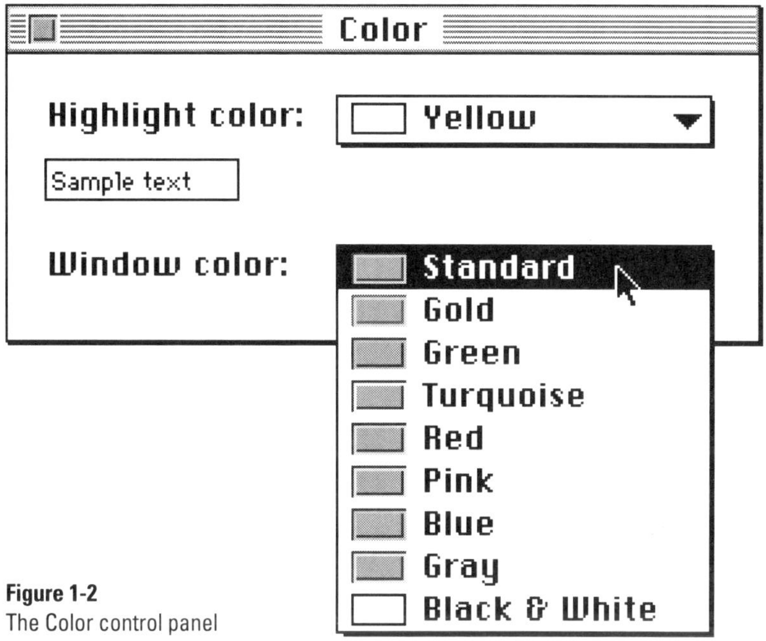

Figure 1-2
The Color control panel

✗ You see traditional black-and-white windows unless your Macintosh is displaying at least 16 grays or 256 colors.

☛ For more information, see "Windows" in Chapter 2.

Color icons

Color icons spruce up the System 7 desktop on systems displaying colors or grays. Apple has taken the same low-key approach with its icons as it has taken with windows, using gray shades and subdued colors to make them look three-dimensional (Figure 1-3). Bright colors are used mainly for highlights.

Prior to System 7, the small icons used in menus and Finder windows were mechanically shrunken from full-size icons. Now any program developer can design separate, better looking small icons (Figure 1-4).

✗ You see the same old black-and-white icons and shrunken icons for programs and documents until software developers update those programs with color icons and small icons.

☛ For more information, see "Icons" in Chapter 2.

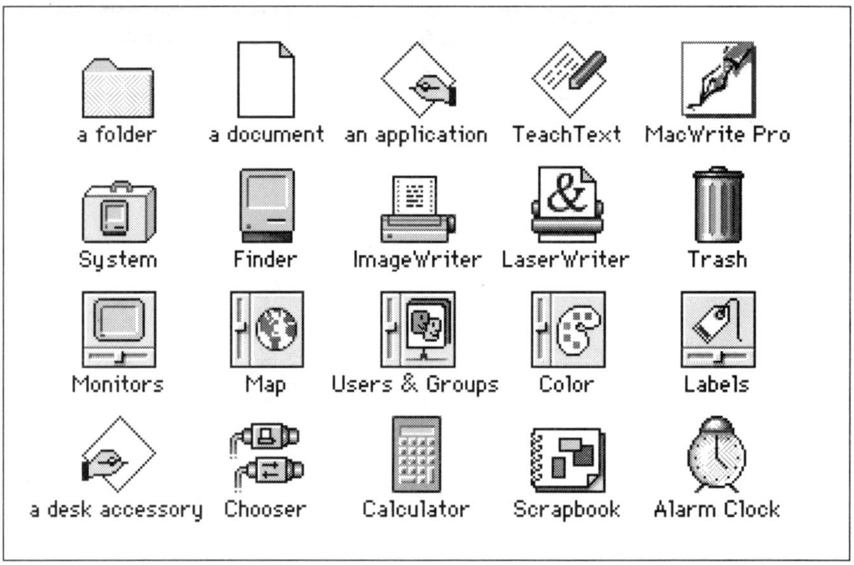

Figure 1-3
Some standard-size color icons

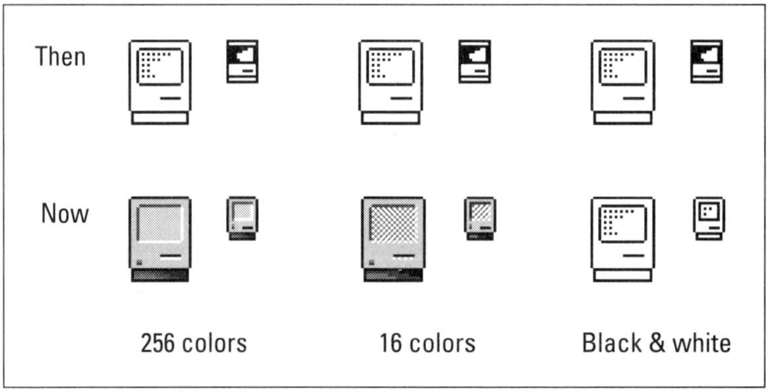

Figure 1-4
Large and small icons

Figure 1-5
Customizing an icon

Custom icons

Tired of the same old icons? Now you can replace individual full-size icons with your own designs (Figure 1-5). First you create a new icon design in color, grayscale, or black-and-white with a paint program. Copy the new icon to the Clipboard. In the Finder, select the icon you want to customize, choose Get Info from the File menu, select the icon in the Get Info window, and paste. The painting you copied replaces the current icon. If your painting is bigger than a standard icon (32 by 32 dots), it will be scaled down to fit the icon space.

✔ You can replace the icon of any unlocked file, folder, or disk. You cannot replace any system software icons such as the System Folder, Finder, Control Panels Folder, and Trash.

☛ For more information, see "Custom icons" in Chapter 3.

Editing icon names

Before you can edit the name of a disk, folder, program, document, or other item in Finder 7, you must carefully select the name. When the name is selected for editing, it has a box around it in addition to being highlighted (Figure 1-6). Clicking an icon no longer also selects the name for editing. The good news is you can no longer accidentally and perhaps unknowingly rename a selected document or folder by bumping the keyboard; the bad news is you have to relearn how to change icon names.

To select the name, you either click the icon and then press Return or Enter, or you click the name itself. After selecting the name, wait until the box appears around the name. Then you can click again to select an insertion point, double-click to select a word, or drag to select a range of text. If you click again too soon, the Finder thinks you're double-clicking the icon and opens it.

Figure 1-6
An icon name selected for editing

✘ Experienced Macintosh users will probably find the new method of editing icon names one of the toughest changes to get used to because old editing habits suddenly cause unexpected behavior.

☛ For more information, see "Editing icon names" in Chapter 3.

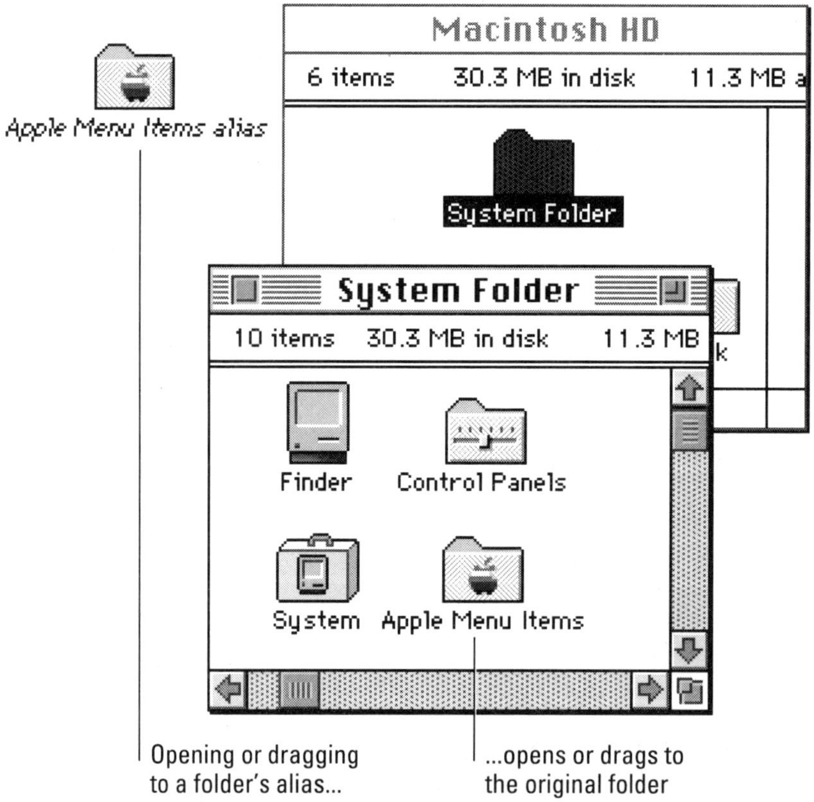

Figure 1-7
An alias and its original item

Aliases

Stop digging for documents, programs, folders, and other items buried deep within nested folders on who-knows-which disk. Instead, make aliases of the items you use frequently and put the aliases on the desktop, in the Apple menu, or in other accessible places. Aliases act like real items when you open them or drag items to them, but they are only small (1K to 3K) stand-ins. An alias looks exactly like the original item except its name is in italics and initially has the word alias as a suffix (Figure 1-7).

Making an alias

You make an alias by selecting an item and choosing Make Alias from the Finder's File menu. You can move the alias, change its name, set options using the Get Info command, classify it using the Label menu, all independently of the original item.

Using aliases

Aliases have a variety of uses (Figure 1-8), some of which are:

❖ Opening frequently used programs, documents, and folders from the desktop while the real items remain buried in nested folders.

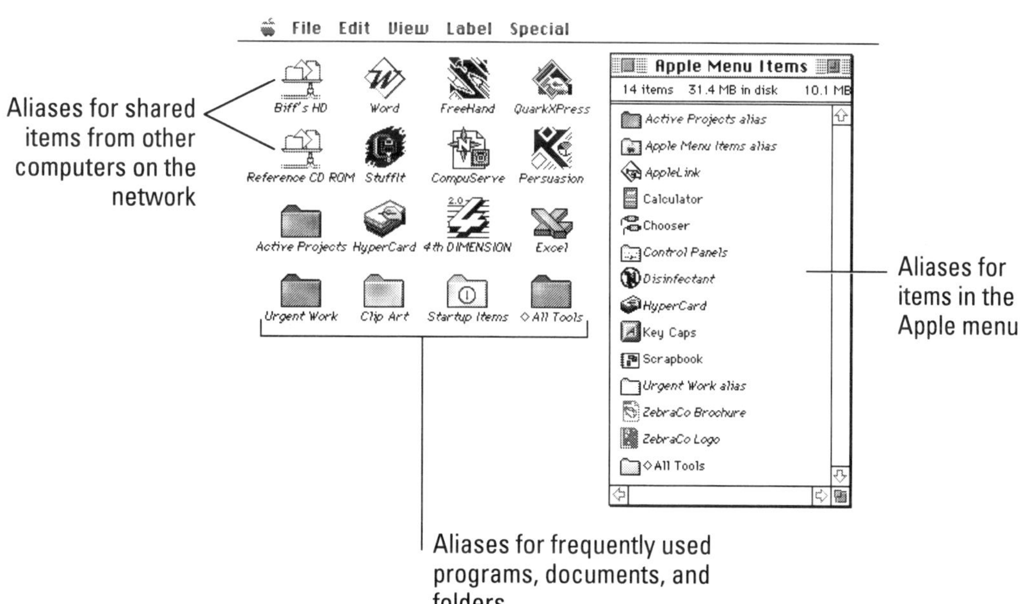

Figure 1-8
Some uses of aliases

❖ Adding items to the Apple menu without moving them from the folders they are in.

❖ Organizing documents and folders according to multiple filing schemes without duplicating items. For example, you could file documents by project, addressee, date, and topic.

❖ Simplifying access to file servers and individual items on servers. Opening an alias of an item on a server makes automatic connection with the server (except for providing the password, which you must type unless you got access to the original item as a guest).

❖ Getting nearly automatic access to your Mac's hard disks using a floppy disk in any other Mac on the same network.

✔ Aliases work with all software and on all Macintosh models that can use System 7.

☛ For more information, see Chapter 6.

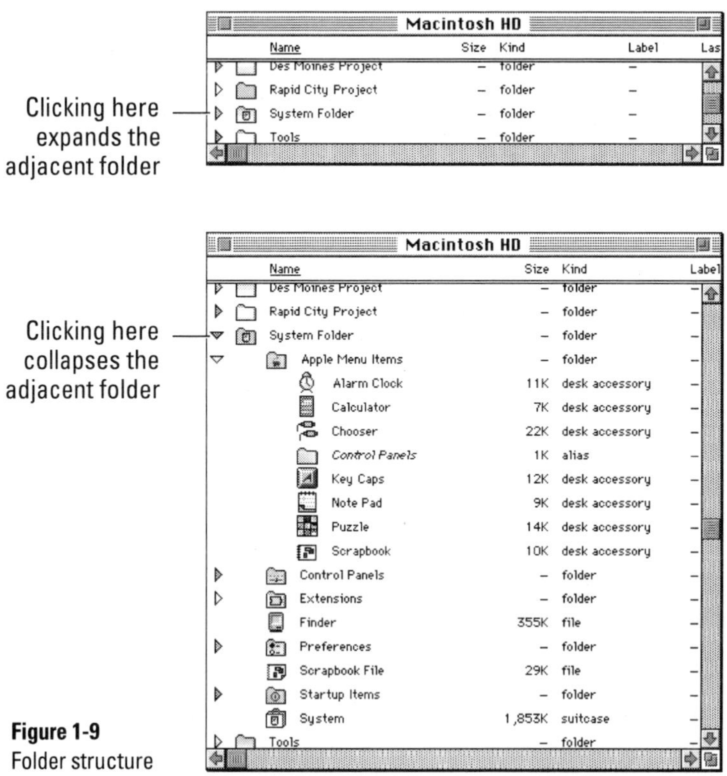

Figure 1-9
Folder structure

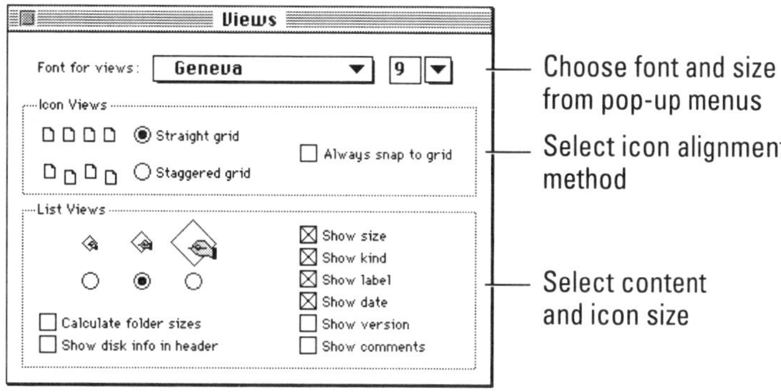

Figure 1-10
The Views control panel

Outlining folder structure

One of Finder 7's myriad improvements lets you see, select, and reorganize items from different folders in the same window. All list views (name, size, kind, and so forth) display folders and their contents in an indented outline format. The levels of indentation in the outline clearly diagram the structure of your nested folders. You can expand or collapse any level in the outline to show or hide the corresponding folder's contents by clicking a triangle next to the folder's icon (Figure 1-9).

Indented outlining works on all Macintosh models that can use System 7.

For more information, see "Outlining folder structure" in Chapter 3.

Custom views

The new Finder gives you control over the format and content of its windows. You select options using the Views control panel (Figure 1-10), and your settings immediately affect all windows. You can set:

- ❖ Font and size of text used for item names and window headings in all views
- ❖ Alignment method in icon and small icon views
- ❖ Content of and icon size in list views

List views (name, size, kind, and so forth) always include an icon and a name for every item. You select which of six other columns of information to include: size, kind, label, date, version, and comments. The last two are new in list views with System 7. You cannot change the order of the columns, only whether each appears or not.

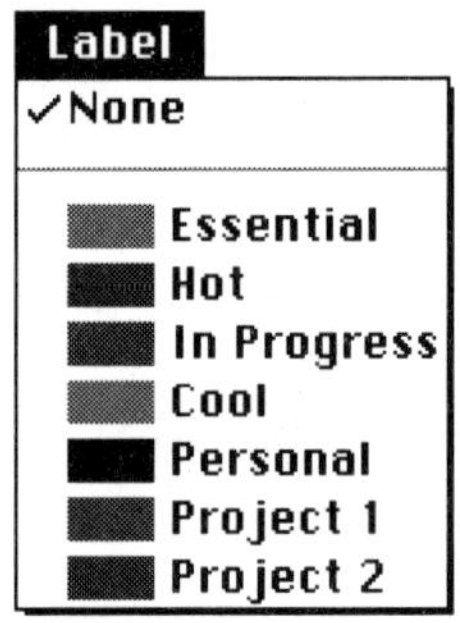

Figure 1-11
The Label menu

The Views control panel also lets you decide whether list views show folder sizes and whether the disk information that formerly appeared only in icon views also appears at the top of list views.

Custom views work on all Macintosh models that can use System 7.

For more information, see "Custom views" in Chapter 3.

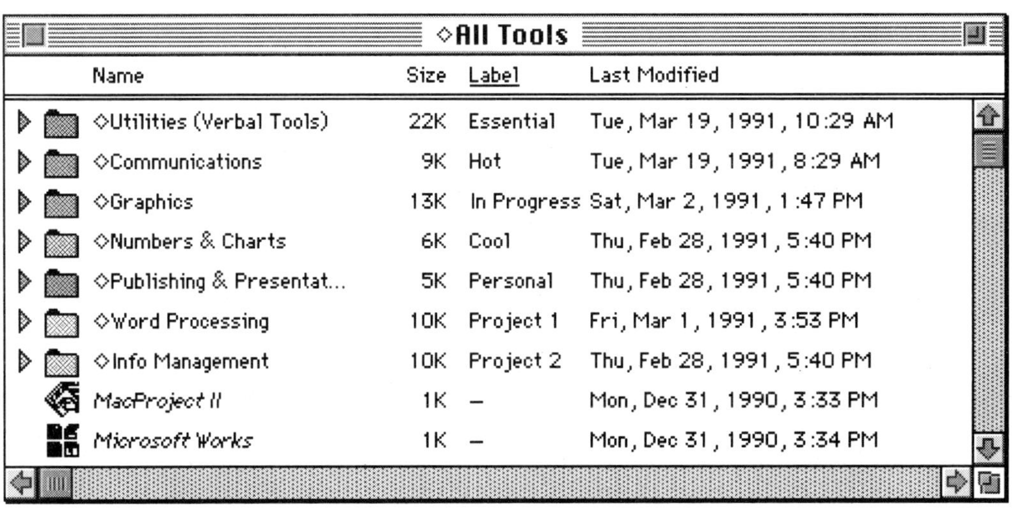

Figure 1-12
Viewing by label

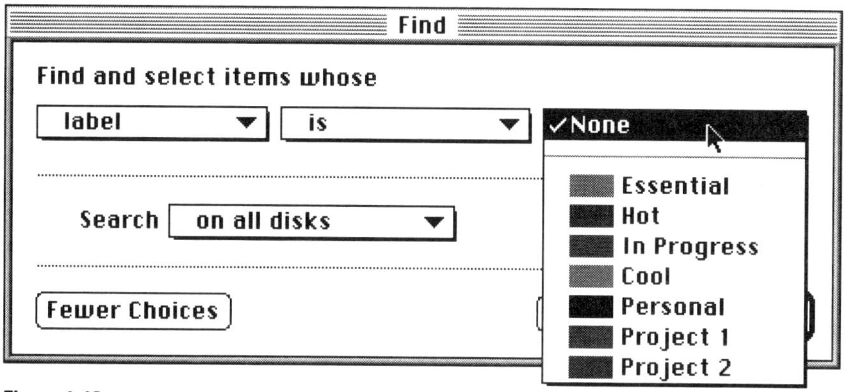

Figure 1-13
Finding by label

Item labels

The Finder now lets you classify folders, programs, and documents by labeling them with a word or phrase. On systems able to display colors, labeling an item also colorizes it. This capability is an extension of an older Finder's ability to colorize items.

Using labels

To label an item, select it and choose a label from the Finder's Label menu (Figure 1-11). After labeling items, you can view Finder window contents arranged by label (Figure 1-12). You can also search for items by label using the Finder's Find command (Figure 1-13).

Changing label names and colors

You change the standard label names and colors using the new Labels control panel (Figure 1-14).

✔ Icon labels work on all Macintosh models that can use System 7. You can see the standard seven label colors only on a monitor displaying at least 16 colors.

☛ For more information, see "Labeling items" in Chapter 3.

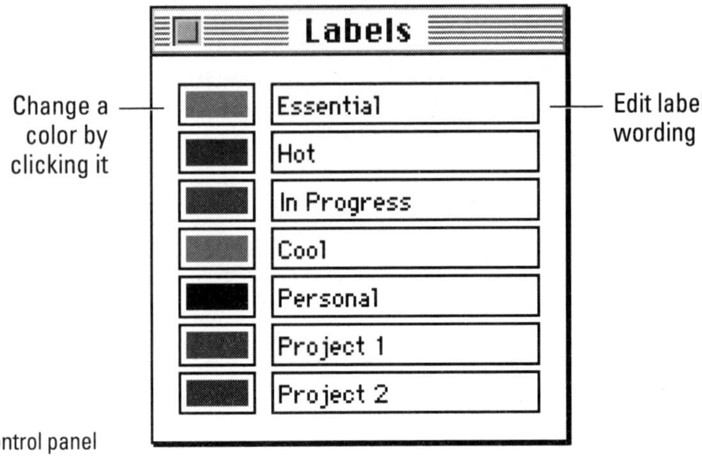

Figure 1-14
The Labels control panel

Smart Finder windows

A number of improvements to the Finder give you more control over its windows (Figure 1-15). You can:

❖ Change the order of items in a list view by clicking a column heading. You can tell the current order by looking for the underlined column heading.

❖ Scroll automatically by dragging an item or a group of selected items past the active area of the window. Dragging into a window corner scrolls diagonally.

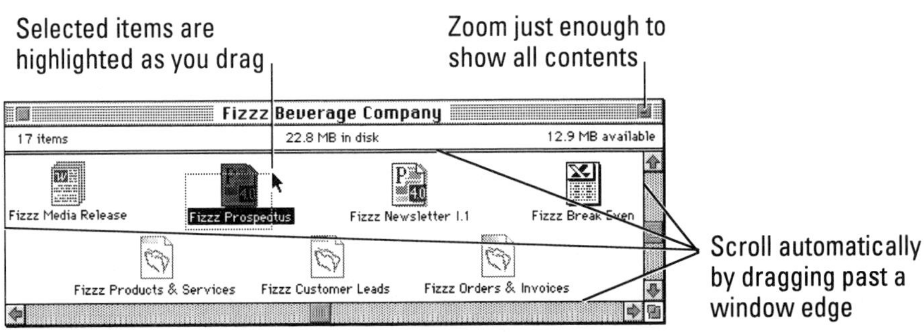

Figure 1-15
Finder window improvements

❖ Zoom a window just enough to show all items in it by clicking the zoom box. The window only covers the whole screen if it contains enough items to fill a screen-size window.

❖ Select multiple items by dragging over them in any view (not just icon and small icon views). Items are highlighted one-by-one as you drag over them, not en masse when you stop dragging.

✔ View switching, auto-scrolling, precise zooming, and drag-selecting in any view work on all Macintosh models that can use System 7.

☛ For more information, see "Smart zooming," "Auto scrolling," "Selecting by dragging," and "Changing list views" in Chapter 3.

Fast file finding

No more hunting through folders and disks for lost items — a chore even with the new outline views — nor waiting for the old slow Find File desk accessory to turn them up. Finder 7's Find command (File menu) finds and fetches lost items for you quickly. In its simplest form, the Find command looks through all disks whose icons are on the desktop for an item whose name contains the text you specify (Figure 1-16). It displays the first item it finds, opening the folder that contains the item to show the item in its native surroundings. You can find additional matching items with the Find Again command.

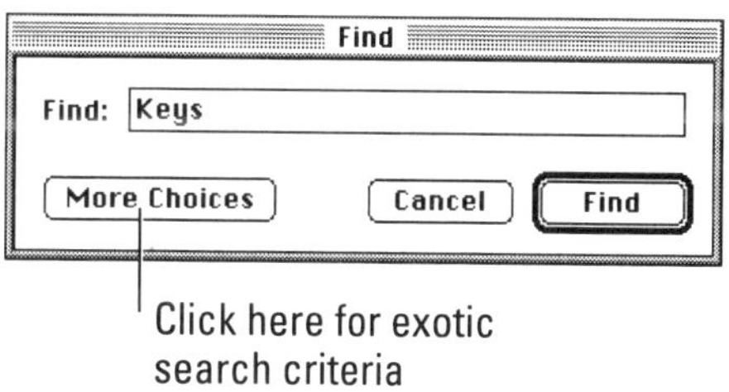

Figure 1-16
A simple find

The Find command has an exotic form as well (Figure 1-17). Clicking the More Choices button lets you specify the type of search: by name, size, kind, label, date created, date modified, version, comments, or lock status. You also specify exactly what you want matched (for example, you enter a date) and how you want it matched (for example, look for items modified before the date you specify). You can restrict the search to a single disk, to the active window, or to a group of items you selected in

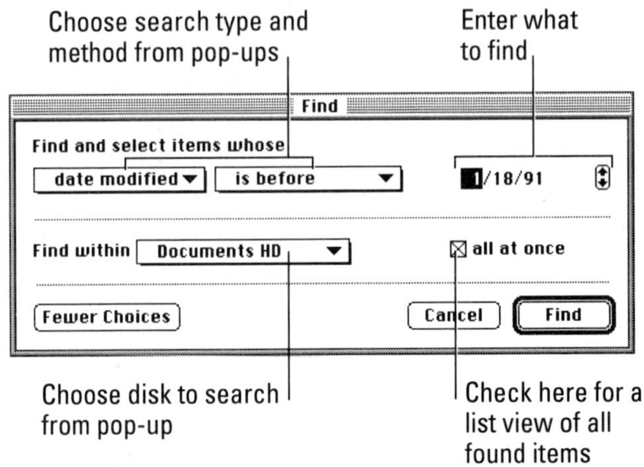

Figure 1-17
An exotic find

the active window before choosing the Find command. The Find command can also select all the items it finds at once in an outline view.

The Find and Find Next commands work on all Macintosh models that can use System 7.

For more information, see "Finding items" in Chapter 3.

Directory dialog improvements

The new directory dialog boxes you get when you use Open and Save As commands work more than ever like a one-window Finder. As always, a single directory window lists the contents of one folder or disk at a time, alphabetically by name. The directory window now uses compressed-style text for names longer than 25 characters.

The desktop

For the first time, directory dialog boxes provide a view of the desktop and let you open disks and other items on it. In fact opening a disk at the desktop level is the new method of switching disk drives (Figure 1-18). The old Drive button has been replaced by a Desktop button, which takes you to the desktop when you click it. You can also get to the desktop by choosing it from the pop-up menu above the directory window.

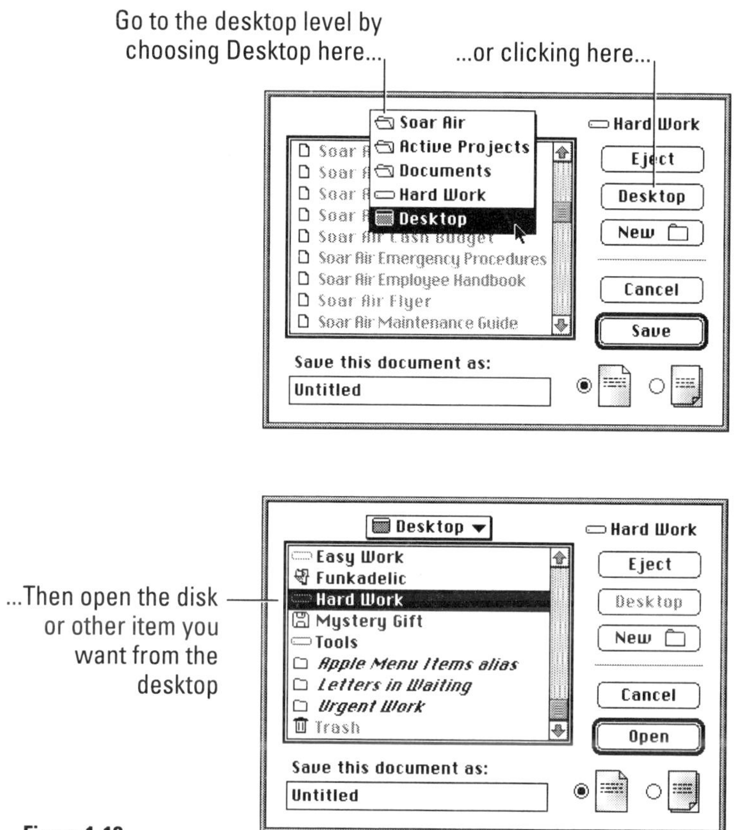

Figure 1-18
At the desktop

Navigating by keyboard

You can now open items and move through folders in any directory dialog box using the keyboard as well as the mouse. For example, typing "k" selects the first item that begins with the letter K or k. Older system software doesn't allow this keyboard navigation in Save or Save As dialog boxes, where you must use the keyboard to edit the name of the item you're saving. In System 7, heavy black border around a Save or Save As dialog's directory window tells you that your typing will select an item in the window (Figure 1-19).

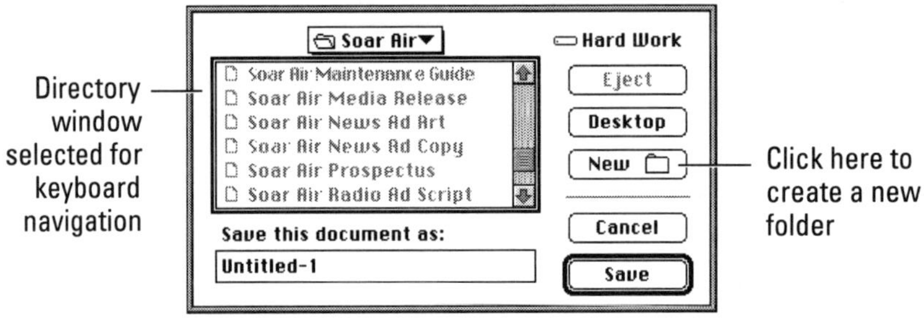

Figure 1-19
Moving around by keyboard

Opening and creating folders

An even more subtle change in Save and Save As dialog boxes further reduces confusion when moving through folders. When you select a folder in the directory window, the Save button becomes an Open button. Clicking it opens the selected folder. In older system software, the button works the same way, but it's always named Save (even when clicking it opens a selected folder).

The Save or Save As dialog boxes of some programs also include a new button you can click to create a new folder. In addition, you can use the Edit menu to cut, copy, and paste while editing the name of an item you're saving.

✗ The New Folder button is missing from the Save and Save As dialog boxes of most programs that have not been updated for System 7.

☛ For more information, see "Directory dialog boxes" in Chapter 2.

System Folder organization

What a mess the System Folder had become! Control panel documents here, startup documents there, preference files everywhere — Finder 7 keeps such items in special new folders inside the System Folder. Other new folders provide new features. All the new folders have distinctive folder icons (Figure 1-20). Moreover, Finder 7 puts many items in their proper places when you drag them to the System Folder icon. The inner folders relieve much of the clutter that plagues System Folders of older system software.

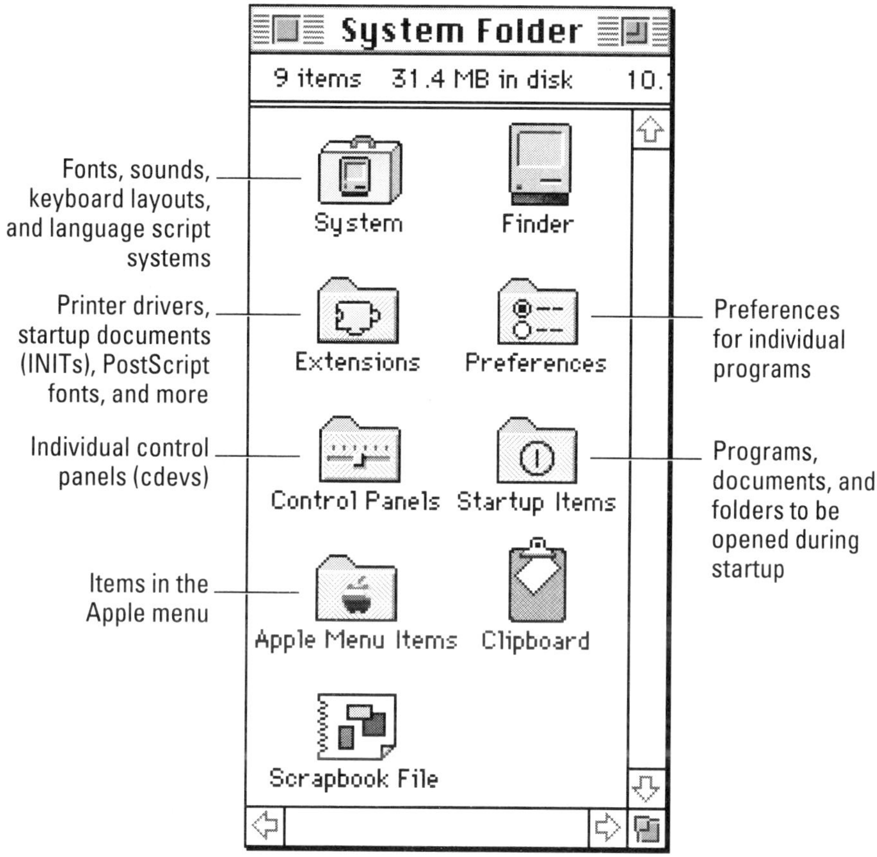

Figure 1-20
Subdivided System Folder

✗ Some items from old System Folders don't work right when they're put in the new Extensions, Control Panels, or Preferences folders. You have to put stubborn old preference files, control panels, and system extensions loose in the System Folder by dragging them to its window (not to its icon).

☛ For more information, see Chapter 4.

Divided control panel

The Control Panel desk accessory, like the System Folder, has become overcrowded and hard to use. In System 7, the sections of the Control

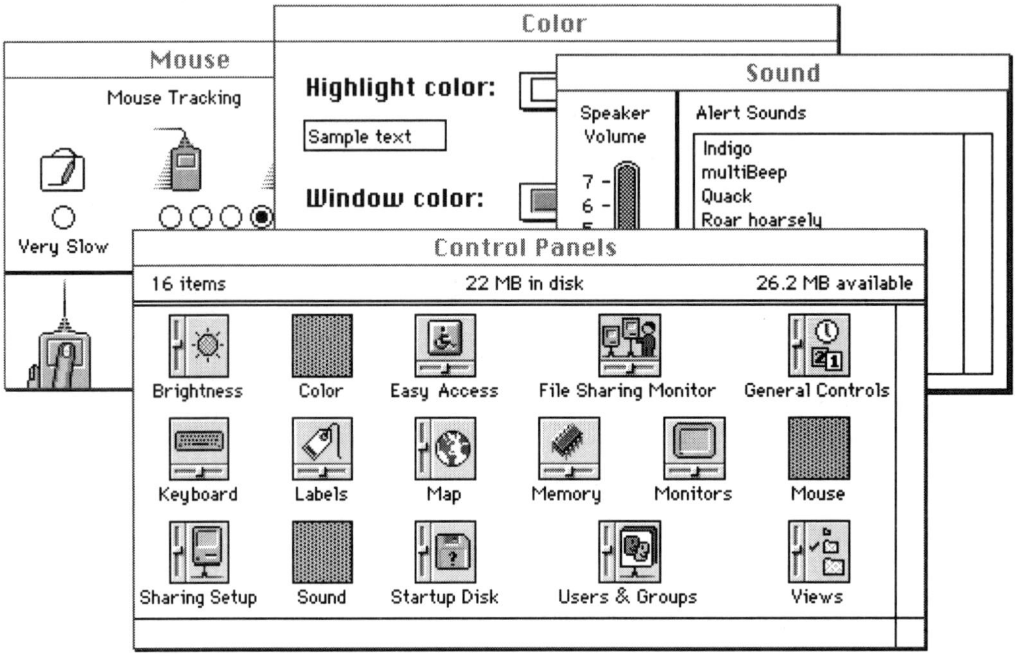

Figure 1-21
Separate control panels

Panel desk accessory are separate control panels, each of which you open like an ordinary document (Figure 1-21). Each open control panel appears in its own window.

Control panel documents are kept in a special Control Panels Folder within the System Folder. For convenience, the Control Panels folder appears in the Apple menu so you can open the folder easily. With the Control Panels folder open, you can rearrange the individual control panels in it by using the View menu or by dragging icons.

✗ Some old control panel documents (also called cdevs) work properly only if you put them in the System Folder itself, not in the Control Panels folder.

☛ For more information, see "Control Panels folder" in Chapter 4 and "Control panels" in Chapter 5.

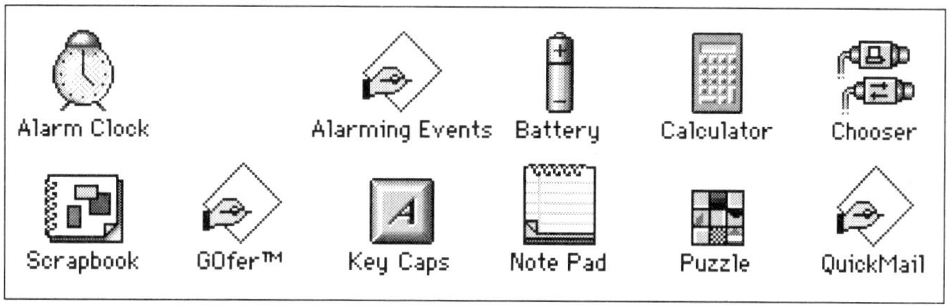

Figure 1-22
Some desk accessory icons

Desk accessories

Desk accessories no longer have to be in the Apple menu. Each has its own icon (Figure 1-22), which you can put in any folder or on the desktop. You now open desk accessories like regular application programs, for example by double-clicking their icons. You can still install desk accessories in the Apple menu by dragging their icons or aliases of them to the Apple Menu Items folder within the System Folder.

You move and copy desk accessories by dragging their icons in the Finder. You do not use the Font/DA Mover utility program. For compatibility with earlier system software versions, desk accessories can exist in suitcase files, which the Font/DA Mover program creates. You must drag desk accessories out of suitcase files before you can open them in System 7, however.

✗ Most old desk accessories work fine with System 7, but some require updating.

☛ For more information, see "Software compatibility" in Chapter 13 and "Desk accessories" in Chapter 5.

Apple menu

The Apple menu has a new role. It now expedites opening anything you use frequently. Any item you can open using the Finder you can put in the Apple menu and open it from there. This includes documents, application programs, desk accessories, folders, control panels, and even fonts and sounds.

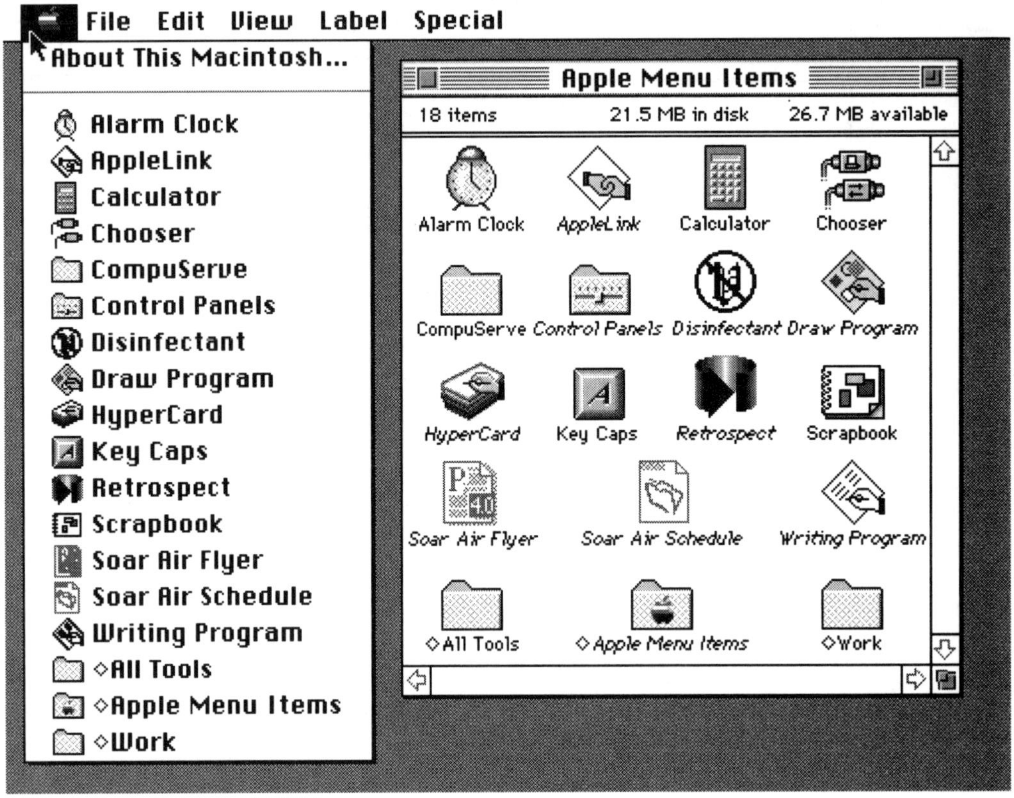

Figure 1-23
An Apple menu and its Apple Menu Items folder

You put an item in the Apple menu by dragging its icon or an alias of its icon into the Apple Menu Items folder (Figure 1-23), which is in the System Folder. The item becomes instantly available in the Apple menu. (No need to restart your Macintosh.)

To remove an item from the Apple menu, drag its icon or alias out of the Apple Menu Items folder.

✔ The new Apple Menu Items folder works with all software and on all Macintosh models that can use System 7.

☛ For more information, see "Apple Menu Items folder" in Chapter 4 and "Your own Apple menu" in Chapter 5.

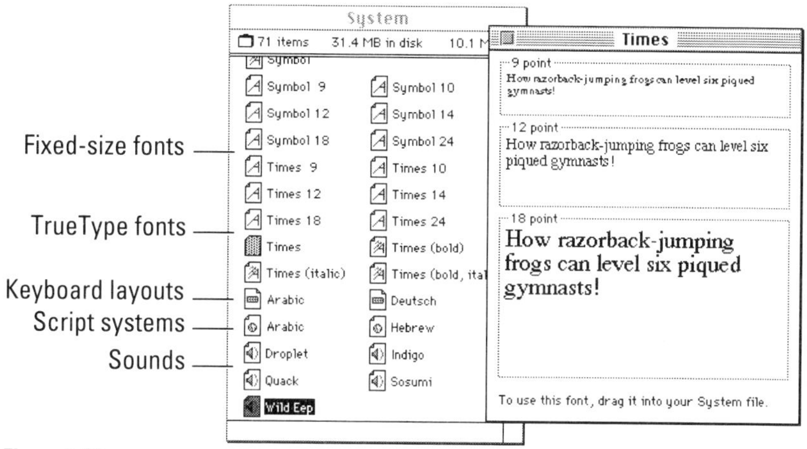

Figure 1-24
Inside the System file

Installing fonts, sounds, and more

Installing fonts and sounds is now simply a matter of dragging their icons to the System file. You don't use the Font/DA Mover utility program any more. Installing fonts makes them available in programs that let you pick fonts. Installing sounds makes them available as system alert sounds selectable in the Sound control panel.

You can open the System file as if it were a folder to inspect or remove the installed fonts and sounds (Figure 1-24). Each installed font and sound is represented by an icon in the System file window. Opening a font icon displays some sample text using that font. Opening a sound icon plays the sound. To remove a font or sound, you drag its icon from the System file window to a folder or the desktop.

You also install keyboard layouts and script systems for foreign languages by dragging their icons to the System file.

✔ All old screen fonts (not PostScript printer fonts) can be installed or removed by dragging to or from the System file.

✘ The sounds used in HyperCard are a special format that don't work properly as system alert sounds.

☛ For more information, see "System file" in Chapter 4.

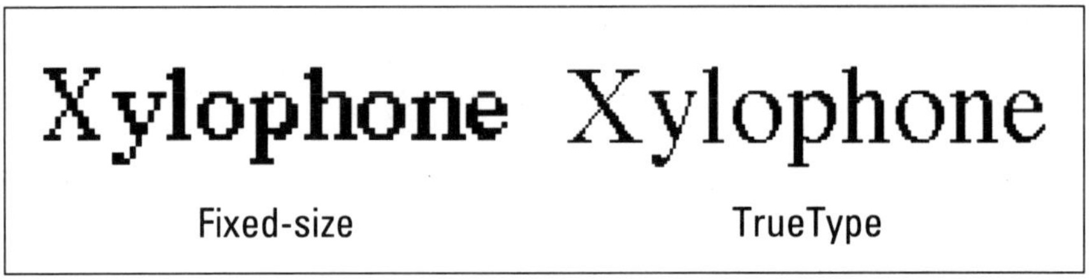

Figure 1-25
36-point Times

Variable-size fonts

Text looks smooth at any size on any screen or printing device thanks to the TrueType font technology built into System 7. TrueType fonts are variable-size outline fonts similar to the PostScript fonts that look so sharp on LaserWriters. System 7 smoothly scales TrueType fonts to any size (Figure 1-25). Old-style fonts still work; they look good at their fixed sizes and look lumpy when scaled to other sizes.

You install a variable-size font by dragging it to the System file. A typical variable-size TrueType font takes up 10K to 20K more disk space than a set of corresponding fixed-size fonts in sizes 9, 10, 12, 14, 18, and 24. However, TrueType fonts save disk space if you use large sizes or if you have a printing device that uses screen fonts. ImageWriters, fax modems, ink-jet printers, and laser printers without PostScript no longer need the double, triple, or quadruple fixed sizes that take up lots of disk space.

LaserWriters and other PostScript devices use PostScript fonts instead of equivalent TrueType fonts. If a document contains a TrueType font that has no PostScript equivalent, System 7 scales the TrueType font to the resolution of the output device.

✔ Variable-size fonts work on all Macintosh models, all printing devices, and with the programs you already have.

✘ Some old programs only provide a fixed list of font sizes and must be upgraded to provide a method for specifying any font size.

☛ For more information, see Chapter 7.

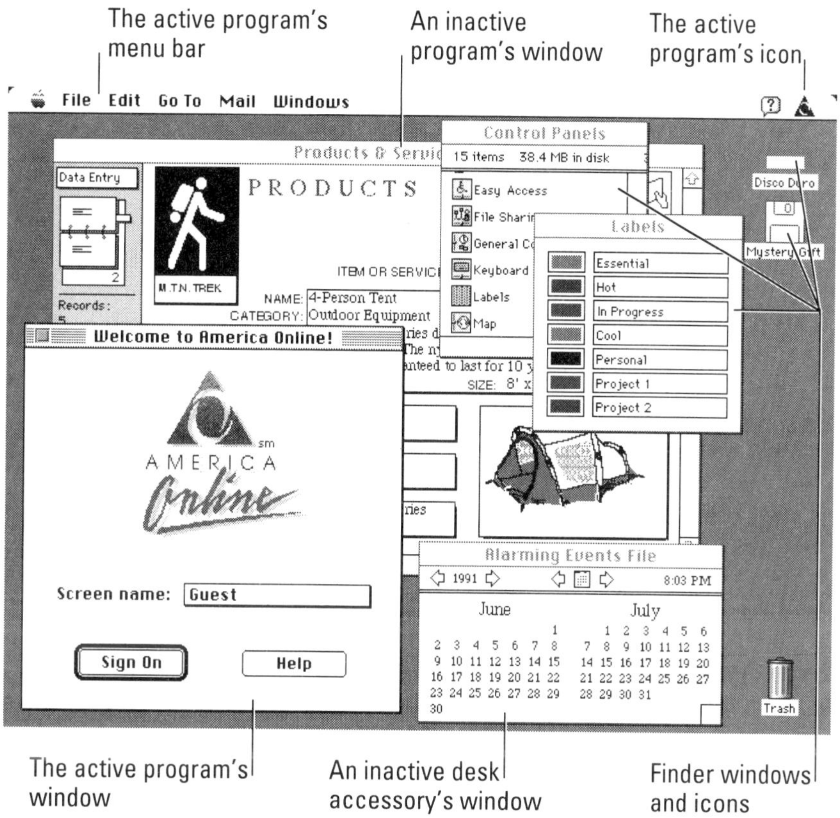

Figure 1-26
Multiple programs open

Multitasking

You will need your wits about you to get used to System 7's multitasking capabilities unless you already use MultiFinder with System 6. With System 7, multitasking is no longer optional. The Finder is always available without quitting the program you're using and you can have as many programs open simultaneously as will fit in your computer's memory (Figure 1-26). You can copy and paste among documents of open programs without closing documents and quitting programs. Also, you can switch to the Finder without quitting programs, and there open other programs, find documents, organize folders and disks, and so on.

Figure 1-27
The Application menu

Multitasking's valuable benefits have disorienting side effects. For instance, you may think the program you're using has unexpectedly quit when actually you switched to another open program. You must condition yourself to look at the menu bar when you need to know which open program is currently active.

The active program's icon appears at the right end of the menu bar. Clicking that icon reveals the new Application menu, which lists the programs that are open (Figure 1-27). Choosing a listed program makes it the active program. You can also make a program the active program by clicking in any of its windows or by opening (double-clicking) its icon or any of its documents' icons in the Finder.

Programs that know how can operate in the background by using System 7's multitasking capabilities. Background programs operate during the intervals — often only split seconds long — when the active program isn't using the computer. Background programs can't use the menu bar or interact directly with you in any other way. They can, however, perform tasks such as:

- recalculating spreadsheets
- making backup copies of disks
- printing documents
- sorting databases

Figure 1-28
Window management

- copying items in the Finder
- sending and receiving electronic mail

System 7's multitasking works with most software and on all Macintosh models that can use System 7. However, you can't use any program with System 7 that doesn't work when MultiFinder is active in older system software.

For more information, see "Opening multiple programs" in Chapter 2.

Hiding window clutter

Having multiple programs open leads to a confusion of windows. You can eliminate window clutter by using Application menu commands to temporarily hide windows (Figure 1-28).

Window hiding works with all software and on all Macintosh models that can use System 7.

For more information, see "Opening multiple programs" in Chapter 2.

Extending memory

Application programs are becoming more memory-hungry all the time, and System 7 has a large appetite itself. Seems like a computer can never have too much memory.

32-Bit Addressing

Some Macintosh models can access more RAM (random-access memory) by using System 7's 32-Bit Addressing capability. Older system software does not have this capability and cannot access more than 8MB

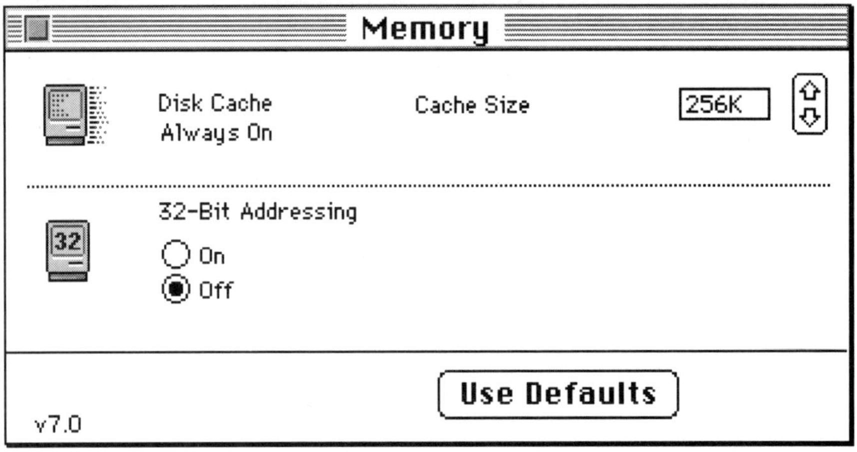

Figure 1-29
The Memory control panel

of RAM regardless of the amount installed. To turn it on and off, you use the new Memory control panel (Figure 1-29). With 4MB RAM SIMMs installed, for example, turning on 32-Bit Addressing lets you use 10MB of RAM on an LC , 17MB on a IIsi, and 32MB on a IIci or IIfx. If 32-Bit Addressing is off, you can only use 8MB of RAM regardless of the amount installed.

Virtual memory

You may be able to increase the amount of memory available on your Macintosh without installing more RAM. System 7 can transparently use part of a hard disk as additional memory. This extra memory, called virtual memory, lets you open more programs at once and increase the amount of memory each program gets when you open it (Figure 1-30). Given more memory, many programs let you open additional documents or larger documents. Virtual memory lets you get by with less RAM. You buy only as much as you need for average use, not for peak use.

Virtual memory only works on a Macintosh equipped with a paged memory management unit (PMMU). The SE/30, IIcx, IIx, IIsi, IIci, and IIfx models all have PMMUs, and a Mac II can be retrofitted with one. An LC can be upgraded with an accelerator card containing a PMMU. However, a Mac Plus, SE, Classic, or Portable cannot use virtual memory even if it has such an accelerator, because the ROMs in those models are missing some information System 7 needs to implement virtual memory.

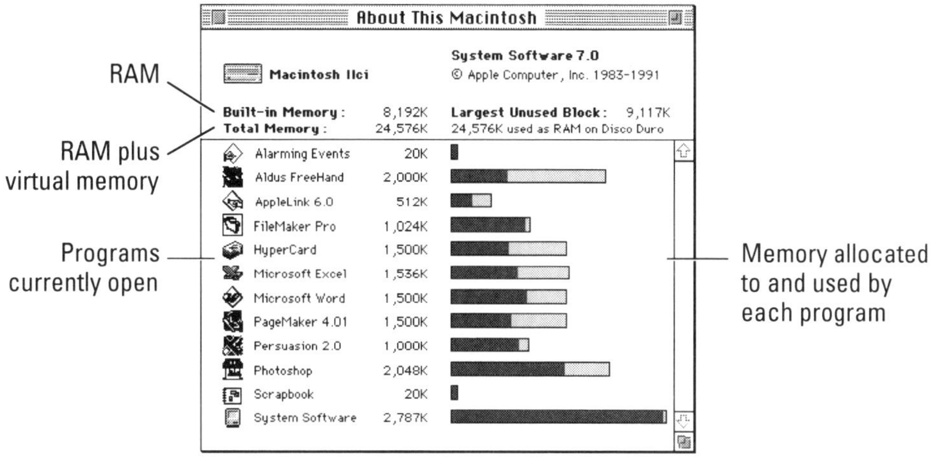

Figure 1-30
Using virtual memory

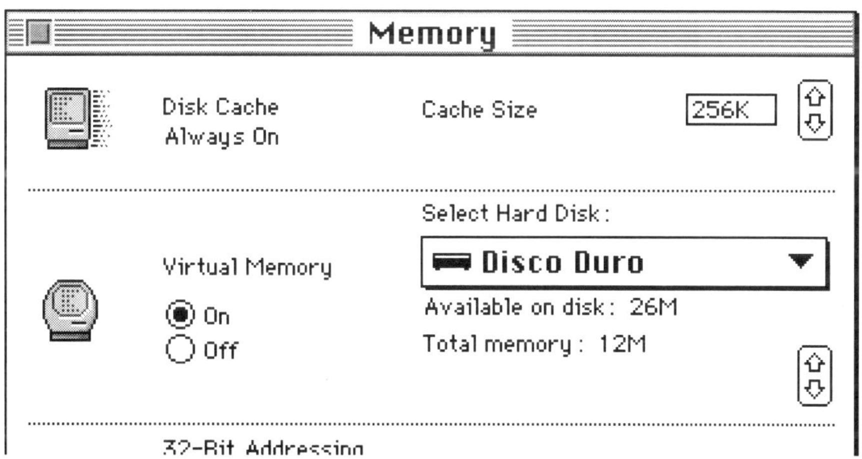

Figure 1-31
Virtual memory settings

Controlling virtual memory

To turn virtual memory on and off, you use the Memory control panel (Figure 1-31). You also set the size of total memory and select a hard disk that has a block of space as large as the total amount of memory you want available (RAM plus virtual memory). These controls are not available on computers that cannot use virtual memory.

Disk Cache

You also use the Memory control panel to adjust the amount of RAM allocated for the Disk Cache, which improves disk performance. You cannot turn off the Disk Cache as you can its equivalent in older system software, the RAM Cache control in the General section of the Control Panel.

✔ The Disk Cache works on all Macintosh models that can use System 7.

✘ Virtual memory doesn't work on a Mac Plus, SE, Classic, or Portable, and a Mac LC or II must be upgraded to use it. The 32-Bit Addressing capability doesn't work on a Mac Plus, SE, Portable, Classic, SE/30, II, IIx, or IIcx. Also, your old application programs may not work when 32-Bit Addressing is on.

☛ For more information, see "Memory management tactics" in Chapter 5.

Chooser changes

In older system software you specified your network name in the Chooser desk accessory. Now you enter it along with your network password and a name for your Macintosh in the new Sharing Setup control panel (described in the next section). In addition, the new, taller Chooser can show more devices and zones (Figure 1-32).

File sharing

If your Macintosh is connected to others in a network, System 7 lets you share hard disks, folders, and the files in them with other network users. You can access folders and disks others have made available to you. You can also make your folders and disks available to others on the network (including those using System 6.x with AppleShare client software).

Sharing someone else's folders

To share another Mac's folder or disk, you use the Chooser desk accessory. It lists as AppleShare file servers the names of all computers that are sharing their folders and disks. After you choose one, the Chooser asks you to connect as a guest or a registered user and then presents a list of items you may share (Figure 1-33).

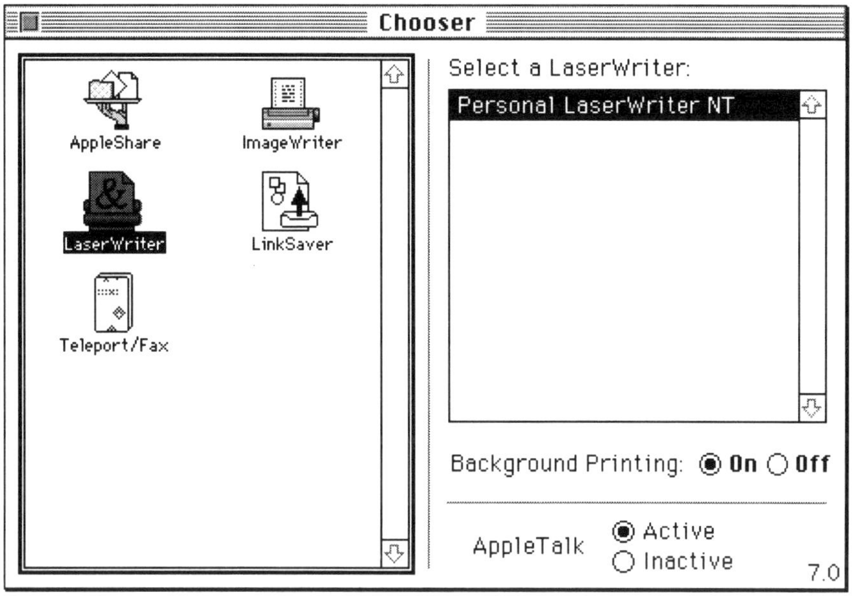

Figure 1-32
The Chooser

Accessing someone else's folders or disks is considerably slower than accessing your own. Also, your computer's performance degrades markedly while others share your folders or disks. For best performance, especially in networks with more than 10 active users, everyone can put folders to be shared on the hard disk of a Macintosh dedicated to sharing its files (a dedicated file server).

Sharing your folders with others

Before you can share your disks or folders, you must configure your Macintosh as an AppleShare file server with the new Sharing Setup control panel (Figure 1-34). It then shows up as an AppleShare file server in the Choosers of other network users who have System 7 file sharing software installed. It also shows up as an AppleShare server in the Choosers of System 6.x users who have AppleShare client software installed.

Sharing your disks or folders with others increases your system memory usage by 250K to 300K. That leaves only about 600K for opening programs on a 2MB Macintosh.

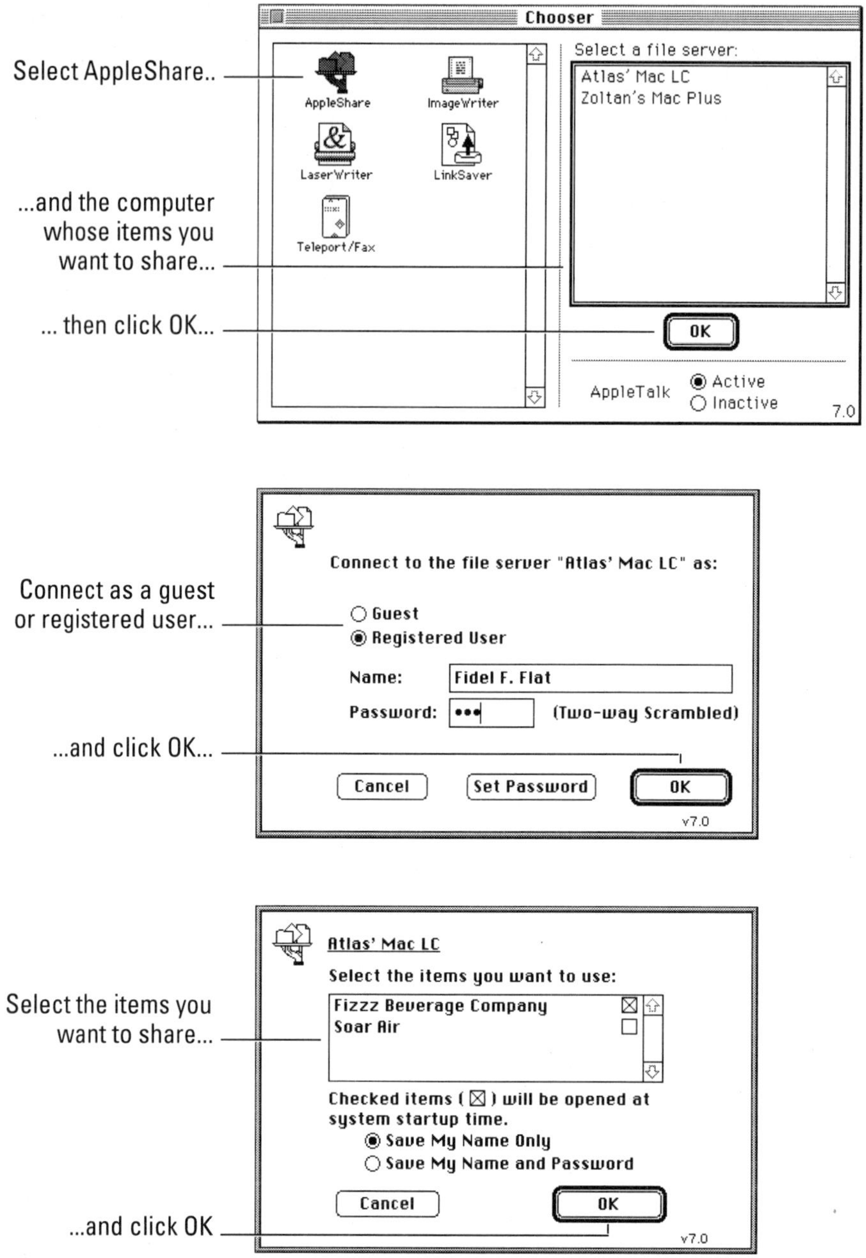

Figure 1-33
Selecting folders to share

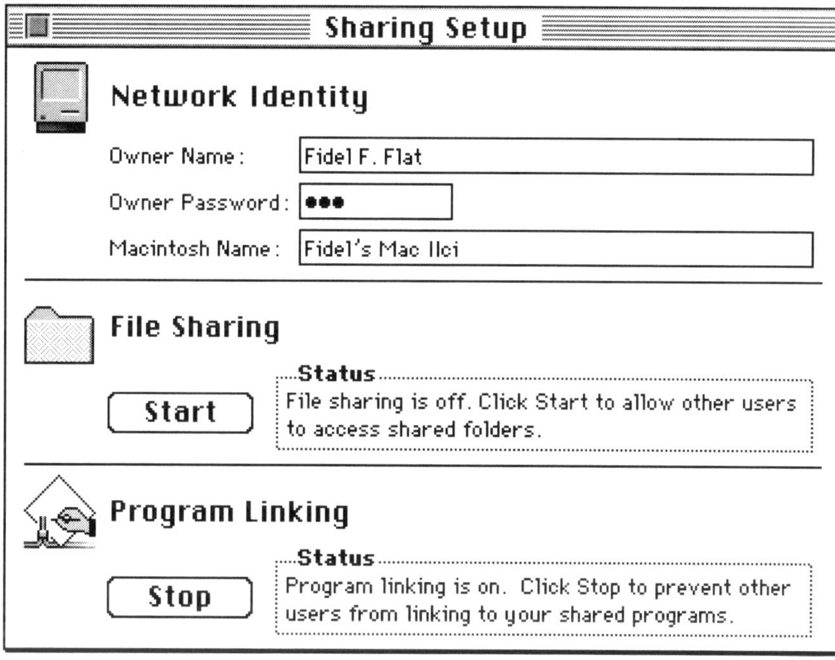

Figure 1-34
The Sharing Setup control panel

To share one of your disks or folders with others, you select it and use the Finder's new Sharing command to display the item's sharing information window (Figure 1-35). There you specify who can see the item's folders, see its files, and make changes to it. You can grant these access privileges differently to the owner of the item (usually you), to one other registered user or group of registered users you designate, and to everyone else.

Users and groups

You identify registered users, set their passwords, and create groups of users with the new Users & Groups control panel (Figure 1-36). Another new control panel, File Sharing Monitor, lets you see who is sharing what and how busy they're keeping your Macintosh. You can also use that control panel to disconnect individual users who are sharing your folders and disks.

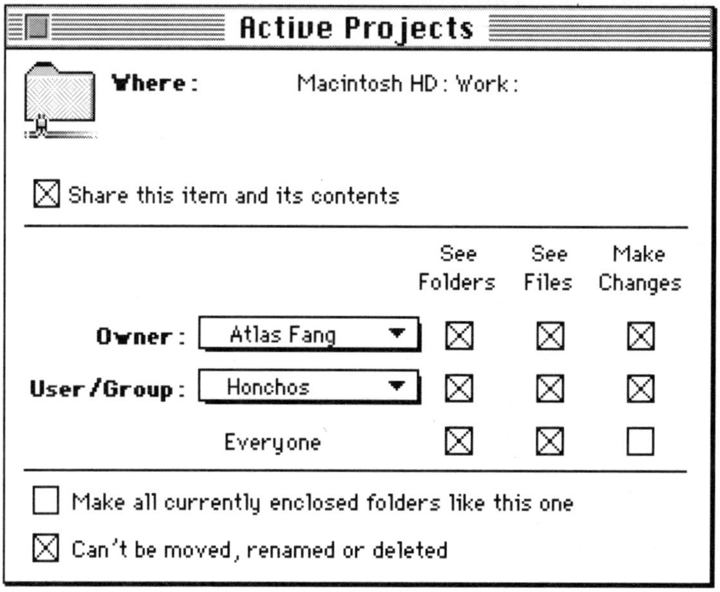

Figure 1-35
Sharing information (access privileges)

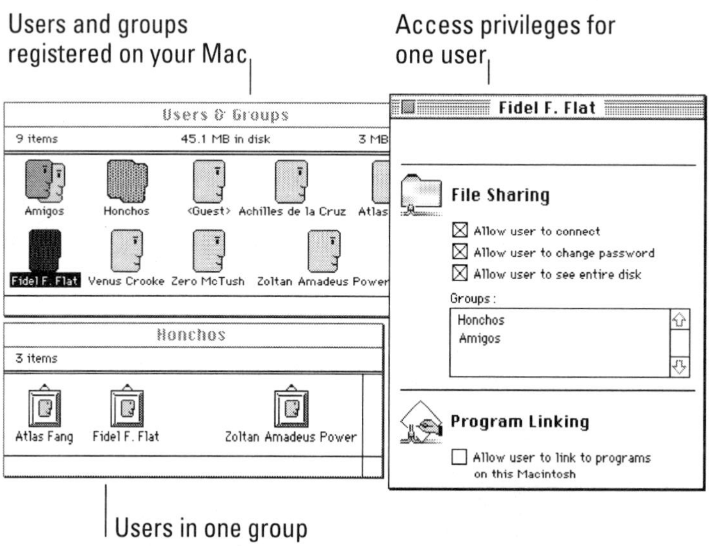

Figure 1-36
Users and groups

✘ File sharing works on all Macintosh models that can use System 7. However, your Macintosh should have at least 2.5MB of RAM if you want to open more than a single mid-size program (say maybe a desk accessory or two) while sharing your folders or disks.

☛ For more information, see Chapter 8.

Interactive help

At last the Macintosh can explain itself. You can get a description of objects you see on screen by turning on System 7's optional balloon help.

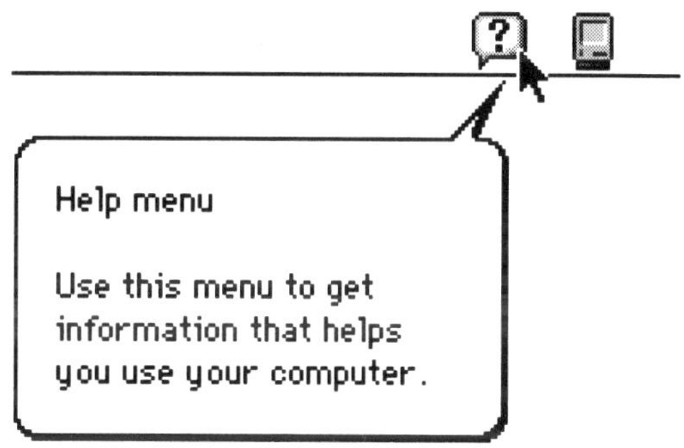

Figure 1-37
A help balloon

With balloon help on, you place the pointer over an object and a concise description of it appears in a cartoon-style balloon (Figure 1-37). Aside from balloons appearing and disappearing, everything works normally when balloon help is on. You may perceive a slight delay as help balloons come and go, especially if you use a slower Macintosh.

To turn on balloon help, choose Show Balloons from the new Help menu, which is always near the right end of the menu bar (Figure 1-38). That command then changes to Hide Balloons, and choosing it turns off balloon help.

Each program can add items to the Help menu for accessing other types of help, such as how-to help. For example, the Finder adds a Finder Shortcuts item that displays a list of tricks for using the Finder.

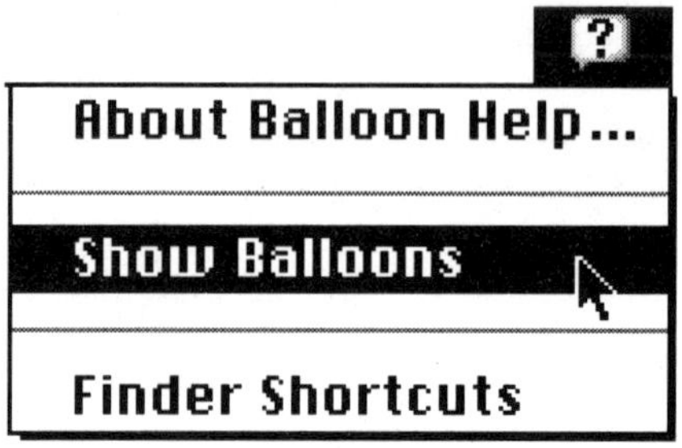

Figure 1-38
The Help menu

✗ Balloon help knows about all standard objects in the Macintosh interface. However, it cannot describe a specific program's menu commands, window contents, dialog boxes, and so forth unless the program has been revised to include the necessary help balloons.

☛ For more information, see "Balloon help" in Chapter 2.

Stationery pads

Stationery pads save time if you regularly create new documents with common formatting, contents, and so on. Opening a stationery pad is like tearing a page from a pad of preprinted forms. You get a new document with all the common elements preset. Stationery pads have a distinctive

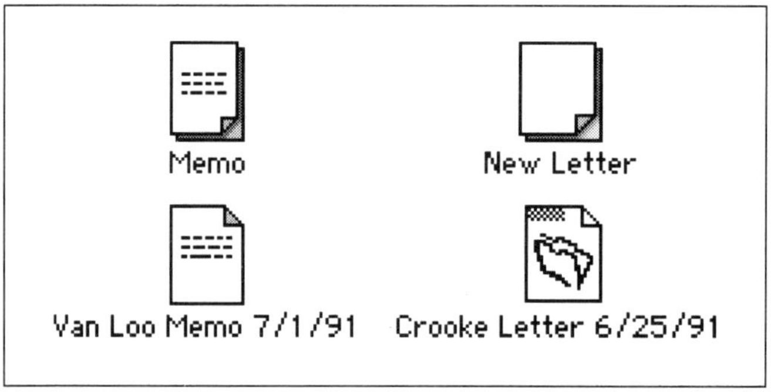

Figure 1-39
Stationery pad icons and ordinary icons

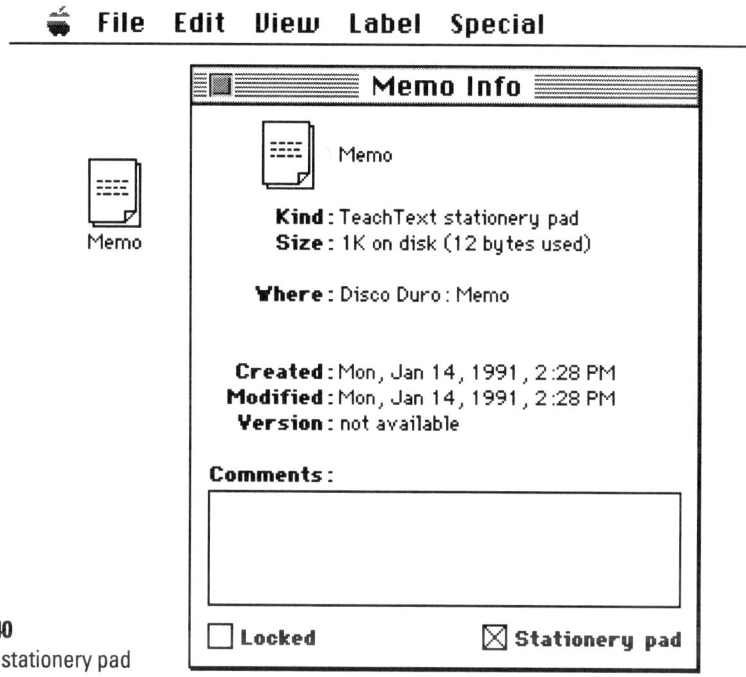

Figure 1-40
Making a stationery pad

icon that looks like a stack of document icons (Figure 1-39). The Finder uses a generic stationery pad icon if the program that handles that type of document doesn't know about System 7's stationery.

You can make any document a stationery pad by setting the Stationery Pad option in its info window (Figure 1-40). To see an item's info window, select the item and choose Get Info from the Finder's File menu. Some programs let you directly save a document as a stationery pad by setting a Stationery Pad option of their Save and Save As commands (Figure 1-41). These programs have been upgraded specifically to work with System 7's stationery pads.

Programs that know about stationery pads open an untitled document identical to the stationery pad. For programs that don't know about stationery pads, the Finder automatically creates a new document by making a copy of the stationery pad, asking you to name it, and having the program open the copy.

✔ Stationery pads work with most software, but work best with software that has been updated to take advantage of them.

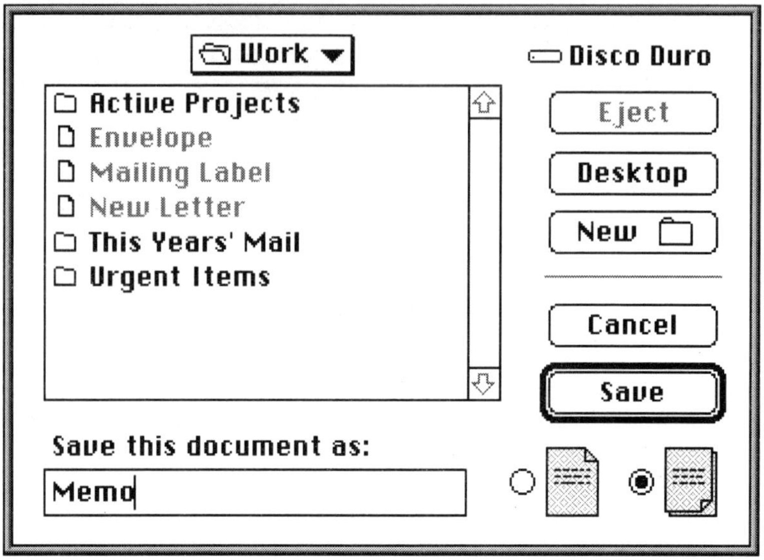

Figure 1-41
Saving a stationery pad

☛ For more information, see "Stationery pads" in Chapter 3.

Folder nesting revealed

A pop-up menu in the title bar of the active Finder window reveals the path through your folder structure from the active window to the disk containing it. The menu pops up when you press Command while clicking the window title (Figure 1-42).

You can open any folder along the path by choosing the folder from the pop-up menu. To close the active window while opening a folder along the path, press the Option key while choosing the folder from the pop-up menu.

✔ All folder windows have a pop-up menu in the title bar.

Smart drag

When you drag an item from one window to a folder in an overlapping window, Finder 7 keeps the destination folder in view (Figure 1-43). Older Finders bring the source window in front of an overlapping target window as soon as you begin dragging, possibly covering the destination

Figure 1-42
Folder path pop-up menu

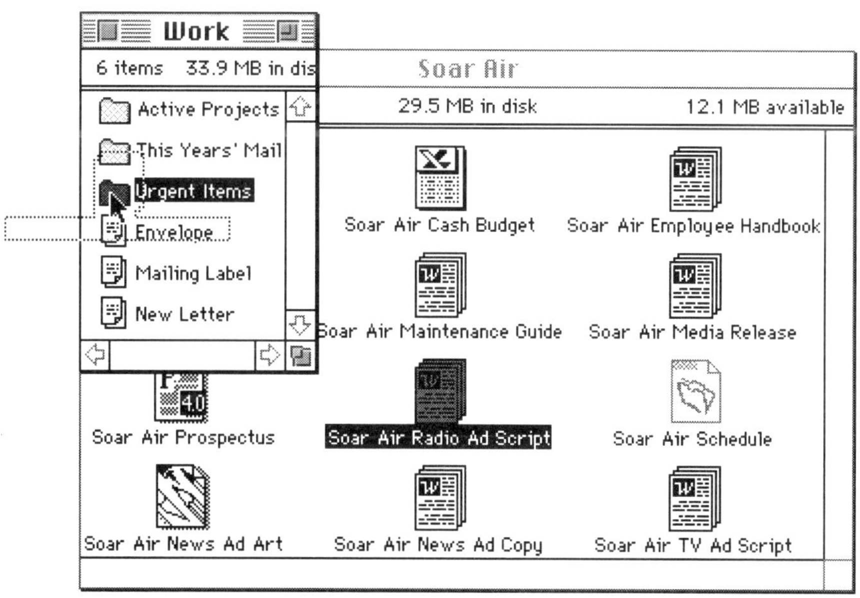

Figure 1-43
Dragging to an overlapping window

Table 1-1: Finder keyboard shortcuts

Objective	Action
Select an item by name	Type the item's full or partial name
Select the next item alphabetically	Tab
Select the previous item alphabetically	Shift-Tab
Select next item up, down, left, or right	Up Arrow, Down Arrow, Left Arrow, or Right Arrow
Select the item nearest upper-right corner of the desktop	Command–Shift–Up Arrow
Open the selected item	Command-O or Command-Down Arrow
Open the selected item and close the active window	Command-Option-O or Command-Option-Down Arrow
Open the parent folder, disk, or volume	Command–Up Arrow
Open the parent folder, disk, or volume and close the active window	Command-Option–Up Arrow
Make the desktop active	Command-Shift-Up Arrow
Begin editing the selected item's name	Return or Enter
Expand the selected folder	Command-Right Arrow
Expand the selected folder and its nested folders	Command-Option-Right Arrow
Collapse the selected folder	Command-Left Arrow
Collapse the selected folder and its nested folders	Command-Option-Left Arrow
Skip installing all system extensions during one startup	Hold down Shift during startup

folder. This feature only works when you drag a single item. Selecting multiple items in an inactive window brings that window to the front.

✔ Dragging from an inactive window works on all Macintosh models that can use System 7.

☛ For more information, see "Smart drag" in Chapter 3.

Keyboard shortcuts

QUICK TIPS

You can select an item in the active Finder window (or the desktop if no window is active) without using the mouse. Typing an item's name or the first part of it selects the item. Other keystrokes select an item near the currently selected item, open the item, and more. Table 1-1 has the details.

✔ The new keyboard shortcuts work on all Macintosh models that can use System 7.

☛ For more Finder shortcuts, see "Finder power" in Chapter 3.

A new opening

You can open a document from the Finder by dragging its icon to the icon of any application program that can open it (Figure 1-44). The

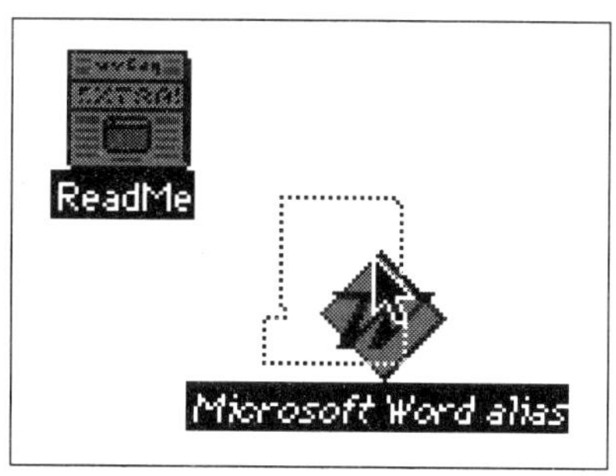

Figure 1-44
Dragging a document to open it

program need not have created the document but must be compatible with it. If the program can't open the document, nothing happens.

✔ This new method of opening documents works with all programs, including those that haven't been updated for System 7.

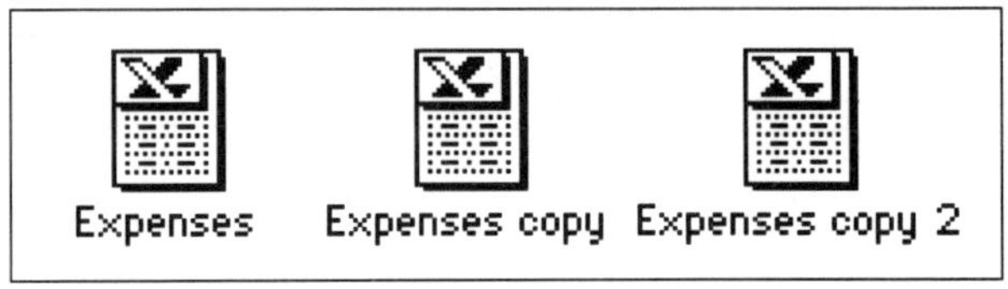

Figure 1-45
Names of duplicate items

Naming duplicates

QUICK TIPS

The Finder constructs names of duplicate items more economically than it used to. Instead of prefixing the name with the words "Copy of," it now simply suffixes the name with the word "copy" (Figure 1-45). Additional copies of the same item also have a serial number suffixed.

✔ The new method of naming duplicate items works on all Macintosh models that can use System 7.

☛ For more information, see "Naming duplicates" in Chapter 3.

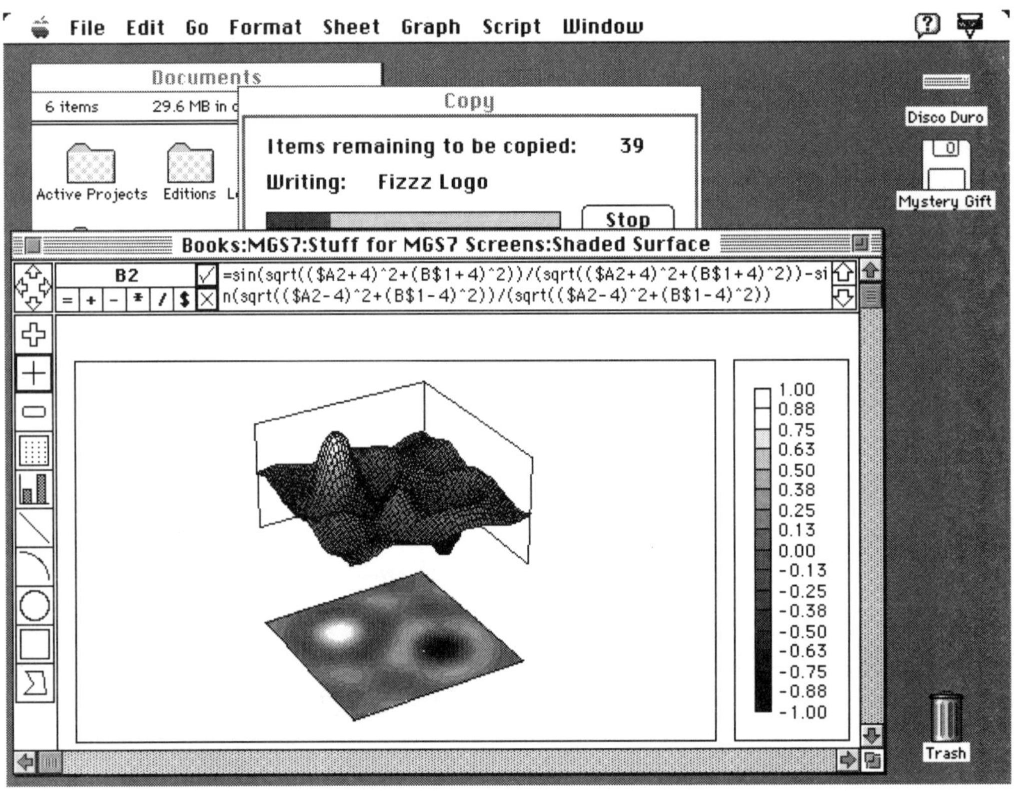

Figure 1-46
Copy while you work

Figure 1-47
The Trash warning

Background copying

You can work with any application program or desk accessory while the Finder copies items in the background (Figure 1-46). This capability is especially useful when copying from or to a shared folder or disk. To switch to another program, click in any of its windows or choose it from the Application menu any time after starting the copy process.

All programs you want to use during the copy must be open before you start the copy process. The Finder can't open a program or do anything else itself while it's copying. Control panels are considered part of the Finder, so you can't use them while copying.

Background copying works on all Macintosh models that can use System 7.

For more information, see "Background work" in Chapter 3.

Trash behavior

Items you drag to the Trash now remain there indefinitely. You must empty the Trash manually using the Finder's Empty Trash command (Special menu). When you do, Finder 7 tells you how many items the Trash contains and how much disk space they occupy (Figure 1-47). You decide whether to discard them all or cancel. To bypass this notice, press the Option key while choosing the Empty Trash command.

You can disable the Trash warning by selecting the Trash, using the Get Info command, and turning off the appropriate option (Figure 1-48).

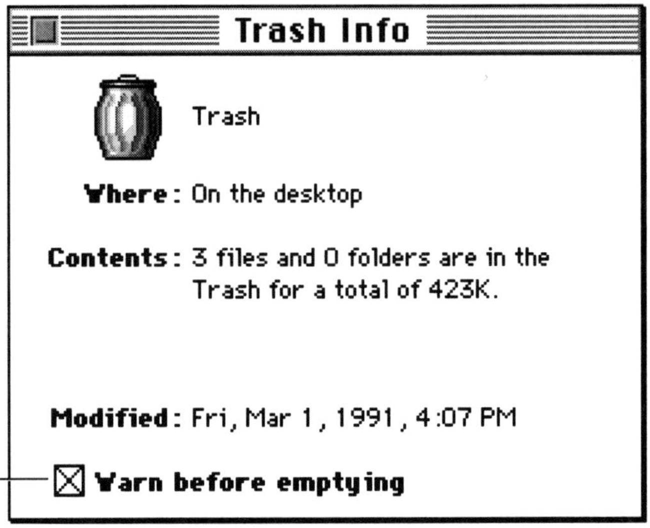

Figure 1-48
Get Info for the Trash

When you drag locked items to the Trash, Finder 7 does not display a warning as older Finders do. Instead, the warning appears when you choose the Empty Trash command with any of the locked items in the Trash. And unlike older Finders, Finder 7 does not confirm whether you want to discard application programs and system files when you drag them to the Trash.

✔ The Trash exhibits its new behavior on all Macintosh models that can use System 7.

☛ For more information, see "Trash disposal" in Chapter 3.

Live copy/paste

Some programs use System 7 to let you share information dynamically from one document with other documents. Because the sharing is dynamic, changing the original information automatically updates copies of it wherever they are. Think of it as live copy-and-paste. The automatic updating extends to computers interconnected on a network, so a document on your computer can dynamically share information from a document on another networked Macintosh. By contrast, copying and pasting shares information statically and on one Macintosh only.

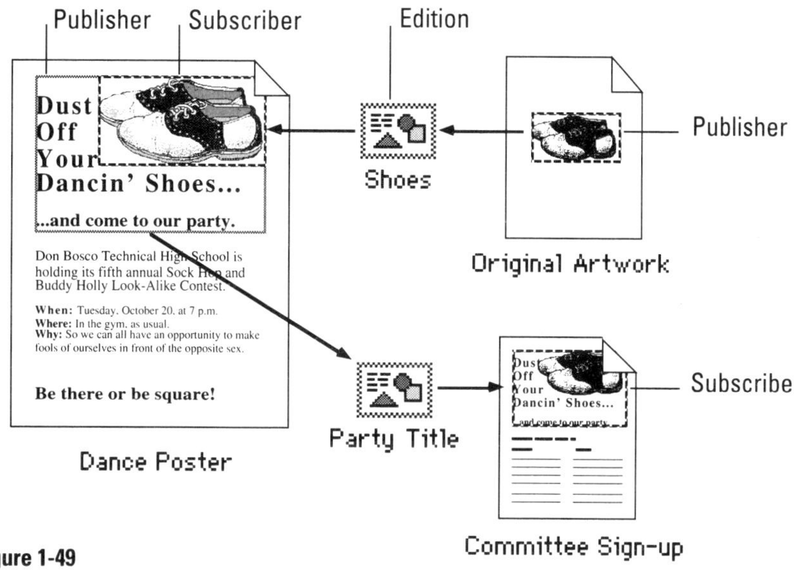

Figure 1-49
Publishing and subscribing

You make a line copy of information by publishing an edition of it. You include copies of the information in a document by subscribing to the edition (Figure 1-49). Publishing material from a document creates a live copy of the material in an edition file on disk. Any number of other documents (on your Mac or others networked to yours) include live copies of the material by subscribing to the edition. When you change the original material and save the document it's in, the edition is automatically updated. Every subscribing document learns of the update the next time it is opened.

Information can only be shared dynamically among documents created by programs that include Edit menu commands for publishing and subscribing (Figure 1-50). You won't find these commands in your old programs, because developers must upgrade their programs to include publishing and subscribing commands.

✘ Old programs require modification to publish and subscribe information.

☛ For more information, see Chapter 9.

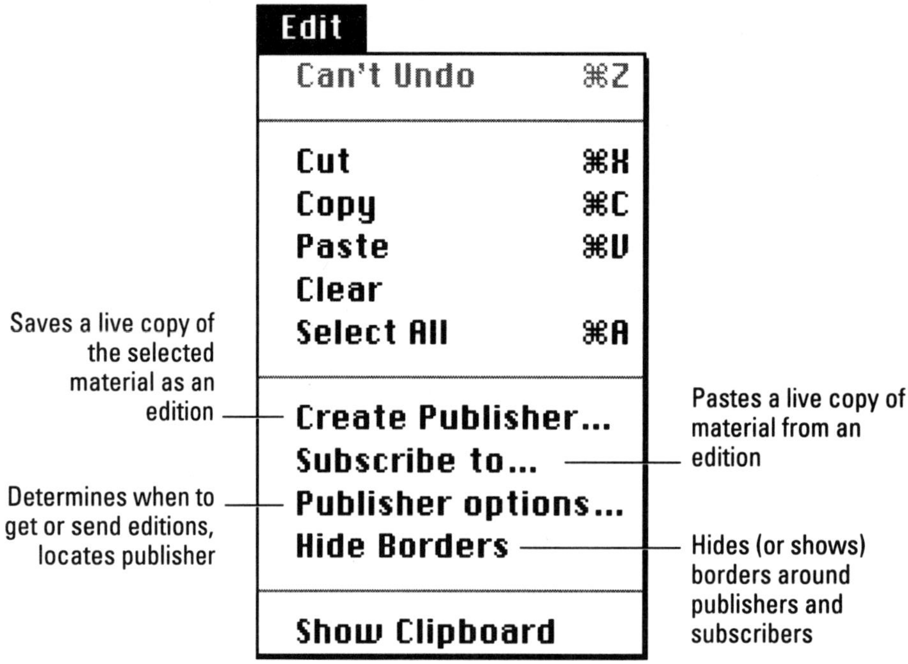

Figure 1-50
Commands for publishing and subscribing

Accessing data

Some programs now let you use System 7's Data Access Manager (DAM). It provides a common, simple method for getting data from a variety of large databases resident on host computers of all brands and sizes. You can usually recognize one of these programs by the Open Query command in its File menu.

To get data, you use the Open Query command to open a query document that describes the type of data you want. A dialog box describes what you will get if you enter the information it requests and click a button to start the query (Figure 1-51).

Behind the scenes the query document and DAM connect to the host computer, request the information using the arcane commands of the host database, obtain the information, and paste it into your document.

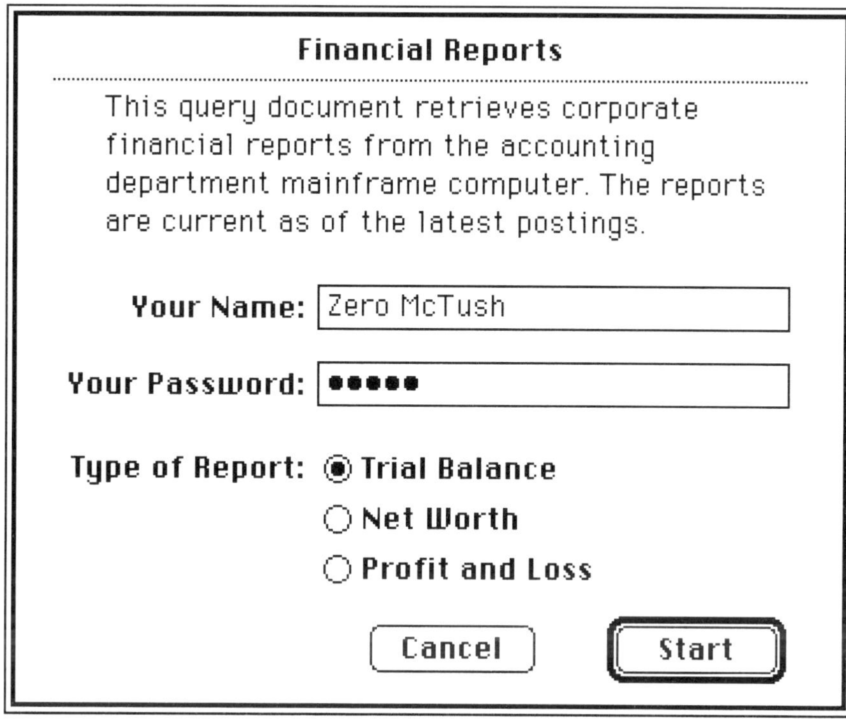

Figure 1-51
A query dialog box

✗ Old programs require modification to use System 7's simplified data accessing capabilities.

☛ For more information, see Data access in Chapter 10.

Linking programs

System 7 paves the way for programs to work together. While you work in one program, you will be able to use the commands and tools of other programs made by different software vendors. For example, an Aldus page layout program could use the functions of a Microsoft word processing program when you wanted to edit a story; a Deneba proofreading program when you wanted to check spelling; an Adobe image editing program when you wanted to edit a photo; a Claris drawing program when you wanted to change a graphic; and so forth (Figure 1-52).

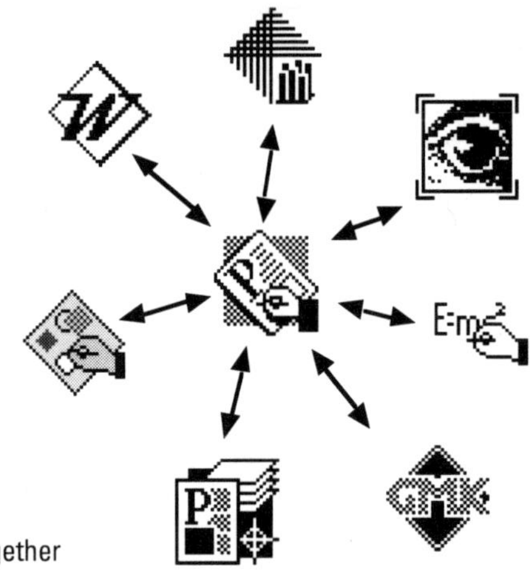

Figure 1-52
Programs working together

Software developers can create specialized program modules that you combine to obtain the set of features and functions best for you. Developers can concentrate on their specialties instead of all trying to create competing monoliths.

Program collaboration relies on System 7's framework for information interchange, called AppleEvents. It lets any program send messages to other programs. System 7 stores AppleEvents messages sent to a closed program and forwards the messages when the program is next opened. It also dispatches messages across a network to programs on another Macintosh.

☛ For more information, see "Program linking" in Chapter 10.

What you need

My how the system software has grown! The About This Macintosh command (which replaces About the Finder) in the Apple menu shows System 7 and Finder 7 together need two to three times as much memory as their immediate predecessors (Figure 1-53). To use the new system software, your Macintosh must have at least 2MB of RAM (random-access memory) and a hard disk.

You'll need more than the minimum 2MB if you use large or complex application programs; if you want to open several programs at once; or if you want to use the new file sharing capability and open any but the smallest program as well. As a rule of thumb, figure you'll need 1MB

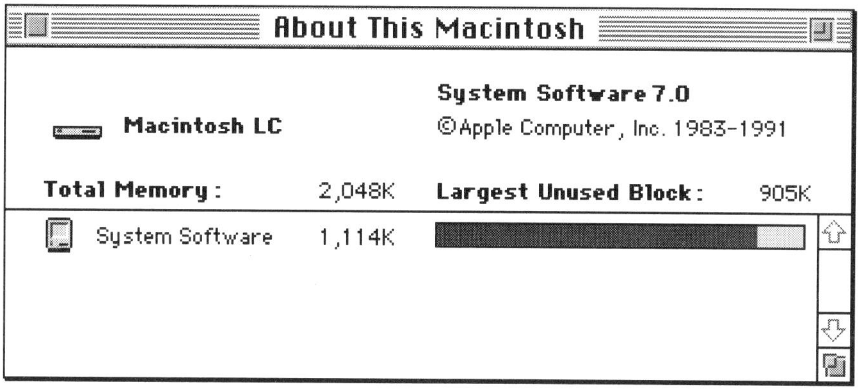

Figure 1-53
System 7 memory requirements

more than you use with older system software. You'll enjoy System 7 more if your Macintosh has at least 4MB of RAM.

To see colorized windows on your Macintosh, it must be displaying at least 256 colors or 16 grays. If it's set at a lower number — or if your Mac has only a black-and-white monitor — your windows and dialog boxes will look like they always have.

Most of System 7 works on all Macintosh models: the Plus, SE, Classic, and up. Only the three oldest models — the 128K, 512K, and XL — can't use System 7 at all.

☛ For more information, see "Equipment requirements" in Chapter 12.

Exploring is the key

So many new features and capabilities may seem intimidating. Remember though, that you can learn how to use most of them at your own pace. Take your time exploring the many Finder improvements. Wait on file sharing, virtual memory, and 32-bit addressing until you need them. Turn on balloon help only when you find it beneficial. Figure out publishing and subscribing (live copy/paste) and data access when you get programs that include them.

System 7 brings only a few changes you must face from the moment you begin using it. You can't dodge multitasking; you must get used to having multiple programs open at once. Also, you have to relearn a few basic skills like editing icon names and using the the standard directory dialog boxes for opening and saving items.

You upgrade to System 7 not for the changes it forces on you immediately, but for the possibilities it offers. Take your time. Upgrade when you can afford to increase your Mac's memory (and get a hard disk, if you don't already have one), but do it. Apple has made it clear that System 7 is the standard system software for Macintosh computers. System 7 capabilities are Macintosh capabilities.

On the whole, Apple engineers have succeeded admirably in making System 7's new capabilities available but not intrusive. The system software's look and feel has changed amazingly little considering all it lets you do.

Summary

- ✔ You can now Access and organize stuff on your disks faster and easier with a greatly improved and omnipresent Finder.
- ✔ System 7's multitasking allows several programs to be open concurrently (memory permitting) and have unattended tasks done in the background while you continue working.
- ✔ Virtual memory allows you to use disk space as if it were memory for opening programs and documents (though not on a Mac Plus, SE, Classic, standard LC, or Portable).
- ✔ File Sharing provides the ability to share files with other computers networked to your Macintosh.
- ✔ Variable-size TrueType fonts are outline fonts similar to PostScript fonts that let you see sharp text at any size on any screen, printer, or other output device.
- ✔ The ability to use color windows and icons adds increased functionality and variety to the Mac interface (requires a color monitor).

Chapter 2

The New Look

In This Chapter

- How to select a desktop pattern as well as customize your own.
- A look into the new windows of System 7.
- System 7 icons: restyled and redesigned for an improved Mac interface.
- Directory dialog boxes used as a one-window Finder.
- Balloon help: how the Mac can now explain itself.
- Opening multiple programs using the new Application menu.
- A summary of System 7's new error messages.

Black and white gets the job done, but color makes the job fun. A colorized desktop is more than a frivolous fad, though. By making your environment more pleasant, color can make you more productive. In addition to this incidental benefit, color can also directly impart information. Traffic lights illustrate this principle. Even though they work for the color-blind, color makes the lights more effective.

On color Macintosh systems, System 7 subtly enhances the desktop with color and shades of gray. Some of the improvements are also visible on systems that display true grays but not color. On a basic black-and-white screen (no colors or gray shades) the desktop looks the same as it does with older system software.

Color isn't the only change System 7 brings to the Macintosh user interface. Two menus — one for program switching and the other for controlling on-screen help — have taken up permanent residence at the right end of the menu bar. Like the Apple menu, the Help and Application menus have small icons instead of words as titles in the menu bar. Those small icons and other small icons no longer look like mutated standard-size icons. In the File menu, the Open, Save, and Save As commands have improved dialog boxes. Also, most of the system dialog boxes contain more detailed information than the messages they replace.

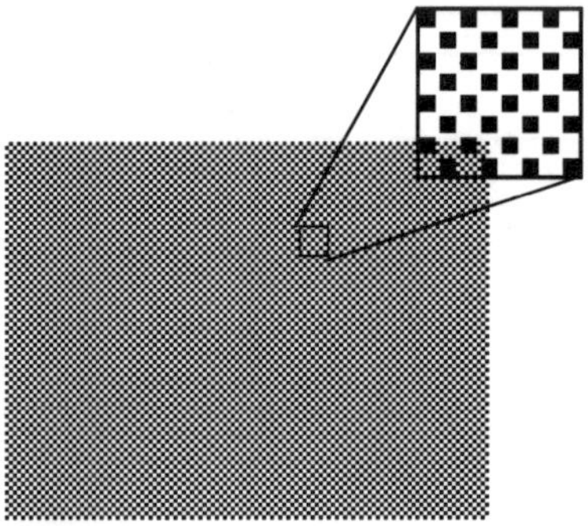

Figure 2-1
Gray desktop (black-and-white screen)

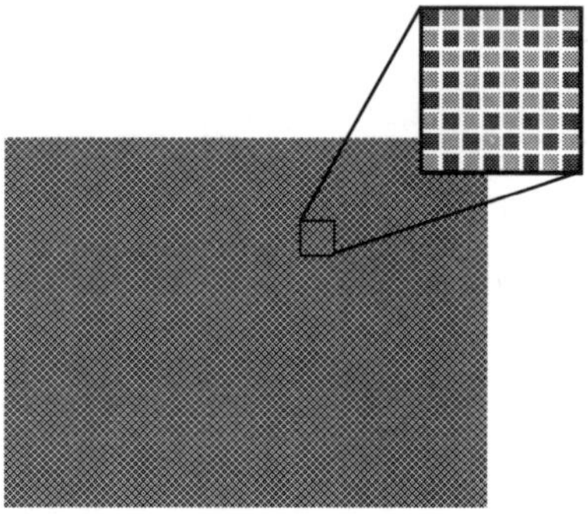

Figure 2-2
Gray desktop (256-color screen)

This chapter describes and illustrates all these ubiquitous changes in detail. Be sure to see the remaining chapters for detailed information on other new aspects of system software, such as the Finder and the System Folder.

Desktop

Look closely at the standard gray desktop prior to System 7 and you see a checkerboard pattern of little black and white dots (Figure 2-1). You see the same thing on a basic black-and-white screen (no colors or gray shades) with System 7.

On a Mac that displays colors or gray shades, however, the standard desktop pattern is made up of two gray shades (Figure 2-2). The overall effect is a smooth, continuous tone.

Selecting a desktop pattern

As always, you can select a different desktop pattern, or create your own pattern, using the General Controls control panel (Figure 2-3). It looks and works the same as the General section of the Control Panel desk accessory in older system software.

To scroll through the available standard patterns, click the miniature menu bar in the Desktop Pattern section of the General Controls control pattern. As you scroll, the pattern below the miniature menu bar changes. System 7 comes with five new color desktop patterns, plus the three of

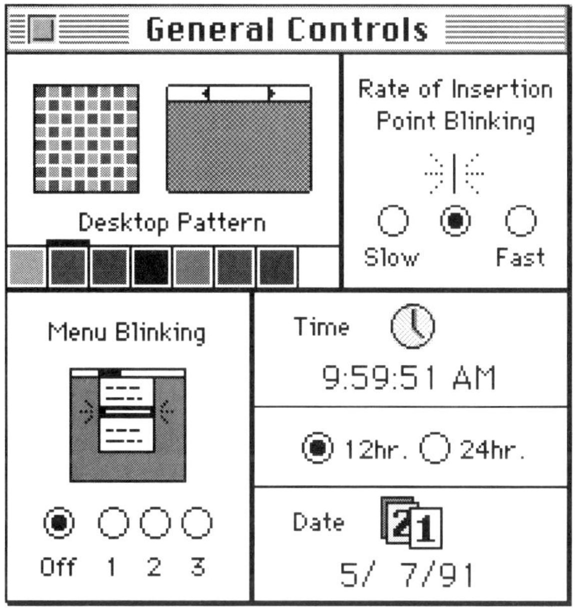

Figure 2-3
The General Controls control panel

old and the standard gray (Figure 2-4). When you see a pattern you like, click it to make it the desktop pattern.

Creating a custom desktop pattern

You create a custom pattern by changing the magnified view of a standard pattern in the General Controls control panel. Select a color from

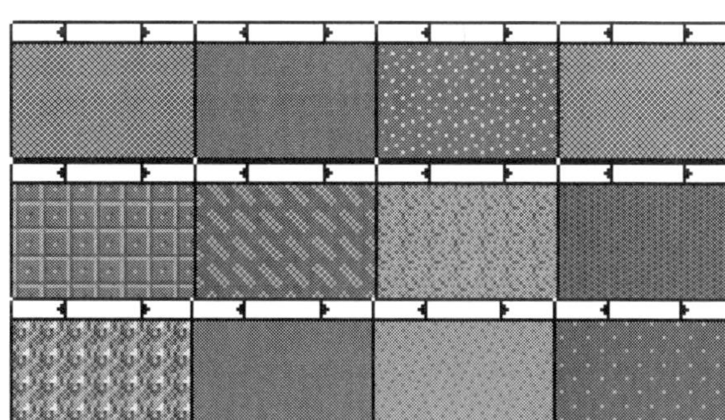

Figure 2-4
All the standard desktop patterns

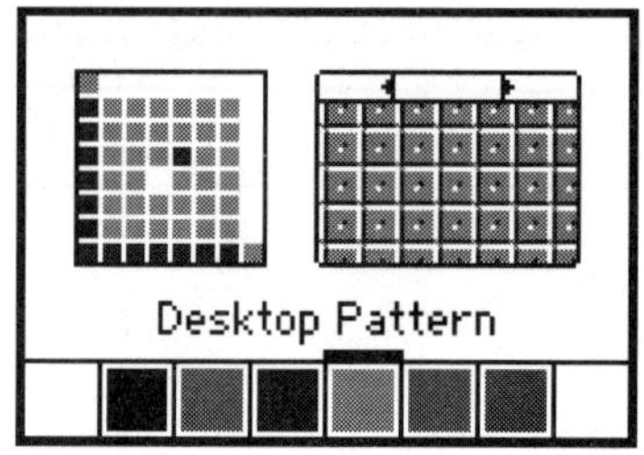

Figure 2-5
Editing a desktop pattern

the eight-color palette in the Desktop Pattern section of the control panel and click a square in the magnified view (Figure 2-5).

To change a color in the palette, double-click it. A dialog box opens in which you can pick another color by clicking a color wheel or by typing values for red, green, and blue or for hue, saturation, and brightness (Figure 2-6). When you've created the pattern you want, click below the miniature menu bar to make it the desktop pattern.

QUICK TIPS

Changes you make to a desktop pattern persist until you select a different pattern. To make a custom pattern revert to its standard configuration, scroll through all available patterns in the General Controls control panel until you see the standard pattern you want and then select it.

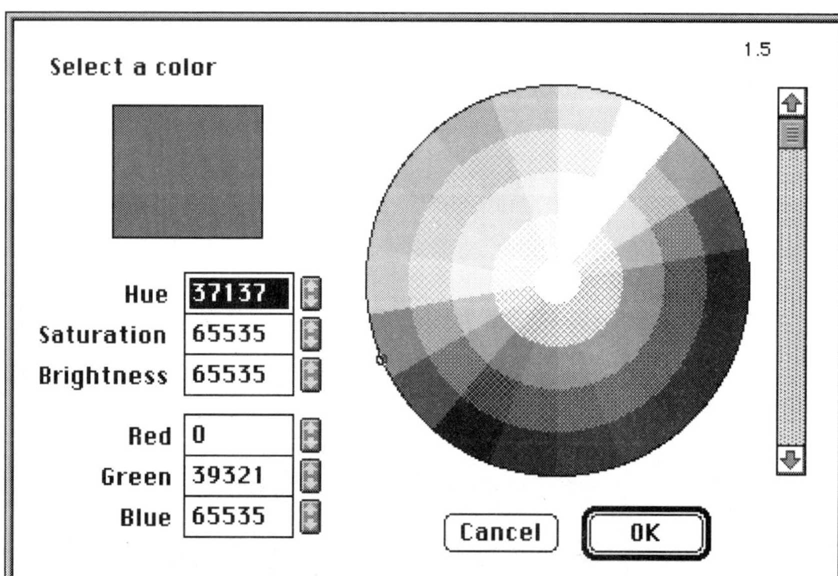

Figure 2-6
Picking a color for a desktop pattern

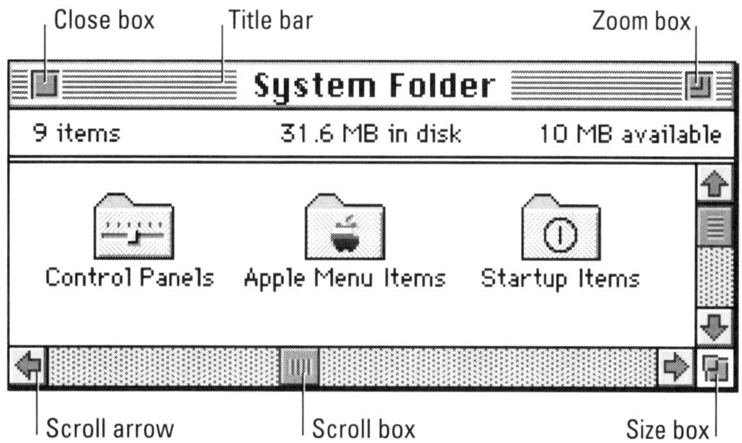

Figure 2-7
Window shades

Windows

The Macintosh windows that looked so avant-garde in 1984 now look dated. System 7 brings them up to date with trendy three-dimensional shading on monitors displaying colors or gray shades.

3-D window controls

Muted colors and shades of gray accent the window components you can manipulate (Figure 2-7): title bar, scroll arrows, scroll boxes, close box, zoom box, and size box. Subtle colors emphasize the window controls without jerking your attention away from your work as bright colors would.

UNDOCUMENTED

3-D motion

Shading tricks also make some of the colorized components seem to work in three dimensions when you use them. Clicking a close box or zoom box, for example, makes it look pressed down (Figure 2-8). (The

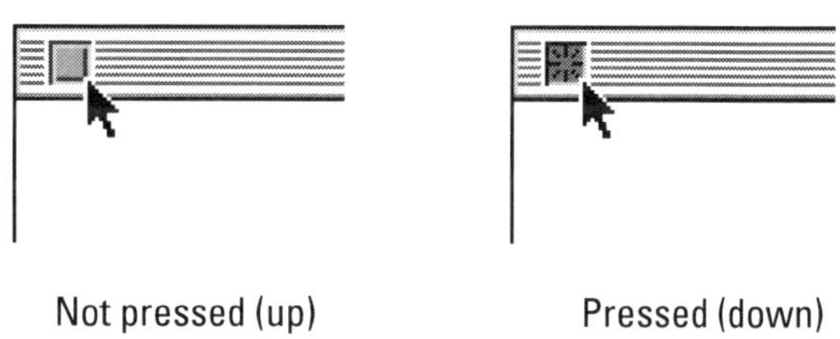

Figure 2-8
Simulated motion

Figure 2-9
The frontmost window stands out

close box and zoom box also flash as they always have.) The title bar, scroll arrows, and size box do not simulate 3-D motion.

Inactive windows pale

UNDOCUMENTED

Only the active window has 3-D shading. It stands out from inactive windows behind it because System 7 displays inactive windows with gray borders and a gray title (Figure 2-9). Older system software displays black borders and titles for inactive windows.

The contents of inactive windows are never dimmed, so you can see the contents easily. Also, window backgrounds are always white. White windows are a fundamental part of the Macintosh interface.

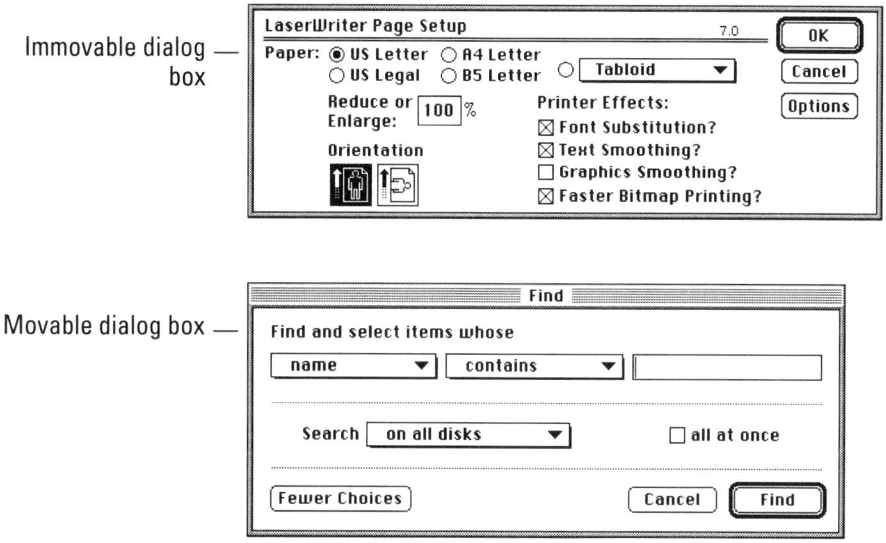

Figure 2-10
Dialog box shading

If the active window is large enough to show the full width or height of its contents without scrolling, System 7 shades its scroll bars a light gray.

Dialog box shading

Three-dimensional shading carries over to standard dialog boxes. System 7 replaces the double-line border of movable and fixed dialog boxes with a narrow half-round molding (Figure 2-10). (Movable dialog boxes have a title bar but no close box or size box.)

Choosing a window color

The standard color for shading window controls is light purple. You can select any of seven other colors or black-and-white as the shading color for window control areas using the Color control panel (Figure 2-11). Your choice of window tint affects all windows immediately, but the Color control panel doesn't save its settings to disk until you close it. The window tint you choose will not apply to tool palettes and special-purpose windows created by some application programs until the programs have been upgraded for System 7. You cannot create your own window-shading color using the Color control panel.

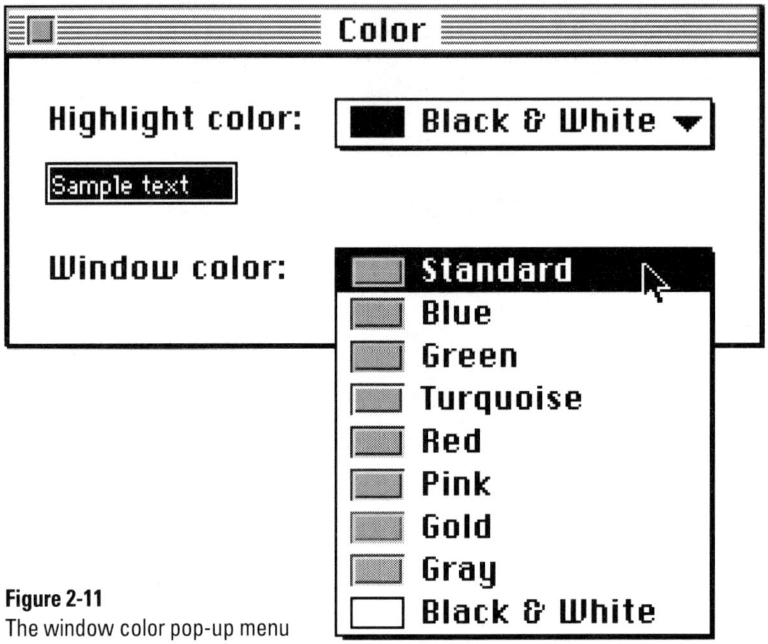

Figure 2-11
The window color pop-up menu

To see colorized windows and shaded dialog boxes on your Macintosh, your Monitors control panel (formerly the Monitors section of the Control Panel desk accessory) must be set for at least 16 grays or 256 colors (Figure 2-12). If it's set at a lower number — or if your Mac has only a black-and-white monitor — your windows and dialog boxes will look like they always have.

Icons

Windows aren't the only colorful part of System 7. Apple has also restyled the icons for folders, the Finder, the System file, the items in the System Folder, Apple utility programs, other Apple software, and generic applications, desk accessories, and documents.

Icon colors

Most of the new icons are shaded using a color similar to the standard purple window color to achieve a 3-D effect. Bright colors are used mainly for highlights (Figure 2-13).

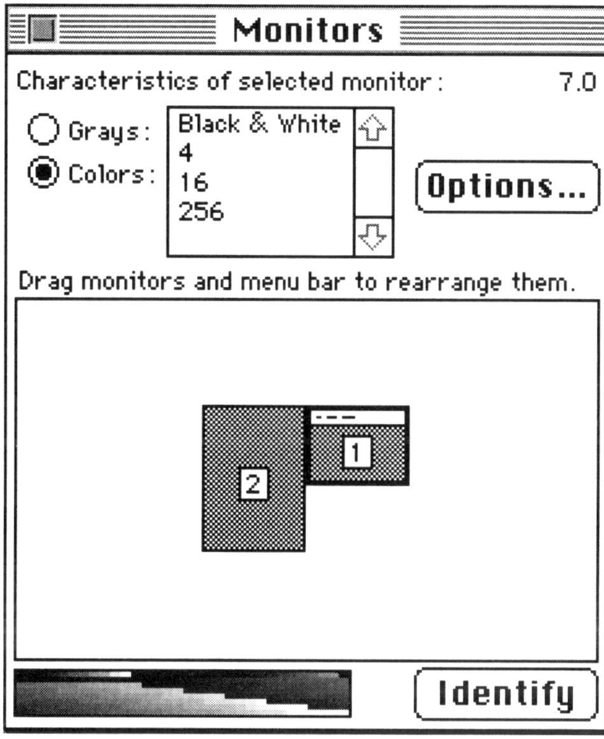

Figure 2-12
The Monitors control panel set for 256 colors

The new icons have three separate color schemes. One of the color schemes is optimized for monitors set to display 256 or more colors or grays. Another color scheme looks best on monitors set to display 16 colors or grays. The third color scheme is used on monitors that display black-and-white or four colors or grays (Figure 2-14).

You can alter an icon's natural color by selecting it and choosing a label from the Finder's Label menu. The Finder blends the label color with the icon colors. It looks like you covered the icon with a piece of acetate the color of the label. Using the Color control panel to select an alternate window color does not affect the color of any icons.

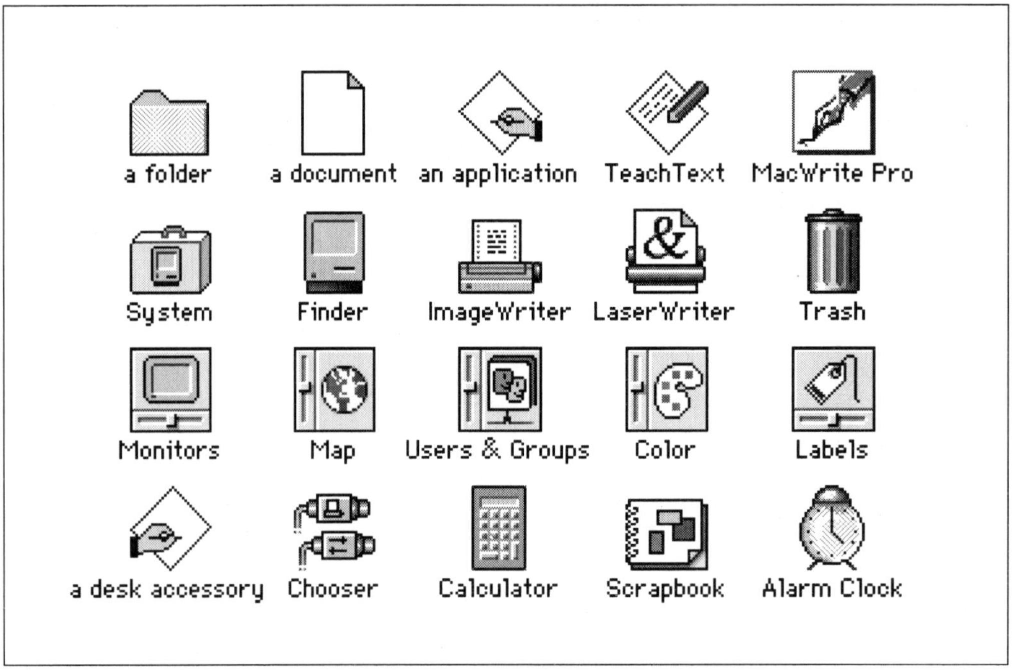

Figure 2-13
Some full-size color icons

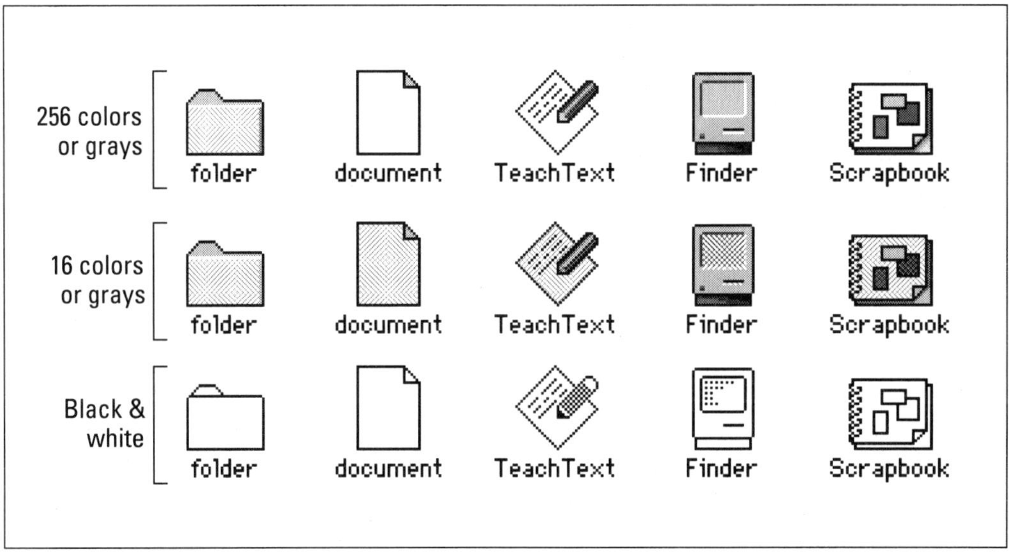

Figure 2-14
The three icon color schemes

Icon sizes

For each of the three color schemes there are two icon designs, one large and one small (Figure 2-15). Large icons appear on the desktop and in the Finder's By Icon view of disk and folder windows. Small icons appear in menus and in the Finder's Small Icon view of disk and folder windows.

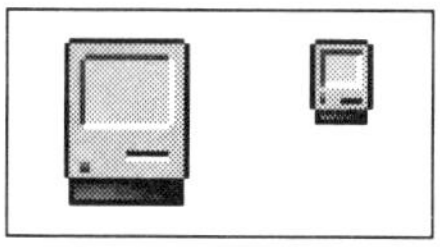

Figure 2-15
Large and small icons

Prior to System 7, the small icons were mechanically shrunken from full-size icons. Now any program developer can design separate, better looking small icons.

UNDOCUMENTED

Icon highlighting

Regardless of icon size and color, System 7 highlights selected icons on monitors displaying 16 or more colors or grays by darkening the icons (Figure 2-16). On a monitor displaying fewer than 16 colors or grays, System 7 highlights selected icons by inverting the colors; white becomes black and black becomes white.

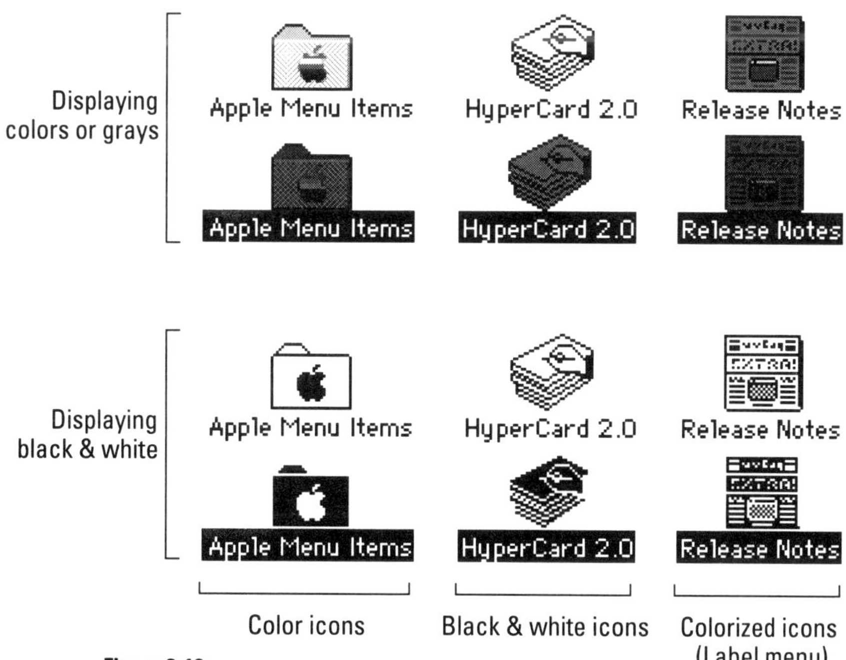

Figure 2-16
Icon highlighting

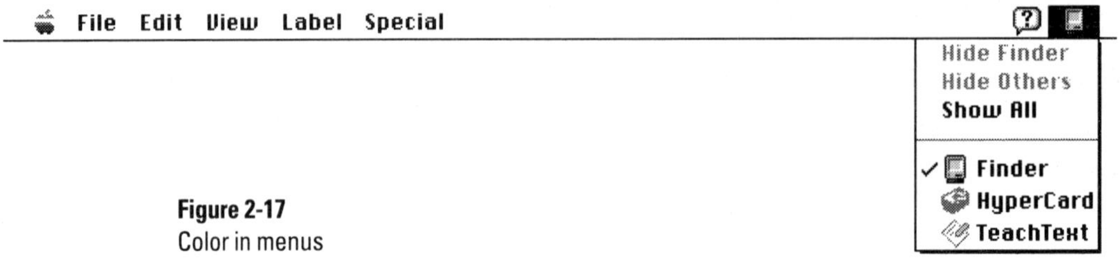

Figure 2-17
Color in menus

Old icons

Just as Apple had to redesign its icons for System 7, so must the developers and publishers of other programs. Until then, the old program and document icons will look like they always have. When you install an updated program that includes redesigned icons on your disk, you will usually have to rebuild the disk's desktop to see the new icons for that program and its documents.

To rebuild the desktop of any disk whose icon normally appears on the desktop after startup, press the Command and Option keys while starting your Macintosh. For each disk in turn, the Finder asks whether you want the disk's desktop rebuilt. To rebuild the desktop of a floppy disk or other removable disk whose icon is not on the desktop, press Command-Option while inserting the disk.

Menus

System 7 enhances menu looks with true grays and colors on monitors that can display them (Figure 2-17). The small icons in the menu bar for the Help and Application menus appear in color or shades of gray on a monitor displaying at least 16 colors or gray shades. In addition, small icons in menus such as the Apple and Application menus appear in color or shades of gray.

On monitors displaying at least 4 grays or 16 colors, System 7 uses true gray text to display inactive menu titles, inactive menu items, and the gray lines that divide sections of menus. In a program with color menus, System 7 displays inactive items in a blend of the menu item color and the menu background color. On a monitor displaying less than 16 colors, System 7 simulates gray text by alternating black and white dots. Older system software simulates gray text at all color or gray levels and does not display color icons in menus or the menu bar (except for the Apple icon).

Figure 2-18
An Open command's dialog box

Menu enhancement works automatically for most existing application programs. However, programs that don't use standard menu management software will not display true gray text and dividing lines in menus until they are revised.

Directory dialog boxes

At first glance the new directory dialog boxes you get when you use Open, Save, Save As, and similar commands look little changed from the older ones. Using them dispels that notion quickly. Directory dialog boxes now work more than ever like a one-window Finder (Figure 2-18).

All directory dialog boxes still have a single directory window, in which you locate an item you want opened or a folder where you want an item saved. The directory window lists the names of items from one folder or disk at a time, always alphabetically by name. System 7 displays longer names than its predecessors by using compressed-style text for names that exceed 25 characters.

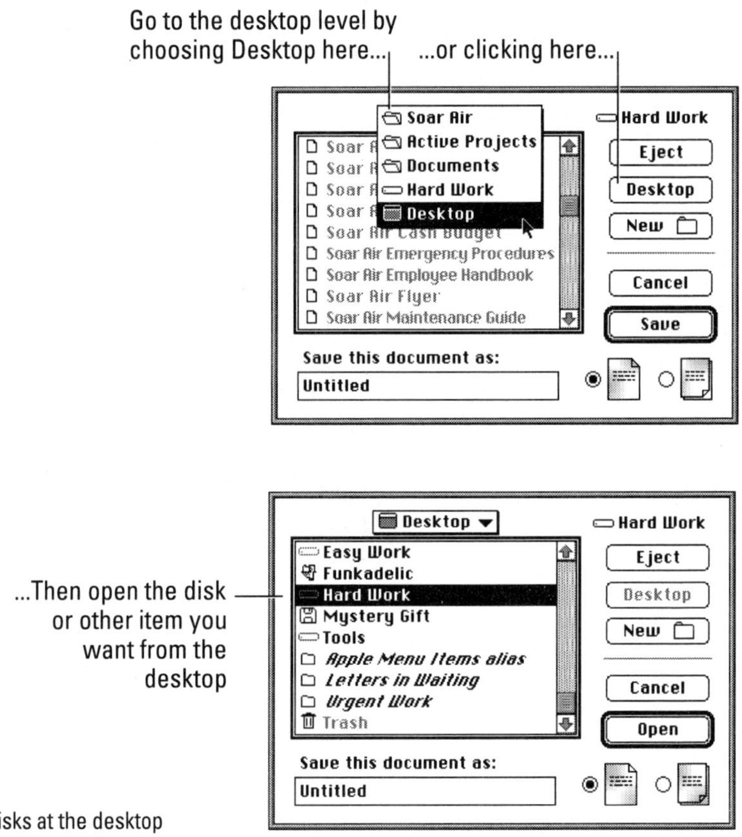

Figure 2-19
Switching disks at the desktop

The new directory dialog boxes display icons in the seven colors assigned by the Finder's Label menu. Also, they show the names of items that can't be opened (such as the names of files in a Save dialog box) using true gray text. Your Monitors control panel must be set for at least 16 colors or 4 grays. Some programs must be upgraded to show icons in color and text in true gray.

The desktop

Directory dialog boxes now provide a view of the desktop and let you open disks and other items on it. No more switching disks using the Drive button. Instead, you go to the desktop level and open the disk whose contents you want to see (Figure 2-19). This new procedure makes switching among more than two disks easier. A new Desktop button replaces the old Drive button and clicking it takes you to the desktop level. You can also go to the desktop by choosing it from the pop-up menu above the directory window.

Navigating by keyboard

Like older system software, System 7 lets you move through folders and open items using the keyboard as well as the mouse. In an Open dialog box, typing an item's name or the first part of it selects the item in the directory window. For example, typing "m" selects the first item that begins with the letter M or m. Typing several letters quickly specifies a longer name to be selected in the directory window. Pausing while typing starts selecting all over. The Key Repeat Rate setting in the Keyboard control panel determines how long you must pause to make a fresh start. Once you have selected an item in a directory window (by any means), pressing the Return or Enter key opens the item.

System 7 makes this keyboard navigation available for the first time in Save and Save As dialog boxes. You also use the keyboard in these dialog boxes to enter a name for the item you're saving. System 7 lets you know when your typing will affect a Save or Save As dialog's directory window by outlining the window with a heavy black border. A flashing insertion point or highlighted text in the text entry box means your typing will go there (Figure 2-20).

You select the directory window or the text entry box by clicking or dragging in the one you want. You can also alternate between them by pressing the Tab key. Prior to System 7, pressing the Tab key in an Open, Save, or Save As dialog box switched to the next disk.

An even more subtle change in Save and Save As dialog boxes further reduces confusion when moving through folders. When you select a folder in the directory window, the Save button becomes an Open button (Figure 2-21). Clicking it opens the selected folder. In older system software, the button works the same way, but it's always named Save (even when clicking it opens a selected folder).

The System 7 directory dialog boxes recognize more keyboard equivalents than older versions. Table 2-1 has the details.

Naming the item you're saving

While you are editing the name of the item you're saving, the Cut, Copy, and Paste commands are available from the Edit menu. You can now cut and paste names. When pasting, only the first 31 characters are used; the rest are omitted. In some programs that haven't been revised for System 7, you must use the keyboard equivalents, Command-X, Command-C, and Command-V.

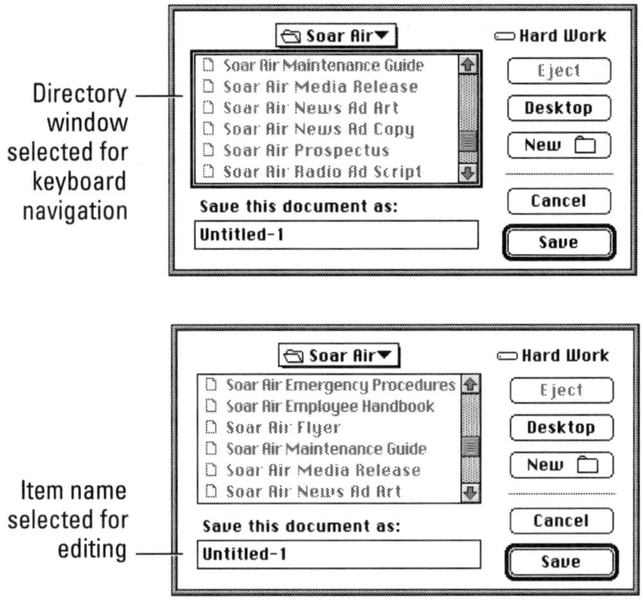

Figure 2-20
Moving around by keyboard

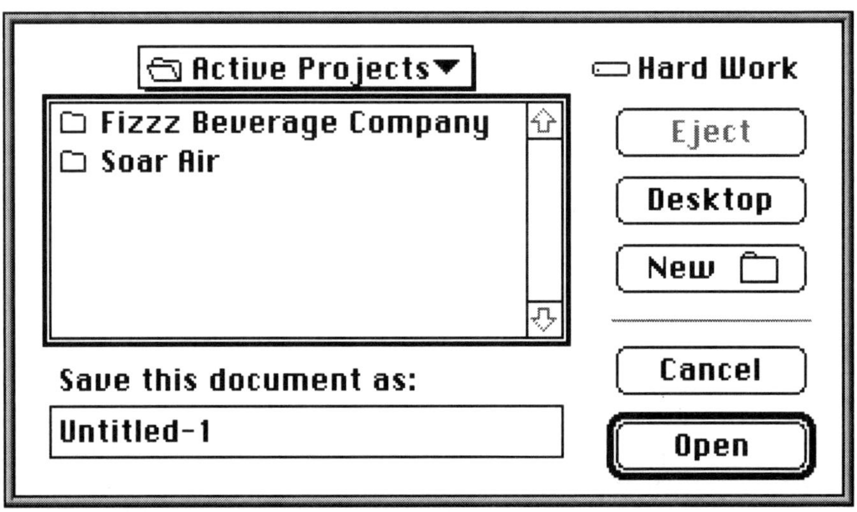

Figure 2-21
Opening a folder while saving

Table 2-1: Directory dialog keyboard equivalents

Objective	Keystroke
Select an item in the active window (or the desktop if no window is active)	Type the item's full or partial name
Scroll up in the directory window	Up Arrow
Scroll down in the directory window	Down Arrow
Open the selected item	Command–Down Arrow or Command–O
Open the enclosing folder, disk, or volume	Command–Up Arrow
Go to the next disk or volume	Command–Left Arrow
Go to the previous disk or volume	Command–Right Arrow
Go to the desktop level	Command–Shift–Up Arrow or Command–D
Eject the disk in drive 1	Command–Shift–1
Eject the disk in drive 2	Command–Shift–2
Move to the next keyboard target	Tab
Click the default button (usually Open or Save)	Return, Enter
Cancel the directory dialog	Escape, Command–Period
Make a new folder (doesn't work with some older programs)	Command–N
Select the original of the selected alias (instead of opening it)	Option–Command–O, Option–double-click, or Option–click Open

Creating a new folder

The System 7 Save and Save As dialog boxes include a new button you can click to create a new folder (Figure 2-22). However, the button is missing from the Save and Save As dialog boxes of most programs that have not been updated for System 7.

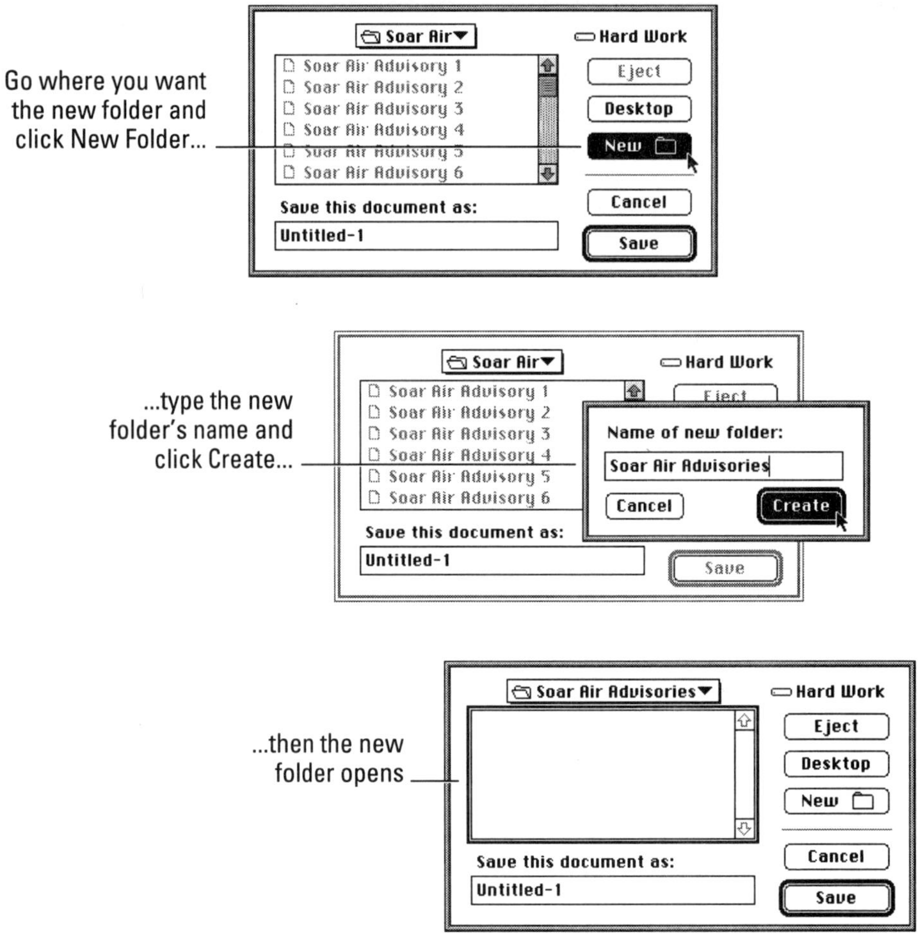

Figure 2-22
Making a folder while saving

Opening an item

As usual, you can open an item in the directory window by double-clicking it. If you double-click the wrong item and realize it before you release the mouse button, continue pressing and drag the pointer to the item you want to open. When you release the mouse button, the currently selected item opens. In older system software, dragging on the second click of a double-click cancels the double-click and nothing is opened. To cancel a double-click in a System 7 directory dialog box, hold down the mouse button on the second click and drag the pointer outside the dialog box before releasing the mouse button.

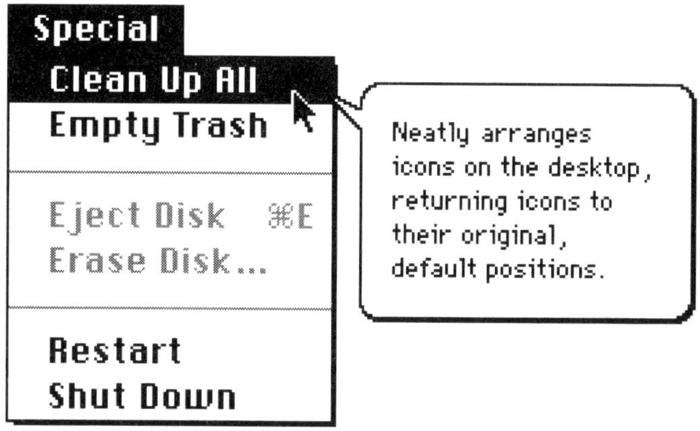

Figure 2-23
A help balloon

Balloon help

When you need immediate information about objects you see on screen, you can turn on System 7's optional balloon help. With balloon help on, you place the pointer over an object and a concise description of it appears in a cartoon-style balloon (Figure 2-23). The balloon points to the object and tells you what the object is, what it does, what happens when you click it, or some portion of this information. You do not have to press any keys or click anything to make a help balloon appear.

Turning balloon help on and off

You turn on balloon help by choosing Show Balloons from the Help menu. That command then changes to Hide Balloons, and choosing it turns off balloon help. The Help menu is near the right end of the menu bar (Figure 2-24).

COMPARISON

The Help menu takes up little space on your menu bar because its title is an icon instead of a word. Moreover, Apple adjusted System 7's menu bar to use no more space with the Help menu than the older system software's menu bar without a Help menu.

Working with balloon help on

Everything works normally when balloon help is on. Using balloon help does not put the Macintosh into a help-only mode. Help balloons appear whether you are pressing the mouse button or not. You click, double-click, and otherwise use programs normally, except that you may

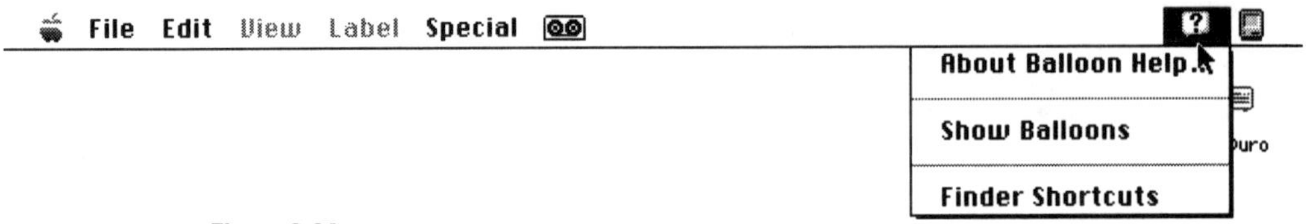

Figure 2-24
The Help menu

perceive a slight delay as help balloons come and go when you move the pointer slowly across items that have balloon help descriptions. It's like someone is standing over your shoulder and describing objects on the screen to you.

The object a help balloon describes may be large or small and individual or collective (Figure 2-25). For example, the close box in the active window's title bar has its own help balloon. In contrast, an inactive window has one balloon for the whole window. Sometimes a help balloon describes a whole group, as in the Mouse control panel where one balloon tells you about the seven settings for the Mouse Tracking option.

UNDOCUMENTED

Moving the pointer slowly over several objects that have help balloons opens and closes balloons in sequence. To prevent excessive flashing of help balloons, they do not appear when you move the pointer quickly. For a help balloon to appear, the pointer must be in the same area for about one-tenth of a second or longer. You cannot change this timing.

What balloon help knows

Balloon help knows about all standard objects in the Macintosh interface. They include the Apple menu, the Help menu, the Application menu (described in the next section), windows in general, and standard parts of directory dialog boxes, the Page Setup dialog box, and the Print dialog box. Balloon help cannot describe a specific program's menu commands, window contents, dialog boxes, and so forth unless its developer or publisher has revised it to include the necessary help balloons. For example, Apple has provided complete balloon help for the Finder, TeachText, standard control panels, and standard desk accessories.

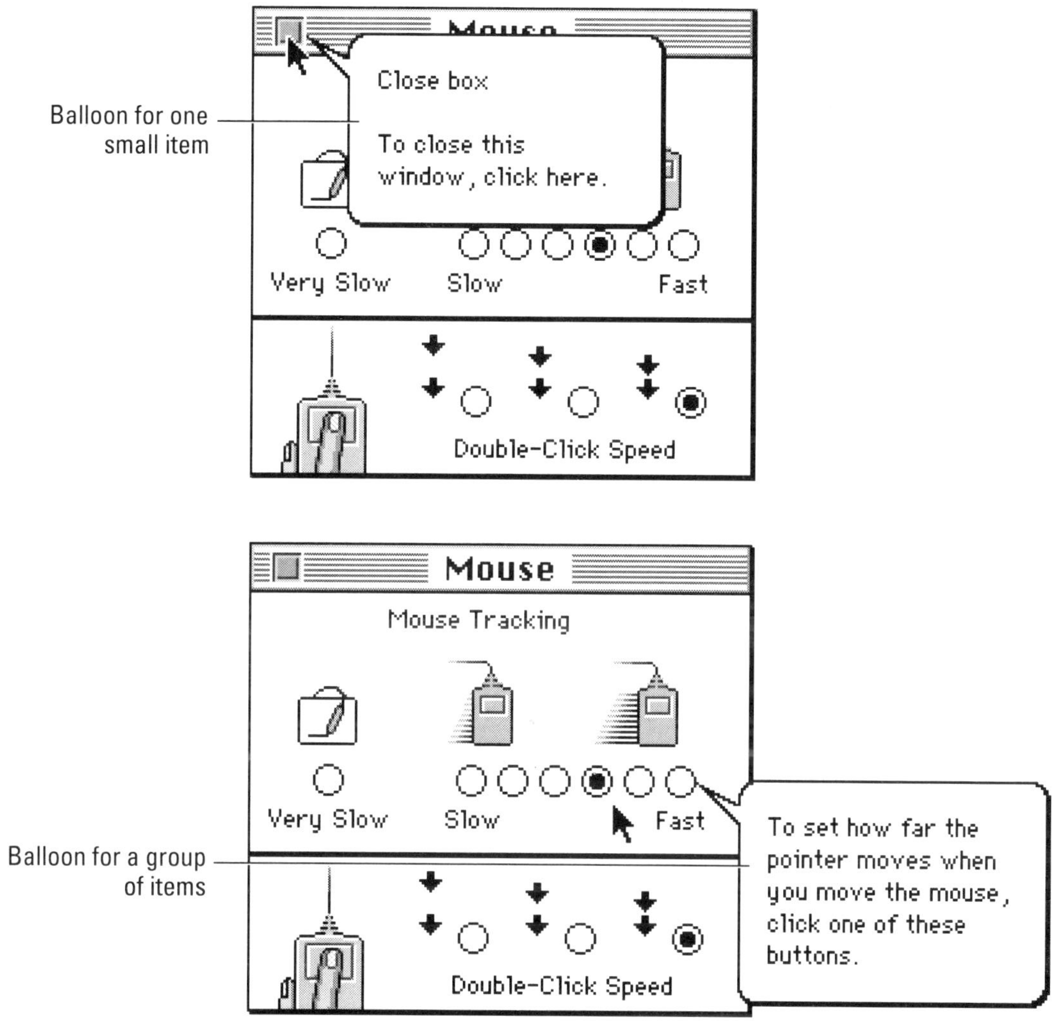

Figure 2-25
Help balloons vary in scope

Other help

Balloon help does not teach you how to combine features of a program to accomplish tasks. However, a program can add how-to help, an on-screen reference, or other items to the Help menu. The Finder, for example, has a Finder Shortcuts item (Figure 2-26) that displays a dialog box containing tricks for using the Finder.

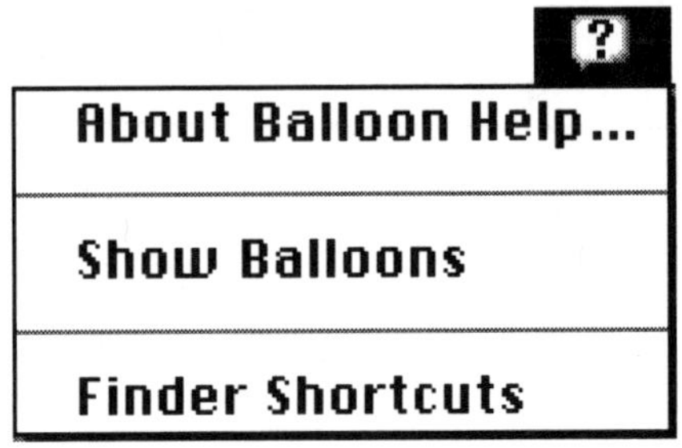

Figure 2-26
The Finder's Help menu

Opening multiple programs

Next to the Help menu is another new menu with System 7, the Application menu (Figure 2-27). It is represented in the menu bar by a small icon that tells you which application program or desk accessory is currently active. You can use the Application menu to switch to another open application program or desk accessory. To this extent the Application menu is like the MultiFinder icon (also called the application icon) of older system software.

MultiFinder's multitasking capabilities are built into System 7. The Finder is always available without quitting the program you're using and you can have as many programs open simultaneously as will fit in your computer's memory (Figure 2-28). You can copy and paste among

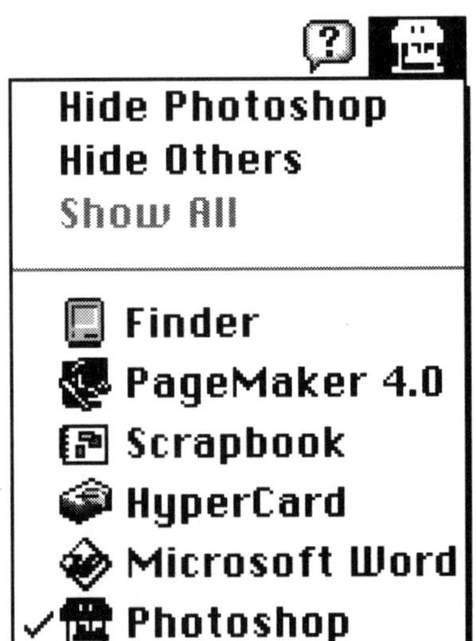

Figure 2-27
The Application menu

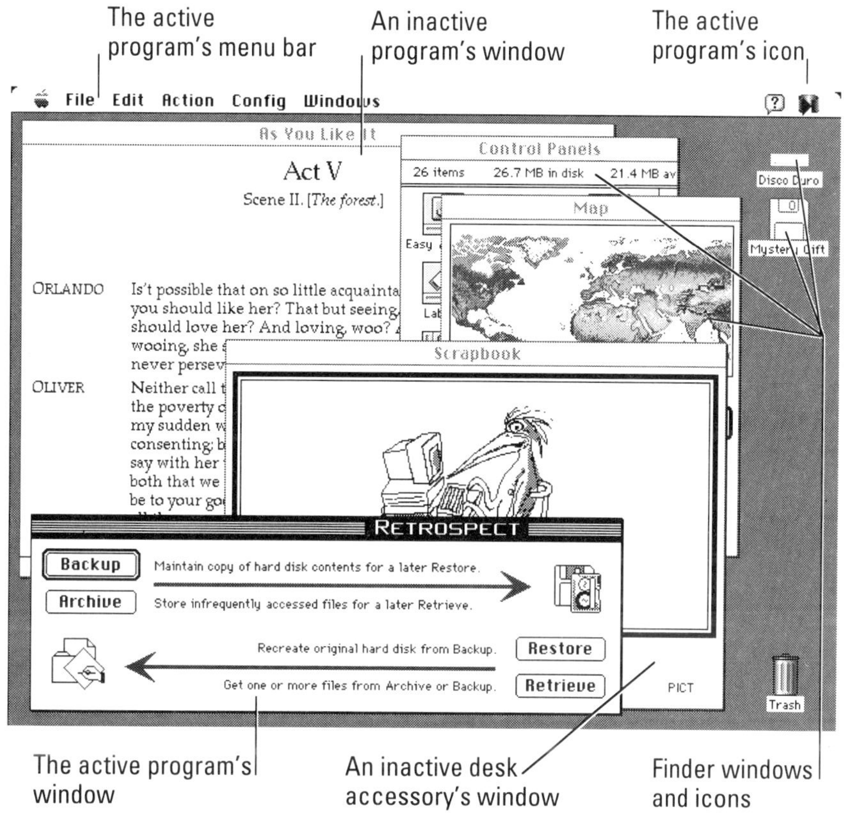

Figure 2-28
Multiple programs open

documents of open programs without closing documents and quitting programs. Also, you can switch to the Finder without quitting programs, and there open other programs, find documents, organize folders and disks, and so on.

Regardless of how many programs you have open, only one can be working at a time. Programs that are open but not working are in a state of suspended animation. In older system software, MultiFinder, and consequently multitasking, can be on or off. System 7's multitasking is always on.

Multitasking's valuable benefits have disorienting side effects. For instance, you may think the program you're using has unexpectedly quit when actually you switched to another open program by clicking one of its windows. You must condition yourself to look at the menu bar when you need to know which open program is currently active. The active program's icon appears at the right end of the menu bar as the placeholder for the new Application menu.

Switching programs

You use the Application menu to switch from one open program to another. All open programs are listed in the Application menu by name and small icon. (With MultiFinder, open application programs are listed near the bottom of the Apple menu.)

To make a program listed in the Application menu the active program, you choose it from the menu. When you do, that program takes over the menu bar and the program's windows come to the front. The program that was active becomes inactive. Its windows drop back but remain visible except for the parts covered by other open programs' windows. You can also make another program the active program by opening its icon or any of its document icons in the Finder or by clicking in any of its windows. Clicking the desktop or a Finder icon makes the Finder active.

Reducing window clutter

With many programs open the desktop quickly becomes a visual Tower of Babel. You can eliminate the clutter by choosing the Application menu's Hide Others command (Figure 2-29). It hides the windows of all programs except the currently active one. The command also dims the icons of open and hidden programs listed in the Application menu. To make the windows of all programs visible again, choose Show All from the Application menu.

You can hide the active program's windows and simultaneously switch to the most recently active program by choosing the first command from the Application menu. The command's name begins with the word Hide and ends with the name of the currently active program.

QUICK TIPS

To hide the active program's windows as you switch to a particular program, press the Option key while choosing the other program from the Application menu. Or press Option while clicking another program's window. You hide windows and switch to the Finder by pressing Option while clicking the desktop or a Finder icon.

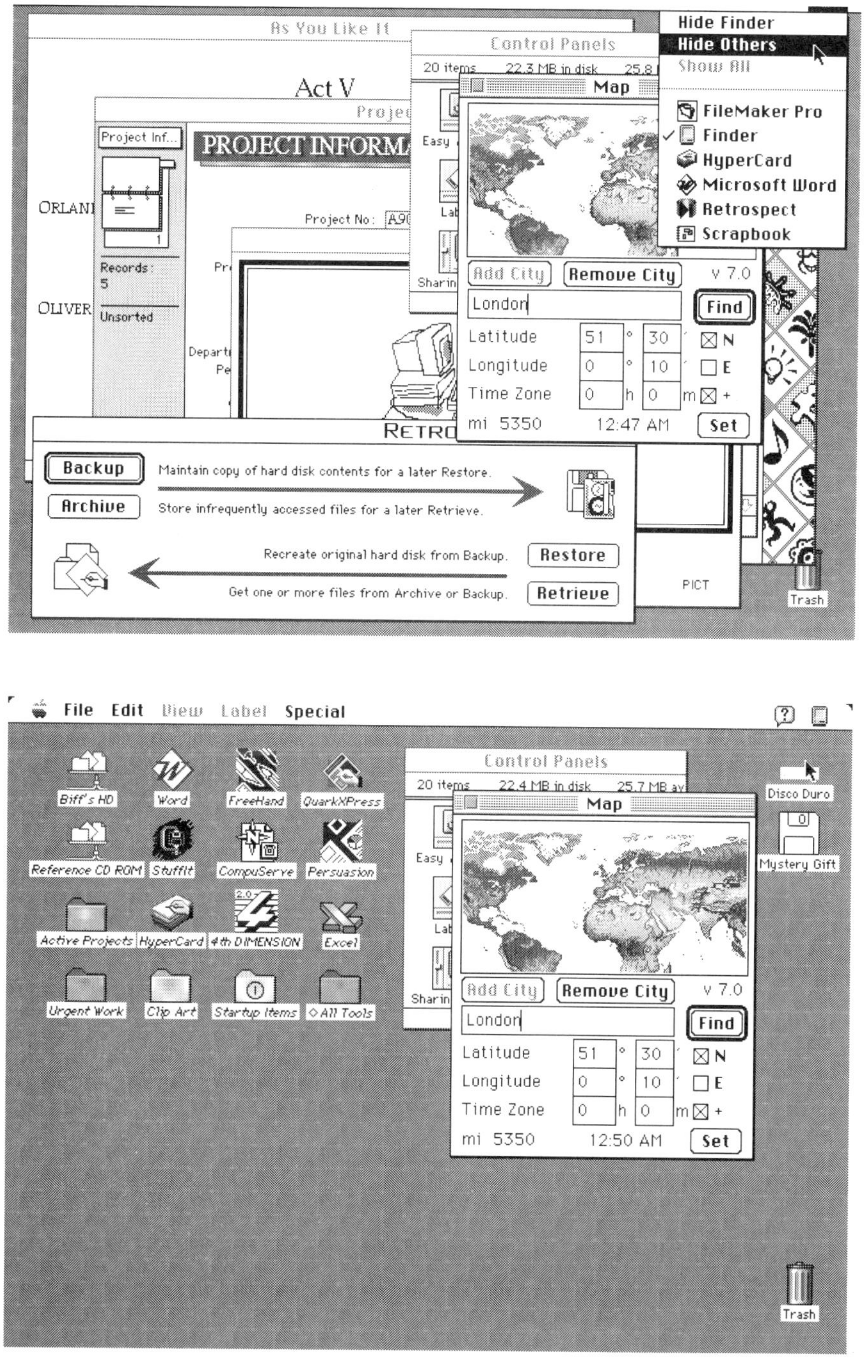

Figure 2-29
Hiding inactive programs

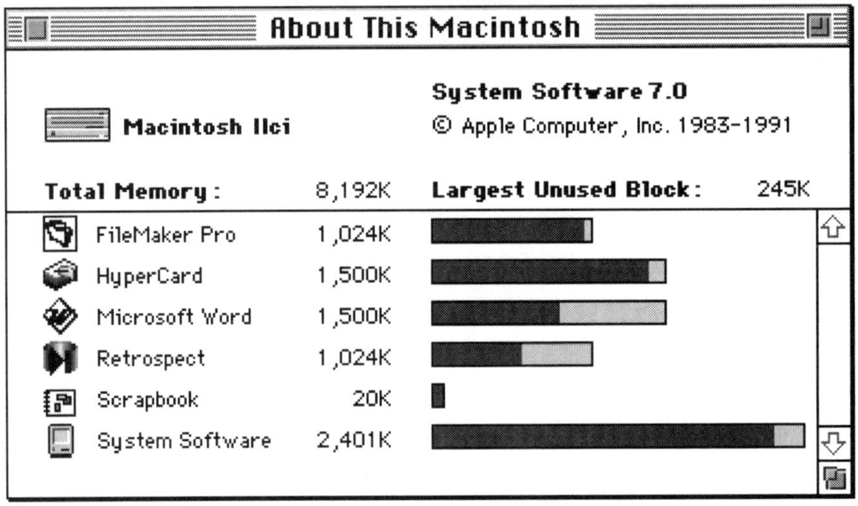

Figure 2-30
Checking on memory use

Memory partitions

Every application program and desk accessory you open has its own memory partition in System 7. (Older system software lumps all open desk accessories together in a single partition if MultiFinder is active or includes them with the open application program if MultiFinder is inactive.) You can see how your computer's memory is partitioned at any time by choosing About This Macintosh from the Apple menu when the Finder is active (Figure 2-30).

Background operations

Programs that know how can operate in the background by using System 7's multitasking capabilities. Background programs operate during the intervals, often only split seconds long, when the active program isn't using the computer. This usually happens while the active program waits for you to do something.

A background program can't use the menu bar or interact directly with you in any other way. It can, however, ask you to activate it by some or all of these means:

❖ Display a diamond symbol next to its name in the Application menu.

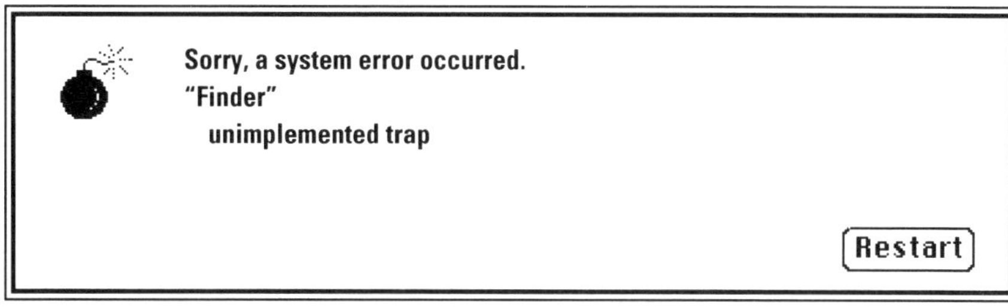

Figure 2-31
The system error (bomb) alert box

- ❖ Flash its icon on top of the Application menu's icon or the Apple menu's icon.
- ❖ Play a sound (commonly a beep).
- ❖ Display a brief alert message which you must dismiss before continuing.

New error messages

Apple hasn't yet managed to eliminate system errors and their dreaded bomb alert boxes (Figure 2-31) from the Macintosh interface, but System 7 does soften their blows a little. Whereas system software versions 6.0.5 and older reports a cryptic error ID number in a bomb box, System 7 reports a brief message that's merely arcane.

Where you used to read "ID = 02," for example, you now read "address error." You still don't know what's going on, but at least you don't feel like a calculator. Table 2-2 lists the error messages that can appear in the system error alert box, their equivalent ID numbers, and likely causes.

Emergency quit

Sometimes you can recover from a system error — or the related problem of a hung or frozen system — without restarting your Macintosh. Pressing Command-Option-Escape may bring up a dialog box asking whether you want to force the Finder (or some other program) to quit (Figure 2-32). If so, click the Force Quit button and cross your fingers. If you get to the Finder, immediately save all open documents and restart the computer.

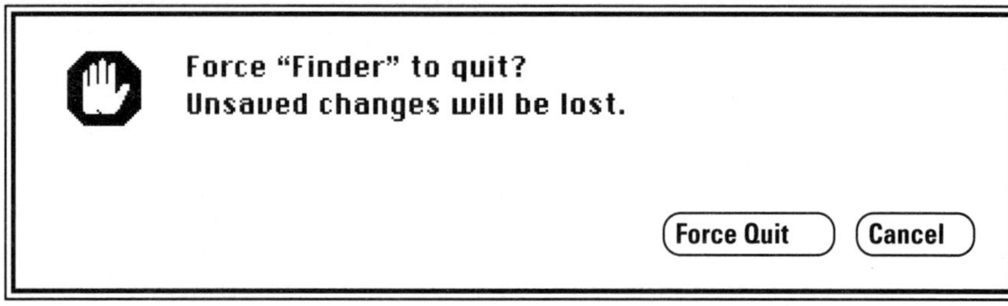

Figure 2-32
Forcing a program to quit

Bomb recovery

If that trick doesn't work and the plastic programmer's switch is installed on your Macintosh, try pressing the Interrupt part of the switch (not the Restart part). On most Macintosh models, the Interrupt part is labeled with a tiny circle and the Restart part is labeled with a tiny arrow. (The Mac LC and IIsi have no programmer's switch.) With luck, you'll see a dialog box containing a greater-than symbol in its upper-left corner (Figure 2-33). Type G FINDER and press Return. If you get to the Finder, immediately save all open documents and restart the computer.

Overall, the changes to the Macintosh desktop interface are the most noticeable in its six-year history, yet they don't disrupt the way you work. Compared to other graphical interfaces — Next's chiseled features and Microsoft Windows 3.0's colorful facade, for instance — System 7 looks quite conservative. While System 7 may not win a fashion award, you'll be able to wear it comfortably for a couple of years after neon colors fade from favor.

None of the cosmetic or functional changes to the Macintosh interface described in this chapter change the basic Macintosh experience. They refine it.

Figure 2-33
Recovering from a system error

Table 2-2: Fatal error messages

Error Message	ID	Likely Cause
bus error	01	Software error or incompatibility
address error	02	Software error or incompatibility
illegal instruction	03	Software error or incompatibility
divide by zero	04	Software error
CHK error	05	Software error
numeric overflow	06	Software error or incompatibility
error type 7	07	Software error or incompatibility
error type 8	08	Hardware error or a programming tool had trouble
error type 9	09	Software error
bad F-line instruction	10	Software error
error type 11	11	Software error or incompatibility
unimplemented trap	12	Software error or incompatibility
unserviceable interrupt	13	Someone pressed the interrupt part of the programmer's switch, hardware malfunctioned, or a programming tool had trouble
Device Manager error	14	Hardware malfunctioned or a programming tool had trouble
Segment Loader error	15	System file probably damaged
SANE error	16	System file probably damaged
List Manager not present	17	System file probably damaged
BitEdit not present	18	System file probably damaged
Disk Initialization package not present	19	System file probably damaged
Standard File not present	20	System file probably damaged
SANE not present	21	System file probably damaged
SANE transcendental functions not present	22	System file probably damaged

☞

Table 2-2 *(cont'd)*

Error Message	ID	Likely Cause
International Utilities not present	23	System file probably damaged
Binary-Decimal Conversion package not present	24	System file probably damaged
out of memory	25	A program unexpectedly ran out of memory
file system map inconsistent	27	System file probably damaged
stack collision with heap	28	A program unexpectedly ran out of memory or a conflict occurred among system extension software
Memory Manager error	33	A program unexpectedly ran out of memory
unserviceable slot interrupt	51	Macintosh malfunction or NuBus card error
bad SANE opcode	81	Software error
menu purged while in use	84	Software error
couldn't load MBDF	85	Software error
couldn't find hierarchical menu's parent	86	Software error
couldn't load WDEF	87	Software error
couldn't load CDEF	88	Software error
floating point coprocessor not installed	90	Software error

Summary

- The cosmetic changes affecting the desktop, windows, icons, and menus only show up on a Macintosh with a color or grayscale monitor. You can see the functional changes on any Macintosh, however.
- On a Mac that displays colors or gray shades, the standard desktop pattern in System 7 is made up of two gray shades resulting in a smooth, continuous tone.
- The updated Mac windows in System 7 include three-dimensional motion and window controls, as well as the ability to select shading color for window control areas.
- System 7's icons have been shaded to achieve a three-dimensional effect and designed in two sizes to allow for better looking small icons.
- New directory dialog boxes allow you to open disks from the desktop without having to use the Drive button as with the older ones; move through folders and open items using the keyboard; and edit the name of an item to be saved using the Cut, Copy, and Paste commands from the Edit menu.
- Balloon help consists of cartoon-like balloons that appear when the pointer is placed over any standard object in the Mac's interface. The balloons point to the object and tell what the object is, what it does, what happens when it is clicked, or some portion of this information.
- System 7 lets you have multiple programs open simultaneously. You use the Application menu to switch from one program to another as well as to hide the windows of all programs except the active one.

Chapter 3

Finder Improvements

In This Chapter

- Zooming, scrolling, and selecting with smart windows.
- Finding and fetching items quickly by simple or complex search criteria.
- New methods for naming documents, folders, disks, and other desktop items.
- Classifying the contents of disks with text labels and colors.
- A look at copying multiple items quickly.
- Working with other programs while copying, duplicating, or finding in the background.
- Making and using stationery pads (template documents).
- Customizing, removing, and aligning icons in windows or on the desktop.
- A summary of shortcuts using the keyboard and mouse.

Ask 100 Macintosh users to name the application program they use most often. Only a few would answer correctly, "the Finder." People don't think of it as a program they use or need to learn to use. In fact, the Finder is a very rich application program that is included with the system software for managing your disks and their contents.

The Finder that comes with System 7 has new capabilities that help you organize your disks more effectively and find items in them more quickly than older Finders. You'll use all of Finder 7's capabilities more often because they're never more than a mouse click away. This chapter describes the new Finder capabilities in detail.

Aliases are covered in Chapter 6 and file sharing is covered in Chapter 8. For more information on the new System Folder organization, see the next chapter.

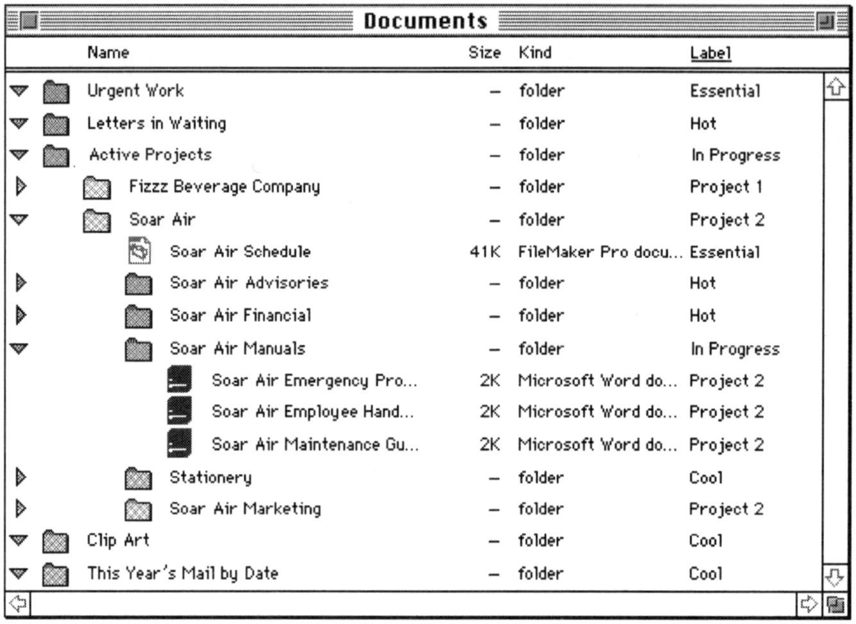

Figure 3-1
Expanded and collapsed folders

Outlining folder structure

Finder 7 displays list views (name, size, kind, and so forth) in an indented outline format (Figure 3-1). The levels of indentation in the outline show how your folders are nested. The indented outline provides a graphical representation of a disk's organization. You can look through and reorganize folders without opening additional windows.

Triangles next to folder names tell you whether the folders are expanded or collapsed. If a triangle points to the right, the folder next to it is collapsed and you cannot see its contents. If the triangle points down, the folder is expanded and you can see a list of the items in the folder indented below the folder name.

Collapsing folders

QUICK TIPS

To collapse a folder, click once on the triangle to the left of the folder's icon (Figure 3-2). To collapse a folder and all the folders nested within it, press Option while clicking the triangle of the outer folder. Resist double-clicking, which causes the folder to expand and then immediately collapse most annoyingly.

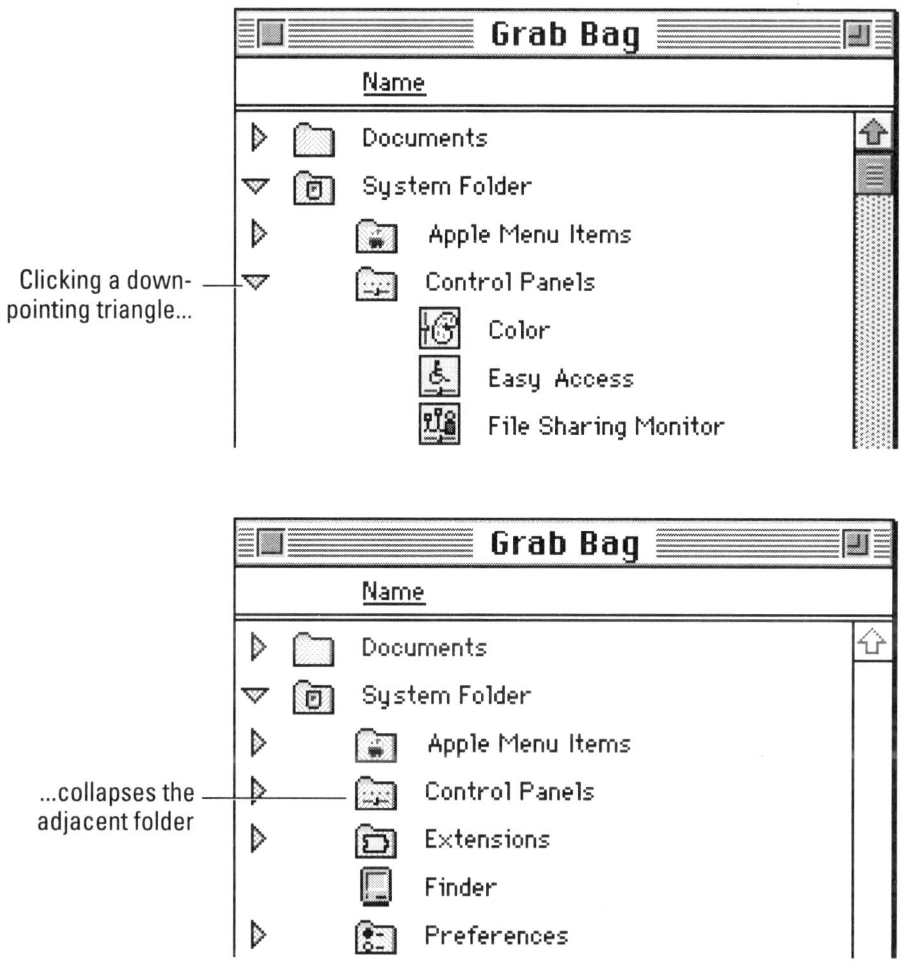

Figure 3-2
Collapsing a folder

Expanding folders

To expand a folder, click once on the triangle to the left of the folder's icon (Figure 3-3). To expand a folder and all the folders nested within it, press Option while you click.

When you expand a folder, the Finder remembers whether folders nested within it were previously expanded or collapsed and restores each to its former state.

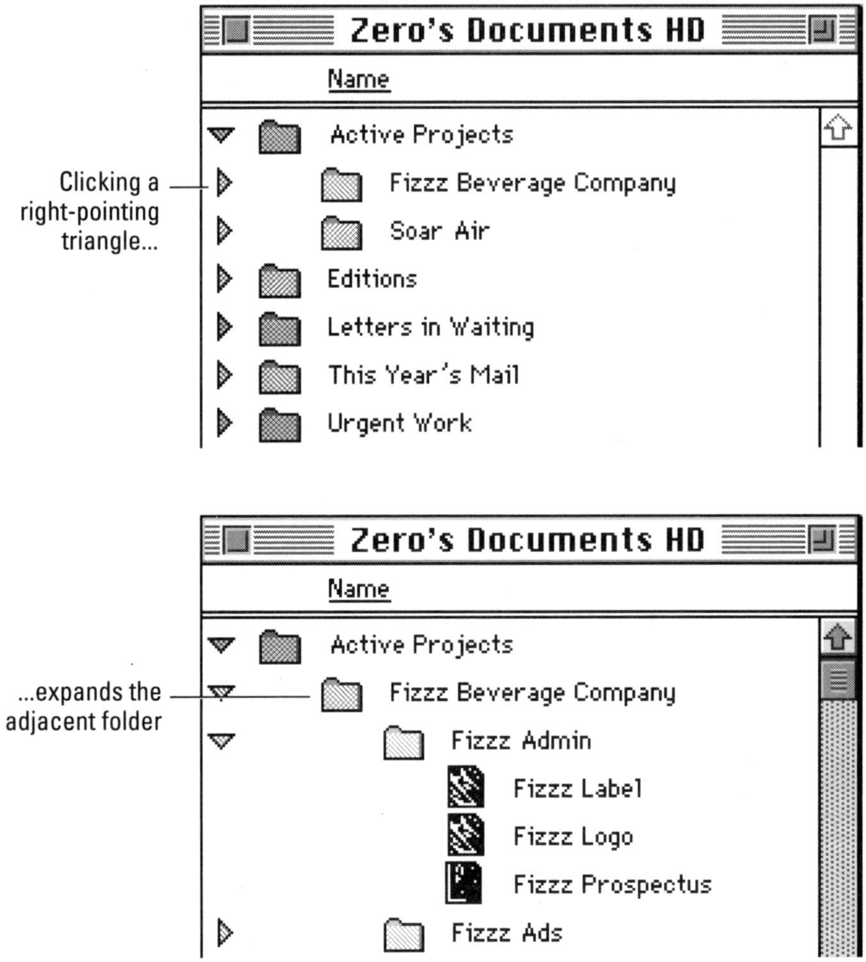

Figure 3-3
Expanding a folder

Selecting from multiple folders

Finder 7's outline views let you select multiple items from any number of folders (Figure 3-4). All folders must be on one disk.

To select an additional item, expand the folder that contains it and press Shift while clicking the item. You can also select consecutive items by pressing Shift while dragging a selection rectangle around them. If you need to deselect a few items, Shift-click each item or Shift-drag across consecutive items.

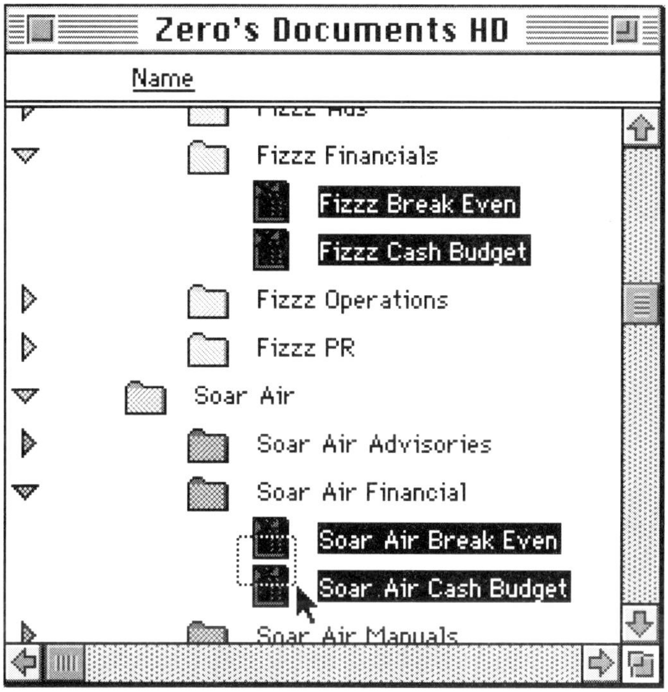

Figure 3-4
Items selected from multiple folders

Smart zooming

After expanding and collapsing folders in an outline view, you may want to make a window just large enough to show all the items currently listed in it. To do that, simply click the Zoom box (Figure 3-5).

Older Finders always zoom up to full-screen size, but Finder 7 zooms up or down to fit a window's contents. The window only covers the whole screen if it contains enough items to fill a screen-size window. This smart zooming helps you make best use of your screen real estate after changing views, adding or removing items, rearranging icons, and so forth. If you do want to zoom a window to fill the screen, press Option while clicking the zoom box.

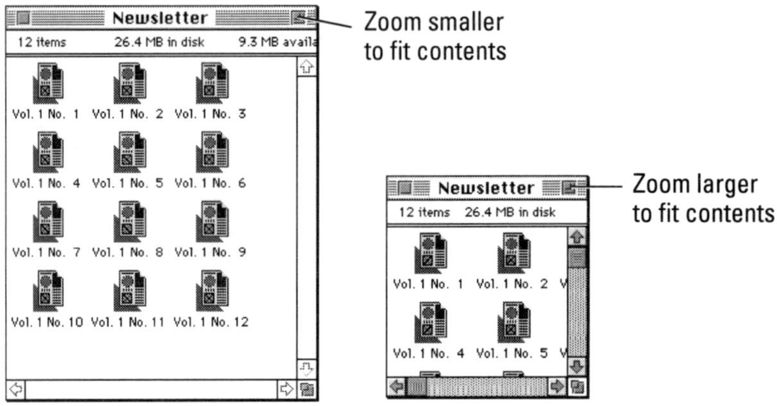

Figure 3-5
Zoom to fit

Finding items

An outline view helps you hunt through folders and disks for items, but Finder 7's Find command finds and fetches lost items with less effort. In its simplest form, the Find command looks through all disks whose icons are on the desktop for an item whose name contains the text you specify (Figure 3-6). It displays the first item it finds, opening the folder that contains the item to show the item in its native surroundings.

UNDOCUMENTED

You can find additional matching items with the Find Again command. If the currently active window doesn't contain any more matches to the Find criteria, the Find looks in other folders and disks. If it finds another match, it closes the active window (unless it was already open) and looks for a match in another folder. If you know the active window contains several matches to the Find criteria but you know none of them is the one you want, you can skip to the next folder by closing the active window.

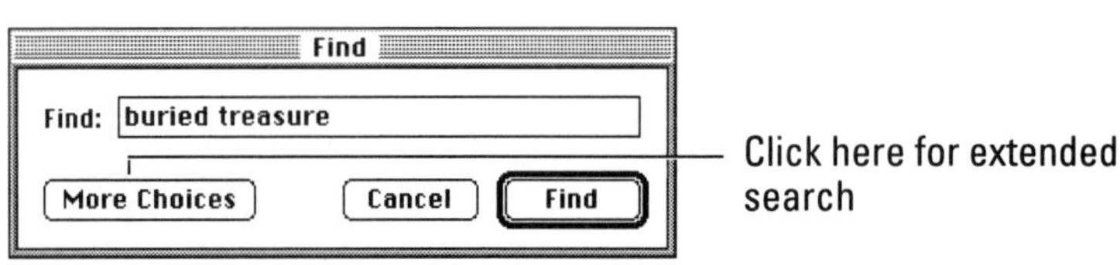

Figure 3-6
A simple find

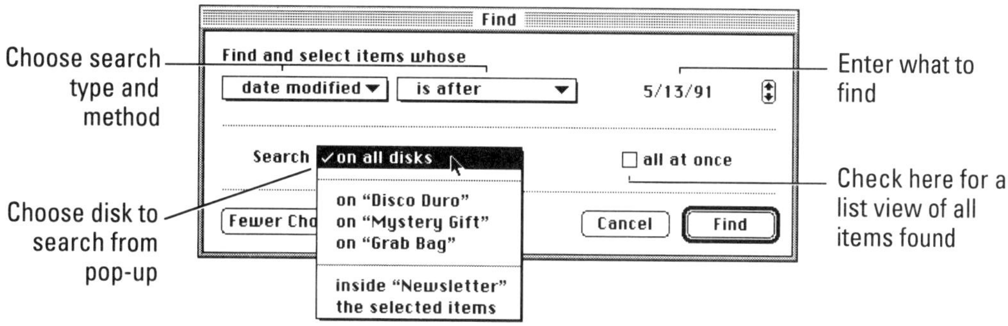

Figure 3-7
An extended find

The Find command has an extended form as well. Clicking the More Choices button lets you specify a wide variety of search criteria (Figure 3-7).

You choose the type of search: by name, size, kind, label, date created, date modified, version, comments, or lock status. You also specify exactly what you want matched and how you want it matched. Table 3-1 enumerates the possible criteria combinations. For all combinations, you can restrict the search to a single disk, to the active window, or to a group of items you selected in the active window before choosing the Find command. If you do, you can also have the Finder select all the items it finds at once, in an outline view.

The Find command does not look inside the System file or suitcase files for fonts, sounds, or desk accessories. It can find those kinds of items in folders and on the desktop, though.

To return to the simple Find dialog box, click the Fewer Choices button. To end searching, click the Cancel button. The Finder remembers whether you were using the simple or the extended Find dialog box and gives you the same one the next time you use the Find command.

Opening an enclosing folder

When you press Command while clicking the active window's title, a menu pops up showing the path from the window through your nested folder structure to the disk that contains the active window (Figure 3-8). You can use the menu to open the folder that contains, or encloses, the active window. The enclosing folder is sometimes called the parent folder.

Table 3-1: Find criteria

Search what	Search how	Search for
name	contains/ starts with/ ends with/ is/ is not/ doesn't contain	text you enter
size	is less than/ is greater than	amount you enter
kind	contains/ doesn't contain	alias/ application/ document/ folder/ stationery/ text you enter
label	is/ is not	label you choose from pop-up menu
date created	is/ is before/ is after/ is not	date you enter
date modified	is/ is before/ is after/ is not	date you enter
version	is/ is before/ is after/ is not	text you enter
comments	contain/ do not contain	text you enter
lock	is	locked/ unlocked

You can also use the pop-up menu to open the other folders along the path or the disk at the root of the path.

To open any folder along the path, or the disk at the end of the path, choose the container you want opened from the pop-up menu. At the same time, you can close the active window by pressing the Option key while choosing from the pop-up menu.

Custom views

You can change the format and content of Finder 7's windows with the new Views control panel (Figure 3-9). Control panel settings affect all Finder windows and the desktop; you can't format each window separately. After changing settings in the Views control panel, you can resize windows to fit the new format by clicking their zoom boxes.

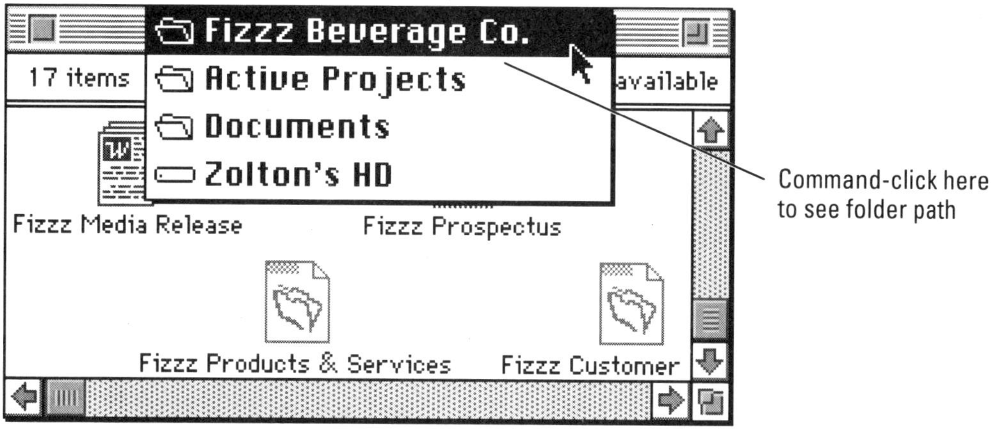

Figure 3-8
Through folders to the disk

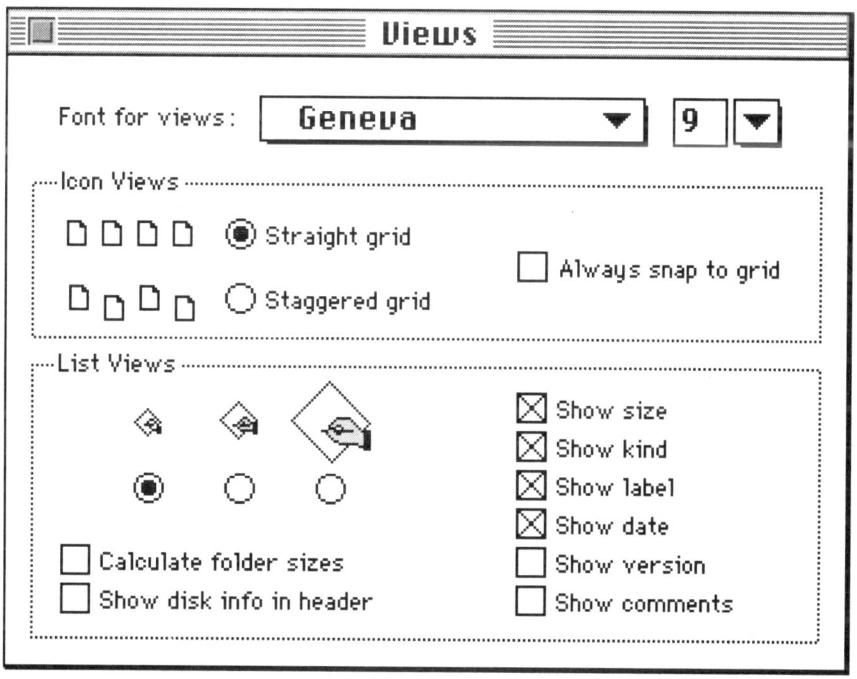

Figure 3-9
The Views control panel

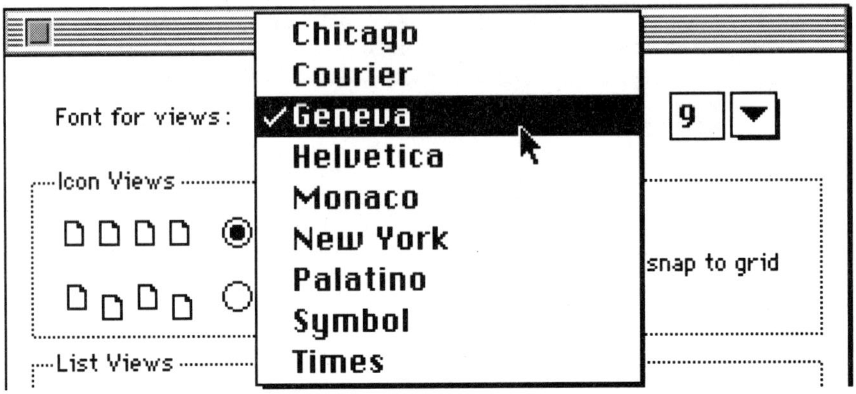

Figure 3-10
Finder text format options

Setting the text font and size

Choose a text font and a text size for icon names and all the text in list views from the pop-up menus at the top of the Views control panel (Figure 3-10). If the text size you want isn't listed, you can enter any size between 6 and 36.

The Finder uses the font and size settings for icon names; the disk information header (number of items, disk space used, and disk space available); and all the text in list views. Your font and size settings affect all windows and icons.

After making the size much larger or much smaller, you may want to use the Clean Up command (Special menu) to adjust the spacing of icons on the desktop and in windows. You must clean up each window separately.

Setting icon alignment

Other settings in the Views control panel determine how the Finder aligns icons (Figure 3-11). The settings affect icons on the desktop and in all windows with icon or small icon views. You can set the type of grid the Clean Up command uses and decide whether icons automatically align with that grid when you drag them.

QUICK TIPS

The Staggered Grid option makes it possible to arrange icons close together without their names overlapping. Turning on the Always Snap To Grid option makes icons you drag align to the Clean Up command's grid.

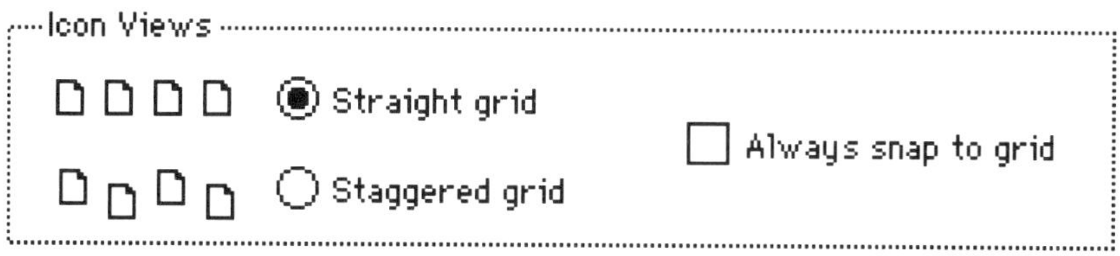

Figure 3-11
Finder icon alignment options

You can temporarily reverse the Always Snap To Grid setting by pressing the Command key while dragging.

Determining list view contents

To determine how much information Finder 7 shows in all windows with list views (name, size, kind, and so forth), you set numerous options at the bottom of the Views control panel (Figure 3-12).

List views always include an icon and a name for every item in the window. In addition, you select which of six other columns of information to include: size, kind, label, date, version, and comments. Your selections appear as choices in the Finder's Views menu. You cannot change the order of the columns or their widths, only whether each appears or not. The version and comments columns, which you otherwise see with the Get Info command (File menu), are new in list views with Finder 7. Only the first 25 characters of an item's comments are shown in a list view.

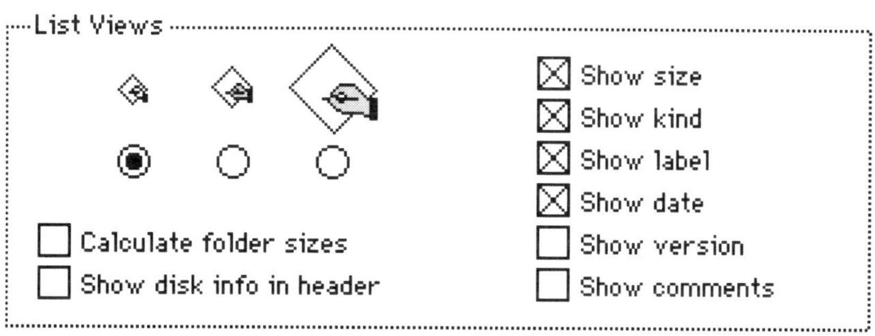

Figure 3-12
Finder list view options

Judicious setting of list view options keeps your list view windows as small as possible. You can make a list view window narrower by reducing the number of items checked in the Views control panel and then clicking the window's Zoom box.

Finder 7, unlike older Finders, lets you pick the size of icons it displays in all list views. Tiny-size icons are like the icons in list views of older Finders. Small-size icons are like the icons in small icon view. Standard-size icons are like desktop icons.

You can also set an option to have Finder 7 calculate and display folder sizes. Adding up the sizes of items in a large folder can take quite a while. Fortunately, Finder 7 only calculates sizes of folders you can see and it does this work in the background so you can get on with other tasks.

Another list view option has Finder 7 show disk information in the header of all list view windows. The disk information includes the number of items in the window, the amount of disk space in use, and the amount of disk space available. This information is standard in icon and small icon views.

Changing list views

You can change a window from one list view to any other available list view directly in the window, without using the Finder's View menu (Figure 3-13). Simply click the column heading that corresponds to the view you want. Finder 7 immediately sorts all the items in the window according to the column you clicked. You can tell the current sort order by looking for the underlined column heading.

Horizontal scrolling

All the information you have requested with the Views control panel for each item in a list view may not fit across a window even at its maximum width. If a window contains more columns out of view on the right or left, Finder 7 activates the window's horizontal scroll bar (Figure 3-14). You can use it to read all of a wide listing. Older Finders never activate the horizontal scroll bar in a list view.

Auto scrolling

You can scroll a window in Finder 7 without using the scroll bars. Simply place the pointer in the window, press the mouse button, and drag toward the area you want to come into view (Figure 3-15). Drag the

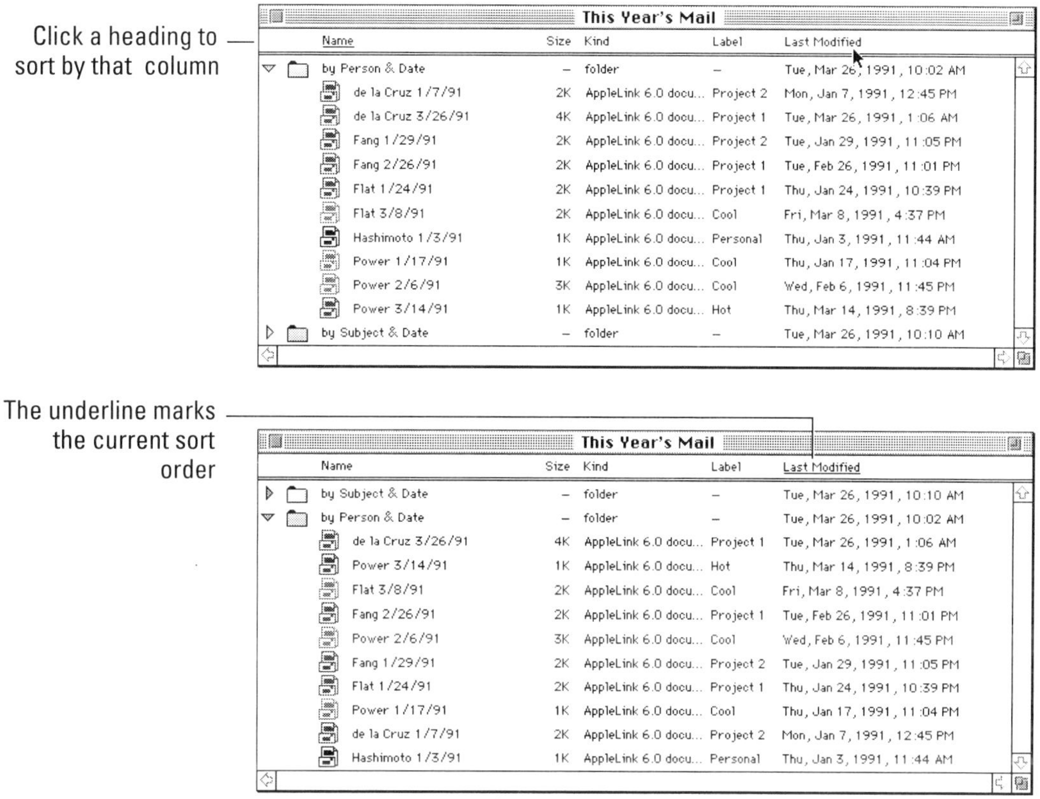

Figure 3-13
Sorting a list view

pointer up, down, left, or right past the window's active area and scrolling begins. Dragging past a window corner scrolls diagonally.

As you drag, you can vary the scrolling speed. To scroll slowly, drag just to the window's edge (and continue pressing the mouse button). Increase scrolling speed by dragging beyond the window's edge.

You can use this scrolling technique, known as auto-scrolling, while:

❖ Moving an icon or group of icons to a new place in the same window (icon or small icon view)

❖ Moving an item or group of items into a folder in the same window (any view)

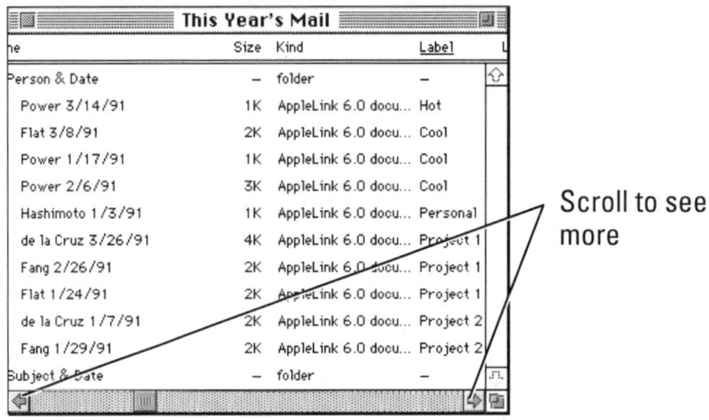

Figure 3-14
Scrolling side to side

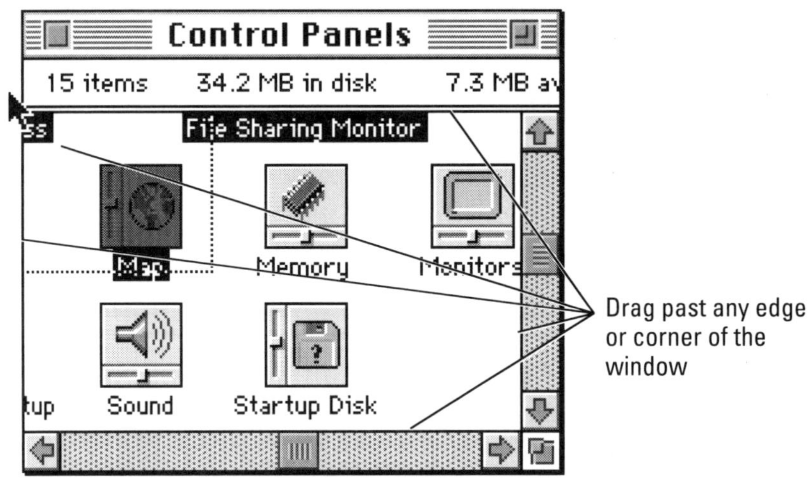

Figure 3-15
Scrolling automatically

❖ Dragging a selection rectangle around adjacent items in the same window to select them all (any view)

Selecting by dragging

All versions of the Finder let you select adjacent icons by dragging a selection rectangle (which looks to some people like marching ants), across them. Finder 7 is the first to allow this type of selection in any view, not just icon and small icon views (Figure 3-16).

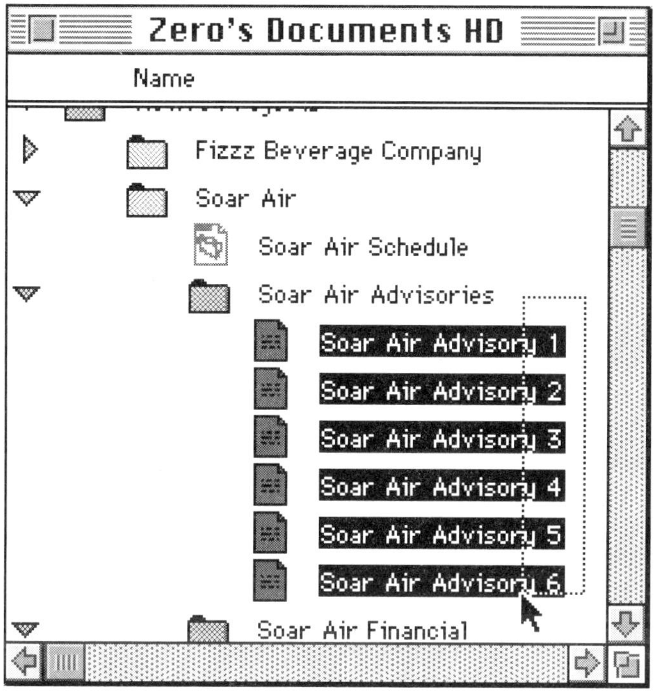

Figure 3-16
Selecting adjacent items

UNDOCUMENTED

The selection rectangle selects every item whose icon or icon name it touches. All items must be on the desktop or in a single window. Items are highlighted one-by-one as you drag over them, not en masse when you stop dragging. As a side effect of this behavior, you must click within some text or on an icon to select an item in any list view. Older Finders select an item when you click anywhere on a line, even in blank spaces.

Renaming items

Clicking an icon selects the icon but no longer also selects the icon name for editing. On the good side, you can no longer accidentally and perhaps unknowingly rename a selected icon by bumping the keyboard. Also, you can now open an icon by double-clicking its name. On the bad side, you have to relearn how to change icon names.

To rename a disk, folder, program, document, or other item, you must explicitly select its name. You either click the name directly or you click the item's icon and then press Return or Enter. When the name is selected

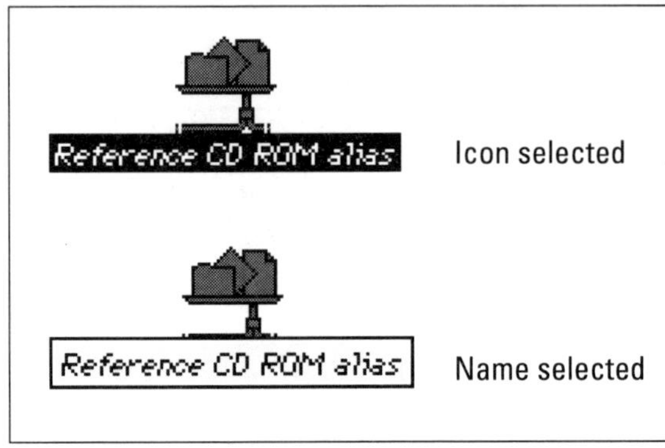

Figure 3-17
Selecting an icon name

for editing, it has a box around it in addition to being highlighted (Figure 3-17). The box does not appear if you just click the icon.

For an additional visual cue that you have selected a name on a color or grayscale monitor, use the Colors control panel to set the text highlight color to something other than black and white. Then you know a name highlighted in color (or gray) is ready for editing, whereas a name highlighted in black and white is not.

After selecting a name, you can replace it completely by typing a new name. If instead you want to select an insertion point, a word, or a range of text, don't click, double-click, or drag right away. Wait until a box appears around the name. The length of time you must wait depends on the duration of a double-click interval — approximately 1.9 seconds, 1.3 seconds, or 0.9 second, as set in the Mouse control panel. If you click again too soon, the Finder thinks you're double-clicking the icon and opens it. If you have trouble editing icon names without opening the item, try setting a briefer Double-Click Speed with the Mouse control panel.

You don't have to wait if you move the insertion point by pressing the arrow keys. Pressing Up Arrow moves the insertion point to the beginning of the name, Down Arrow moves it to the end, Left Arrow moves it left, and Right arrow moves it right.

While editing a name, you can use the Undo, Cut, Copy, and Paste commands in the Edit menu. You cannot undo your changes to a name after you finish editing it, only while it is still selected for editing. You can also copy the entire name of any item by selecting its icon (or its whole name) and using the Copy command (Edit menu). This capability comes

Figure 3-18
Names of duplicate items

in handy when you're copying a disk and want to name the copy the same as the original.

The name of a locked item can't be changed. (Unlock an item with the Get Info command, or if it's a disk, by sliding its locking tab.) However, you can copy its entire name as just described.

Naming duplicates

The Finder constructs the name of a duplicate item you create with the Duplicate command (File menu) by suffixing the name with the word "copy." Additional copies of the same item also have a serial number suffixed (Figure 3-18).

UNDOCUMENTED

If any suffixes would result in a name longer than 31 characters, the Finder removes characters from the end of the original item's name. For example, duplicating an item named 5/91 Income and Expense Report would result in an item named 5/91 Income and Expense Re copy.

These same rules come into play when an item you drag to the Trash has the same name as another item already there. Suppose, for example, the Trash contained an item named Untitled and you dragged another like-named item there. The Finder would rename the item already there to Untitled copy. If you later added another item named Untitled, the Finder would change Untitled copy to Untitled copy 2, change Untitled to Untitled copy, and leave the name of the item you just added unchanged. In other words, the item most recently added has the plain name and the next most recently added has the highest number suffix.

The Finder uses similar rules to construct names of aliases. See Chapter 6.

Labeling items

Finder 7 lets you classify folders, programs, and documents by labeling them with a word or phrase. On monitors displaying at least 16 colors, labeling an item also colorizes it.

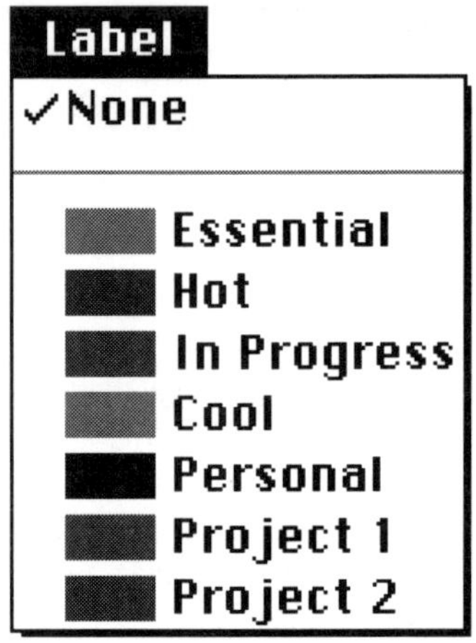

Figure 3-19
The Label menu

Using labels

To label an item, select it and choose a label from the Finder's Label menu (Figure 3-19). If the icon has an icon with natural color, the Finder blends the label color as if you covered the icon with a piece of acetate the color of the label. To label an item without colorizing it, change the label color to solid black as described in the next section.

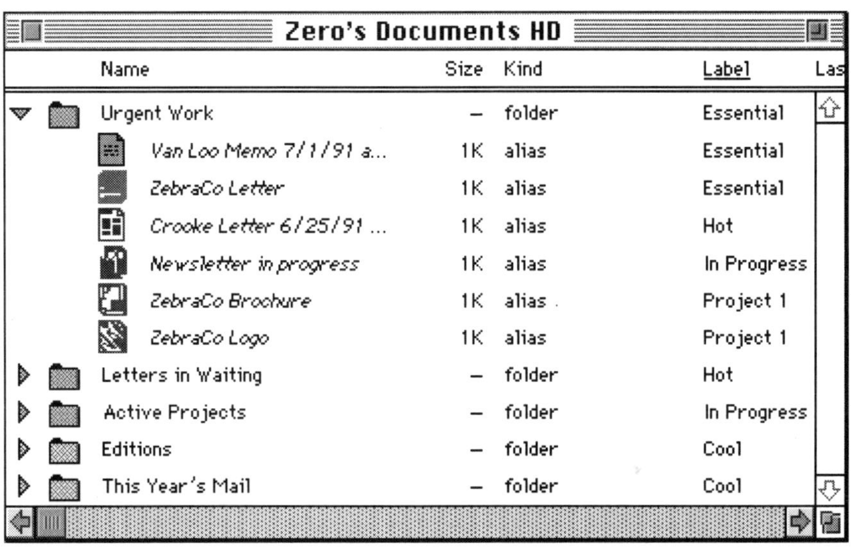

Figure 3-20
Viewing by Label

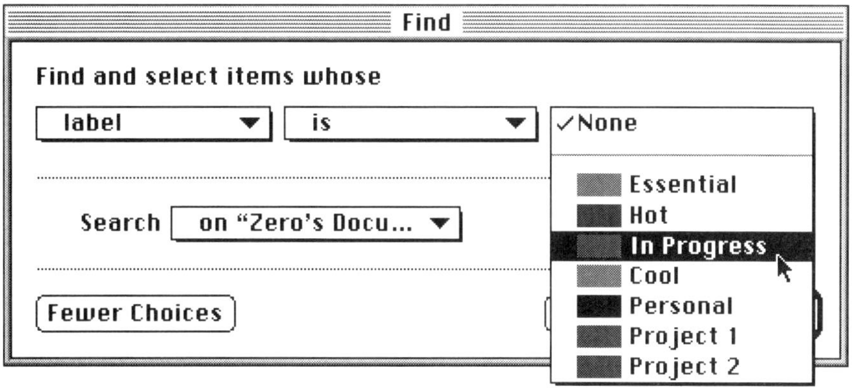

Figure 3-21
Finding by label

After labeling items, you can view Finder window contents arranged by label (Figure 3-20). You can also search for items by label using the Finder's Find command (Figure 3-21). Label colors also show up in the Apple menu and in the directory dialog boxes used by many programs' Open and Save commands.

UNDOCUMENTED

Changing label names and colors

You change the standard label names and colors using the Labels control panel (Figure 3-22). If you click a label color to change it, the Finder displays a dialog box in which you specify a new color. You can

Figure 3-22
The Labels control panel

Table 3-2: Values for standard label colors

Label	Hue	Saturation	Brightness
Essential	4223	64884	65535
Hot	108	63573	56683
In Progress	59733	63286	62167
Cool	35756	64907	60159
Personal	43690	65535	54272
Project 1	23764	65535	25775
Project 2	5332	61619	22016

click a color on the color wheel or you can enter values between 0 and 65535 either for hue, saturation, and brightness or for red, green, and blue. Table 3-2 lists the hue, saturation, and brightness values for the standard colors (in case you want to reset them after experimenting).

Polite drag

When you move or copy an item by dragging it from one window to a folder in an overlapping window, Finder 7 keeps the target window in front of the source window so the destination folder is always in view (Figure 3-23). Older Finders rudely bring the source window in front of an overlapping target window as soon as you begin dragging, sometimes covering the destination folder.

In other words, Finder 7 brings a window to the front only if the pointer is in it when you release the mouse. In contrast, older Finders bring a window to the front if the pointer is in it when you press the mouse button.

If you want to drag more than one item at a time to a folder in an overlapping window, the Finder can't always keep that destination folder in view. Selecting a group of items brings the window that contains them to the front, possibly covering the destination folder.

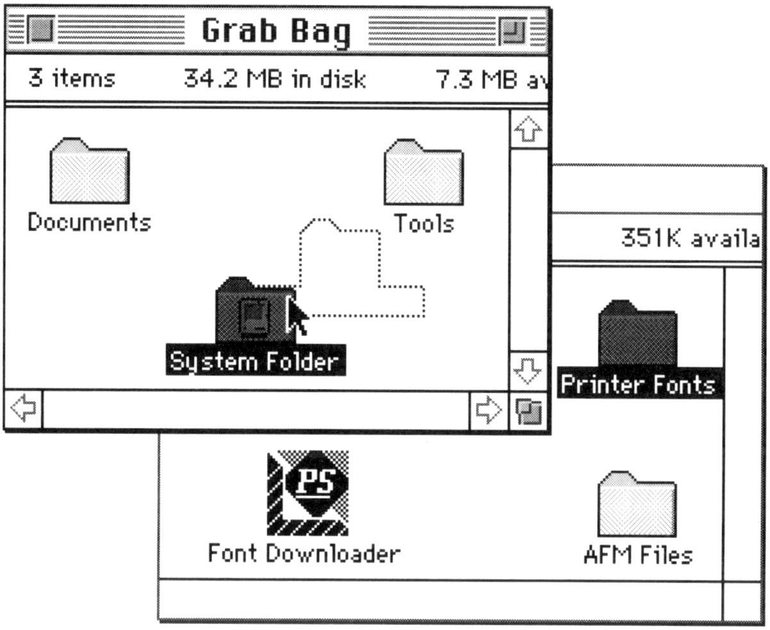

Figure 3-23
Dragging to an overlapping window

Desktop database

When you copy items to a hard disk containing hundreds or thousands of items, Finder 7 often finishes a full minute or more faster than would an older Finder doing the same job. The increased efficiency comes from System 7's improved desktop database, which keeps track of:

- ❖ How icons look
- ❖ What kind of file each icon refers to
- ❖ Where programs are
- ❖ Comments you have entered with the Finder's Get Info command

System 7 creates a new desktop database on every disk larger than 2MB. Each smaller disk has an old-style desktop file, because those disks can usually be ejected and inserted into other systems that are using old system software.

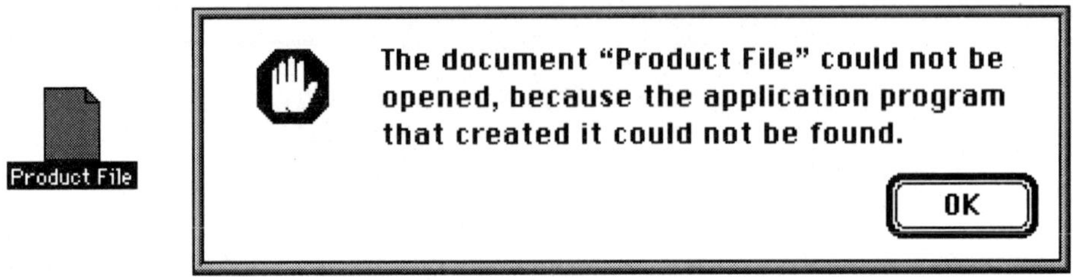

Figure 3-24
Signs of a corrupt desktop

A desktop database (or old-style desktop file) can become corrupt, not through greed or false pride, but as a side effect of programs quitting unexpectedly or system crashes. Typical symptoms are blank icons or the Finder being unable to find the program to open a document (Figure 3-24). These symptoms also occur when the program that created a document is on an ejected disk (or you don't have the program).

QUICK TIPS

Restarting your Macintosh may eliminate the blank icons. If not, rebuilding the desktop usually does the trick. To rebuild the desktop, simply press the Command and Option keys while starting up, and wait for the Finder to inquire whether you indeed wish to rebuild the desktop on the startup disk. If you have multiple hard disks, the Finder asks about rebuilding each one in turn. To rebuild the desktop on a floppy disk, hold down Command and Option while inserting the floppy.

WARNING

Rebuilding the desktop erases all comments you have entered in Get Info windows for items on the disks involved.

Background work

Not only can the Finder copy files faster than ever before, it can do the work in the background while you use another program (Figure 3-25). Background copying is especially useful during a lengthy copy, such as from or to a shared folder or disk. In addition, Finder 7's Duplicate, Empty Trash, and Find commands work in the background.

After starting a copy process, you can switch to another program by clicking in any of its windows or choosing it from the Application menu. Any program you want to use during the copy process must be open before the Finder starts copying. The Finder can't open a program or do

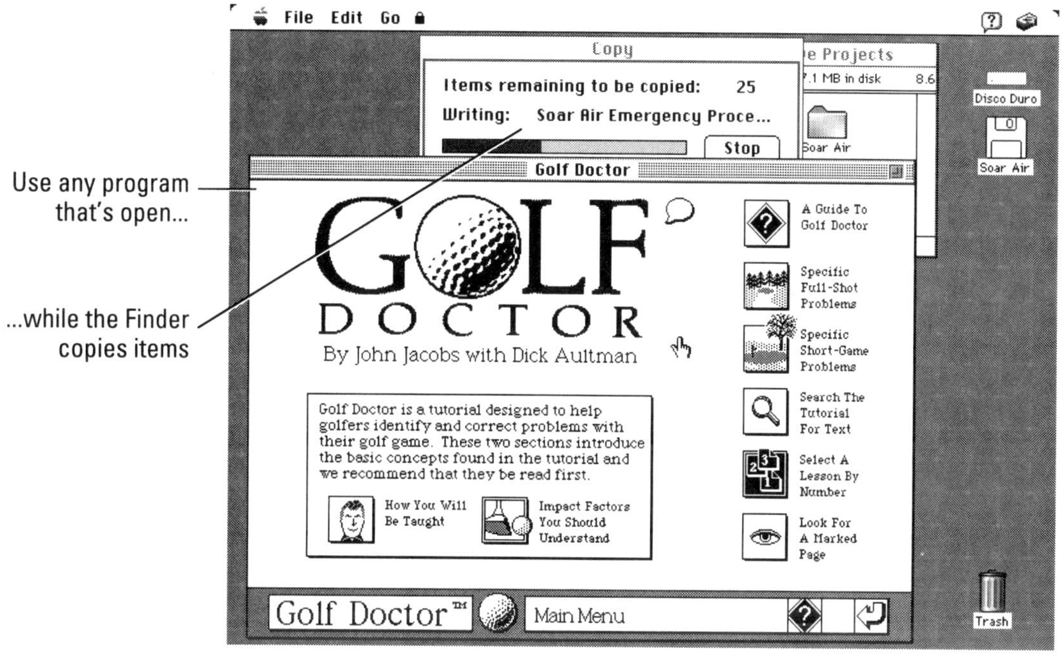

Figure 3-25
Work while you copy

anything else itself while it's copying. Control panels are considered part of the Finder, so you can't use them while copying. Notice the copy dialog box has a title bar; you can use it to move the dialog box.

The performance of your Macintosh suffers while background copying is underway. Copying proceeds more slowly than it would in the foreground. The pointer jerks across the screen. The mouse button and keyboard may seem to stop working for a few seconds from time to time. If you keep typing blind (characters are not displayed on screen), the system remembers the most recent 20 characters you type (about five seconds of typing at 40 words per minute). The system can also remember one click or double-click, or it can catch up with your dragging as long as you don't release the mouse button.

Smarter copying

When you copy an item to a disk or folder that already contains an item by the same name, Finder 7 does more than older Finders. It asks you whether you want to replace the item at the destination and it tells you which item is newer (Figure 3-26).

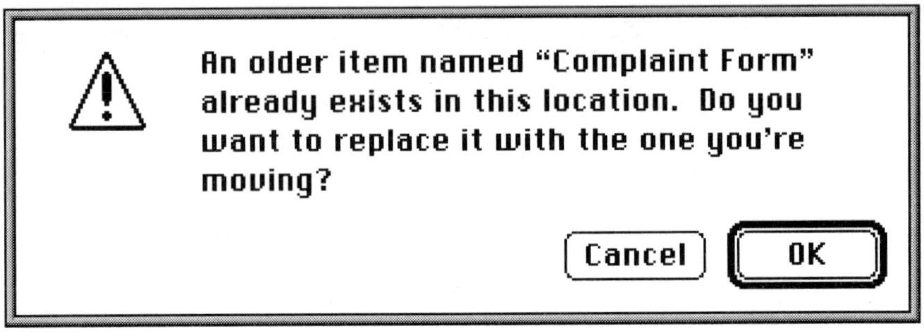

Figure 3-26
Verifying replacement

Finder 7 is also smart about copying a floppy disk to a hard disk. It puts the floppy disk's contents into a new folder on the hard disk and names the folder the same as the floppy. You can even copy a floppy to a folder on a hard disk.

Stationery pads

Rather than copy a document for its format and content, you can make it a stationery pad. Opening a stationery pad with the Finder is like tearing a page from a pad of preprinted forms. You get a new document with preset format and contents.

Stationery pad documents have a distinctive icon that looks like a stack of document icons (Figure 3-27). The Finder uses a generic stationery pad icon if the program that handles that type of document doesn't know about System 7's stationery.

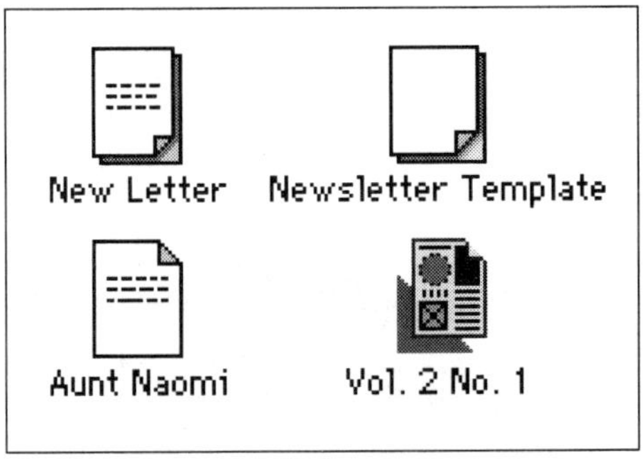

Figure 3-27
Stationery pad icons and ordinary icons

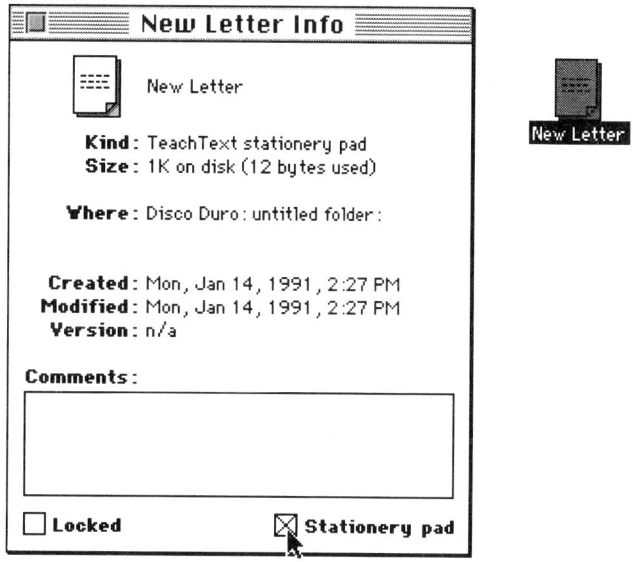

Figure 3-28
Making a stationery pad

Making stationery pads

You can make any document a stationery pad by selecting it in the Finder and setting the Stationery Pad option of the Get Info command (Figure 3-28). Some programs let you directly save a document as a stationery pad by setting a Stationery Pad option of their Save and Save As commands (Figure 3-29). These programs have been upgraded specifically to work with System 7's stationery pads.

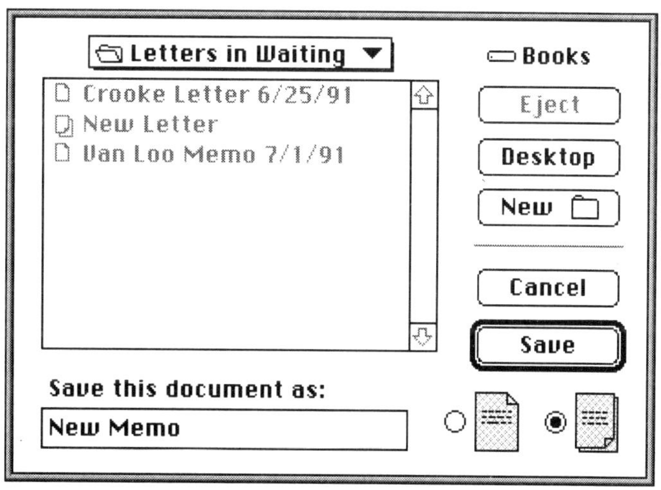

Figure 3-29
Saving a stationery pad

Figure 3-30
Opening stationery within a program

Using stationery pads

Programs that know about stationery pads open an untitled document with the format and contents of the stationery pad. For programs that don't know about stationery pads, the Finder automatically creates a new document by making a copy of the stationery pad, asking you to name it, and having the program open the copy. However, opening a stationery pad from within a program that doesn't know about them (as opposed to opening from the Finder) opens the stationery pad itself, not a copy. A message warns you that you are opening a master stationery pad (Figure 3-30).

QUICK TIPS

If you don't want to save a copy of a template document every time you use it, don't make it a stationery pad unless the program that created it supports stationery pads. Instead, make the template an ordinary document, but lock it using the Finder's Get Info command. You might want to use this method with templates for printing single envelopes and mailing labels, for example. Then you could open the locked template, type or paste the recipient's address, print, and close without saving.

Custom icons

Would you like to see dinosaurs or hummingbirds on your desktop instead of ordinary icons? Finder 7 lets you replace the icons of individual documents, programs, folders, and disks with your own pictures (Figure 3-31).

Figure 3-31
Icons your way

The color, grayscale, or black-and-white picture you use for an icon can come from a variety of sources:

- ❖ Clip-art disk
- ❖ Photo or drawing on paper, converted to an electronic image with a scanner
- ❖ Video image captured with special hardware accessories
- ❖ Your own picture made with a painting or drawing program

Making a custom icon

To replace an icon with your icon, first select the picture and copy it with the Copy command (Edit menu). Then go to the Finder and find the icon you want to replace. Select the icon (click it once) and choose Get Info from the Finder's File menu. In the Get Info window, click the icon to select it and use the Paste command (Edit menu) to replace it with the picture you just copied (Figure 3-32). You can also copy an icon from a Get Info window and paste it into a different Get Info window.

For best results, your picture should measure 32 by 32 pixels (dots), or at least 64 by 64, 128 by 128, or 256 by 256. If your picture is larger than 32 by 32, the Finder reduces it proportionally to fit that amount of space when you replace an icon with it. Reducing a picture distorts it, especially if the original size is an odd or fractional multiple of the final size. If your picture is smaller than 32 by 32, the Finder centers it on a white 32 by 32 square.

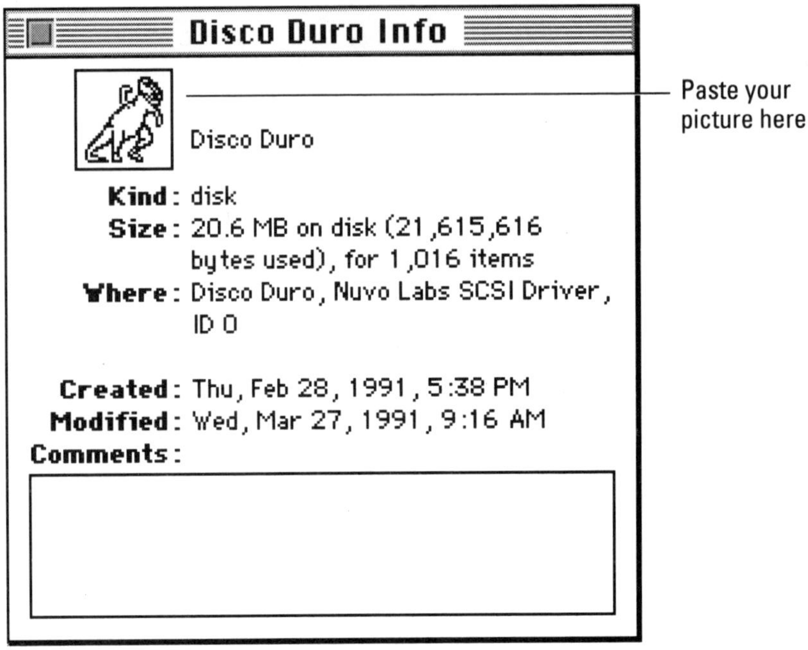

Figure 3-32
Customizing an icon

When an item with a custom icon appears in a small icon view, in the Apple Menu, or in the Application menu, the Finder reduces the standard-size icon by half (Figure 3-33). If you duplicate or make an alias of an item with a custom icon, the duplicate or alias inherits the custom icon.

You cannot replace the icon of a locked item, an open document., or an open program. Nor can you replace any system software icons such as the System Folder, Finder, Control Panels Folder, and Trash. (You can replace individual control panel icons, however.)

Figure 3-33
Custom icons in standard and small sizes

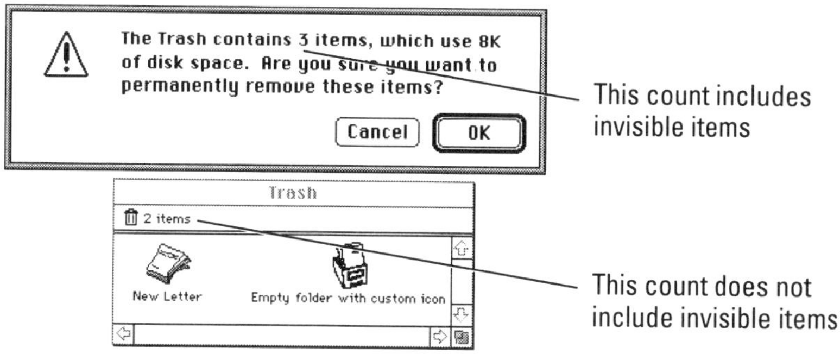

Figure 3-34
The Trash warning

Reverting to a standard icon

To revert to an item's standard icon, select the item, choose Get Info from the Finder's File menu, select the icon in the Get Info window, and choose Clear or Cut from the Edit menu.

Trash disposal

The Trash icon looks the same with System 7 as with older system software, but the Trash works differently. The Finder no longer automatically empties the Trash. You must remove items from the Trash explicitly by choosing Empty Trash from the Finder's Special menu. Until you do, the contents of the Trash remain there even if you open another program, shut down, or restart.

Finder 7 doesn't allow you to leave items from 400K (single-sided) disks in the Trash, however. When you drag items from a 400K disk to the Trash, a message asks whether you want to delete them immediately or cancel.

Trash warnings

When you choose the Empty Trash command, Finder 7 tells you how many items the Trash contains and how much disk space they occupy (Figure 3-34). Invisible items in the Trash also count toward the total number of items to be permanently removed. (For example, any folder that has a custom icon contains an invisible item named Icon.) You decide whether to discard them all or cancel.

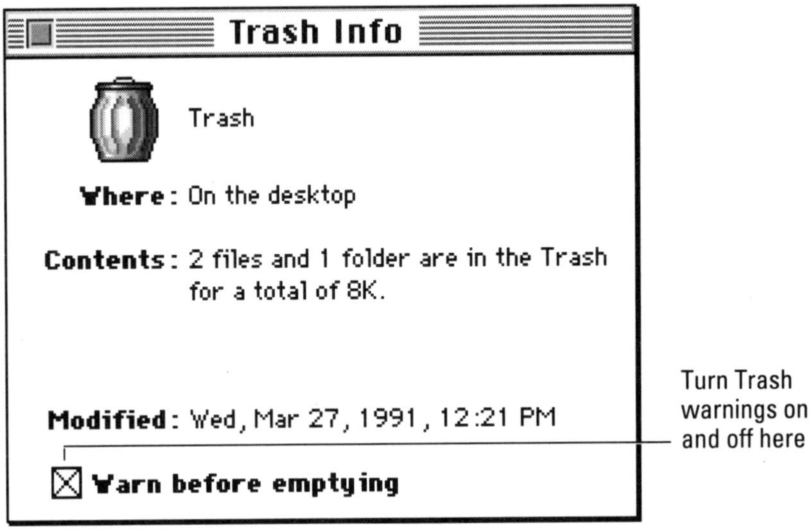

Figure 3-35
Get Info for the Trash

You can disable the Trash warning by pressing the Option key while choosing the Empty Trash command. To more permanently muzzle the warnings, select the Trash icon, choose the Get Info command, and turn off the appropriate option (Figure 3-35).

Unlike older Finders, Finder 7 does not display a warning when you drag locked items, application programs, or system software items to the Trash. However, the Finder will not remove locked items. It advises you the Trash contains locked items, and asks whether you want to remove the other items or cancel. Before you can remove a locked item, you must use the Finder's Get Info command to unlock it.

Trash retrieval

To put items now in the Trash back where they came from, open the Trash, select the items, and choose Put Away from the Finder's File menu. The Finder returns the each selected item to its previous folder, though not necessarily to the same place in the folder window.

Trash contents

The Trash contains all the items that have been dragged to it from all the disks whose icons are on the desktop. The Empty Trash command removes the items from all disks involved. To remove items from only one disk, you must open the Trash and drag the items you don't want removed to the desktop or to another folder. Then use the Empty Trash Command.

If you eject a disk (and put away its icon) after dragging items from that disk to the Trash, those items disappear from the Trash but the Finder has not deleted them. They will reappear in the Trash the next time you insert that disk. If you insert that disk in another Mac, they will appear in its Trash. They appear in a folder named Trash when you use that disk with older system software.

If you're sharing someone else's disk or folder over a network and you drag an item from the shared disk to the Trash on your desktop, the item does not go into the Trash on the Mac where the shared disk or folder resides. The item is removed from that disk or folder if you use the Empty Trash command on your Mac, however. From the opposite viewpoint, this means you do not know if someone sharing your disk or folder drags items from it to his or her Trash. (The owner of a shared disk or folder can set access privileges to keep unauthorized people from dragging items from it to their Trash.)

Sometimes the Trash contains a folder named Rescued Items. It contains formerly invisible temporary files found when you started up your Macintosh. The Rescued Items folder only appears after a system crash. You may be able to recreate your work up to the time of the system crash from the contents of the Rescued Items folder.

Removing disk icons

Dragging a disk icon to the Trash does not permanently remove anything from the disk, as you might reasonably fear. Instead this process, known as unmounting a disk, removes the icon from the desktop and makes the disk's contents unavailable. If the disk is a floppy disk or other removeable disk, dragging its icon to the Trash ejects the disk from the disk drive.

With Finder 7, you can also remove a disk icon by selecting the disk icon and choosing Put Away from the File menu (Figure 3-36). The Put Away command ejects floppy disks and other removeable disks.

To eject a disk without removing its icon from the desktop, select the icon and choose Eject from the Special menu. The ejected disk's icon becomes gray to show it is unavailable. With older Finders, the Eject command is in the File menu and you put away a disk by pressing Option while choosing the Eject command.

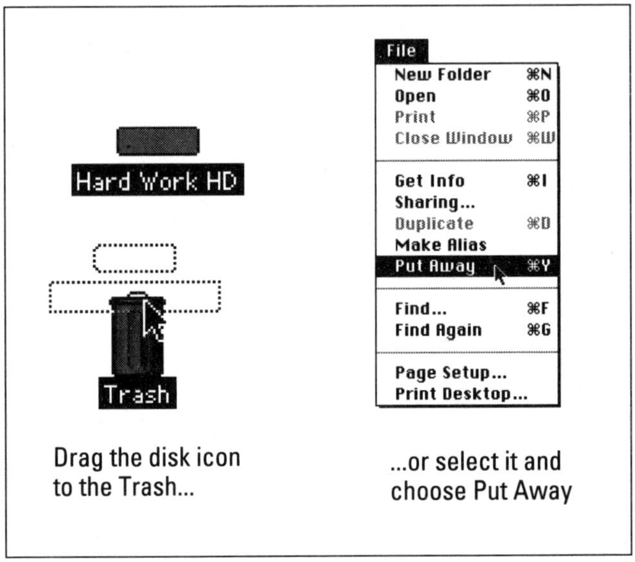

Figure 3-36
Unmounting a disk

Drag open

You can open a document from the Finder by dragging its icon to the icon of any application program that can open it. The program need not have created the document but must be compatible with it. For example, most ReadMe documents are plain text documents that any word processor can open. Dragging a document over a compatible program without releasing the mouse button highlights the program's icon, as if you had dragged the document over a folder (Figure 3-37). Then releasing the mouse button removes the highlighting, opens the program (unless it's already open), and opens the document. If a program can't open a document you drag to it, nothing happens — no highlighting, no opening.

Clean up options

New wrinkles in Finder 7's Clean Up command help keep your icons neat and organized. As in older Finders, choosing Clean Up from the Special menu aligns the active window's icons (or the desktop icons, if no window is active) in neat rows and columns. But Finder 7 doesn't move icons into positions that make their names unreadable. If aligning an icon would make its name overlap a neighboring icon's name, the Finder moves it somewhere nearby where the names won't collide.

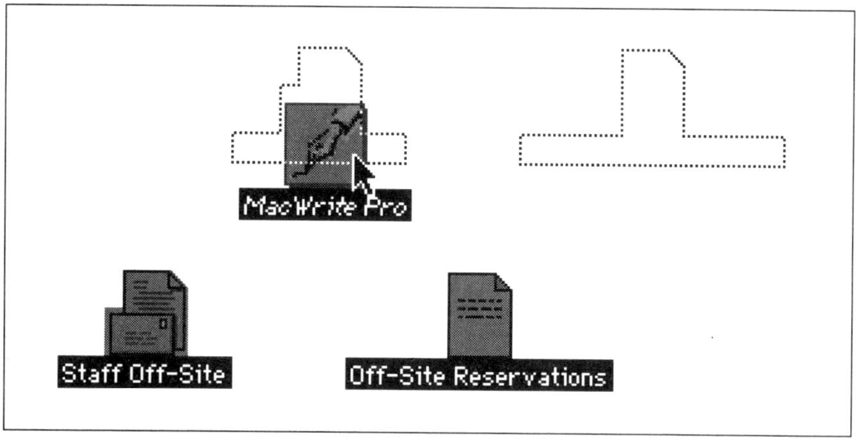

Figure 3-37
Dragging a document to open it

As Finder 7 cleans up your icons, you can have it sort them by any of the choices in the View menu. First you choose the sort order you want from the View menu (temporarily changing the view). Then use the View menu again to choose by Icon or by Small Icon. Finally, press the Option key while you choose the Clean Up command. The Finder rearranges all icons in the window, putting the one lowest in the sort order in the upper left corner and then filling the window from left to right and top to bottom.

If you press Option while cleaning up the desktop (instead of a window), the Finder aligns all desktop icons in a standard configuration. It moves the startup disk's icon to the upper right corner of the desktop; lines up other disk icons below it; puts the Trash in the lower right corner; and arranges all other desktop icons in rows and columns next to the disk icons.

You can also use System 7's Clean Up command to align just the icons you have selected in a window or on the desktop. Pressing Shift changes Clean Up to Clean Up Selection.

Table 3-3: Selecting items

Objective	Action
Select an item	Type the item's partial or full name
Select the next item alphabetically	Press Tab
Select the previous item alphabetically	Press Shift-Tab
Select the next item up	Press Up Arrow
Select the next item down	Press Down Arrow
Select the next item left	Press Left Arrow
Select the next item right	Press Right Arrow
Select the desktop item nearest upper right corner	Press Command-Shift-Up Arrow
Select multiple items	Press Shift while clicking each item or while dragging to enclose them

Finder power

The Finder has a great deal of hidden power, which you tap by pressing the Command and Option keys at the opportune moment. In addition, much of what you can do with the mouse you can also do with the keyboard alone. Tables 3-3, 3-4, 3-5, and 3-6 list power methods and keyboard equivalents for selecting items in windows or on the desktop; opening and closing items; expanding and collapsing outlines of folders in list views; and more. For the most part, these tables do not list keyboard equivalents for menu commands because you can review them on screen by pulling down the menus.

Table 3-4: Opening and closing

Objective	Action
Open the selected item	Press Command-O or press Command-Down Arrow
Open the selected item and close the active window	Press Command-Option-O or press Command-Option-Down Arrow
Open the folder or disk that contains the selected item	Press Command-Up Arrow
Open the folder or disk that contains the selected item and close the active window	Press Command while clicking the window's title or press Command-Option-Up Arrow
Close a window while opening an item in it	Press Option while opening the item
Close all windows	Press Option while clicking the active window's Close box

Table 3-5: Manipulating outlines of folders

Objective	Action
Expand the selected folder	Press Command-Right Arrow
Expand the selected folder and its nested folders	Press Option while clicking the triangle next to the folder or press Command-Option-Right Arrow
Expand all folders in the active window	Press Command-A and then press Command-Option-Right Arrow
Collapse the selected folder	Press Command-Left Arrow
Collapse the selected folder and its nested folders	Press Option while clicking the triangle next to the folder or press Command-Option-Left Arrow
Collapse all folders in the active window	Press Command-A and then press Command-Option-Left Arrow

Table 3-6: More power methods

Objective	Action
Make the desktop active	Press Command-Shift-Up Arrow
Begin editing the selected item's name	Press Return or Enter
Zoom a window to fill the screen	Press Option while clicking the window's zoom box
Move a window without making it active	Press Command while dragging the inactive window
Copy an item to another folder on the same disk	Press Option while dragging the item to the folder or to the folder's open window
Copy an item to the desktop	Press Option while dragging the item to the desktop
Align (or don't align) icons to invisible grid as you move them (revokes the Views control panel's Always Snap To Grid setting)	Press Command while dragging the icons
See the path from the current window to the disk it's on	Press Command while clicking the window's title or Press Command-Option-Up Arrow
Erase a disk	Press Command-Option-Tab as you insert the disk
Skip installing all system extensions during one startup	Hold down Shift during startup
Rebuild the desktop	Hold down Command-Option during startup or when inserting a disk
Force the active program to quit your Macintosh (restart as soon as possible afterwards)	Hold down Command-Option Escape

Summary

- The new versatile Find command locates items in your disks quickly.
- Outlines of folder structure in all list views let you see, select, and reorganize items from different folders in one window.
- You can now customize the format and content of Finder windows.
- Under System 7, all Finder windows are smarter about zooming, scrolling, and selecting.
- Copying items in Finder 7 is both quicker (improved desktop database) and more convenient (background copying).
- Finder 7 no longer automatically empties the Trash; you must explicitly remove items by choosing the Empty Trash command.
- Stationery pads, which are documents with preset format and contents, simplify working with document templates.
- You can classify items in a window or on the desktop using words and colors.

Chapter 4
Organized at Last

In This Chapter

- Exploring the new folders inside the System Folder that make it more manageable.
- Working with some of the System file's contents for the first time.
- A look at the additional special folders outside the System Folder.
- Putting control panels, system extensions, fonts, sounds, keyboard layouts, or language scripts where they belong.
- Assisting the Finder in placing items in the special folders.
- Removing items from the System Folder.
- Tips on troubleshooting conflicts between system extensions.

Your Macintosh has one, my Macintosh has one, everyone's Macintosh has one. It stores the essential software that gives your Macintosh its unique appearance and behavior. It has become overcrowded and unmanageable with dozens if not hundreds of items. What is it? The System Folder!

System 7 organizes this chaos at last. Many of the items that formerly floated loose inside the System Folder now go in one of several new folders inside it. All the new folders have distinctive folder icons (Figure 4-1). In addition, the System file has a new look and a new openness.

Still at large in the System Folder are the Finder, the Scrapbook File, and the Clipboard. If you use Adobe Type Manager 2.0, the PostScript fonts it needs must go in the System Folder. Moreover, many preferences files and other items crowd the System Folder to maintain compatibility with older application programs and desk accessories. These leftovers will gradually find their way into the Preferences folder and other special folders as the programs that use them are upgraded for System 7.

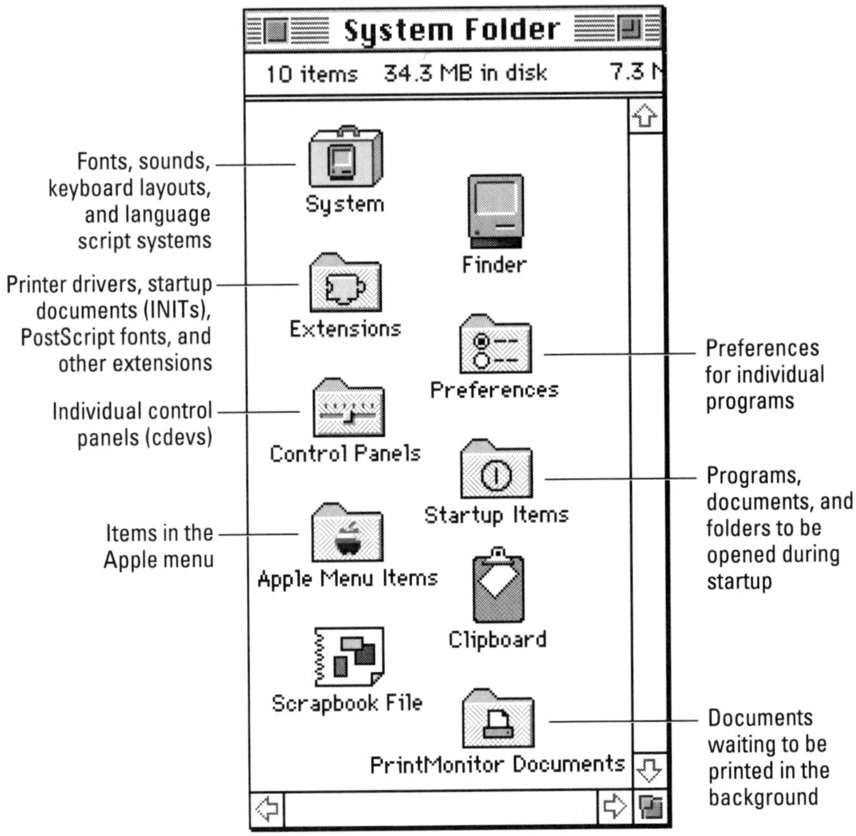

Figure 4-1
Inside a System Folder

This chapter describes each new folder and the System file in a separate section. Another section describes some other special folders outside the System Folder. At the end of the chapter are four sections that explain some new ways to work with the new folders and the System file.

System file

The System file has long been terra incognita to all but the most intrepid resource-hacking Macintosh users. Although a large part of it remains an uncharted wilderness of basic system software, Finder 7 lets

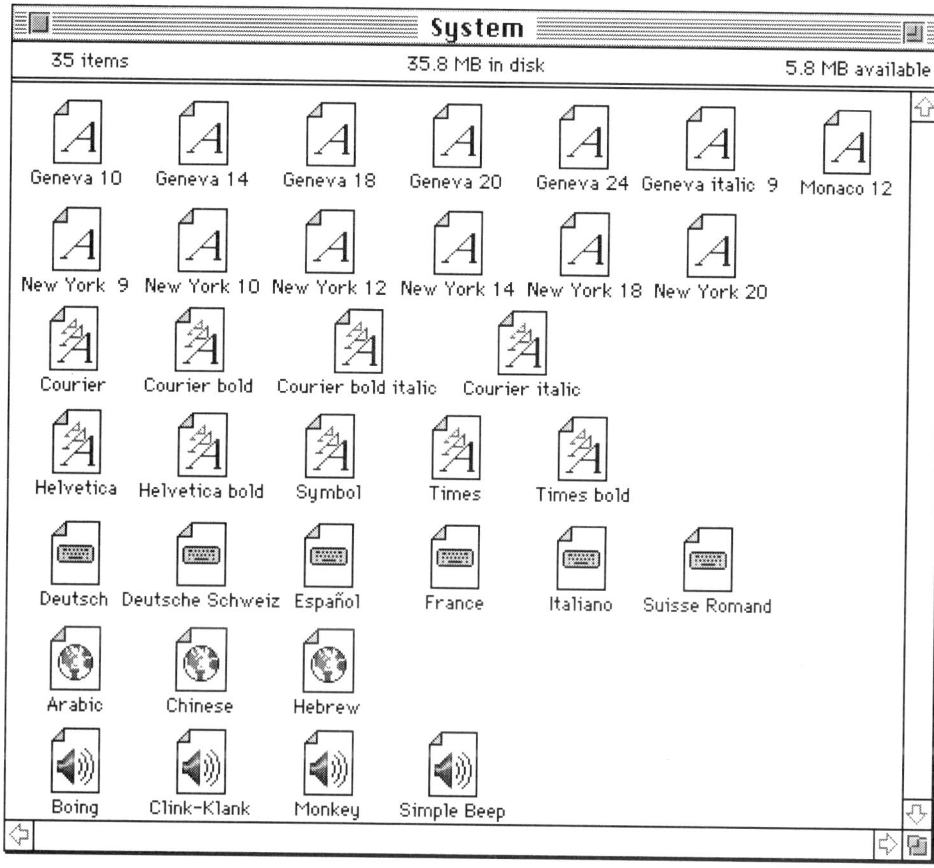

Figure 4-2
System file contents

everyday Macintosh users see and work with some of the System file's contents for the first time.

Seeing System file contents

You can open the System file as if it were a folder and see which fonts, alert sounds, keyboard layouts, and script systems for foreign languages it contains (Figure 4-2). The System file can contain two types of fonts: fixed-size (also called bitmap) and TrueType (also called variable-size or outline). PostScript printer fonts go in the Extensions folder or in the System Folder as they always have. (For more information on fonts, see Chapter 7.)

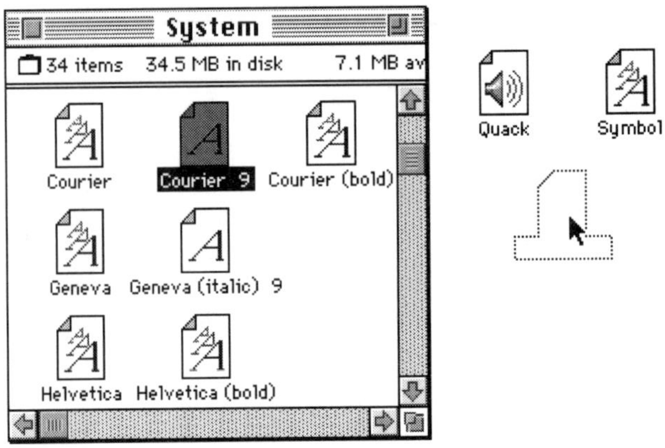

Figure 4-3
Fonts and sounds on the desktop

Several items do not appear when you open the System file because they are permanently installed in every Macintosh that can use System 7. The permanent items are:

- Geneva 9, Geneva 12, Chicago 12, and Monaco 9 fixed-size fonts
- Standard beep sound (sounds different from the Simple Beep)
- US keyboard layout
- Roman script system for Western languages

In older system software, the System file also contains desk accessories. In System 7, desk accessories stand alone in folders or on the desktop like application programs (see “Desk Accessories” in Chapter 5).

Working with System file contents

Not only can you see the contents of the System file, you can also drag items in and out of it as if it were a folder. Your changes take effect as soon as you close the System file; no need to restart your Macintosh first. However, the Finder doesn't let you drag items in or out of the System file if other programs are open. You must quit all open programs, make your changes to the System file contents, and then open the programs again.

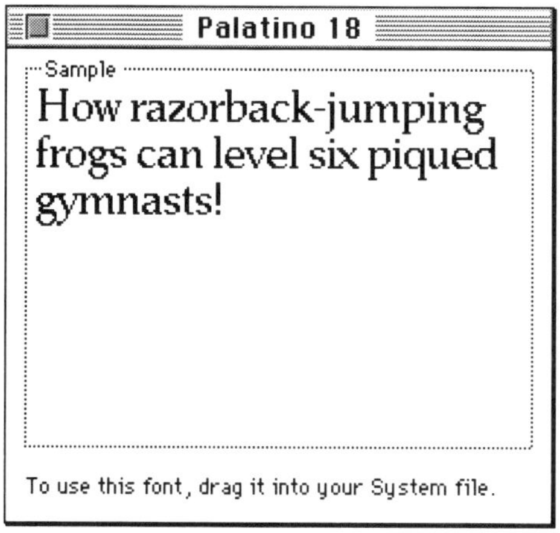

Figure 4-4
Sample text windows

Items you drag out of the System file become independent files. You can move them to any folder or the desktop and copy them to other disks (Figure 4-3). You can rename sounds but not fonts.

Whether fonts and sounds are inside the System file or out, you can open them as you would any ordinary document. Opening a font displays some sample text using that font (Figure 4-4). Opening a sound makes the Macintosh play it.

Installing fonts in the System file makes them available in programs that let you pick fonts. Some programs have you choose a font from a menu. Others have you select a font in a dialog box.

Installing sounds makes them available as the system alert sound, which you choose with the Sound control panel. These sounds are not HyperCard sounds. The sounds used in HyperCard are a special format that don't work properly as system alert sounds.

Keyboard layouts you install appear in the Keyboard control panel. Selecting a different keyboard layout there changes how your Mac sees

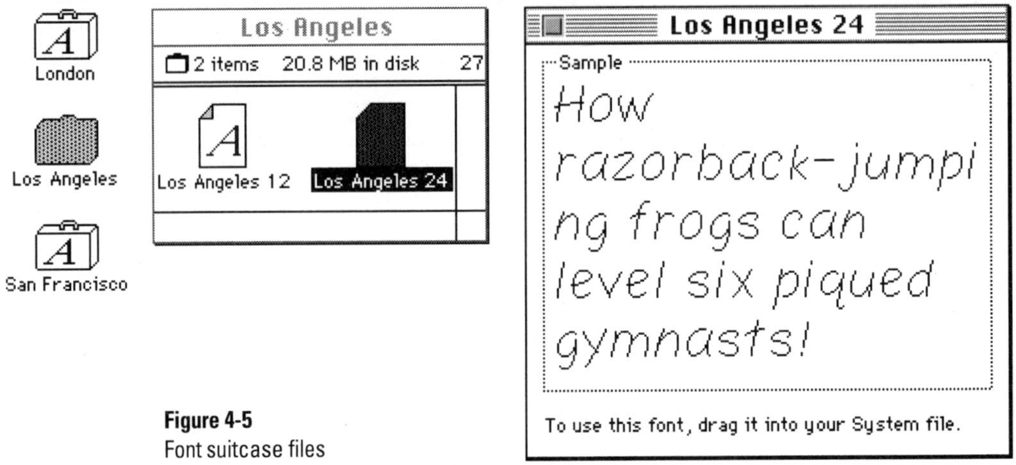

Figure 4-5
Font suitcase files

the arrangement of keys on your keyboard. Selecting the Español (Spanish) layout, for example, makes the semicolon key on a US keyboard produce an ñ.

If your System file contains more than one language script system, a Keyboard menu appears between the Help menu and the Application menu near the right end of the menu bar. You choose a keyboard layout and language script from it.

Exchanging with older systems

With System 7 you can also open font suitcase files and old System files (Figure 4-5). You can drag items in and out of these files. Old System files contain fonts, sounds, and desk accessories. Font suitcase files contain only fonts.

You only need font suitcases if you use the Font/DA Mover program to move fonts with older system software. You do not need the Font/DA Mover program with System 7 because it lets you manipulate fonts directly. You can create a new font suitcase file with System 7 by duplicating an existing font suitcase file, opening the duplicate, and dragging its contents to the Trash. You can also create font suitcase files using version 4.1 of the Font/DA Mover with System 7.

Apple Menu Items folder

The Apple Menu Items folder lets you quickly open anything you use often. All the items in the folder appear on the Apple menu (Figure 4-6) and choosing an item from the menu has the same effect as opening

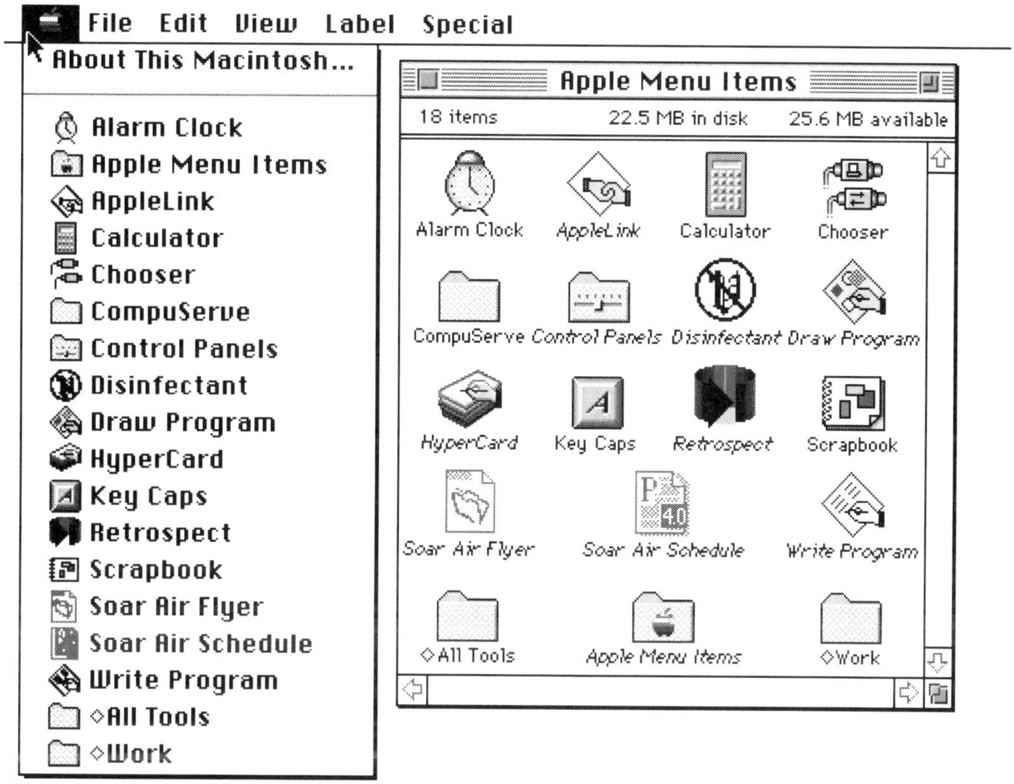

Figure 4-6
Apple Menu Items folder and Apple menu

(double-clicking) the corresponding item in the folder. The Apple menu plays a larger role in System 7 than in older system software because it isn't needed for opening desk accessories or for switching among open programs any more. (For more information, see "Opening multiple programs" in Chapter 2 and "Your own Apple menu" in Chapter 5.)

Startup Items folder

Everything you put in the Startup Items folder — application programs, desk accessories, documents, control panels, and so forth — gets opened when you start up your Macintosh (Figure 4-7). Items in the folder are opened in alphabetical order.

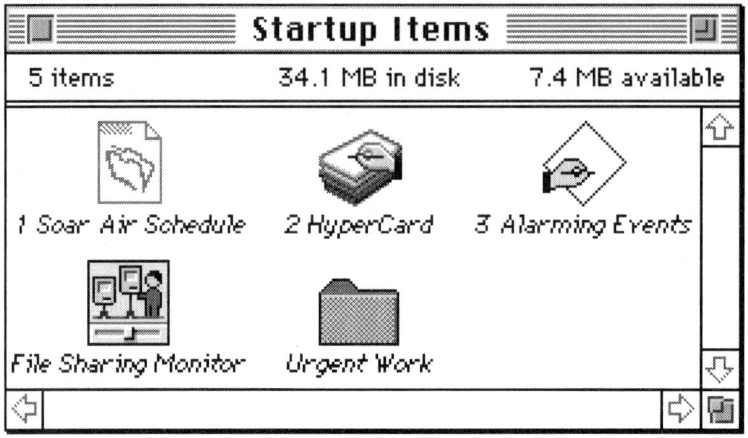

Figure 4-7
Inside a Startup Items folder

To have an item opened for you at startup time, drag it or an alias of it to the Startup Items folder. Dragging it out of that folder removes it from the startup sequence.

If you have several programs opened during startup, you may later have to quit some of them to free up memory for opening another. Naturally you'll want to quit the programs least important to you. You'll get maximum benefit from quitting them if they were the last items opened during startup. To make that happen, rename the programs in your Startup Items folder so the most important comes first alphabetically, the next-most important comes second, and so on. You can avoid renaming original programs by putting aliases in the Startup Items folder, as described in Chapter 6.

Don't bother renaming desk accessories, control panels, folders, or the aliases of any of those items that are in the Startup Items folder, however. During startup, the Finder first opens all those items alphabetically as a group after it has first opened all application programs alphabetically, along with their documents, as a group. For example, the Finder opens MacDraw Pro, QuarkXPress, and any of their documents included in the Startup Items folder before it opens the Control Panels folder, the File Sharing Monitor control panel, or the Key Caps desk accessory.

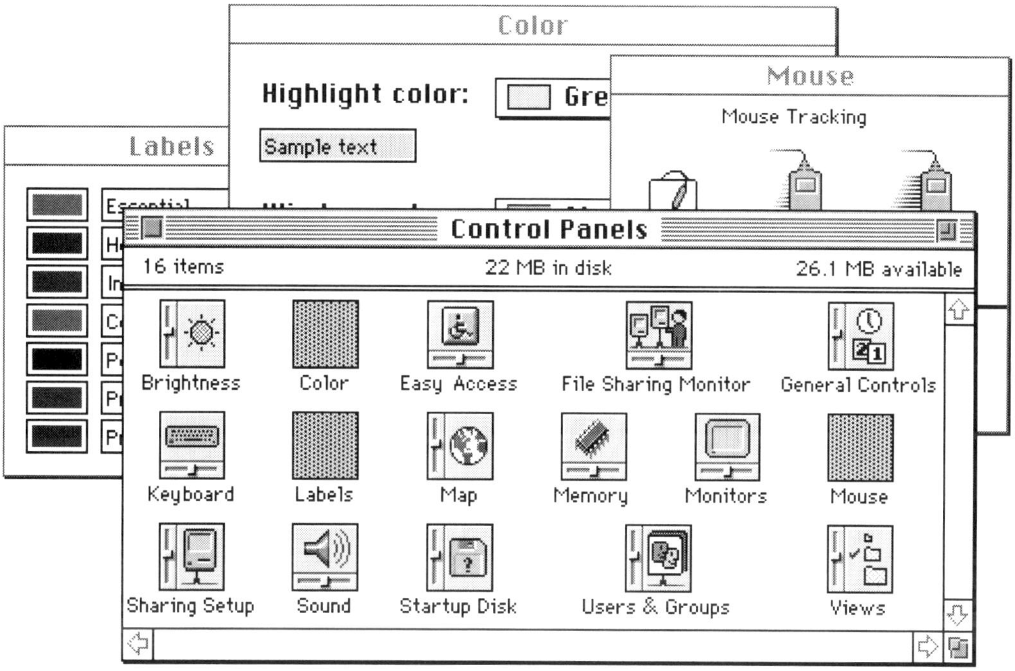

Figure 4-8
Control panels

Including desk accessories and folders or control panels in the Startup Items folder can disrupt the automatic startup sequence. Whenever a folder or control panel follows a desk accessory alphabetically, the Finder stops opening items and flashes its icon at the right end of the menu bar. You must switch to the Finder, for example by choosing it from the Application menu, whereupon it opens the folders and control panels that come next alphabetically. For example, you must manually switch to the Finder after it opens the Alarming Events desk accessory before it will open the Control Panels folder.

Control Panels folder

The items in the Control Panels folder give you control over system appearance and behavior as do the sections of the Control Panel desk accessory found with older system software. The folder contains small programs now called control panels (Figure 4-8). They are also known as

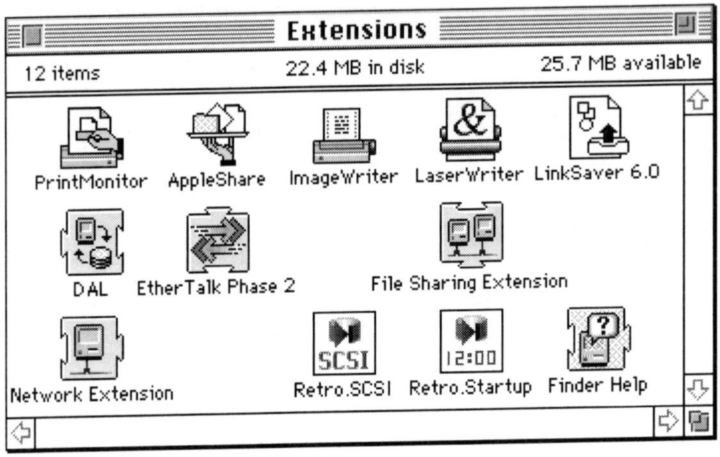

Figure 4-9
Inside an Extensions folder

control panel devices, control panel sections, and cdevs. Each affects one aspect of the system. Some control panels also add functions to the basic system software during startup. (For information on using individual control panels, see "Control panels" in Chapter 5.)

Extensions folder

The items in the Extensions folder customize your Macintosh by extending the services and functions of the system software (Figure 4-9). These items, which are small software modules called system extensions, include the following:

❖ ImageWriter, LaserWriter, and other Chooser extensions that enable your system to print on a specific type of printer (also called printer drivers).

❖ The PrintMonitor program, which allows you to continue working while documents print on a LaserWriter printer.

❖ Fonts for PostScript printers.

❖ AppleShare, a Chooser extension that lets you share folders and disks from other computers connected to yours.

- ❖ File Sharing Extension and Network Extension, which allow you to share your folders and disks with other people in your network.
- ❖ DAL, which adds simplified database-accessing services to programs designed to use them.
- ❖ EtherTalk and TokenTalk, which permit connecting some Macintosh models to EtherTalk and Token-Ring networks.
- ❖ Help systems like Finder Help, which provides on-screen help for the Finder.

To use a system extension, you simply put it in the Extensions folder and restart your Macintosh. If you remove a system extension from the Extensions folder, you must again restart for the removal to take effect.

Note that Aldus Pagemaker versions 4.01 and earlier and Adobe Type Manager (ATM) versions 2.0 and earlier can't find PostScript fonts in the Extensions folder. If you use these products or if text looks bad on your PostScript printer, you should put PostScript fonts in the System Folder itself.

Preferences folder

Some programs save preference settings in the Preferences folder. Programs with commands for publishing and subscribing information also save an alias named Last Edition Used whenever they save an edition (as described in Chapter 9). Also, the system software saves the following items in the Preferences folder (Figure 4-10):

- ❖ DAL Preferences: procedures the system software uses for connecting to relational databases.
- ❖ File Sharing folder: file sharing access privileges for your disks and folders.
- ❖ Finder Preferences: many of the settings you make with control panels.
- ❖ Users & Groups Data File: names and privileges for registered users and groups to whom you have given access to your computer.

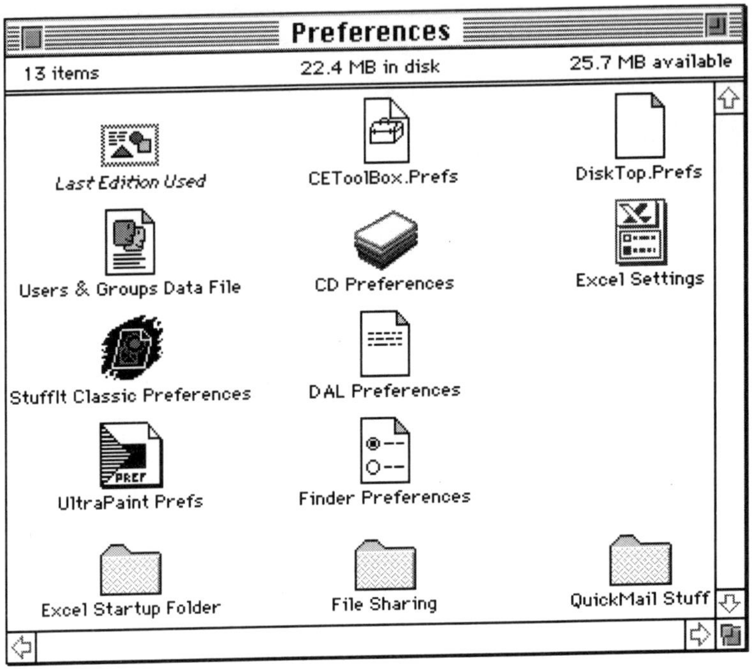

Figure 4-10
Inside a Preferences folder

Most of the preference files of older programs are loose in the System Folder, where they must remain until the programs are upgraded to work with System 7. If you drag a preferences file from the System Folder to the Preferences folder, the program that uses it probably won't be able to find it and will use its standard settings by default.

UNDOCUMENTED

More special folders outside

System 7 further organizes your disks with additional special folders outside the System Folder. The Finder creates the following special folders as needed on each disk:

❖ Temporary Items folder: Contains temporary files created by programs you are using. A program automatically deletes its temporary files when you quit it normally. This folder is invisible.

❖ Trash folder: Contains the items you have dragged from the disk to the Trash icon. Your disks' Trash folders are invisible, but you see their consolidated contents when you open the Trash icon. A visible Trash folder in a shared disk contains items from the disk that are in the owner's Trash.

❖ Network Trash folder: Contains items that people who are sharing the disk have dragged from the shared disk to their Trash icons. Inside this folder are folders named Trash Can #2, Trash Can #3, and so on. They contain items from your shared disk or folder that someone has dragged to the Trash — but has not yet permanently removed — on another Macintosh. These items appear in his or her Trash, not yours.

❖ Rescued Items folder: Contains items the Finder found in the Temporary Items folder when you restarted after a system crash (or after switching off the power without using the Shut Down command — tsk, tsk!). You may be able to reconstruct your work from them. If the Rescued Items folder exists, you can always see it by opening the Trash.

❖ Desktop Folder: Contains items located on the desktop. This folder is invisible on your disks, but the visible Desktop Folder of a shared disk is visible and contains items from the disk that are on the owner's desktop.

All these special folders become visible if you start up your Macintosh with older system software.

Adding to the System Folder

Putting control panels, system extensions, fonts, sounds, keyboard layouts, or language scripts where they belong is just as easy as putting them all in the System Folder. You simply drag the items to the System Folder icon. The Finder recognizes items that go in special folders or the System file and asks whether you want the items put into their proper places (Figure 4-11).

If you consent, the Finder puts control panels in the Control Panels folder; Chooser extensions, the PrintMonitor program, PostScript fonts, database extensions, network extensions, and system extensions in the Extensions folder; desk accessories in the Apple Menu Items folder; and fonts, sounds, keyboard layouts, and language script systems into the System file. All other items go into the System Folder itself.

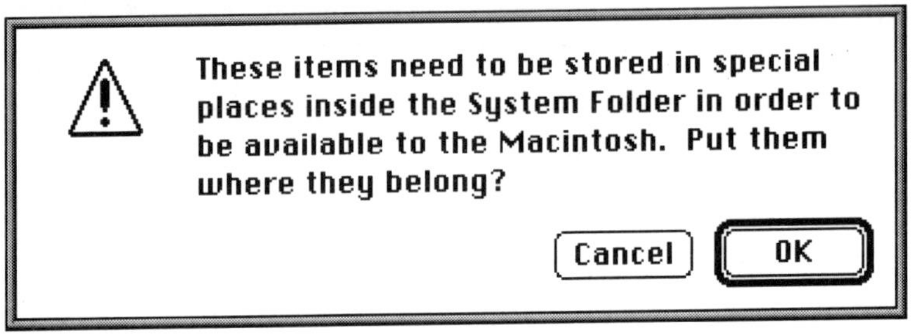

Figure 4-11
Upon dragging items to the System Folder

If you drag folders to the System Folder, the Finder looks inside them and puts items it recognizes in the Control Panels, Extensions, or Apple Menu Items folders. If a folder you drag contains items the Finder doesn't recognize, the Finder leaves them in the folder and puts the folder loose in the System Folder. If an item you drag to the System Folder has the same name as an item already there, the Finder not only asks whether you want to replace the latter with the former, but tells you which is newer.

When the Finder finishes putting items into their places, it tells you how many items of each type it moved (Figure 4-12). (It counts a folder and its contents as one item no matter how numerous the contents may be.)

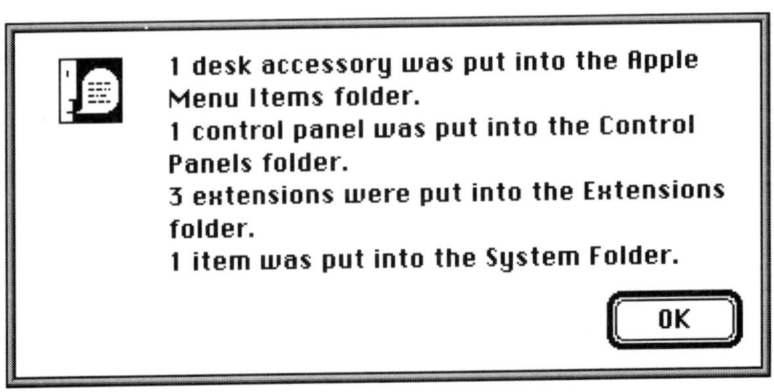

Figure 4-12
After dragging items to the System Folder

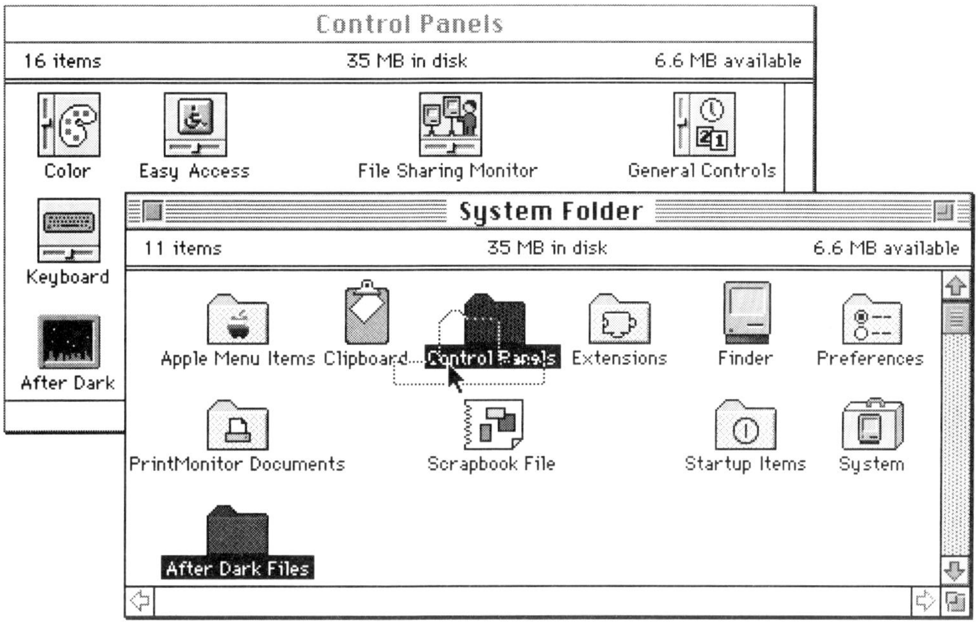

Figure 4-13
Correcting Finder mistakes

If you drag items to the System Folder window instead of the System Folder icon, the Finder does not put them in the inner folders for you.

QUICK TIPS

Should you happen to discard one of the special folders, you can make a replacement using the Finder's New Folder command (File menu). After creating a new folder, change its name to be the same as the special folder you want. Wait a few seconds and you'll see its icon get the distinctive look of the special folder you're creating.

Fooling the Finder

The Finder sometimes makes mistakes when it puts items in the special folders for you. It may put some items in the correct places and incorrectly leave others in the System Folder itself. For example, it may put a control panel in the Control Panels folder but leave that control panel's auxiliary folder in the System Folder. That control panel won't work right because it expects to find its auxiliary folder in the same folder as it is in. You must open the System Folder and drag the auxiliary folder to the Control Panels folder yourself (Figure 4-13).

Additionally, the Finder never puts anything you drag to the System Folder icon into the Preferences folder or the Startup Items folder. You must open the System Folder and drag items to those folders directly.

Some items from old System Folders don't work right when they're put in the new Extensions, Control Panel, or Preferences folders. If you have trouble with an item in one of the special folders, try dragging the item from the special folder to the System Folder window.

Removing from the System Folder

Before you can remove an item from the System Folder, you must know which inner folder it is in. If you're not sure, use the Finder's Find command to locate the item (see "Finding items" in Chapter 3). Be sure to put items you drag from the special folders within the System Folder onto the desktop or into an ordinary folder. Many items you drag out of special folders are still effective if you merely drag them to the System Folder window.

Troubleshooting a conflict

If items you add to the System Folder, Extensions folder, or Control Panels folder don't work, or if your Macintosh refuses to start up, then some of the system extensions in those places may be in conflict during startup. Sometimes changing the order in which the Macintosh installs system extensions resolves the conflict.

Whereas older system software installs system extensions in strict alphabetical order, System 7 installs them in three groups. First it goes through the Extensions folder in alphabetical order. Then it installs the extensions that are built into items in the Control Panels folder, again alphabetically. Finally it checks the System Folder itself and alphabetically installs system extensions it finds there. This change in the installation sequence can cause problems for older system extensions and control panels.

Some system extensions and control panels have peculiar names meant to put the items first or last in the installation sequence (Figure 4-14). Names of items meant to come first usually begin with blank spaces. Names meant to come last often begin with a tilde (~) or diamond (◊).

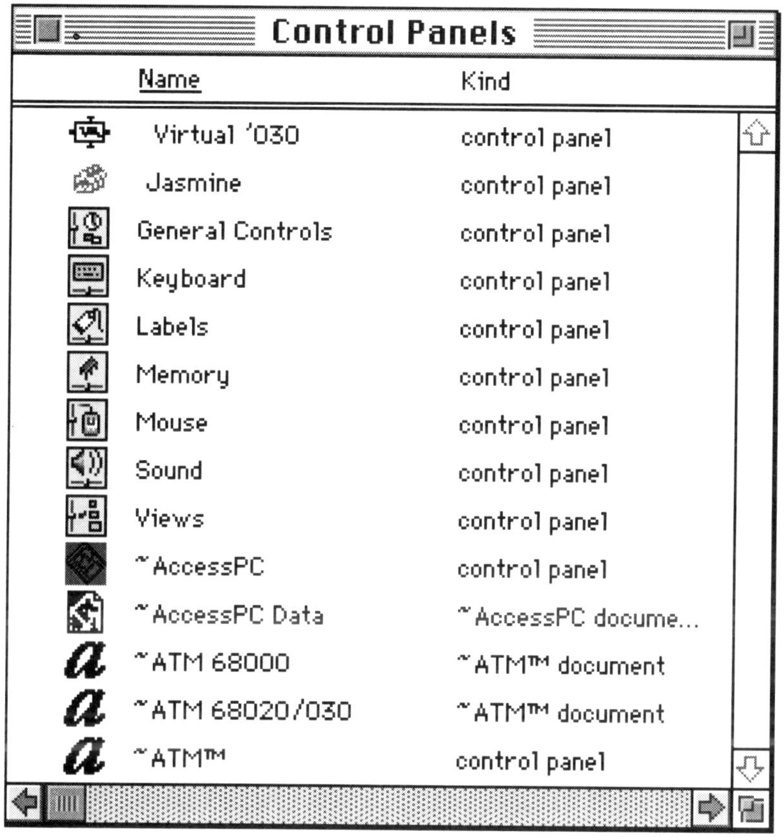

Figure 4-14
Name prefixes affect startup sequence

To have control panels whose names begin with blank spaces installed first during startup, put them in the Extensions folder. To have control panels whose names start with tildes or diamonds installed last during startup, put them in the System Folder. For convenient access to the control panels you move out of the Control Panels folder, make aliases for them and put the aliases in the Control Panels folder.

To have system extensions whose names begin with tildes and diamonds installed last during startup, drag them from the Extensions folder to the System Folder. Leave system extensions whose names begin with blank spaces in the Extensions folder so they will be installed first during startup.

Fixing other conflicts between system extensions and control panels involves experimenting. Start by removing all the items you have added to the System Folder and its inner folders since the trouble began. Then add them back one at a time, restarting your Macintosh each time. When you find an item that causes a conflict, try renaming it so it comes before or after other system extensions in the same folder. By experimenting with names you may find a startup sequence that works.

As a last resort, remove all system extensions and control panels to the desktop. Then put them in the System Folder (not the Extensions or Control Panels folder) one at a time, from most important to least. Restart your Macintosh each time you add another item to the System Folder. When you find an item that causes a conflict, discard it and try the next item you previously moved to the desktop. You may be able to resume using the items you discarded when they are next upgraded.

(If a conflict prevents starting up from your hard disk, start from a floppy disk with any version of system software. Make a change to the System Folder on the hard disk and try restarting from it.)

Summary

- Three new folders — the Control Panels folder, the Extensions folder, and the Preferences folder — go a long way toward cleaning up the sprawling growth going on in so many System Folders. Other new folders inside the System Folder improve your access to programs, documents, and other items that can be opened.
- The Apple Menu Items folder lets you decide what items are listed on the Apple menu for quick opening.
- The Startup Items folder contains the things you want opened automatically at startup time.
- The Finder helps you keep the System Folder organized by putting many of the items you drag to its icon into the proper inner folders.
- In addition to the new folders found inside the Sysem Folder are special folders — Temporary Items, Trash, Network Trash, Rescued Items, and Desktop — created by the Finder as needed on each disk.
- To round out the redevelopment of the System Folder, System 7 unseals the System file. You now add and remove fonts, sounds, keyboard layouts, and language systems by dragging them in and out of the System file.

Chapter 5

Tailored to Fit

In This Chapter

- Desk accessories move to the desktop and behave like ordinary application programs.
- A look at the Apple menu's expanded role: opening any program, document, folder, or other desktop icon.
- Individual control panels that look and act like independent Finder documents.
- Opening more programs and bigger documents with virtual memory and 32-Bit Addressing.
- Managing your memory in the face of increasingly intense memory usage.

Fitting the Macintosh to your work environment just got easier. System 7 removes the special rules of older system software for installing and using desk accessories and control panels. Now you put them where you want and use them in a manner more consistent with ordinary programs and documents. At the same time, ordinary programs and documents acquire a trait formerly unique to desk accessories: being in the Apple menu where you can find and open them quickly.

System 7's multitasking capabilities let you keep multiple programs open simultaneously if your Macintosh has enough memory available. Virtual memory lets you use hard disk space as additional memory, and 32-Bit Addressing increases the amount of memory some Macintosh models can use. To effectively use your computer's memory, you must adjust program memory size and monitor when you open and quit programs.

Related topics discussed elsewhere in this book include aliases (Chapter 8), multitasking ("Opening multiple programs" in Chapter 2), installing fonts ("Adding and removing fonts" in Chapter 7), custom views of Finder windows ("Custom views" in Chapter 3), making and using template documents ("Stationery pads" in Chapter 3), customizing icons ("Custom icons" in Chapter 3), and system folder organization (Chapter 4).

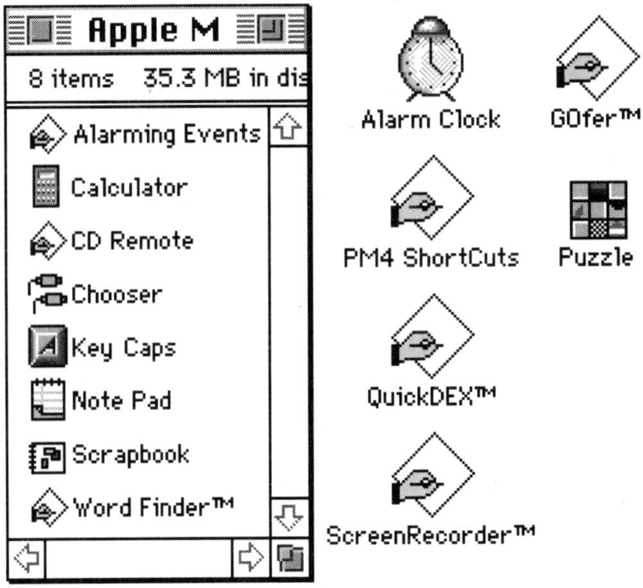

Figure 5-1
Some desk accessories

Desk accessories

Very little differentiates desk accessories and application programs in System 7. You can put both in folders, on the desktop, or in the Apple menu (Figure 5-1). Each desk accessory can have its own family of icons, consisting of small and standard sizes each in black-and-white, 16 colors, and 256 colors. However, most older desk accessories use the generic desk accessory icons, which look like generic application program icons.

You move and copy desk accessories by dragging their icons in the Finder. If you want to install a desk accessory in the Apple menu, you simply drag it to the System Folder icon. You do not use the Font/DA Mover utility program. For compatibility with older system software, desk accessories can exist in suitcase files, which the Font/DA Mover program creates. You can use Font/DA Mover version 4.1 (but not earlier versions) with System 7.

Opening desk accessories

System 7's full-time multitasking always lets you open any desk accessory or application program without quitting the program you're using (available memory permitting). You open a desk accessory like an application program, by double-clicking it or by selecting it and using the Finder's Open command. Unlike an application program, however, you can't open a desk accessory by opening one of its documents. Also, desk accessories in a suitcase file can't be opened. You must first drag them out of the suitcase into a folder or onto the desktop.

Using desk accessories

System 7 puts each desk accessory you open in its own memory partition and adds its name to the Application menu. You make a single desk accessory the active program by choosing it from the Application menu or clicking its window, just like an application program. While a desk accessory is the active program, it has its own About command in the Apple menu that includes the name of the desk accessory. Older system software lumps all open desk accessories together in one partition when MultiFinder is active or includes them with the open application program when MultiFinder is inactive.

All desk accessories have a File menu with Close and Quit commands. These commands work differently in System 7 than in older system software. The Close command closes the desk accessory's active window and — in most desk accessories — it quits the active desk accessory. The Quit command quits the active desk accessory (not all open desk accessories as in older system software).

Some older desk accessories depend on being open in the same memory partition as an application program. They don't work quite right with System 7, where they must be independent. A thesaurus desk accessory, for example, may be unable to automatically look up a word you have selected. A screen capture utility may be unable to take a picture of a program's menu. In older system software with MultiFinder active you could work around these problems by pressing the Option key while opening the desk accessory. That trick does not work in System 7.

System 7 comes with the same seven desk accessories as older system software: Alarm Clock, Calculator, Chooser, Key Caps, Note Pad, Puzzle, and Scrapbook. The System 7 versions of these standard desk accessories use color and gray shades on color and grayscale monitors; on black-and-white monitors they look similar to their older counterparts. These desk accessories are described in the following sections.

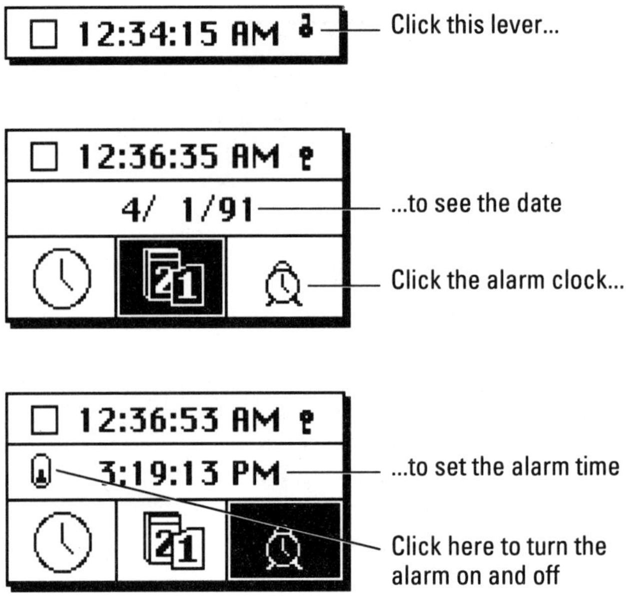

Figure 5-2
The Alarm Clock desk accessory

Alarm Clock

The Alarm Clock desk accessory shows the time of day (Figure 5-2). It can be expanded to show the date, set the time or date, or set an alarm. When the alarm goes off, you hear the system alert sound (as set in the Sound control panel) and the Alarm Clock icon flashes on top of the Apple Menu icon at the left end of the menu bar. To stop the flashing, you need only open the Alarm Clock desk accessory.

Calculator

The Calculator desk accessory adds, subtracts, multiplies, and divides numbers you enter (Figure 5-3). You can type numbers and operation symbols or click the keys in the desk accessory. In addition, you can copy the text of a calculation — for example, 69.95+26.98+14.99*.0725 — and paste it into the Calculator.

Chooser

The Chooser desk accessory lets you select a printer or other output device and make connections with other computers networked to yours (Figure 5-4). Chooser 7 is larger than older versions to make room for

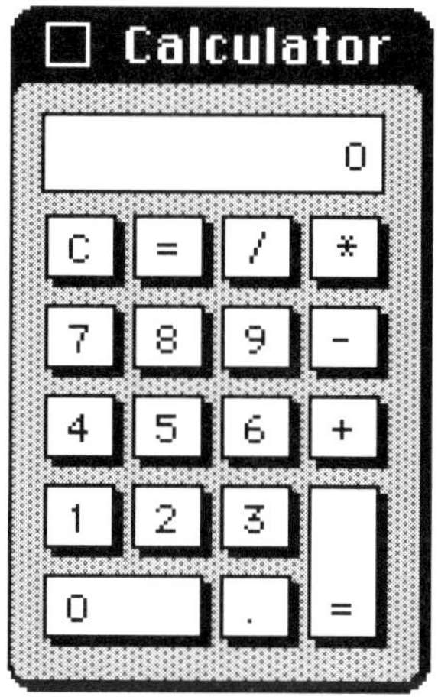

Figure 5-3
The Calculator desk accessory

more devices and network zones. Also, you no longer enter the Macintosh owner's name in the Chooser, but in the Sharing Setup control panel (described in Chapter 8).

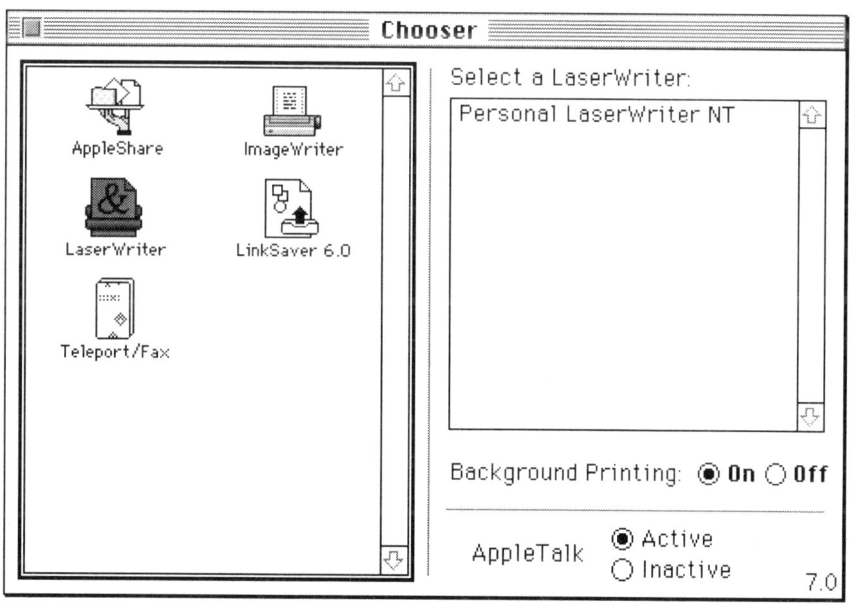

Figure 5-4
The Chooser desk accessory

Figure 5-5
The Key Caps desk accessory

Key Caps

The Key Caps desk accessory shows all the characters you can type in any font installed in your system (Figure 5-5). You choose the font from the Key Caps menu, which appears to the right of the Edit menu when the Key Caps desk accessory is active. Key Caps changes to show the effect of pressing the Shift, Option, or Control keys separately or in combination.

In Key Caps 7, pressing the Option key outlines the keys that, when pressed along with the Option key, don't directly produce a character (Figure 5-6). Each of those Option-key combinations, called dead keys, adds an accent or other diacritic to certain subsequently typed keys. Pressing a dead key, for example Option-E for an accent, outlines the keys that can have that diacritic added.

You might like to print Key Caps as a handy reference, but it has no Print command. To work around this, take a picture of the screen and print that as follows: Open Key Caps, choose the font you want it to show, and press any modifier keys (Shift, Option, Control, or Command) you want in effect. Move the pointer to an empty area of the menu bar, hold down the mouse button, temporarily release the modifier keys, press Command-Shift-3, again press the modifier keys you released temporarily, and finally release the mouse button. Your gyrations should be rewarded by the sound of a camera shutter as the system snaps a picture of the screen. Open your startup disk and look for a document named Picture 1.

Figure 5-6
Reviewing dead keys

Print this document using TeachText or any graphics program. Cut out the Key Caps window with scissors after printing or crop it out with a graphics program before printing. If you take additional snapshots, they will be numbered sequentially.

Note Pad

The Note Pad desk accessory records brief messages you type or paste into it (Figure 5-7).

Puzzle

The Puzzle desk accessory is a game in which you unscramble tiles to make a picture (Figure 5-8). Push a tile in the same row or column as the vacant space toward the vacant space by clicking the tile. Also, Puzzle 7 has two games, one with numbered tiles and another with a picture of the Apple logo. Choose Clear from the Edit menu to switch between them.

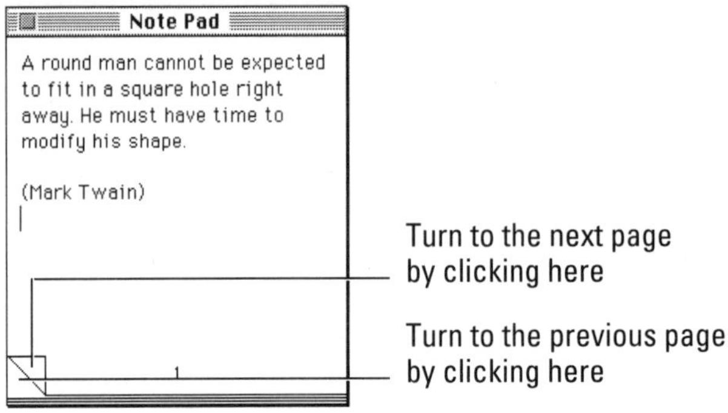

Figure 5-7
The Note Pad desk accessory

You can replace the picture of the Apple logo. Just copy a picture in another program, switch to the Puzzle, and paste.

Scrapbook

The Scrapbook desk accessory stores and retrieves text, pictures, sounds, and other types of information that you paste into it, one item at a time (Figure 5-9). Scrapbook 7 can play sounds as well as show pictures and text.

QUICK TIPS

After extensive use, your Scrapbook may become cluttered with old clippings. If you can't bear to throw them out, make a copy of the Scrapbook File in your System Folder (use the Finder's Duplicate command) before you start weeding. Later you can use the old copy you made by

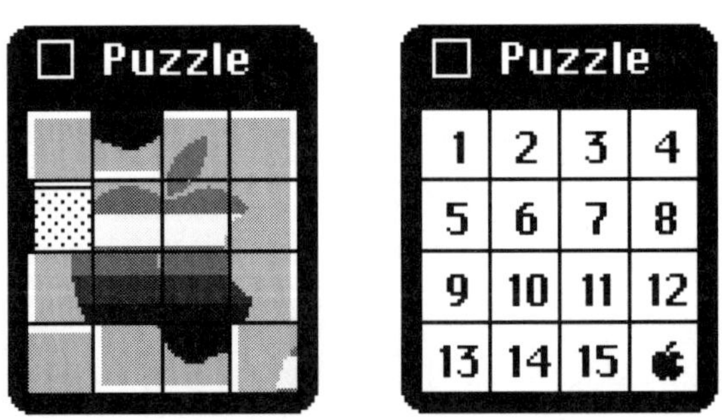

Figure 5-8
The Puzzle desk accessory

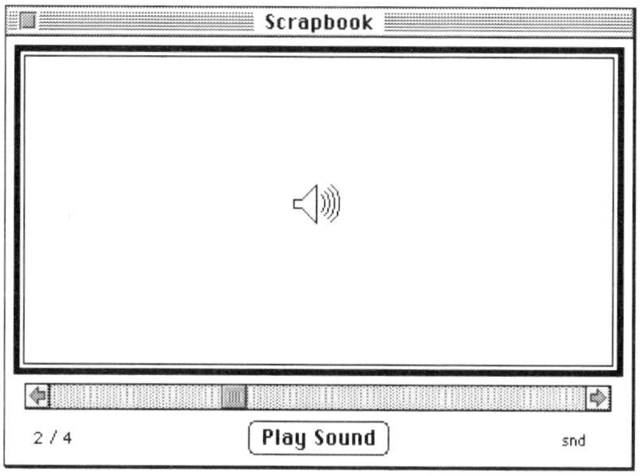

Figure 5-9
The Scrapbook desk accessory

dragging the current Scrapbook File out of the System Folder, dragging the old copy in, and changing its name to Scrapbook File.

Your own Apple menu

The Apple menu's role has expanded because desk accessories do not have to be in it any longer. Now the Apple menu expedites opening anything you use frequently. Anything you could double-click in the Finder you can put in the Apple menu and open it by choosing it there. This includes documents, application programs, desk accessories, folders, control panels, and even fonts and sounds (Figure 5-10).

You put an item in the Apple menu by dragging it into the Apple Menu Items folder, which is inside the System Folder (Figure 5-11). The item becomes instantly available in the Apple menu. (No need to restart your Macintosh.)

Items are always listed alphabetically in the Apple menu using plain Chicago 12-point text. Alias names are not italicized in the menu even though they are italicized in the Apple Menu Items folder. Rearranging the contents of the Apple Menu Items folder by dragging icons in its window, clicking column headings in a list view, or using the Finder's Views menu doesn't affect the Apple menu.

QUICK TIPS

You can make an item appear at the top of the Apple menu by prefixing its name with a blank space. Alternatively, you can prefix the name with an Apple logo or solid diamond ♦ symbol. You do that by setting

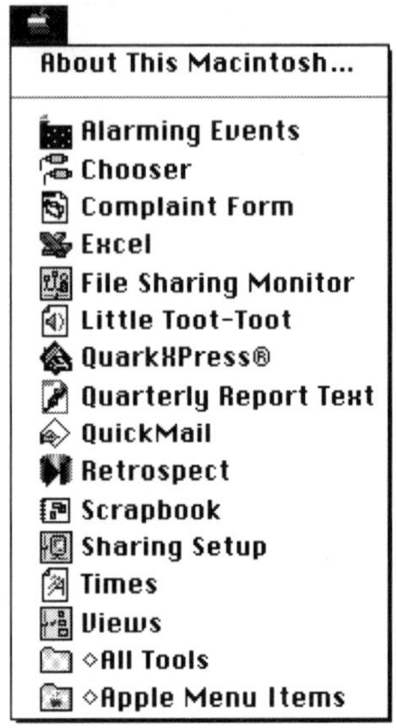

Figure 5-10
An Apple menu

the Key Caps desk accessory to the Chicago font, typing Control-T for the Apple logo or Control-S for the solid diamond, copying the symbol, and pasting it at the beginning of the item name. These special symbols look like boxes in the Apple Menu Items window because they're not part of the Geneva font, which the Finder uses for text in windows unless you specify another font with the Views control panel. They look right in the Apple menu, which uses the Chicago font.

To make items appear at the bottom of the Apple menu, prefix with a hollow diamond (◊) or a bullet (•). Type Shift-Option-V for the hollow diamond or Option-8 for the bullet.

To remove an item from the Apple menu, drag its icon or alias out of the Apple Menu Items folder onto the desktop or into another folder.

Control panels

Like desk accessories, control panels are more versatile in System 7 than in older system software. You open one or more individual control panels as you would any document, for example by double-clicking it. Each open control panel appears in its own window. Control panels now come in all sizes and shapes because they no longer have to fit in a fixed-size section of the old Control Panel desk accessory.

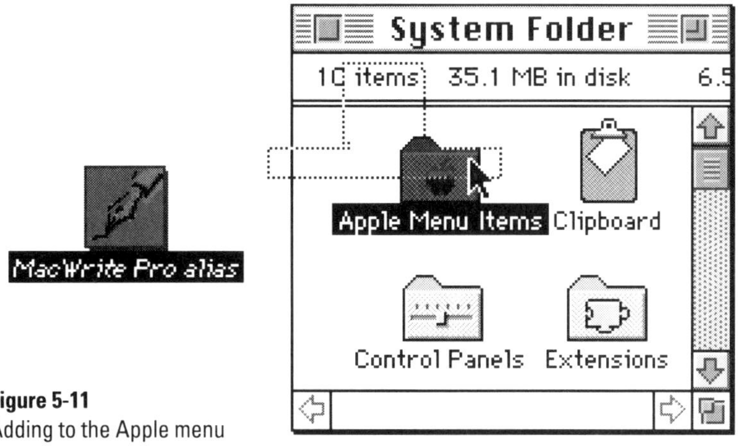

Figure 5-11
Adding to the Apple menu

By convention control panels go in the special Control Panels folder inside the System Folder. When you open the Control Panels folder, its window acts as a master control panel (Figure 5-12). You can rearrange the individual control panels in it by using the Finder's View menu or by dragging icons. So that you can open the Control Panels folder easily, it is listed in the Apple menu. (The Apple Menu Items folder contains an alias of the Control Panels icon.)

Many control panels work fine if you drag them out of the Control Panels folder. However, control panels that extend the system software during startup won't work unless they're located in the Control Panels folder, the Extensions folder, or the System Folder. The system only looks in those places during startup for system software extensions.

Control panels aren't listed in the Application menu at the right end of the menu bar along with application programs and desk accessories. They're considered part of the Finder. To use one that's already open, switch to the Finder (by choosing it from the Application menu or by clicking the desktop) and find the control panel's window.

Some old control panel documents (also called cdevs) work properly only if you put them in the System Folder itself, not in the Control Panels folder. You should make an alias of each control panel you put in the System Folder and put the alias in the Control Panels folder so you can open that control panel from the Control Panels window (which you see upon choosing Control Panels from the Apple menu).

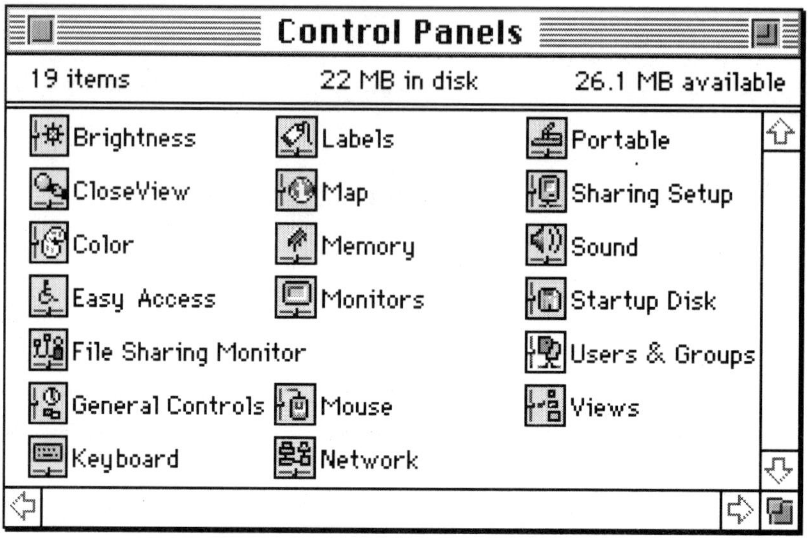

Figure 5-12
An open Control Panels folder

Standard control panels

System 7 comes with 19 control panels. The following seven are covered in other chapters:

- ❖ Color has settings for text highlighting color and window shading color. See "Choosing a window color" in Chapter 2.
- ❖ File Sharing Monitor lists the disks and folders you're sharing with others, identifies who is connected to your Macintosh, and lets you disconnect them individually. See "Monitoring file sharing activity" in Chapter 8.
- ❖ Labels sets the names and colors (on a color or grayscale monitor) of items in the Finder's Labels menu. See "Changing label names and colors" in Chapter 3.
- ❖ Network determines which network connection to use if your Macintosh has more than one available. See "Selecting your network" in Chapter 8.

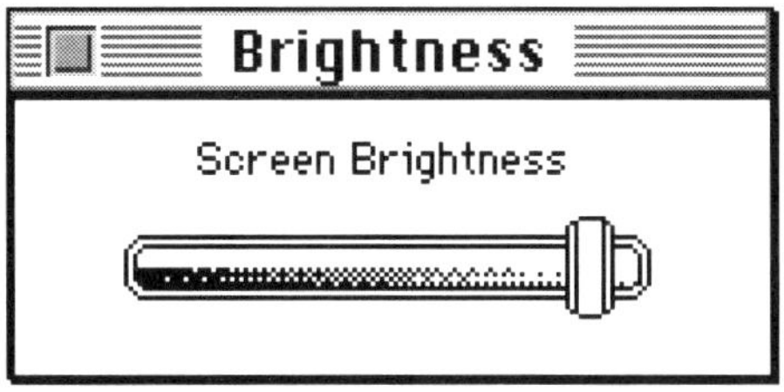

Figure 5-13
The Brightness control panel

❖ Sharing Setup names your Macintosh and its owner on its network, sets the owner's network password, and starts or stops file sharing and program linking. See "Starting file sharing" in Chapter 8 and "Using program linking" in Chapter 10.

❖ Users & Groups identifies people and groups whom you allow specific access privileges for file sharing and program linking. See "Who can access your shared item?" in Chapter 8.

❖ Views sets format and content options for Finder windows. See "Custom views" in Chapter 3.

The other 12 standard control panels are described in the following sections of this chapter.

Brightness

On some Macintosh models, you adjust the brightness of your monitor by dragging the slide control in the Brightness control panel (Figure 5-13). If a message advises that you can't use the Brightness control panel when you try to open it, use the brightness knob on the monitor instead.

CloseView

You can use the CloseView control panel to magnify your screen 2 to 16 times and to invert the displayed colors (Figure 5-14). CloseView must be in the Control Panels folder at startup time.

Easy Access

The Easy Access control panel sets up three alternative methods of using the keyboard and mouse (Figure 5-15): Mouse Keys, Slow Keys,

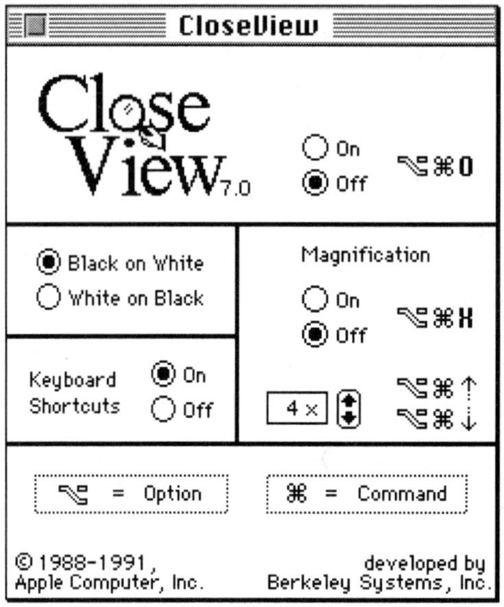

Figure 5-14
The Close View control panel

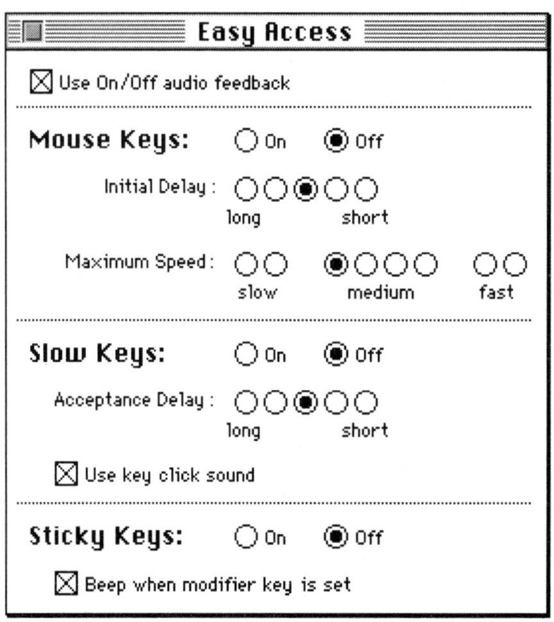

Figure 5-15
The Easy Access control panel

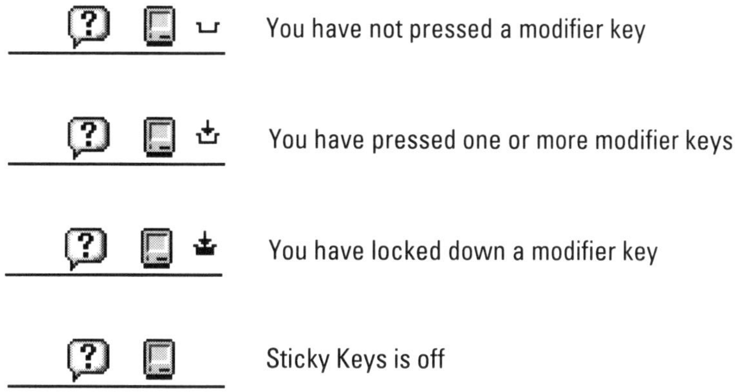

Figure 5-16
Sticky Keys status

and Sticky Keys. In System 7, Easy Access whistles when you turn any of these features on or off. You can silence the whistle by turning off the audio feedback option at the top of the Easy Access control panel.

Mouse Keys lets you click, drag, and move the pointer with the keypad instead of the mouse. You can turn on Mouse Keys by pressing Command-Shift-Clear instead of using the Easy Access control panel. You can also turn it off by pressing Clear. With Mouse Keys on, the 5 key on the keypad acts like a mouse button. Press once to click; press twice to double-click; or hold it down. The eight keys around the 5 key move the pointer left, right, up, down, and diagonally. Pressing the 0 key locks the mouse button down until you press the Period key on the keypad.

Slow Keys makes the Macintosh wait before it accepts a keystroke, thereby filtering out accidental keystrokes.

Sticky Keys lets you type combination keystrokes such as Command-Shift-3 (which puts a snapshot of your screen in a picture document most graphics programs can open) one key at a time. Sticky Keys also lets you lock down any modifier key by pressing it two times in a row. You can turn on Sticky Keys by pressing the Shift key five times in succession. When Sticky Keys is on, an icon at the right end of the menu bar shows its status (Figure 5-16). You can turn Sticky Keys off by pressing Shift five times again or by pressing any two modifier keys simultaneously.

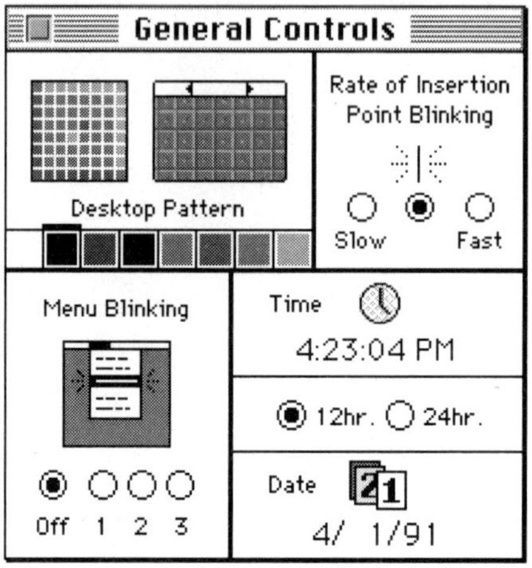

Figure 5-17
The General Controls control panel

General Controls

The General Controls control panel sets the desktop pattern, clock, calendar, menu flashing, and insertion point flashing (Figure 5-17). Selecting a pattern and making a custom pattern are covered in the "Desktop" section of Chapter 2.

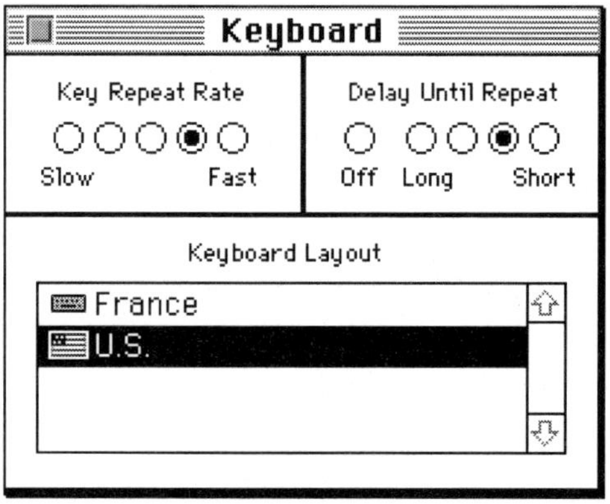

Figure 5-18
The Keyboard control panel

Keyboard

The Keyboard control panel sets the key repeat rate and the delay time until key repeating begins (Figure 5-18). If your system has multiple keyboard layouts installed, you can select among them using the Keyboard control panel.

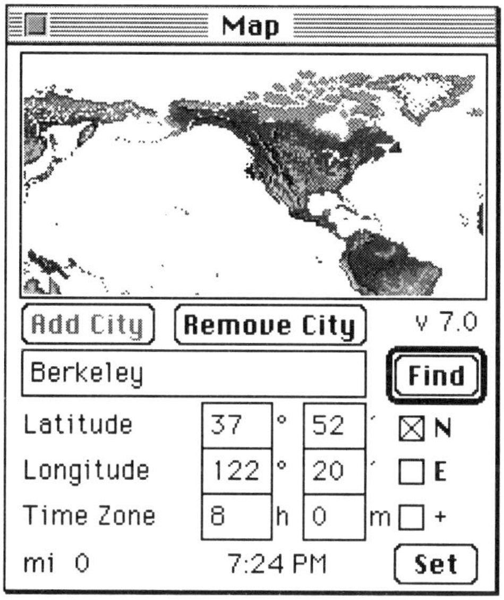

Figure 5-19
The Map control panel

Map

The Map control panel sets the world location (latitude and longitude) and the time zone of your Macintosh (Figure 5-19). It can also compute the time difference and distance between any two places. Tiny flashing dots on the map mark known places. Click one to see its name or drag the pointer around until a name comes up. The map scrolls if you drag beyond its boundaries. You can also type a place name in the space provided and click the Find button or go through the list of known places alphabetically by pressing Option while clicking Find. The latitude, longitude, and time zone pertain to the most recently selected place. Map marks that location with a flashing star.

To add a new place, specify its latitude and longitude by clicking, by dragging, or by typing the coordinates in the spaces provided. Then type the place name and click the Add City button. After adding a new place, verify the estimated time zone and correct it if necessary.

Map marks the location of your Macintosh with a flashing dark cross. Set it by finding or adding the proper location and then clicking the Set button. Map automatically adjusts the time and date of your system's clock

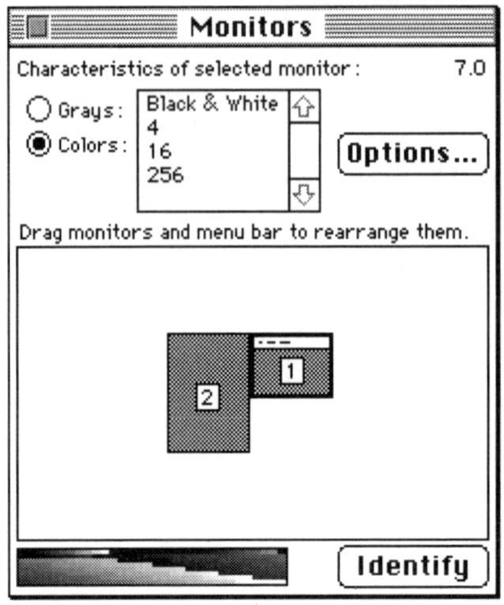

Figure 5-20
The Monitors control panel

according to the difference between the old and new locations. Your Macintosh stores its location in battery-powered memory along with the time of day and other semipermanent settings.

The distance or compass direction from your Macintosh to the place marked with the flashing star appears at the bottom of the control panel along with the time at the distant place. Change from distance in miles to distance in kilometers or direction in degrees by clicking the unit of measure in the lower left corner of the control panel. To see the time difference between that place and your Macintosh, click the words Time Differ in the control panel.

You can enlarge the map by pressing the Option key while opening the Map control panel. To magnify more, press Shift-Option while opening.

Monitors

The Monitors control panel sets the number of colors or grays of one or more monitors (Figure 5-20). Changes to these settings take place immediately.

QUICK TIPS

If your Macintosh has multiple monitors, you can drag images of them around to determine their relative positions and can drag the menu bar to the monitor on which you want it to appear. You can also designate

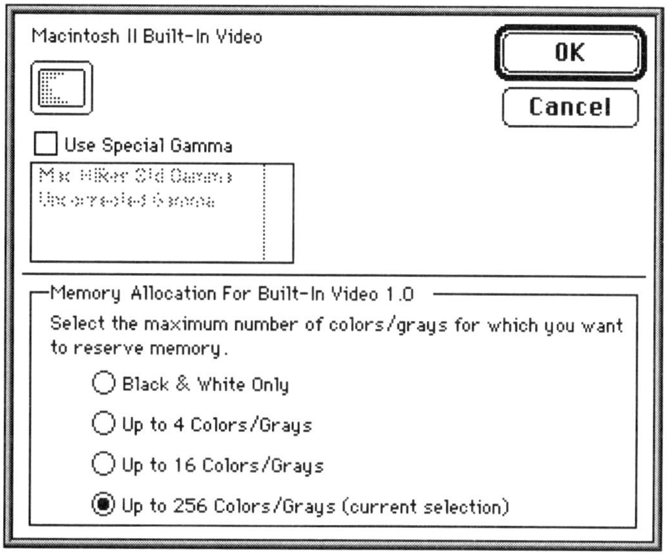

Figure 5-21
The Monitors Options panel

which monitor displays startup messages and icons. Press the Option key to reveal a tiny Macintosh icon and drag it to the monitor you want used during startup. Settings that affect multiple monitors take place when you next restart your Macintosh.

On a Macintosh IIci or IIsi, you can also use the Monitors control panel to limit the number of colors or grays available with built-in video. The higher the limit, the more memory the built-in video uses. You set the limit in the Monitors Options panel (Figure 5-21). To see it, press the Option key while clicking the Options button in the Monitors control panel. With a 640 by 480 color monitor, 256 colors require 320K, 16 colors require 160K, 4 colors require 96K, and black-and-white requires 74K.

Mouse

The Mouse control panel sets the mouse-to-pointer tracking speed and the double-click interval (Figure 5-22).

Portable

The Portable control panel sets special features of the Macintosh Portable (Figure 5-23).

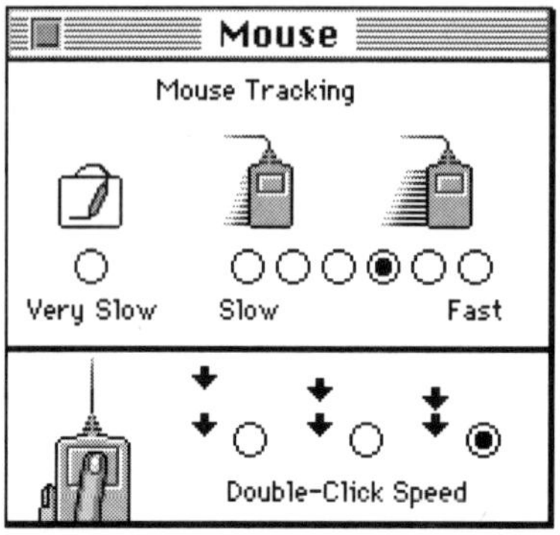

Figure 5-22
The Mouse control panel

Sound

The Sound control panel sets the speaker volume and the system alert sound (Figure 5-24). It also includes controls for recording new alert sounds if your Macintosh has sound input equipment.

Startup Disk

The Startup Disk control panel sets which hard disk your Macintosh will use the next time it starts up (Figure 5-25). This control panel doesn't

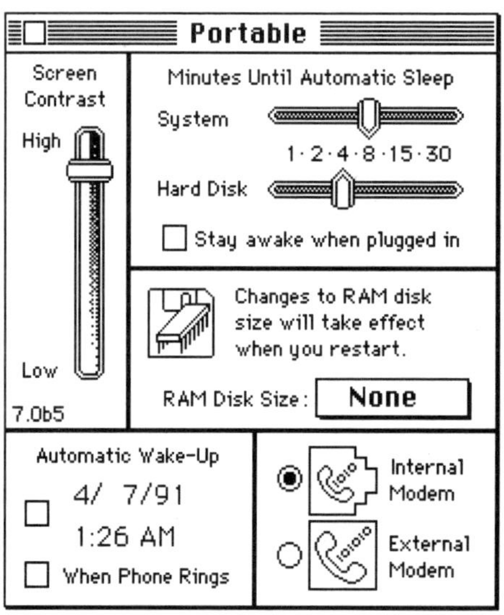

Figure 5-23
The Portable control panel

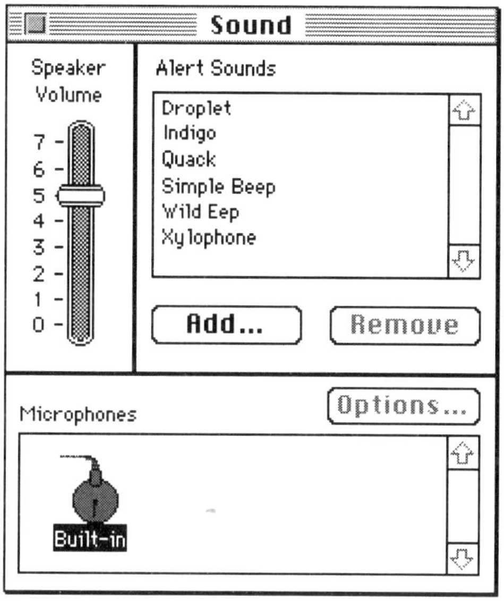

Figure 5-24
The Sound control panel

work with a Macintosh Plus. It has no effect unless your Macintosh has more than one hard disk with a System Folder. And in most cases it won't let you choose among multiple partitions on a single hard disk.

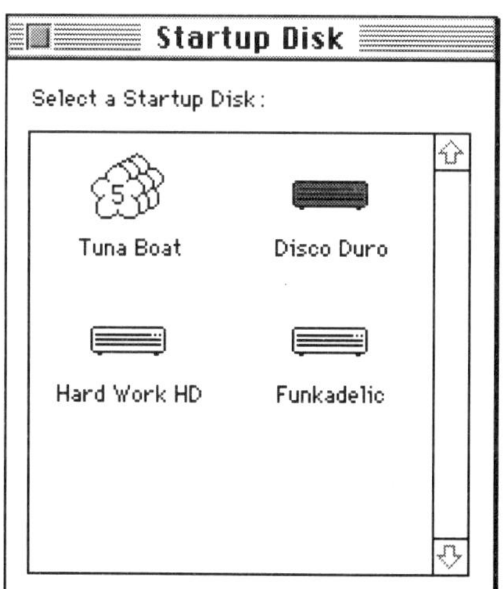

Figure 5-25
The Startup Disk control panel

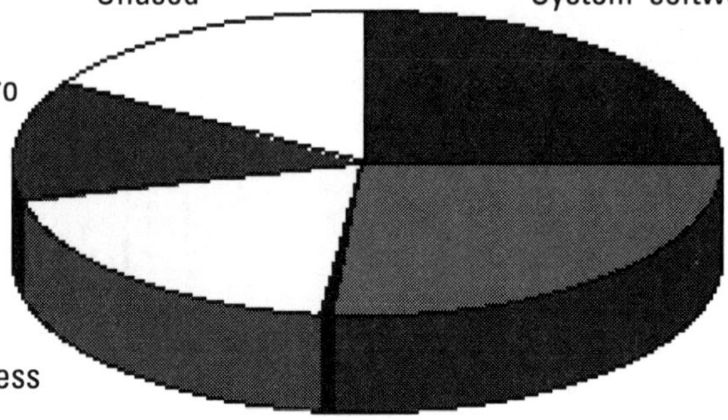

Figure 5-26
Memory pie

Memory management tactics

The Memory control panel, new with System 7, helps you manage your computer's memory. You can ignore that control panel and the burden of memory management in general if you never open more than one program at a time and don't care about your computer's performance or effectiveness (not to mention your own). To get the most from your Macintosh, you must pay attention to how you use its memory.

Think of your computer's memory as a pie (Figure 5-26). You need to know the size of the pie, how much of the pie each open program uses, and how much is unused and available for opening additional programs. You also need to know how big a piece of the memory pie each of those additional programs would need if you opened it.

Analyzing memory use

For information on the condition of your Macintosh memory pie, switch to the Finder and choose About This Macintosh from the Apple menu. The Finder displays a window that reports the total amount of memory installed in your Macintosh and the largest amount available for opening another program. It also graphs the amount allocated to and currently used by the system software and by each open program (Figure 5-27).

Program memory size

When you open a program, the system software gives it a chunk of the memory pie. You can change how much an application program gets by

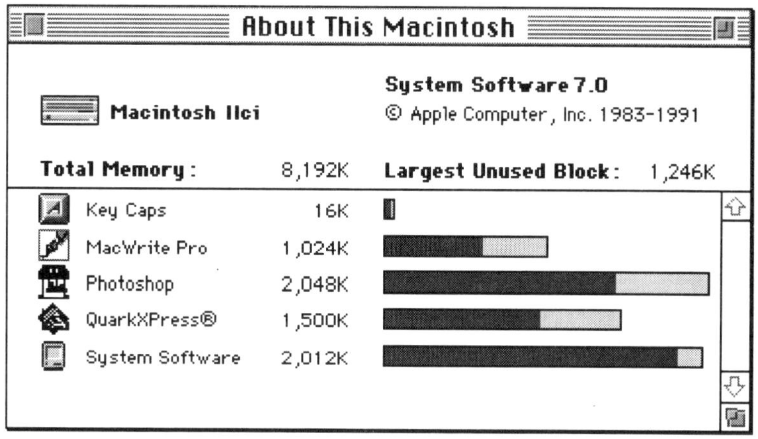

Figure 5-27
An About This Macintosh window

setting its memory size in its info window (Figure 5-28), which the Finder's Get Info command displays. You must quit an open program before changing its memory size.

The info window lists a suggested memory size, which the program's developer has recommended for best performance. Setting the memory size higher than the suggested size may improve performance or allow you to open more documents or larger documents. Setting the memory

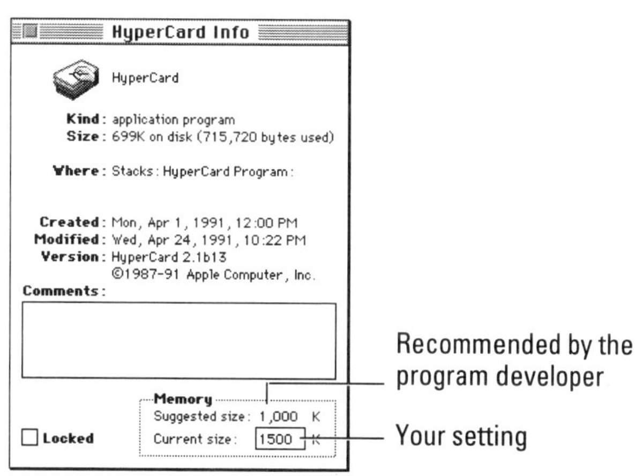

Figure 5-28
A memory size setting

size below the suggested size usually has the opposite effect. For example, setting HyperCard's memory size below the suggested 1000K reduces the number of stacks you can have open simultaneously, limits your access to painting tools and scripting, and prevents opening some stacks altogether.

If your Macintosh has just the minimum 2MB of RAM required to use System 7, you should pare program memory sizes to the bone. For example, giving your favorite word processing program the full amount of memory available after the system software takes its chunk leaves you no room to use the Chooser to select a printer or share someone's files. (Though you can work around the file sharing limitation by making aliases of the items you most often share, as described in Chapter 8.) Also, there wouldn't be any memory left for background printing.

After setting the memory size below the suggested size a message may ask whether you're sure you want to set the memory size "to less than the recommended minimum." This means you have set the memory size so low the developer is not sure the program will work properly. The Finder will duly attempt to open the program in that amount of memory. If it fails, it usually informs you politely that the memory size you set is too small. If the program does open in the small memory size, proceed with caution. The program may quit unexpectedly. Spectacular system crashes are always a possibility.

You can't change the memory size of a desk accessory. Each desk accessory gets 20K and it increases the system software memory size, generally by a good deal more.

Memory fragmentation

As you open and quit a series of programs, the unused portion of the memory pie tends to become fragmented into multiple small chunks (Figure 5-29). You may find yourself unable to open a program because it needs a chunk of memory bigger than the biggest unused chunk (the Largest Unused Block amount in the About This Macintosh window). The total of all unused chunks may be large enough to open the program, but System 7 cannot consolidate fragmented memory nor open a program in multiple chunks of memory.

To check for fragmentation, add up the memory sizes of all the open programs and the system software as listed in the About This Macintosh window. If you have a monitor connected to the built-in video on a Macintosh IIsi or IIci, add another 320K (or less if you have limited the

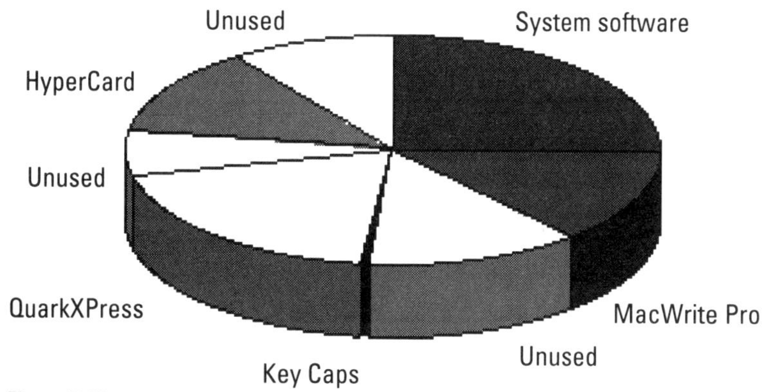

Figure 5-29
Fragmented memory

number of colors to less than 256 as described in "Monitors" earlier in this chapter). If the total exceeds the Largest Unused Block amount by more than 50K or so, then the unused memory is fragmented into two or more chunks.

To consolidate fragmented memory, quit all open programs and then open them again. Restarting your Macintosh also fixes fragmentation and may reduce the amount of memory used by system software as well.

You can avoid memory fragmentation by planning the order in which you open and quit programs. Open the programs you're least likely to quit first, and open the programs you're most likely to quit last. When you need more memory to open another program, quit the most recently opened program. If that doesn't free enough memory, quit the next most recently opened program, and so on. This method frees up a contiguous chunk of memory. Quitting programs helter-skelter leads to memory fragmentation.

Disk Cache

The system software takes up a considerable chunk of your memory pie. A goodly portion of that goes to the Disk Cache, which improves system performance. You can use the Memory control panel to adjust the amount of memory allocated for the Disk Cache (Figure 5-30). You cannot turn off the Disk Cache as you can its equivalent in older system software, the RAM Cache control in the General section of the Control Panel.

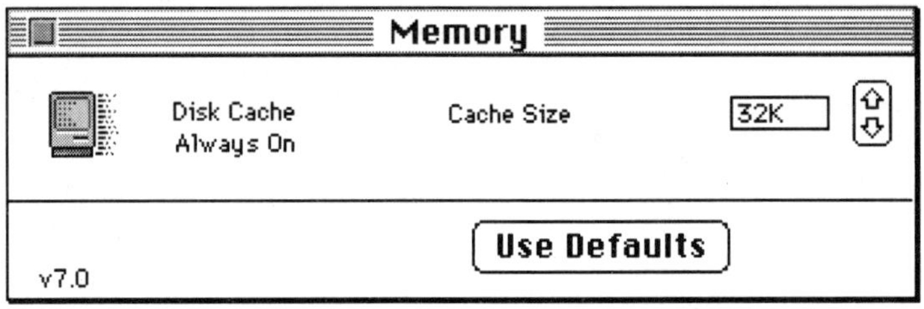

Figure 5-30
The Disk Cache setting

The Disk Cache improves system performance by storing frequently used information from disk in memory. When the information is needed again, it can be copied quickly from memory instead of slowly from disk.

QUICK TIPS

If you have a Mac IIsi and you set the number of colors or grays for its built-in video to 4 or more, you can improve system performance by setting the Disk Cache to 768K. Then the Disk Cache and the built-in video together use up all the memory that's soldered to the main circuit board. This forces the system software and your programs into the part of memory in the four SIMM sockets. Programs may work much slower if they are located in the soldered-on memory along with the built-in video.

The same trick works on a Mac IIci with 5MB, 9MB or 17MB of RAM. To get the performance boost, the 256K SIMMs must be installed in the four sockets nearest the disk drive. Realizing a performance increase on a IIci with other RAM capacities isn't feasible because you would have to set the Disk Cache so high as to waste a large amount of memory.

32-Bit Addressing

Some Macintosh models can access a larger memory pie by using System 7's 32-Bit Addressing capability. To turn it on and off, you use the Memory control panel (Figure 5-31).

With 4MB RAM SIMMs installed, for example, turning on 32-Bit Addressing lets you use 10MB of RAM on an LC, 17MB on a IIsi, and 32MB on a IIci or IIfx. If 32-Bit Addressing is off (as it always is with older system software), you can only use 8MB of RAM regardless of the amount installed.

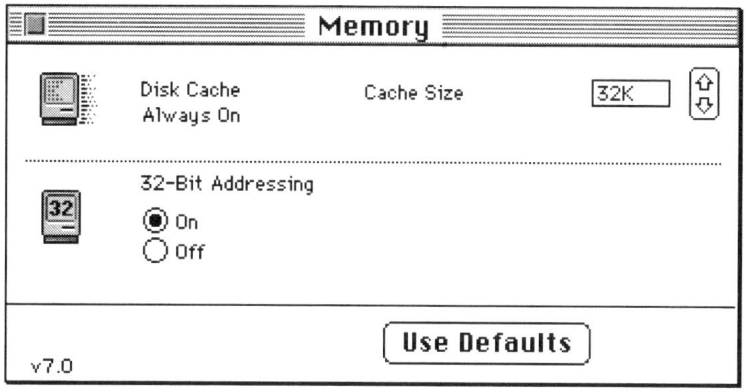

Figure 5-31
The 32-Bit Addressing setting

QUICK TIPS

Your programs may not all be compatible with 32-Bit Addressing. Apple began exhorting developers to make their products "32-Bit Clean" in 1987, but not all have. Mac II, IIx, IIcx, and SE/30 models cannot use 32-Bit Addressing because their ROMs (permanent read-only memory) are incompatible with it. Mac Classic, SE, Plus, and Portable models can't use 32-Bit Addressing because their 68000 central processing units don't support it. Macintosh models that can't use 32-Bit Addressing can access larger amounts of memory by using the MODE 32 utility software from Connectix (415/324-0727).

Virtual memory

You may be able to increase the size of your memory pie without buying and installing more RAM modules. System 7 can transparently use part of a hard disk as additional memory. This extra memory, called virtual memory, lets you get by with less RAM. You buy only as much as you need for average use, not for peak use.

To turn virtual memory on and off, you use the Memory control panel (Figure 5-32). You also set the size of total memory and select a hard disk that has a block of available space as large as the total amount of memory you want available (RAM plus virtual memory). The hard disk space cannot be on a removable hard disk.

Virtual memory controls are only available on a Macintosh equipped with a PMMU (paged memory-management unit). The SE/30, IIcx, IIx,

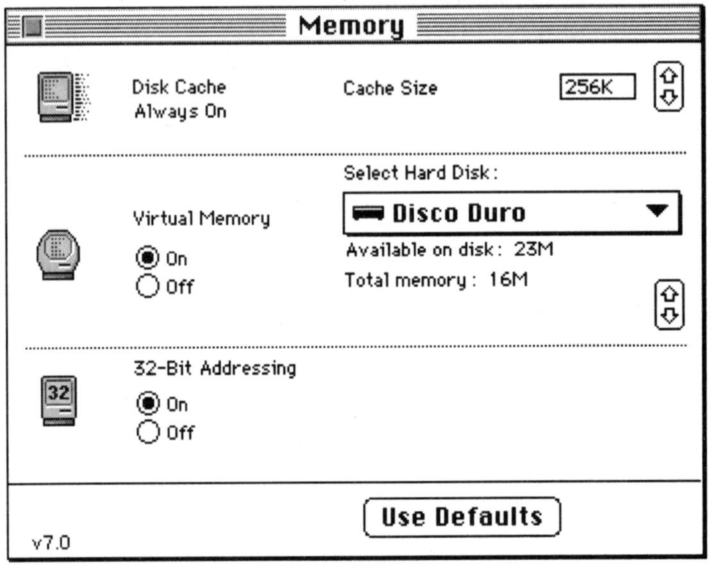

Figure 5-32
Virtual memory settings

IIsi, IIci, and IIfx models all have PMMUs, and a Mac II can be retrofitted with one. An LC can be upgraded with an accelerator card containing a PMMU. However, a Mac Plus, SE, Classic, or Portable with such an accelerator can't use virtual memory because its ROM lacks some necessary information.

With virtual memory on, the About This Macintosh window reports the total amount of memory and the amount of built-in memory (that is, RAM). It also tells you how much disk space is used for virtual memory storage and on which disk the storage file is located (Figure 5-33).

Total memory size (virtual memory plus RAM) cannot exceed 14MB unless you turn on the 32-Bit Addressing option in the Memory control panel. On Macintosh models with NuBus cards installed, that limit is 1MB lower for each installed card. Furthermore, virtual memory will be fragmented unless you install all NuBus cards consecutively starting at one end slot or the other. On a IIcx, fill slots from left to right.

With 32-Bit Addressing on, the limit on total memory is 1 gigabyte (1024MB). NuBus cards are not an issue.

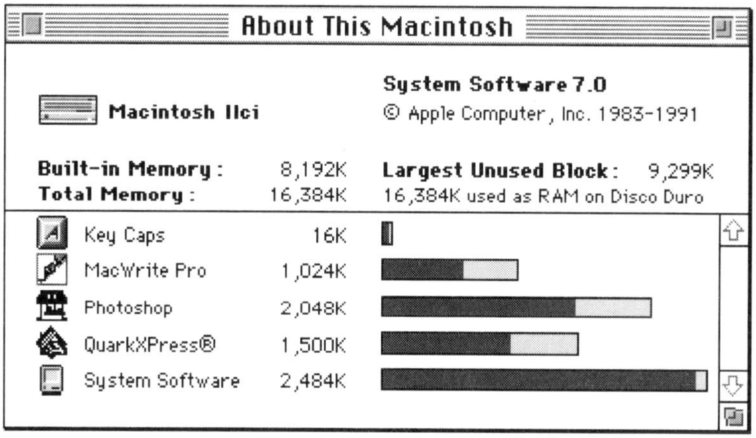

Figure 5-33
Virtual memory statistics

Virtual memory works by keeping the most active program and document segments in RAM. Less-used segments of open programs and documents are kept in an invisible file named VM Storage on the hard disk. When a program needs a segment not currently in physical memory, System 7 automatically swaps the least-used segment in RAM with the needed segment on disk. A swap often occurs when you switch programs, for example.

Because a hard disk is much slower than RAM, using virtual memory can degrade system performance. The performance penalty is barely noticeable if a swap happens when you switch programs. The slowdown may be severe if you use virtual memory to open a program that's bigger than the amount of RAM left after system software gets its share. The disk may thrash for several minutes as it tries to swap segments back and forth. For best results, set virtual memory no higher than double the installed RAM and use it for opening multiple small programs.

QUICK TIPS

You can usually improve system performance by using the Hide Others command in the Application menu. Hidden windows don't require updating, which may require disk access when virtual memory is on.

Summary

- ✔ Desk accessories now work outside the Apple menu, in folders and on the desktop, and can be used like ordinary application programs. The standard Chooser, Key Caps, Puzzle, and Scrapbook desk accessories get minor improvements.
- ✔ The Apple menu lists every item you put in the Apple Menu Items folder. Choosing an item from the Apple menu opens the item.
- ✔ The old Control Panel desk accessory gives way to individual control panels that you open like Finder documents. There are eight new (or revised) control panels: Color, Easy Access, File Sharing Monitor, Memory, Labels, Sharing Setup, Users & Groups, and Views.
- ✔ Virtual memory lets you use disk space as memory, and 32-Bit Addressing increases the amount of memory some Macintosh models can use.
- ✔ Managing memory becomes more important as you use more of it and as you use it for keeping more programs open at the same time.

Chapter 6
Fast Access with Aliases

In This Chapter

- Learning what aliases are, how to make them, and how to use them.
- Opening any item from the desktop without moving it from its folder.
- Cutting laterally across your folder structure in directory dialog boxes.
- Adding items to the Apple menu or the Startup Items folder without moving the items from their folders.
- Organizing documents and folders according to multiple filing schemes without duplicating items.
- Opening items on floppy disks that are not inserted.
- Accessing files, folders, and disks shared from other computers on your network.
- Using a floppy disk on any Macintosh in your network to access your hard disks.

The hierarchical order of the Macintosh universe allows you to organize programs and documents into folders. Nesting folders within folders keeps related items together but can turn your disk into a labyrinth. Finder 7's Find command helps you locate items without digging through folders but it's no substitute for well-organized disks.

Finder aliases cut through the organizational maze. Aliases act like real items when you open them or drag items to them. Think of an alias as a stand-in or an agent for a real program, document, folder or disk. You can place these agents at your beck and call in any handy location such as the desktop or the Apple menu. When you open aliases or drag items to them, they act like the real items they represent. Aliases even look like the items they represent, except their names are italicized.

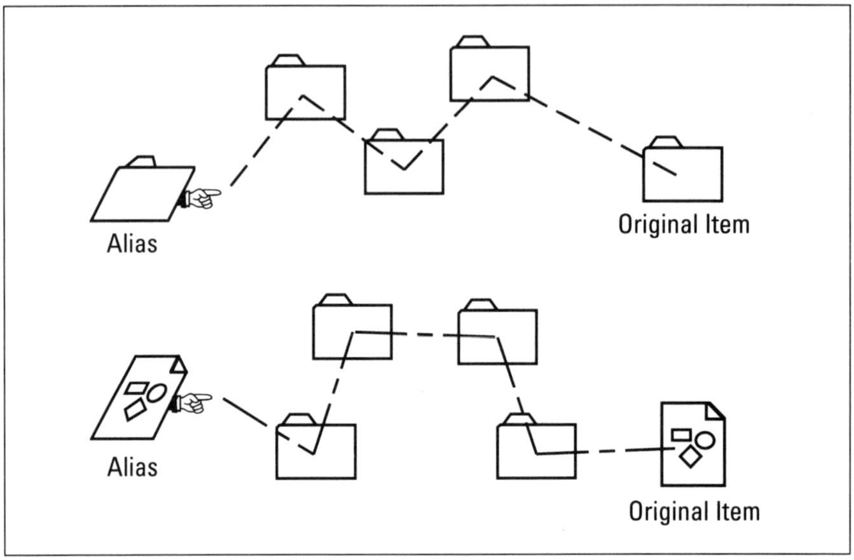

Figure 6-1
An alias points to another item

Understanding aliases

Like the documents, programs, and other items on your disks, aliases are files. Each alias contains a pointer to the original item it represents (Figure 6-1). An alias always remembers where its original item is located, even when you move or rename the original item. The only way you can break the connection between an alias and its original item is to drag the original item to the Trash and empty the Trash.

When you open an alias, the Finder follows the pointer to the original item and actually opens the original. Dragging an item to the alias of a folder or disk has the same affect as dragging it to the original folder or disk: the Finder follows the pointer to the original folder or disk and that's where it places the item you dragged. Likewise, a document you drag to an alias of a compatible program follows the pointer to the program itself, which opens the document. You can even drag an alias to an alias; the Finder follows both pointers and deals with the original items.

Aliases vary in size from 1K to 3K, depending on the capacity of the disk they're on. For example, an alias takes up 1K of a floppy disk, a

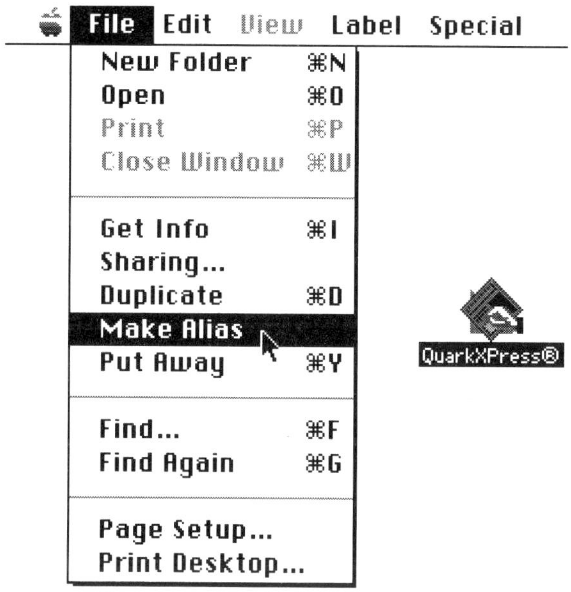

Figure 6-2
Using the Make Alias command

20MB hard disk, or a 40MB hard disk. On an 80MB hard disk, an alias takes up 2K. If a hard disk is partitioned into multiple volumes (each having its own icon on the desktop), the volume capacity determines the size of aliases on it.

Making an alias

You can make an alias for any item you can open from the Finder. That includes documents, application programs, desk accessories, folders, disks, control panels, and even fonts and sounds. Making an alias is a simple procedure. Select the item you want to create an alias for and choose Make Alias from the File menu. A new item appears with the same icon as the original item and an italicized name the same as the original item's name plus the suffix "alias" (Figure 6-2).

QUICK TIPS

Immediately after creating an alias, its name is selected for editing. You can change the name by typing a replacement or by using other standard text-editing techniques (see "Renaming items" in Chapter 3). To keep the name as is, click anywhere outside the name or press the Return or Enter key.

You can create multiple aliases for the same original item to access the original item from different locations. The number of aliases you can create is limited only by disk space.

To make aliases for several items in the same window at once, select them all and use the Make Alias command. An alias appears for every item you selected. All the new aliases are automatically selected so you can immediately drag them to another place without having to manually select them as a group.

Changing an alias

Once you make an alias, you can manipulate it as you would any item. Move it to another folder on the same disk or to the desktop. The alias still knows where to find its original item.

Copy an alias by using the Finder's Duplicate command or by dragging the alias to another disk or to a folder on another disk. To copy an alias or other item to another folder on the same disk, press Option while dragging. All copies of the alias point to the same original item.

You rename an alias as you would any other item on the desktop or in a Finder window (see "Renaming items" in Chapter 3). If you want an alias to have the same name as its original item, they can't be in the same folder. You must move one out.

To quickly remove the word "alias" from the end of the name, click the name once to select it for editing, pause briefly, double-click the last word of the name, and press the Delete key twice. If you double-click too quickly after selecting the name, the Finder opens the alias instead of selecting the last word of the name. Alternatively, you can select the name for editing, press the Down Arrow key or Right Arrow key to move the insertion point to the end of the name, and press the Delete key six times to erase the last word. To conclude your name editing, click anywhere outside the name or press the Return or Enter key.

Like any item, you remove an alias by dragging it to the Trash. Remember, throwing away an alias doesn't affect the original item. You're throwing away just the alias, not the item it points to.

An alias inherits its icon from the original item. If you subsequently change the original item's icon, the alias icon is updated automatically the next time you open (but not drag something to) the alias. Like most other

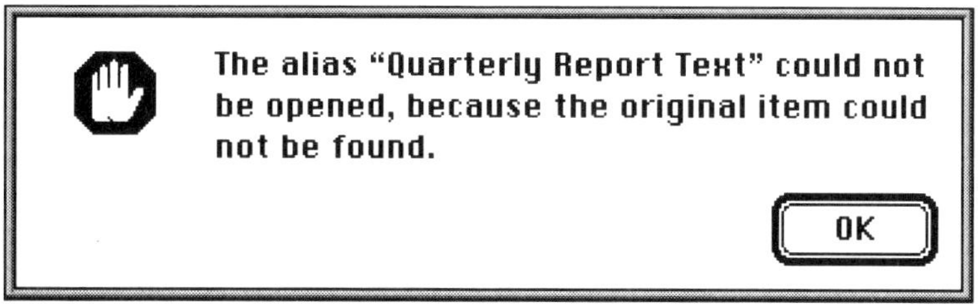

Figure 6-3
After deleting an original item

icons, you can customize an alias's icon in its info window. You see the info window by using the Finder's Get Info command (see "Custom icons" in Chapter 3). The alias's custom icon won't be affected by changes to the icon of the original item. You can also type comments about the alias and lock it in its info window.

Changing an original item

Aliases are truly amazing at finding items. Not only can you rename and move an alias's original item, you can replace it with another file having the same name, all without breaking the alias. You might wonder how an alias can find the original item after you rename or move the original item. If the alias can't find an item having the same name and folder location as the original, it searches for the original item's unique file ID number, which the system software internally assigns to each file. Once the alias finds the original item using this ID number, it remembers the original item's current name and folder location.

If you copy the original item referenced by an alias, the alias still points to the original item, not the copy. Sounds reasonable unless you forget the difference between copying an item and moving it. In many cases, copying and moving an item feels and looks the same. Both copying and moving involve the same action — dragging an item to another place. If that other place is a folder in the same disk as the item you're dragging, the item is moved and the item's alias knows where to find the moved item. If the other place is a folder in another disk, the item is copied. The alias knows where the original item is, but not the copy. Deleting the original item breaks the alias's link to the item, even though a copy of the item exists on another disk. If you use an alias for which the original item has been deleted, the Finder tells you it couldn't find the original item (Figure 6-3).

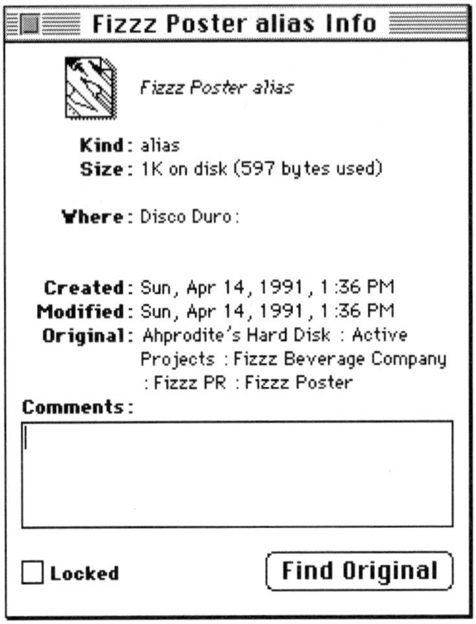

Figure 6-4
An alias's info window

Finding an original item

You can find an alias's original item by using the Get Info command to display the alias's info window (Figure 6-4). The disk and folder path to the original item appears above the Comments box next to the heading Original. Clicking the Original button in the info window opens the folder that contains the original item and selects the original item.

Using aliases

There are many useful applications for aliases. The most common is quick access to programs and documents you frequently work with. For example, you can make an alias of a spreadsheet you regularly use for updating sales figures and place the alias in a convenient location, such as the desktop. Some of the most important uses of aliases include adding items to the Apple menu or to the list of items opened at startup time, adding desktop convenience for accessing items, accessing archived information from floppy disks, streamlining access to shared items, and more. The following sections provide a collection of scenarios to leverage the power of aliases, providing express service to a wide range of items.

Aliases in the Apple menu

With System 7, the most convenient place from which to open application programs, desk accessories, control panels, documents, folders, and other items is the Apple menu. Because the Apple menu is always on the menu bar, items in the Apple menu are never more then a mouse click away. You can add any item to the Apple menu that you can open using the Finder, including aliases.

Placing an alias in the Apple menu is as easy as dragging the alias icon to the Apple Menu Items folder, which is in the System Folder. The alias and the original item it points to become instantly available without having to restart your Macintosh. Items in the Apple Menu are displayed alphabetically in plain (not italic) text. You may want to change the name of your alias to adjust its position in the Apple menu.

You can add as many aliases as you want to the Apple Menu Items folder. However, it's a good idea to keep the number within a reasonable range to prevent constant scrolling through a large number of options. To remove an alias from the Apple menu, drag its icon out of the Apple Menu Items folder.

QUICK TIPS

One of the most useful aliases you can add to the Apple menu is an alias of the Apple Menu Items folder. Adding this alias allows you to quickly open the Apple Menu Items folder and easily customize the Apple menu anywhere, anytime.

Aliases as startup items

Every time you start up (or restart) your Macintosh, Finder 7 automatically opens everything in the Startup Items folder. For example, if you regularly use a program, such as PageMaker, you may want it ready to go immediately after starting up your Macintosh. But some programs don't work correctly from the Startup Items folder. Furthermore, returning items to their previous locations when you no longer want them opened at startup time can be a drag. Moving an alias of a program, document, or other item to the Startup Items folder has the same effect as moving the original item there. To remove an alias from the startup sequence, drag the alias out of the folder.

Application programs in the Startup Items folder open in alphabetical order, so you can rename the alias of an application program to determine when it starts relative to other application programs in the folder. Aliases of other types of desk accessories, control panels, and folders open alphabetically after all application programs have opened. For more information on the Startup Items folder, see "Startup Items folder" in Chapter 4.

Aliases on the desktop

QUICK TIPS

Next to the Apple menu, the desktop is the most accessible place for opening items, and it's the most accessible place for folders to which you want to drag items. Rather than drag frequently used programs, control panels, documents, and folders themselves into the desktop, make aliases of them and put the aliases on the desktop. Putting aliases of nested items on the desktop gives you quick access to the folders without digging through folders to find them.

Putting aliases of programs on the desktop avoids problems that can occur if you move the programs themselves onto the desktop. Such programs depend on support files being in the same folder (or on the desktop) with them. For example, a word processor on the desktop may also need a dictionary file on the desktop in order to check spelling. Aliases save you the hassle of guessing which support files a program needs in order to run correctly and avoid the mess that results if you place those support files on the desktop. By creating an alias for an application, the alias accesses the original application in its folder, saving you from moving the application and supporting files to get full access to the application.

By making aliases of documents and programs you use frequently and putting the aliases on the desktop, you never have to remember where you have put the original items. Also, you can open several related items at the same time, even if the original items happen to be in different folders or on different disks, by opening aliases on the desktop.

QUICK TIPS

If the windows of open programs obscure desktop aliases, you can hide those windows by choosing Hide Others from the Application menu while the Finder is active. If Finder windows cover desktop aliases, you can close all those windows at once by pressing Option while clicking the close box of any Finder window.

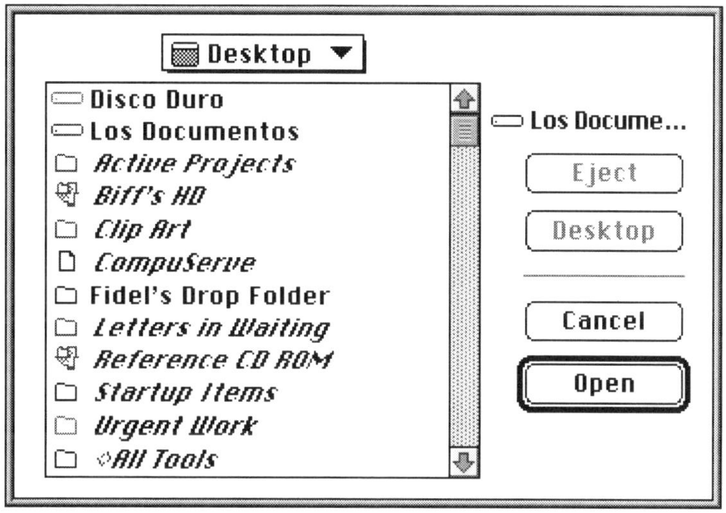

Figure 6-5
Aliases in a directory dialog box

If your desktop becomes too cluttered with aliases, you can put related aliases together in a desktop folder.

Aliases in directory dialogs

Aliases on the desktop appear at the desktop level in the directory dialog boxes you get when you use Open, Save, and other disk-related commands. Alias names appear in italics in directory dialog boxes (Figure 6-5), and opening an alias there opens its original item. You can also quickly go to an alias's original item in a directory dialog box by pressing the Option key while opening the alias (by double-clicking it, for example). In this case, System 7 opens the folder containing the original item and selects the original item.

Aliases for favorite folders

Putting aliases of your favorite folders on the desktop or inside disk windows allows you to quickly open a favorite folder from a directory dialog box. Instead of working your way down through one branch of your folder structure and then working your way up another branch to the folder you want, you zip to the desktop level or the disk level and there open the alias of the folder you want. It's as if you could jump from one branch of a tree to the root level and then jump to a spot on another branch without crawling up the trunk and along the other branch.

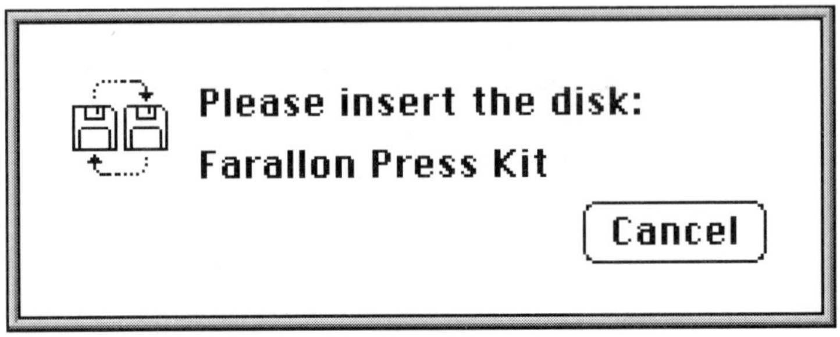

Figure 6-6
Opening an item archived to a floppy disk

You can quickly get to aliases of favorite folders on the desktop by clicking the Desktop button. Get to aliases at the disk window level by choosing the disk from the directory dialog's pop-up menu.

Aliases of items on floppy disks

You can use aliases to keep track of and quickly open items on floppy disks — even floppies that aren't inserted in your Macintosh. For example, suppose you're keeping track of your company's bills, and one month, March, doesn't balance. You want to close out the quarter, and archive the monthly detail files to floppy disk but you know that you may need to access the file for March later. Instead of keeping the monthly detail files on your hard disk, go ahead and copy them all to a floppy with a unique name, such as First Qtr. Select the March file on the floppy and choose Make Alias from the File menu. Copy the alias to your hard disk. When you need the March file again, open its alias on the hard disk. The system tells you the name of the disk to insert so it can open the alias's original item (Figure 6-6). If you change your mind or can't find the needed disk, click the Cancel button.

Keeping aliases on your hard disk and the original items on floppies saves valuable hard disk space because aliases almost always take up less space than the original items they represent. Just be sure you make aliases of the archived items after copying them to floppies, not before. If you make aliases of the items while they are still on the hard disk, the aliases stop working when you delete the original items from the hard disk after copying them to floppies. (Remember, aliases point to the original items, not to copies of the originals on other disks.)

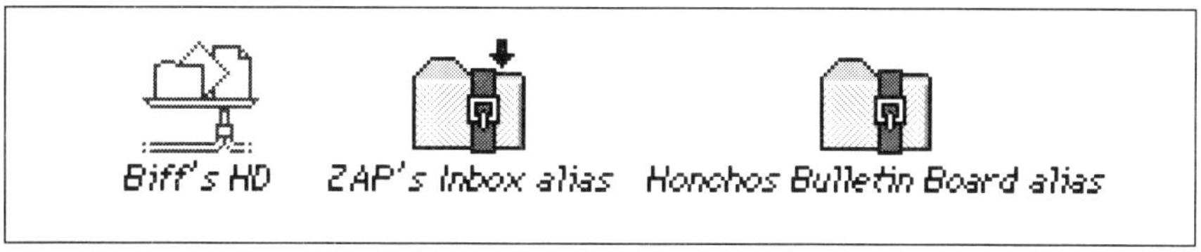

Figure 6-7
Aliases of shared items

Aliases and CD ROM

Slowly wading through folders on a CD ROM can be a royal pain (unless you can somehow see the experience as stately pomp and circumstance). Cut through the drudgery by making aliases of items inside the CD ROM folders. Because CD ROMs are permanently locked, you must put the aliases on your hard disk (or a floppy disk). Opening an alias makes a beeline to the original item on the CD ROM.

Aliases of shared items

System 7's file sharing capabilities allow you to share items from someone else's Macintosh connected to the same network as yours, but getting access to shared items involves wading through a fair amount of bureaucracy. Aliases cut through the red tape. Here's how: You access a shared disk or folder once using the Chooser desk accessory described in Chapter 8. Next you select the shared item or any folder or file in it and choose Make Alias from the File menu. Finally, you copy the alias to your desktop or hard disk (Figure 6-7). An alias keeps track of its original item even if the original item is on another networked Macintosh.

Once you have made an alias of a shared item, you can access the shared item by opening the alias either from the Finder or from an Open command's directory dialog box. Dragging something to the alias of a shared disk or folder also automatically accesses that shared item. You still must enter a password unless you initially accessed the original item as a guest. If the shared item is not available — for example because the Macintosh where it resides is turned off — a message tells you that.

Aliases keep shared documents current

Besides providing easy access to shared items from other computers, aliases can help you make sure others who share your documents have the latest version. Suppose, for example, you create a letter template that you want the rest of your group to share. By making an alias of the

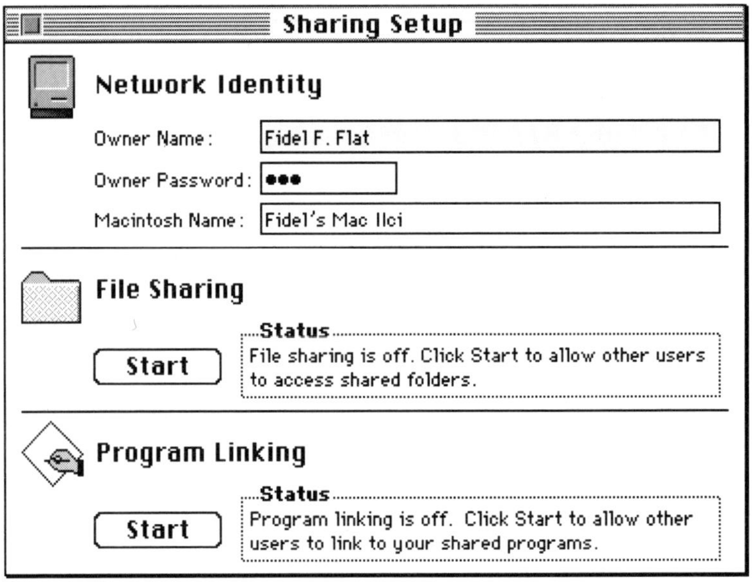

Figure 6-8
The Sharing Setup control panel

template and copying it to a shared folder, other users can copy the alias to their disks and use the alias to open the original template. If you later replace the original template with a version having the same name, the aliases people already copied will open the new version. People who share the alias always get the newest version of the original item it represents, even if the original frequently changes.

The only drawback to using an alias to share a template is that unless you're using a program that allows more than one person to open the same document, only one person can have access to the template document at a time. However, anyone who opens the template can quickly and easily save it with a different name and then close it to free it for someone else to open.

Your office on a disk

QUICK TIPS

Aliases can give you nearly automatic access to your Macintosh's hard disks using a floppy disk in any other Macintosh on the same network. To easily access your disks from another Macintosh open the Sharing Setup

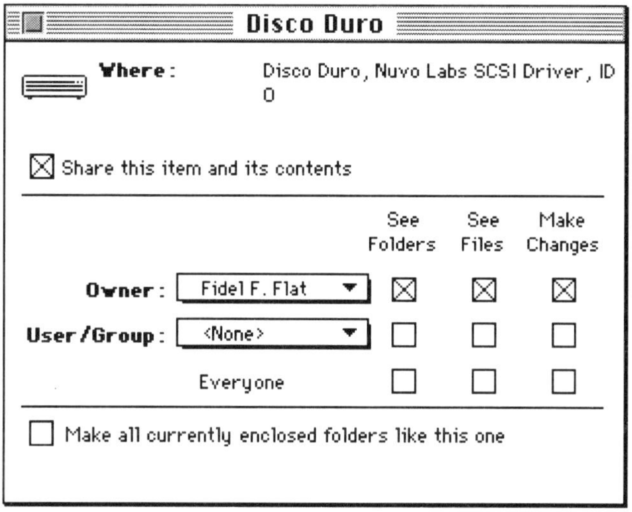

Figure 6-9
Access privileges for your office on a disk

control panel (Figure 6-8) and check the File Sharing status. If it is off, click the start button and wait until it is on (the Start button becomes a Stop button).

Next select all your hard disk icons and choose Sharing from the File menu to open a Sharing info window for each disk. In each window turn on the "Share this item and its contents" option and turn off the See Folders, See Files, and Make Changes options for the User/Group and Everyone categories (Figure 6-9). These settings restrict access to your disks so that only you can make changes or see files or folders. Make an alias of each hard disk and copy the aliases to a floppy disk. As long as file sharing is active on your Macintosh, you can use that floppy disk to access your hard disk from any Macintosh on your network. You simply insert the disk, open the alias for the disk you want to use, and enter your password when asked. Correctly entering your password allows you access to all applications, folders, and documents on your disk from any remote Macintosh. You don't have to bother with opening the Chooser, selecting Apple Share, selecting your computer, and typing your name as the registered user.

Summary

- Aliases look and act like the real programs, documents, folders, disks, or other items they represent. But aliases are actually small pointer files.
- Use aliases to add items to the Apple menu without moving those items from the folders they are in.
- Use aliases to increase the flexibility of the Startup Items folder.
- Use aliases to open frequently used programs, documents, folders, and control panels from the desktop while the real items remain buried in nested folders.
- Use aliases to speed access from directory dialog boxes to items buried in nested folders.
- Use aliases to speed access to archived items stored on disks that are not inserted and to items buried on CD ROMs.
- Use aliases to streamline access to shared items from another Macintosh on your network and to keep items you share with other network users current.
- Use aliases to get nearly automatic access to your Macintosh's hard disks using a floppy disk in any other Macintosh on the same network.

Chapter 7
Smooth Text Everywhere

In This Chapter

- Comparing TrueType, fixed-size, and PostScript font technologies.
- Displaying samples of TrueType and fixed-size fonts.
- Installing and removing fonts.
- When to mix and not to mix TrueType with fixed-size fonts.
- Printing with TrueType, PostScript, and fixed-size fonts.
- How TrueType fonts work.
- Samples of standard TrueType fonts.

Text looks great when displayed or printed with old Macintosh font technology if you stick to a half-dozen font sizes, usually 9, 10, 12, 14, 18, and 24 points. Apple's TrueType font technology, a standard part of System 7, makes odd sizes and big sizes like 11, 13, 36, 100, and 197 look just as good.

TrueType fonts work with the programs you already have. You can mix them with the fixed-size fonts and PostScript fonts you already have. They work with all Macintosh models and all types of printers, including PostScript printers.

Three font technologies

Your Macintosh can display and print text using three types of fonts: fixed-size, TrueType, and PostScript. Which looks best depends on the font size and the output device (display screen or type of printer).

About fixed-size fonts

Before the advent of TrueType fonts, the Macintosh system software used fixed-size fonts for displaying text on screen and for printing on many types of printers. A fixed-size font contains exact pictures of every letter, digit, and symbol for one size of a font (Figure 7-1). Fixed-size fonts are often called bitmap fonts because each picture precisely maps the dots, or bits, to be displayed or printed for one character.

Each fixed-size font looks great in one size only, so fixed-size fonts are usually installed in sets. A typical set includes 9-, 10-, 12-, 14-, 18-, and 24-point sizes. If you need text in a size for which no fixed-size font is installed, the system must scale a fixed-size font's character bitmaps up or down to the size you want. The results are lumpy, misshapen, or blocky (Figure 7-2).

Figure 7-1
Times capital A and G bitmaps in sizes 12, 14, and 18 (enlarged to show detail)

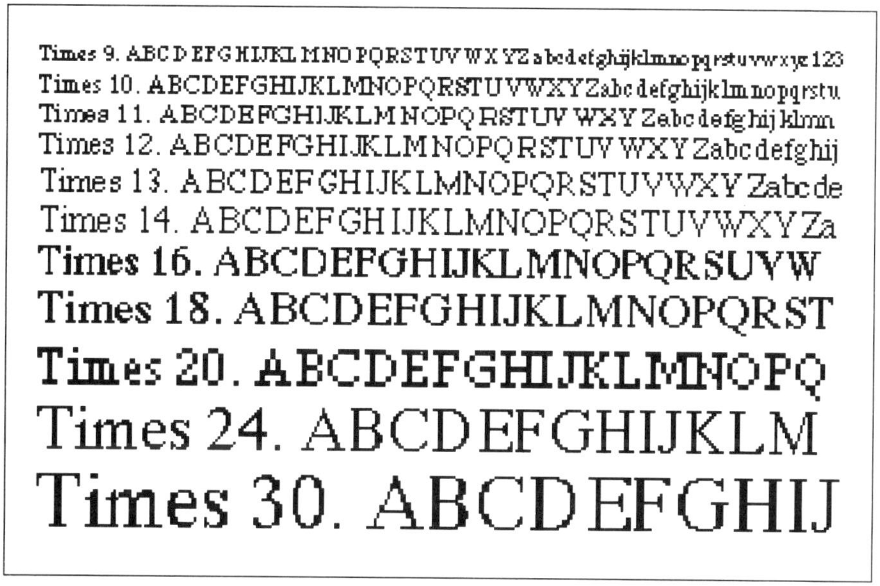

Figure 7-2
Fixed-size Times (9, 10, 12, 14, 18, and 24 installed)

About TrueType fonts

TrueType fonts don't use fixed bitmaps to define characters. Instead they use curves and straight lines to outline each character's shape. Because of this methodology, they are sometimes called outline fonts (Figure 7-3).

Figure 7-3
Outline for TrueType Times capital G

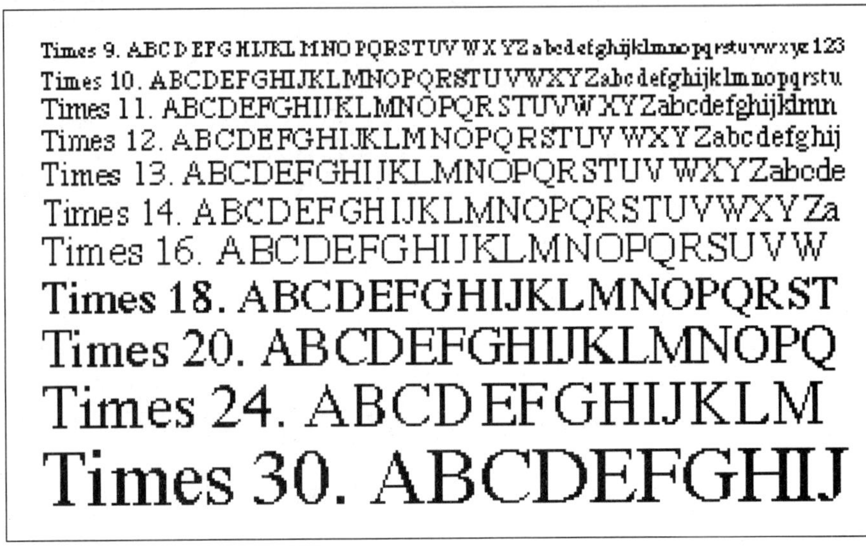

Figure 7-4
TrueType Times

TrueType fonts are variable-size fonts. The Macintosh system software can smoothly scale a single TrueType font's character outlines to any size, large or small, with good results (Figure 7-4).

About PostScript fonts

Like TrueType fonts, PostScript fonts use outlines to define character shapes and consequently they look good any size. PostScript fonts were originally designed for printing on LaserWriters and other PostScript output devices. A set of matching fixed-size fonts were used for screen display.

UNDOCUMENTED

Today the more common PostScript fonts have TrueType equivalents for screen display and for printing on devices that don't use the PostScript page description language. Alternatively, your Macintosh can now display PostScript fonts on screen after you install the Adobe Type Manager (ATM) software and the PostScript fonts in your System Folder.

Recognizing best font sizes

You can usually tell which font sizes will look good on screen by inspecting the Font menu of a program you're using. The program

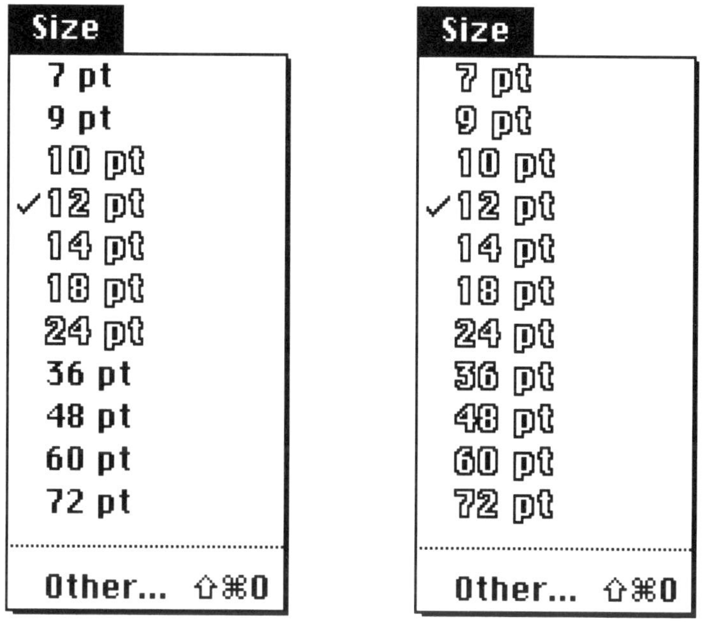

A fixed-size font   A TrueType font

Figure 7-5
Smooth sizes are outlined

highlights the best-looking sizes with outline-style numbers. All sizes of a TrueType font are so highlighted. Only the installed sizes of fixed-size fonts are highlighted (Figure 7-5).

UNDOCUMENTED

About font styles

Text varies by style as well as size. The Macintosh system software can display and print four basic styles — plain, bold, italic, bold italic — and many others (as listed in your friendly Style menu). The system can derive various styles by modifying the plain style, but you get better-looking results by installing separate styled versions of fonts (Figure 7-6).

Many fixed-size, TrueType, and PostScript fonts come in the four basic styles. Some PostScript font families include 20 or more styled versions. Collectively, all the styled versions together with the plain version of a font are known as a font family.

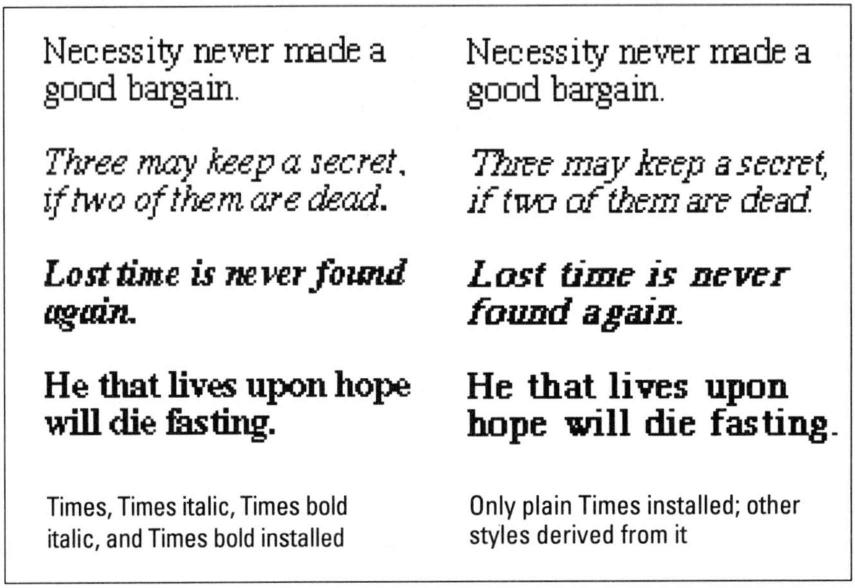

Figure 7-6
Installed styles versus derived styles

Seeing font samples

In System 7 all fonts are individual items, each with its own icon (Figure 7-7). Icons of fixed-size fonts have a single capital A on them. Icons of TrueType fonts have three capital A's, each a different size to suggest the variable sizing of the font. Icons of PostScript fonts may look like a generic laser printer or they may have custom graphics designed by the companies that make the fonts.

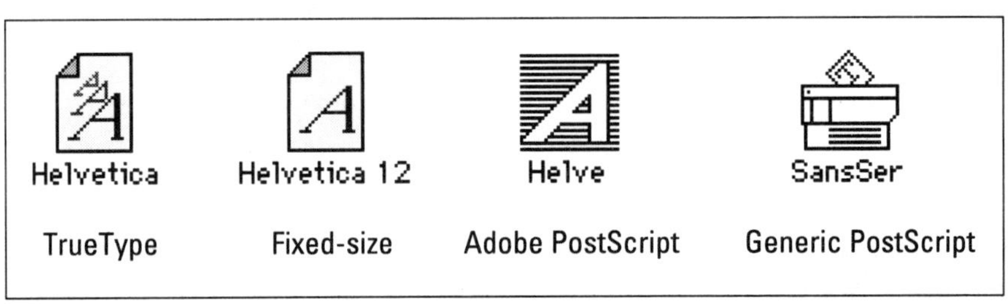

Figure 7-7
Font icons

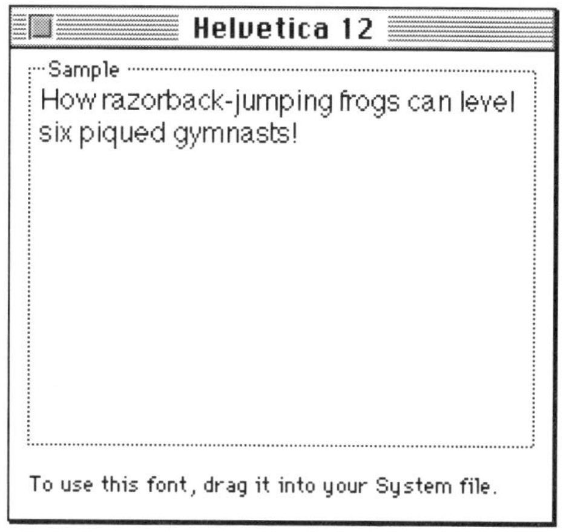

Figure 7-8
TrueType and fixed-size font samples

You can see a sample of any TrueType or fixed-size font by opening the font from the Finder (Figure 7-8).

The fonts you're not using can be kept in any folder or on the desktop. You can also store spare TrueType and fixed-size fonts in font suitcases. They are created with the Font/DA Mover program for storing and distributing fonts in older system software. You do not need the Font/DA Mover program with System 7 because it lets you manipulate fonts directly. You can create a new font suitcase file with System 7 by duplicating an existing font suitcase file, opening the duplicate, and dragging its contents to the Trash. You can also use version 4.1 of the Font/DA Mover with System 7 to create font suitcases.

The System file is the place you install the TrueType and fixed-size fonts you want to show up in your Font menus. The PostScript fonts you want to use go in the Extensions folder, which is inside the System Folder (or in the System Folder itself, as with older system software). You should put PostScript fonts in the System Folder itself (not the Extensions Folder) if text prints incorrectly on a PostScript printer. For example, Aldus PageMaker versions 4.01 and earlier and Adobe Type Manager (ATM) versions 2.0 and earlier can't find PostScript fonts in the Extensions folder.

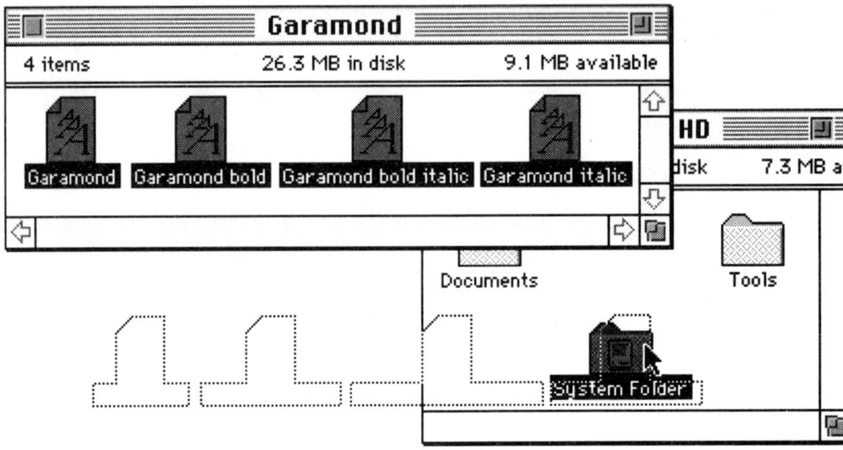

Figure 7-9
Installing TrueType or fixed-size fonts

Adding and removing fonts

Apple's Installer program puts a basic set of TrueType fonts in the System file for you, along with some basic fixed-size fonts, when you install System 7. You can add or remove both types of fonts at any time with Finder 7.

To add TrueType or fixed-size fonts, you must first quit all programs that are open except the Finder. Then you drag the additional fonts to the System Folder icon (Figure 7-9). You can drag font suitcases, folders containing fonts, or loose fonts to the System Folder icon. You do not use the Font/DA Mover program as in older system software.

When you drag fonts to the System Folder icon, Finder 7 knows to put them in the System file where they belong (Figure 7-10). It automatically extracts fonts from folders and font suitcases that you drag to the System Folder icon. If a folder contains items other than fonts, Finder 7 puts the other items in the places where they belong (see "Adding to the System Folder" in Chapter 4). The Finder does not distribute items for you if you drag them to the System Folder window instead of the System Folder icon.

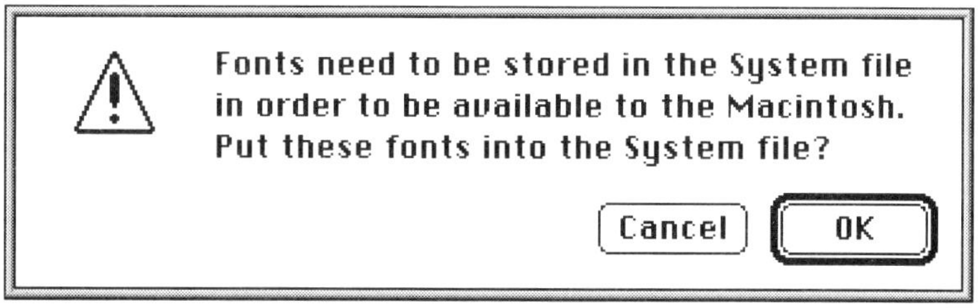

Figure 7-10
The Finder knows where fonts go

If you prefer, you can drag TrueType fonts directly to the System file icon (Figure 7-11). You can also open the System file and drag TrueType fonts to its window.

To remove TrueType fonts from your system, open the System file as if it were a folder and drag the fonts from the System window to a folder, the desktop, or the Trash (Figure 7-12). You must quit all open programs before removing fonts from the System file.

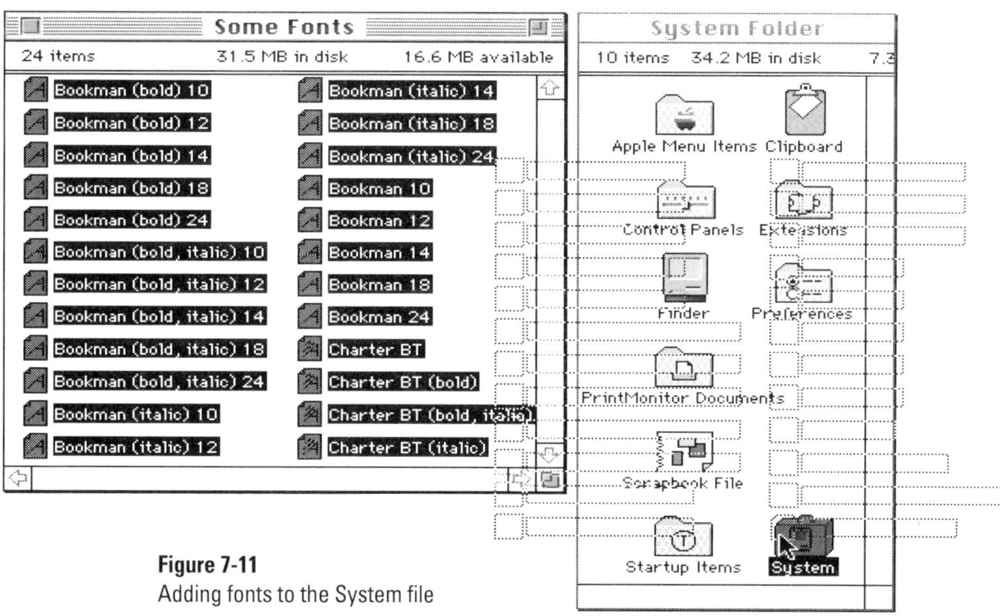

Figure 7-11
Adding fonts to the System file

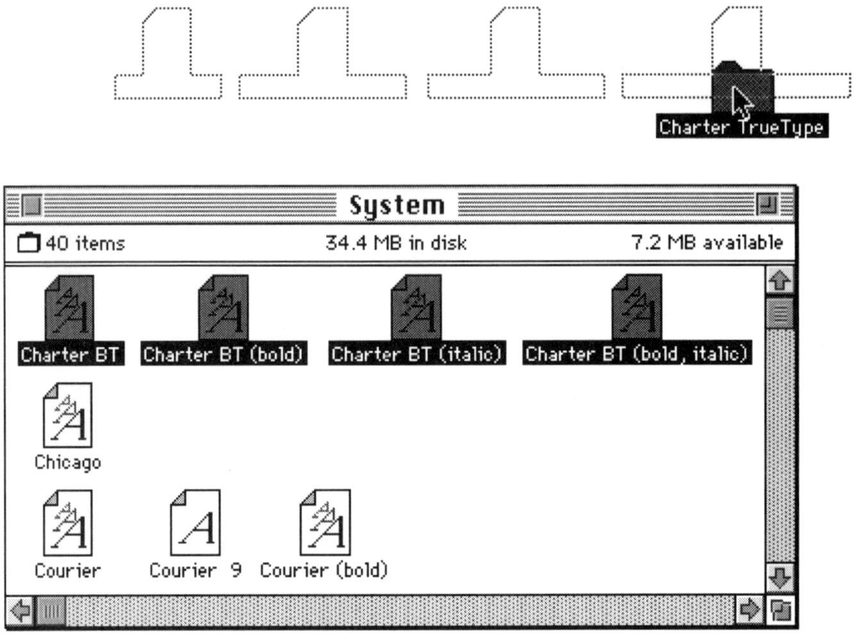

Figure 7-12
Removing fonts from the System file

You can add fonts to the System file or remove them from it at any time when the Finder is the only open program. (Inspect the Application menu to see what's open.) The changes take effect immediately, without restarting your Macintosh.

Combining fixed-size and TrueType fonts

Look closely at some text in a TrueType font and the same text in an equivalent fixed-size font. You'll see differences in letter shape, width, and height that may affect text spacing (Figure 7-13). The TrueType fonts match the PostScript fonts used on printers better than fixed-size fonts.. Fixed-size fonts display faster and many of them look better on screen in sizes below 18 points, however.

You can install TrueType and fixed-size versions of the same font together in the System file. For each font and size, the system software's first choice is a fixed-size font with its hand-tuned bitmaps. If the system can't find the right fixed-size font, it scales a TrueType font to the needed

TrueType Times
12-point plain

Fixed-size Times
12-point plain

Fixed-size Times
12-point bold italic

TrueType Times
12-point bold italic

Figure 7-13
Comparison of letter shape, width, and height

size. Note that when you install both fixed-size and TrueType versions of the same font, the system software always derives styled fonts from the fixed-size version, even if a styled TrueType version is installed. For example, if you have a fixed-size 12-point Times and a TrueType Times italic installed (but no fixed-size 12-point Times italic), the system software derives a 12-point Times italic by slanting the fixed-size 12-point Times.

UNDOCUMENTED

Individual programs can tell the system to ignore fixed-size fonts if a TrueType equivalent is available. You may be able to turn this behavior on and off in some of your programs. Check each program's preference settings for one that tells the program you prefer outline fonts. A decision to ignore fixed-size fonts in one program does not affect other programs. The general system preference for fixed-size fonts dominates in a program unless specifically overridden for that program.

Printing with TrueType

As much as TrueType fonts improve text displayed on screen, they improve printed text more. They work directly with printers that don't use PostScript. TrueType fonts also work in conjunction with PostScript fonts on printers that use them.

TrueType alone

With TrueType fonts in your System file, you're no longer limited to a few font sizes when printing on an ImageWriter or other non-PostScript output device. You can print any font size that fits on the page at the best resolution the printer can manage (Figure 7-14).

Without TrueType fonts, printers that don't use PostScript require extra-large fixed-size fonts to achieve their highest resolution. When you select Best quality for an ImageWriter II, for example, the system prints double-size fonts at a 50 percent reduction to get 144 dpi resolution, twice the screen's 72 dpi. The scarcity of extra-large fixed-size fonts limits the number of font sizes you can print. Moreover, the extra-large fixed-size fonts take up 25K to 50K apiece on your startup disk. After installing System 7, you no longer need these extra-large fixed-size fonts. Remove them to free up disk space.

TrueType and fixed-size

If you have both fixed-size and TrueType fonts installed, text may not look quite the same on screen as it does on paper. Character shapes may be different. More importantly, spacing of words on the line may not match. When this happens, the system software has used a fixed-size font for display (at 72 dots per inch) and a TrueType font for printing (at a higher resolution). You can fix the problem by removing the fixed-size font from your System file. Some programs may also allow you to set an option that causes fixed-size fonts to be ignored.

TrueType and PostScript

Where System 7 displays TrueType fonts on screen, LaserWriters and other PostScript devices print PostScript fonts if the system software can find ones that match the screen fonts. The printer contains a basic set of

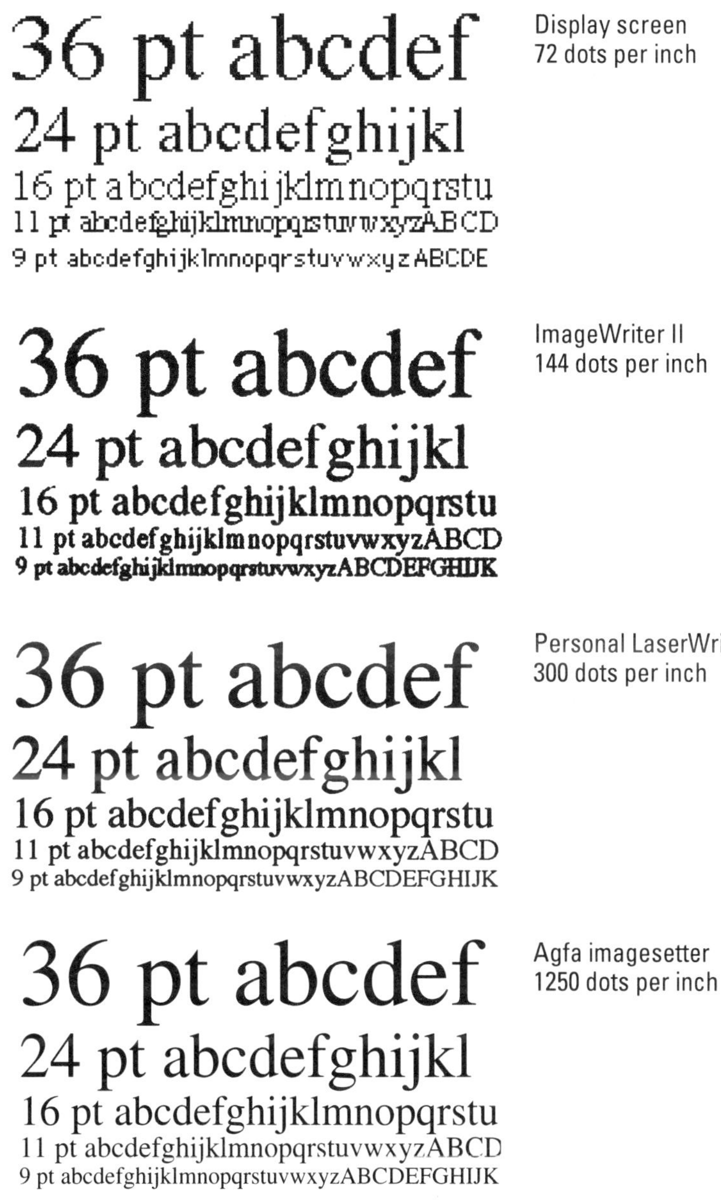

Figure 7-14
TrueType on various output devices

PostScript fonts and you can put others in your System Folder. When used in conjunction with PostScript fonts, smoothly scaled TrueType fonts provide a much better match than fixed-size fonts between the screen and the printed page.

If the system can find no PostScript equivalent for a TrueType font, it smoothly scales the TrueType font to the resolution of the printer. The PostScript printer prints the scaled TrueType font with quality equal to a PostScript font.

TrueType fonts do not signal an end to PostScript output devices for a number of reasons. For one, there are far more PostScript fonts available than TrueType fonts. In addition, PostScript can set text at any angle or along a curve or other nonlinear path. Also, PostScript offers more than outline fonts; it is a complete page description language.

Understanding TrueType fonts

To understand why TrueType fonts look different from equivalent fixed-size fonts, you need to know how outline font technology works. Like any outline font, a TrueType font defines each character mathematically as a set of points that, when connected, outline the character's shape. The Macintosh system software can vary the font size by moving the points closer together or farther apart and drawing the character again.

After scaling the outline to the size you want, the system fills the outline with the dots that make up the text you see on screen and on paper. The dot size, which is determined by the resolution of the screen or other output device, governs how smooth the result is at a given size (Figure 7-15). Devices with more dots per inch produce smoother results, particularly at smaller point sizes.

At small sizes, however, simply scaling the font outlines results in text with unpleasant problems, such as gaps in diagonal lines or unwanted dots on the edges of curves. These imperfections happen because the outline does not precisely fit the grid of small point sizes, especially if the dots are relatively large as they are on the Macintosh's 72 dpi screen. On the display screen the system software must draw a typical 12-point letter in a space eight dots square. At small sizes and relatively low resolutions, deciding which dots to darken is difficult. The system reduces the TrueType outline, lays it over the grid, and darkens the dots whose center points fall inside the outline (Figure 7-16).

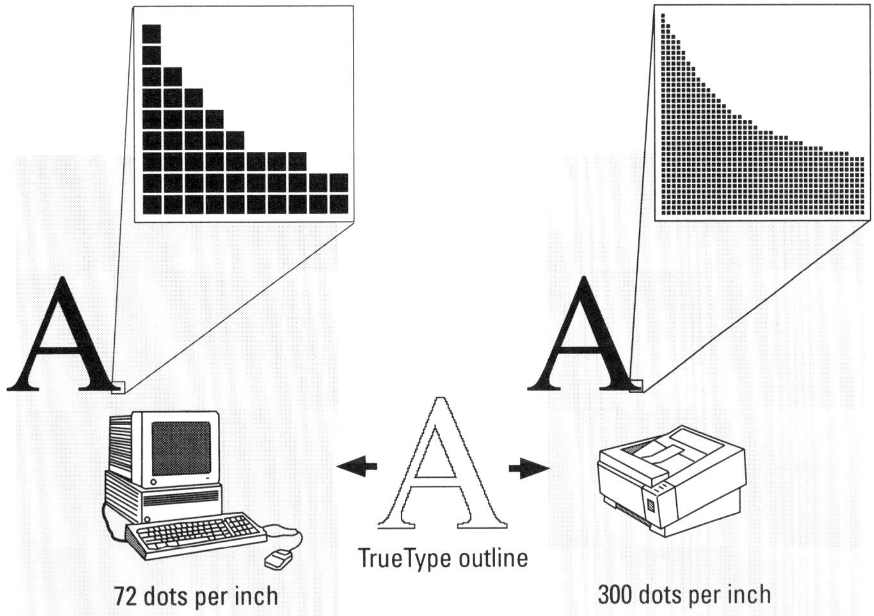

Figure 7-15
Output device resolution affects smoothness

TrueType includes a mechanism for adjusting the outline at small sizes on low-resolution devices. The font designer provides a set of instructions, also known as hints, that tell the system how to modify character outlines so they fit the grid (Figure 7-17). This process is called grid fitting.

High-resolution devices such as typesetters and film recorders usually don't need grid-fitting instructions. Their grid is so fine that the character outlines don't need adjusting to get filled with dots. A 300 dpi grid is four times finer than a 72 dpi grid, and a 1270 dpi grid is over 16 times finer.

Scaling and grid fitting happens so quickly you may not even notice it, especially if you have a fast Macintosh model. However, TrueType fonts are not as fast as fixed-size fonts and the lag is perceptible on screen.

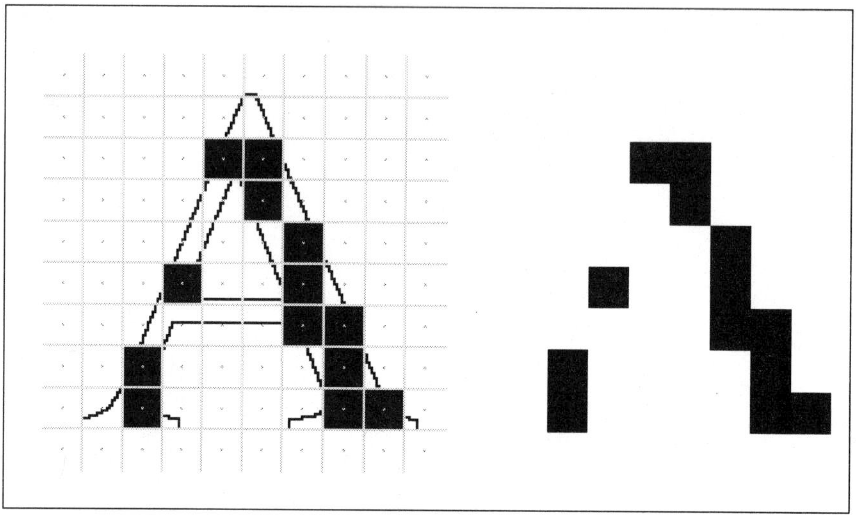

Figure 7-16
Grid fitting problems at small sizes

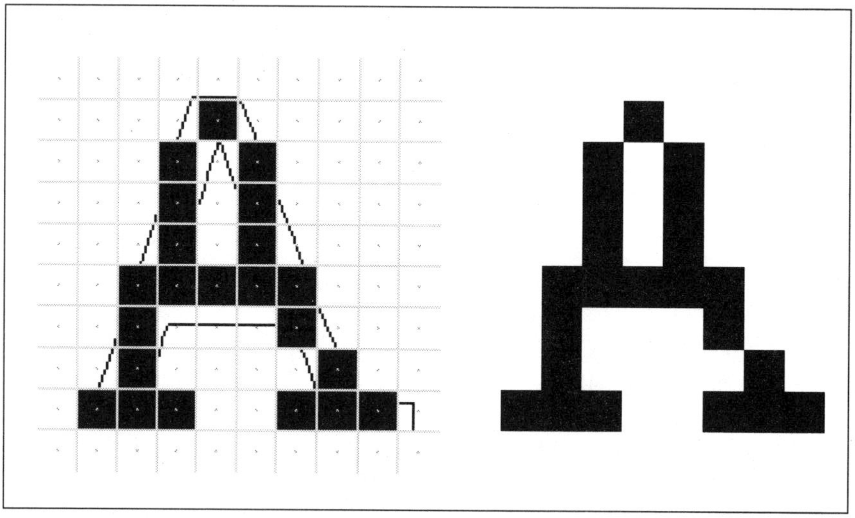

Figure 7-17
Hints modify outlines at small sizes

TrueType font availability

System 7 comes with a standard set of TrueType fonts. They include TrueType versions of the PostScript fonts Times, Helvetica, Courier, and Symbol; and the standard Apple fonts Chicago, Geneva, Monaco, and New York. Apple may add other TrueType fonts to System 7 over time, and may make more fonts available separately. In addition, many type companies make TrueType fonts, including:

Agfa Compugraphic
200 Ballardvale Street
Wilmington, MA 01887
508 658-5600

Bitstream Inc.
215 First Street
Cambridge, MA 02142-1270
617 497-6222

Casady & Greene, Inc.
P. O. Box 223779
Carmel, CA 93922
408 624-8716

Letraset
40 Eisenhower Drive
Paramus, NJ 07653
201 845-6100

Linotype-Hell Company
425 Oser Avenue
Hauppauge, NY 11788
516 434-2000

Monotype Typography Inc.
53 West Jackson Boulevard, Suite 504
Chicago, IL 60604
312 855-1440

Kingsley/ATF Type Corp.
2559-2 E. Broadway
Tucson, AZ 85716
602 325-5884

Summary

- Fixed-size fonts look best at their installed sizes; TrueType fonts look good at any size on any screen or printer; and PostScript fonts look good on any PostScript printer.
- You can see samples of fixed-size and TrueType fonts by opening them in the Finder.
- You add and remove fonts by dragging icons in the Finder.
- Fixed-size fonts look better on the display screen than many TrueType fonts at sizes below 18 points, but TrueType fonts look better when printed. You can mix both types in the same system.
- The system chooses the fixed-size version of a font over the TrueType version when both are present.
- Where System 7 displays TrueType or fixed-size fonts on screen, PostScript printers substitute PostScript fonts if the system software can find ones that match the screen fonts.

Chapter 8

File Sharing for the Rest of Us

In This Chapter

- A description of networks and network services, including file sharing.
- Building a network, identifying yourself on it, and making your Macintosh available to others on the same network.
- Designating which folders and disks you want to share, with guidelines for optimizing sharing and preventing potential problems.
- Who can access your shared items: all about the owner, guests, and registered users.
- Granting privileges that determine who can see and change your files and folders, with instructions for making a private in-box folder and a bulletin-board folder.
- Seeing which folders and disks you are sharing and who is connected to your computer.
- Sharing folders and disks from someone else's Macintosh.

Similar to a library, file sharing allows you to share files, folders, and disks with people whose computers are connected to yours in a network. You can share items from your Macintosh with others, they can share their items with you, and they can share their items with each other. In effect, these network users become librarians of their shared information, controlling who has access to shared items and determining what a user can do to files. This chapter explains how to use System 7's new file sharing capabilities to manage the flow of shared information across a network.

Understanding networks

System 7's built-in networking capabilities make sharing items across a network surprisingly easy. Previously, to create a network to share items, you needed to purchase additional networking software, such as

AppleShare or Tops. With System 7 and LocalTalk or LocalTalk-compatible connectors, you can easily create a ready-to-use network for sharing files, folders, and disks. File sharing is one type of network service; networks can also provide printing services, modem and fax modem services, and more.

File sharing can be implemented in either a distributed or centralized fashion. In a distributed file sharing network, each Macintosh user makes files, folders, and disks available to other users on the network. The user sharing files is free to use his or her Macintosh for normal tasks. A centralized file sharing network allows users to share items from a computer dedicated to provide file sharing services, referred to as a dedicated file server. Usually, the Macintosh acting as a dedicated file server needs above-average processing capabilities, like a Macintosh SE/30 with a large hard disk, to handle network demands.

System 7's file sharing capabilities are designed for distributed file sharing among 10 users at once. (More than 10 can be connected to the network, but only 10 can share files at the same time.) You can also use System 7's file sharing capabilities on a Macintosh dedicated to sharing files, making it a dedicated file server. In addition, System 7's file sharing capabilities are compatible with AppleShare, which is Apple's file sharing software designed specifically for dedicated file sharing on larger networks. Because AppleShare works with older system software, you can share files with other users even if they are not using System 7. They can use AppleShare client software to share your files, and you can use System 7's file sharing capabilities to share files on a dedicated AppleShare file server.

Only one person can use a shared item at a time unless the application program involved is a network version, which allows multiple users to work with the same program or document. For best performance, multiuser application programs and their documents are usually kept on a dedicated file server.

The network connection

You establish a LocalTalk network by simply plugging Apple's LocalTalk connectors into the printer ports of two or more Macintosh computers and connecting them with LocalTalk wiring. For a less expensive network that actually performs better, you can also use Farallon's PhoneNet connectors and ordinary telephone cables. Either way you have a basic LocalTalk network.

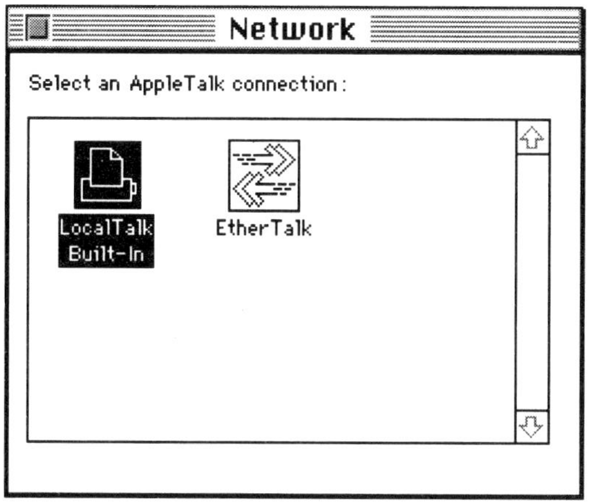

Figure 8-1
The Network control panel

System 7 includes optional software for connecting your Macintosh to two other types of networks: EtherTalk and TokenTalk. These are sophisticated networking options that provide more powerful networking capabilities than LocalTalk, but require more expensive wiring and extra-cost internal or external adapters. You install EtherTalk or TokenTalk software using the same Installer program that installs System 7.

Selecting your network

If your Macintosh has an EtherTalk or TokenTalk network connection, you switch between LocalTalk and the other network or networks using the Network control panel. You will not usually find the Network control panel in your Control Panels folder unless your Macintosh is directly connected to more than one network.

The Network control panel displays the network option icons (Figure 8-1). To select a network, click its icon. A message warns that you'll lose any network services you're using with your current network connection, because you can only maintain a connection to one network at a time. When you switch to a different network, you'll no longer be able to access any file servers, printers, or other network services on the original network.

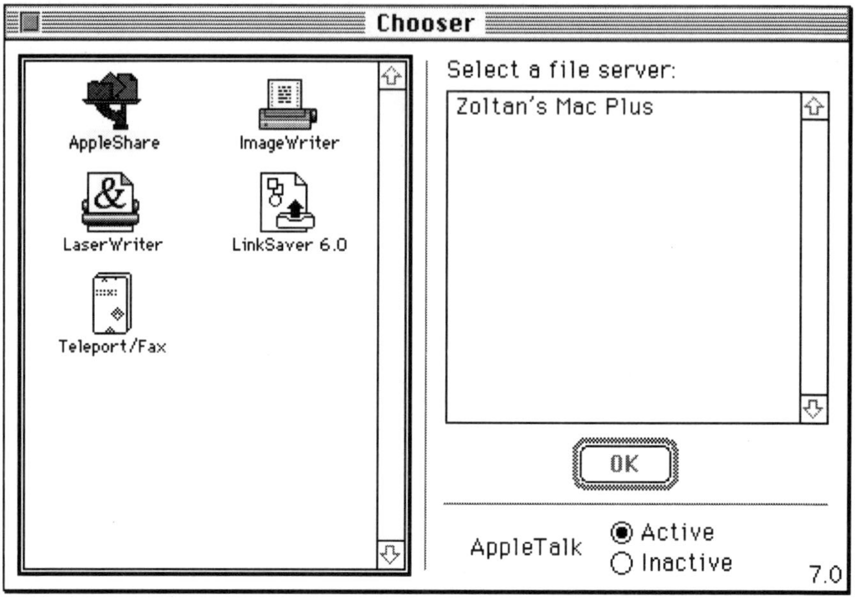

Figure 8-2
The Chooser desk accessory

Turning AppleTalk on and off

As soon as you connect to a network and turn on your Macintosh, AppleTalk is automatically turned on for you. AppleTalk is the built-in software that allows your Macintosh to communicate with a network. In some cases, you may need to turn AppleTalk off, meaning you want to disconnect your Macintosh from the network. To turn AppleTalk off, use the Chooser desk accessory (Figure 8-2). Click the Inactive button to turn AppleTalk off. If you attempt to turn off AppleTalk when you're currently connected to a network service, such as file sharing, you get a message warning you these services will be disconnected. In this case, click the Cancel button, close the Chooser, and then close any shared items. Remember, if you turn off AppleTalk, it remains turned off until you turn it on again by clicking on the Active button in the Chooser.

Identifying your Macintosh

Before you can begin sharing files, you must identify your Macintosh to the network using the Sharing Setup control panel (Figure 8-3). Identifying your Macintosh involves entering the name of its owner, a password

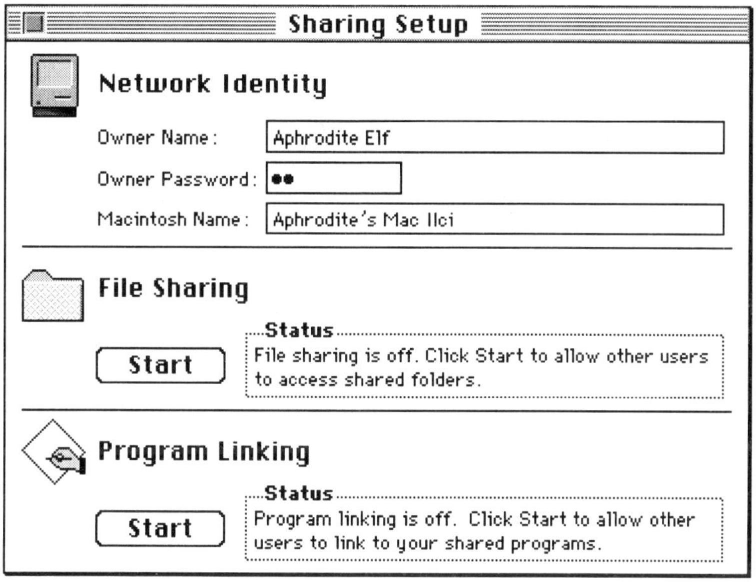

Figure 8-3
The Sharing Setup control panel

to prevent other users from connecting to your Macintosh as its owner, and a name for your Macintosh. Identifying the owner of your Macintosh plays an important role in determining who has access to your shared items. When people on the network want to share items from your Macintosh, they first select your Macintosh by name from a list in their Chooser.

QUICK TIPS

The Owner Password can be up to eight characters in length. A password is case sensitive, meaning if you enter a password that includes uppercase and lowercase letters, when using the password, it must be entered using the same uppercase and lowercase letters. Select a password that is easy to remember but difficult for others to guess. For better security mix letters with numbers; try replacing the letters I and O with the numbers 1 and 0. You must know the Owner Password to access your Macintosh from another Macintosh on the network. After entering your password, the Sharing Control panel displays bullets in place of the actual password to prevent others from seeing the password.

In the Macintosh Name text box, give your Macintosh a name that others will easily recognize when they see it in their Choosers. If a name already appears in the Macintosh Name text box, you can use that name or type a new one. You can change any of these settings at a later time by returning to the Sharing Setup control panel.

Starting file sharing

You also use the Sharing Setup control panel to start up, or activate, file sharing. This allows the network users to access your computer and its shared items. To start file sharing, click the Start button in the File Sharing section of the Sharing Setup control panel. The Start button's label changes to Cancel, and the status message next to the button describes what is happening while file sharing is starting up. When the status line says, "File sharing is now enabled" and the button's label changes to Stop, your Macintosh is ready to share files. You can close the Sharing Setup control panel any time after clicking the Start button, but you won't know precisely when file sharing is enabled if you do.

If you shut down or restart your Macintosh while file sharing is on, System 7 automatically starts up file sharing when the Macintosh is next started up. In other words, file sharing stays on until you explicitly stop it.

You can stop file sharing so other users on the network cannot access your computer. Stopping file sharing does not unshare items you've already designated as shared (as described in the next section), but instead denies other users on the network all access to any of your shared items until you turn on file sharing again. To stop file sharing, click the Stop button in the Sharing Setup control panel. The system asks you to enter the number of minutes' warning to be given to anyone sharing items from your Macintosh. Allow enough time for people sharing items from your Macintosh to be able to close any shared items. Every Macintosh sharing items from your Macintosh sees a message indicating that access to your computer is going to be disconnected at the end of the time you specified (Figure 8-4).

If you're planning to share a CD-ROM or removable hard disk, you must insert the disk before starting up file sharing with the Sharing Setup control panel. You can only share disks whose icons are on your desktop when you start up file sharing.

Sharing your folders and hard disks

After identifying your Macintosh and activating file sharing, you designate the folders and hard disks you want to share. You can share up to ten folders and hard disks (including CD-ROMs and removable hard

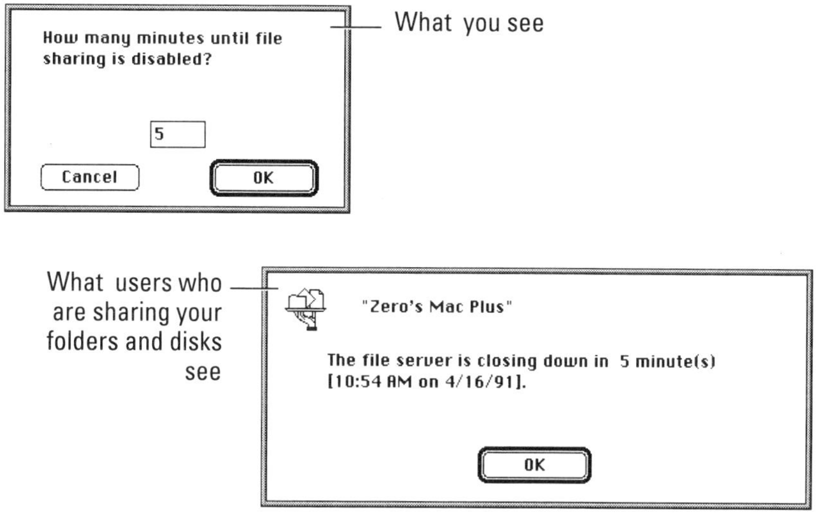

Figure 8-4
When you stop file sharing

disks) at one time. To share just one file, you must drag it into a folder and share the folder.

When you share a folder or hard disk, every item it contains is shared, including enclosed folders. You can't share a document by itself (outside a folder) or an item located on a floppy disk. Once you share a folder or hard disk, you can drag unshared items into the shared folder or hard disk to share them.

To make a folder or hard disk available for sharing, select the item and then choose Sharing from the File menu to see the Sharing info window, in which you specify access privileges (Figure 8-5). Turn on the "Share this item and its contents" option. The remaining options in the Sharing info window establish which users can access the shared item and what privileges they have, as explained in "Controlling access to shared items" later in this chapter. The initial settings for a shared item allow anyone on the network to access it and make any changes he or she wants. When you close the Sharing info window, the system asks if you want to save the changes to the access privileges that you've just made. If you click the Save button, the item is shared and available to everyone on the network. All items contained within the selected folder or hard disk are also available.

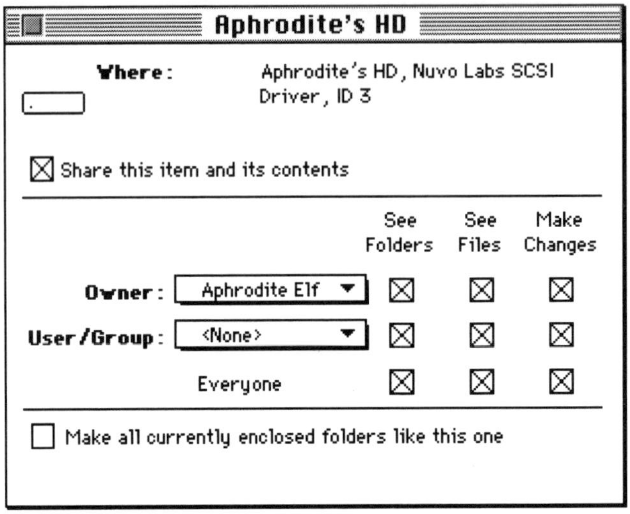

Figure 8-5
A disk's Sharing info window

Settings you make in an item's Sharing info window persist until you use the Sharing command again to change them. Shutting down or restarting your Macintosh does not affect Sharing info window settings; nor does stopping file sharing with the Sharing Setup control panel.

The icon of a shared folder on your Macintosh appears with network cables and a tabbed folder, indicating its shared status. When people on your network are connected to a shared folder, the folder icon displays faces in the center to indicate that it's in use (Figure 8-6). Note that shared hard disk icons, unlike folders, don't change. You can use the Views control panel to set icon size so you'll see the network folder icons. You can move a shared folder anywhere on your Macintosh, except a floppy disk.

You can't rename a shared folder or disk. Neither can you drag it to the Trash. Also, you can't eject and put away a removable hard disk or CD ROM that you are sharing. To do any of these things, you must first stop sharing with the Sharing Setup control panel or unshare the item.

You unshare any folder or disk with the Sharing command. In the item's Sharing info window, turn off the "Share this item and its contents" option and close the Sharing info window.

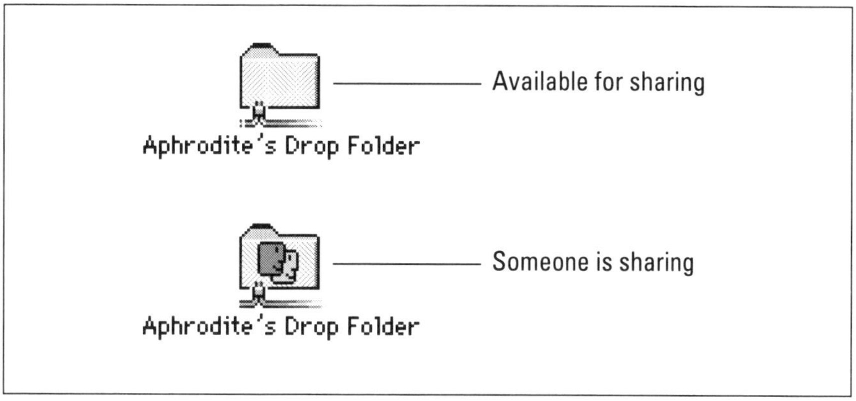

Figure 8-6
Shared folders on your Macintosh

If another user throws away a shared item from your Macintosh, a folder appears on your Macintosh with the label Network Trash Folder. As long as the user doesn't empty the Trash, the items thrown away appear inside the Network Trash Folder in folders labeled Trash Can #1, Trash Can #2, and so on, one for each Macintosh with something of yours in its Trash. To restore an item someone else has trashed, simply drag it out of the Trash Can # folder and rename it. You can set access privileges to prevent others from trashing your shared items, as described in "Controlling access to shared items" later in this chapter.

Guidelines for sharing folders and disks

There are several things you can do to optimize file sharing and prevent potential problems. The following are some guidelines and tips for sharing folders and disks:

- **Share aliases rather than the actual items themselves so the original item can remain in its folder**. Sharing items using aliases prevents the shared items from being thrown away by another user. The other person can open an alias and save changes to its original item but can only remove the alias, not the original item. Creating and working with aliases is explained in Chapter 6.

- **Share from the highest level of your disk and folder structure**. For example, a disk can't be shared if it contains an already-shared folder (no matter how deeply nested in the unshared disk). If you attempt to share a disk or folder that contains an already-shared folder, you get a message telling you the disk or folder cannot be shared because there is a shared folder inside it. To work around this situation, use the File Sharing monitor to identify the shared items (as explained in "Monitoring file sharing activity" later in this chapter), unshare it, and then share the enclosing disk or folder.

❖ **Share as few folders as possible**. The more shared folders being accessed, the greater the memory demands on your Macintosh. Sharing too many folders can slow your system to a crawl.

❖ **Check with any applicable licensing agreements before sharing folders containing programs, artwork, or sounds**. Often licensing agreements or copyright laws restrict use of these items to a single computer.

❖ **Set up a dedicated Macintosh to act as a centralized file server for the shared information**. This is often the most efficient way to share numerous files or share folders simultaneously with several users.

Who can access your shared items

When you initially share a folder or disk, it's made available to every user on the network. Every network user can access the shared items on your Macintosh as a guest without any restrictions. This arrangement may be fine if you know and trust absolutely everyone who might use another network Macintosh to access your shared items. Otherwise, you should take steps to restrict access.

The Users & Groups control panel allows you to specify which users can access the shared folders and disks on your Macintosh (Figure 8-7). When you first open the Users & Groups control panel, there are two user icons already created. The one with the dark border is for your Macintosh's owner and the other is for guests (that is, anyone on your network). You create additional icons for registered users to whom you want to grant greater access privileges than guests have. Registered users must enter their names and any passwords you've assigned them before they can access your Macintosh to share information.

Once you create your set of registered users, you can use the Sharing command to specify the kind of access each has to an individual shared item. You can also create groups of registered users and assign a group special access privileges to any item (again with the Sharing command). As many as 100 registered users and groups can be created in the Users &

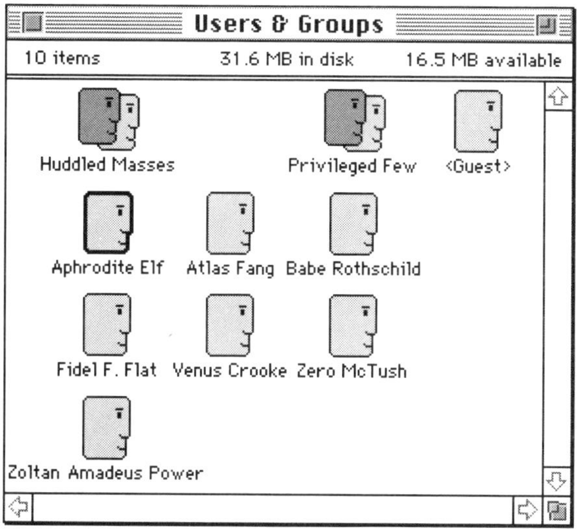

Figure 8-7
Users & Groups control panel

Groups control panel; however, you shouldn't name more than 50 for optimal performance.

The Owner

The Owner icon in bold outline in the Users & Groups control panel represents the owner of your Macintosh as a registered user. It's created automatically when you identify your Macintosh using the Sharing Setup control panel. The name of the Owner icon comes from the name in the Sharing Setup control panel's Owner Name text box. You have special access rights when you connect to your Macintosh as its owner from any other Macintosh on the network. Opening the Owner icon displays the owner privileges window (Figure 8-8). Turning on the "Allow user to connect" option allows you access to your Macintosh from another Macintosh connected to the network. Turning on the "Allow user to change password" option allows you to change your password remotely. The option "Allow user to see entire disk" allows you to see and use any items on any hard disk attached to your Macintosh. This setting lets you work with all shared or unshared disks and folders on your Macintosh (while connected to it from another Macintosh), whether or not you're named the owner of a shared folder and regardless of the privileges assigned to them.

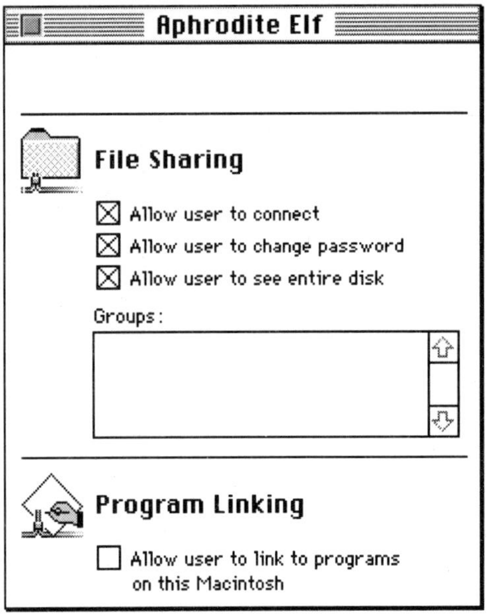

Figure 8-8
The Owner's access privileges

Guests

The Guest icon in the Users & Groups window allows anyone connected to the network to access your shared information; however, you can restrict Guest access to your Macintosh. Generally, it's a good idea to prevent unwelcome users from accessing your Macintosh by restricting Guest access and granting specific access privileges to registered users. To restrict access privileges for individual shared items, see "Controlling access to shared items" in this chapter. To disallow all Guest access, open the Guest icon in the Users & Groups control panel to display the Guest privileges window (Figure 8-9) and turn off the "Allow guests to connect" option in it. Now only registered users will be allowed to share items on your Macintosh.

Registered users

Establishing registered users helps secure your shared items from unauthorized access. To identify a registered user, first open the Users & Groups control panel. Next, choose New User from the File menu to create a New User icon in the Users & Groups control panel (Figure 8-10). The New User command is only available when the Users & Groups control panel is opened.

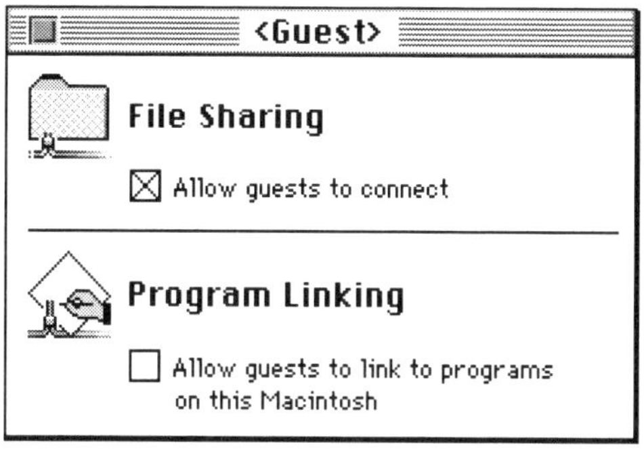

Figure 8-9
A Guest's access privileges

Replace the name New User with the name of the user you want by typing the user's name while the icon name is selected. Registered user names are not case sensitive, so it doesn't matter how you mix uppercase and lowercase letters. You can save the user's time when connecting to your Macintosh if you use the Owner Name from his or her Sharing Setup control panel. Contact the user to get the right name. If you use a different name than the Owner Name, you need to notify the user of the name you enter here, since the user must type the exact name to be able to connect to your Macintosh. The user is now registered on your Macintosh and you can grant him or her special access privileges to specific shared items on your Macintosh. For information on setting access privileges of your shared items, see "Controlling access to shared items" in this chapter.

You can add another level of security by assigning a registered user a password that he or she will need to type to access your shared items. You assign a password by opening the user's icon to see the registered-user privileges window (Figure 8-11). Enter a password up to eight characters long. Keep in mind that the user must type the password exactly as you type it here, including uppercase and lowercase letters.

Two additional settings in the registered-user privileges window allow you to specify the user's general access privileges. Turning on the "Allow user to connect" option allows the user access to your Macintosh. If you want this user to be able to change the password you assign, turn on the "Allow user to change password" option. When you're done setting the registered user's access privileges, close the registered-user privileges window to make them take effect.

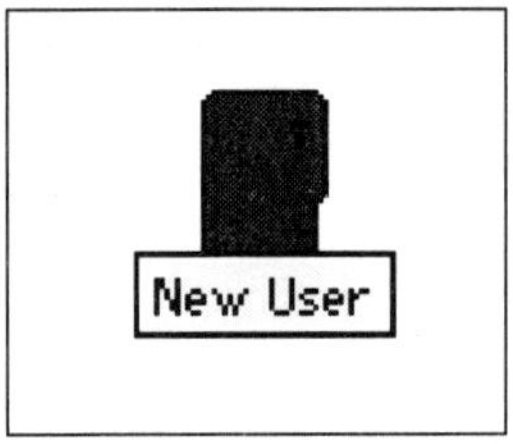

Figure 8-10
A new registered user

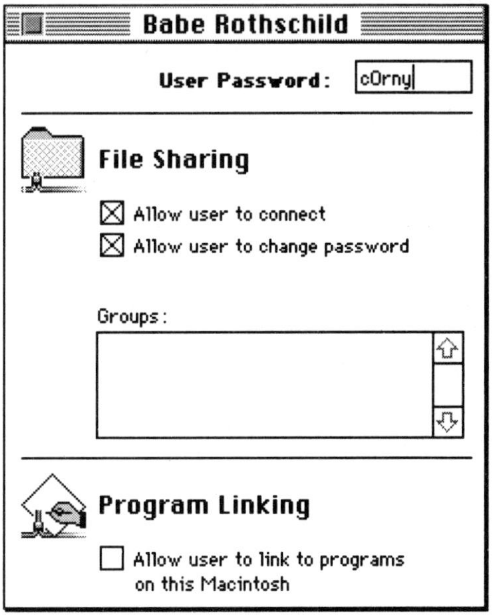

Figure 8-11
A registered user's access privileges

You can modify a registered user's access privileges or remove the user from your set of registered users at any time. To remove a registered user, drag its icon from the Users & Groups control panel to the Trash.

Groups of users

Office or work environments usually consist of groups of people, such as departments or project teams, who need to share common items. System 7 lets you specify special access privileges for groups as well as individual users. Groups are simply collections of individual registered users. Creating groups lets you grant specific access privileges for a shared item to a group instead of a single user. See "Controlling access to shared items" for information on setting access privileges of your shared items.

To establish a group of users, open the Users & Groups control panel and choose New Group from the File menu. A new icon named New Group appears in the Users & Groups control panel (Figure 8-12). Notice the group icon is different from the single-user icon. Replace the name New Group with your own group name by typing while the icon name is selected.

Figure 8-12
A new group

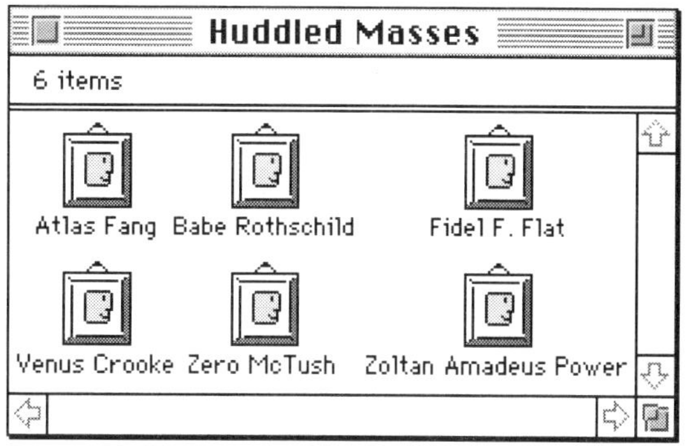

Figure 8-13
Members of a group

To add registered users to a group, drag their icons to the group icon. The system displays a message indicating the user or users are being added to the group. The registered-user icons are copied into the group icon. You can also drag the group icon to a user icon to add the user to the group. To speed up the process of adding users to groups, Shift-click to select all the registered users at once and then drag them to the group icon. You don't need to include the owner icon in groups.

To see the members of the group, open the group icon. The group window shows a member icon for every user in the group (Figure 8-13). If you want to see or change information for a registered user, you can open either the user icon or the member icon. You cannot create a new registered user from within the group window however.

To see all the groups that an individual user belongs to, open the registered or member user icon. In both cases, the user's access privileges window displays a list of groups the registered user belongs to (Figure 8-14).

Controlling access to shared items

Anyone can use and make changes to a shared folder or disk and its contents when you first share the folder or disk. System 7 provides access privilege settings that allow you to control who can see and change your shared files, folders, and disks. You specify access privileges for three categories of users: the owner, one user or group, and everyone. For example, you might want to ensure that a user or group of users can

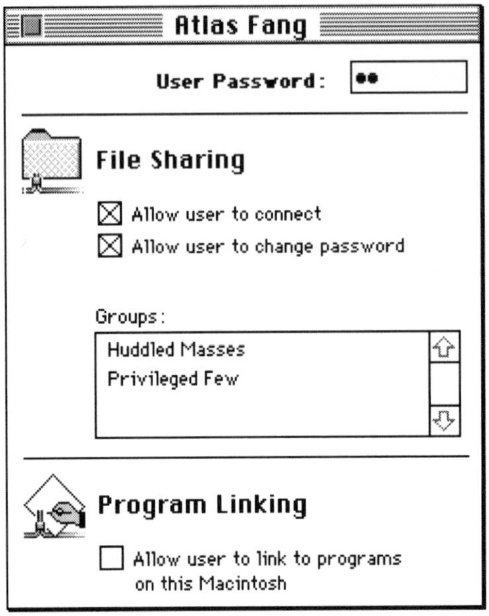

Figure 8-14
The groups a registered user belongs to

access templates on your Macintosh but not be allowed to modify them. Access privileges also let you selectively share confidential documents, such as an employee's review.

You set the access privileges of a folder or disk in its Sharing info window, which appears when you select the folder or disk and choose Sharing command from the File menu (Figure 8-15). You can't set a file's access privileges directly. Instead you put the file in a shared folder and set the folder's access privileges.

Setting access privileges

There are three types of access privileges you can grant to each user category in the Sharing info window. Table 8-1 describes each of these access privilege settings.

Additional settings in the Sharing info window allow access privilege uniformity and more security for shared items. Turning on the "Make all currently enclosed folders like this one" option for a shared disk or folder assigns its privileges to folders you have recently moved into it and to folders in it that previously had different privilege settings. This option

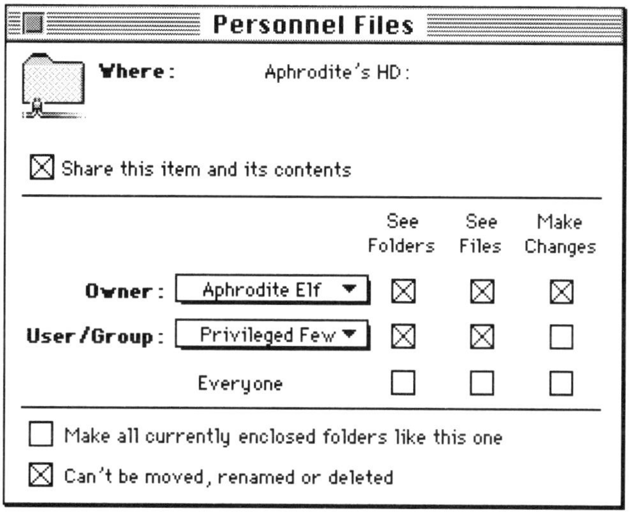

Figure 8-15
A folder's Sharing info window

makes the privileges of all enclosed folders the same as the enclosing folder. When you're sharing a disk or folder for the first time, you don't need to turn on this option because the shared item's contents, as well as any new folders you later create in it, are automatically set to the same privileges as the shared item.

Table 8-1: Disk and folder access privilege settings

Privilege	Purpose
See Folders	Shows or hides folders enclosed in a shared folder or disk. Users who don't have this privilege can't see the folders enclosed in the shared folder or disk.
See Files	Shows or hides files enclosed in a shared folder or disk. Users who don't have this privilege can't see files enclosed in the shared folder or disk.
Make Changes	Allows designated users to make changes to the shared item, including duplicating, deleting, and saving.

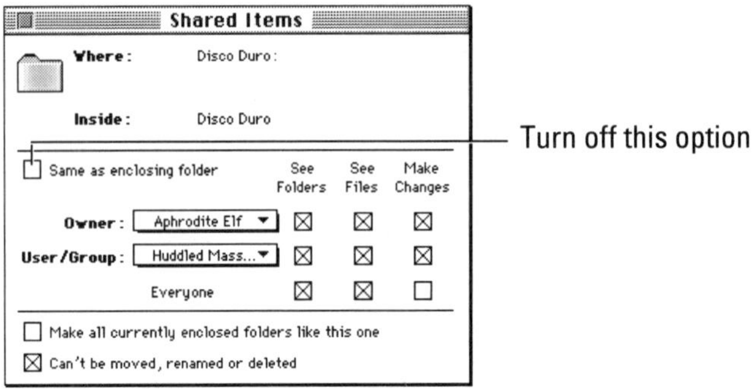

Figure 8-16
Making an enclosed folder's privileges unique

To prevent anyone on the network, including yourself, from moving, deleting, or renaming a shared folder, turn on the "Can't be moved, renamed, or deleted" option. This option is always in force for shared disks so it is not listed for them. You can set different privileges for a folder inside a shared folder or disk by turning off the "Same as enclosing folder" option in the enclosed folder's Sharing info window (Figure 8-16).

Specifying who has access privileges

The Sharing info window displays three categories of users to whom you can grant or deny access privileges. The Owner category is the person or group that created the shared folder (not necessarily your Macintosh's owner). The User/Group category refers to one registered user or one group of users. The Everyone category refers to anyone who connects to your Macintosh as a guest. The three categories of users appear dimmed if the "Share this item and its contents" option is off or, for enclosed folders, if the "Same as enclosing folder" option is on.

Ownership of a folder or disk allows you to modify its access privileges. You can transfer ownership of a folder or disk to a registered user, to a group, or to any user on the network. To change ownership of a folder or disk located on your Macintosh, use the Owner pop-up menu in the Sharing info window. The Owner pop-up menu lists the registered users and groups to whom you can transfer the ownership of the folder (Figure 8-17). You can also change ownership of a folder or disk you own on someone else's Macintosh. In this case there is no Owner pop-up menu so you must type the new owner's name.

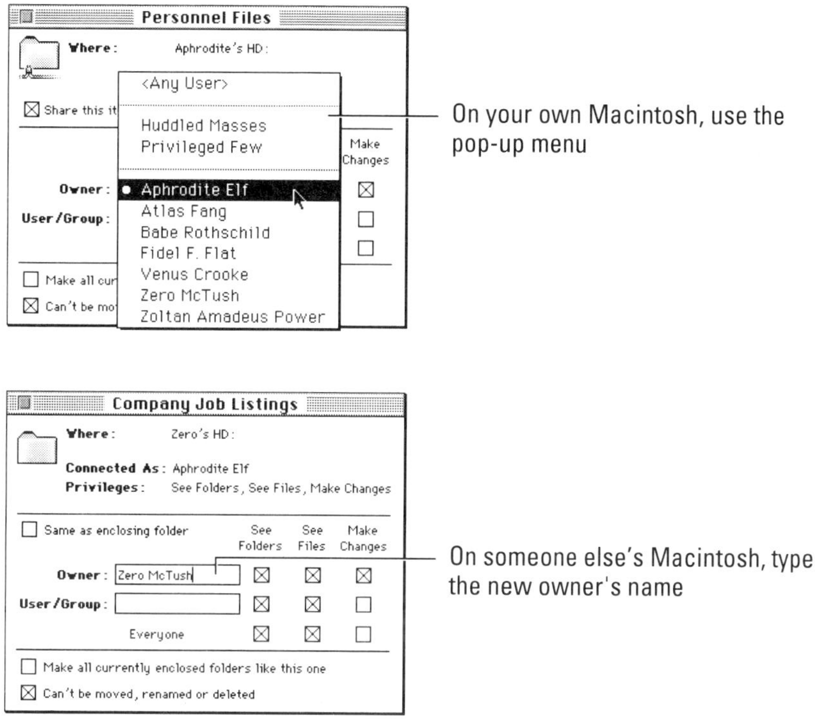

Figure 8-17
Changing an item's owner

Keep in mind that once you transfer ownership of a folder or disk, the new owner can restrict your access to that item and its contents — but only when you try to access the folder over a network. Giving away ownership to a folder or disk on your Macintosh doesn't take away your ability to open, use, or modify it. In effect an item can have dual ownership, allowing two users ownership privileges. If you make another user the owner of an item on your Macintosh, both you and that other user have ownership privileges. Of course, you can reclaim sole ownership at any time by making yourself the owner in the item's Sharing info window.

You choose the registered user or a group to which you want to grant specific access privileges by choosing from the User/Group pop-up menu. It lists all the registered users and groups in your Users & Groups control panel (Figure 8-18). You can also change the User/Group setting for an item you own on another computer (or on your computer when you're

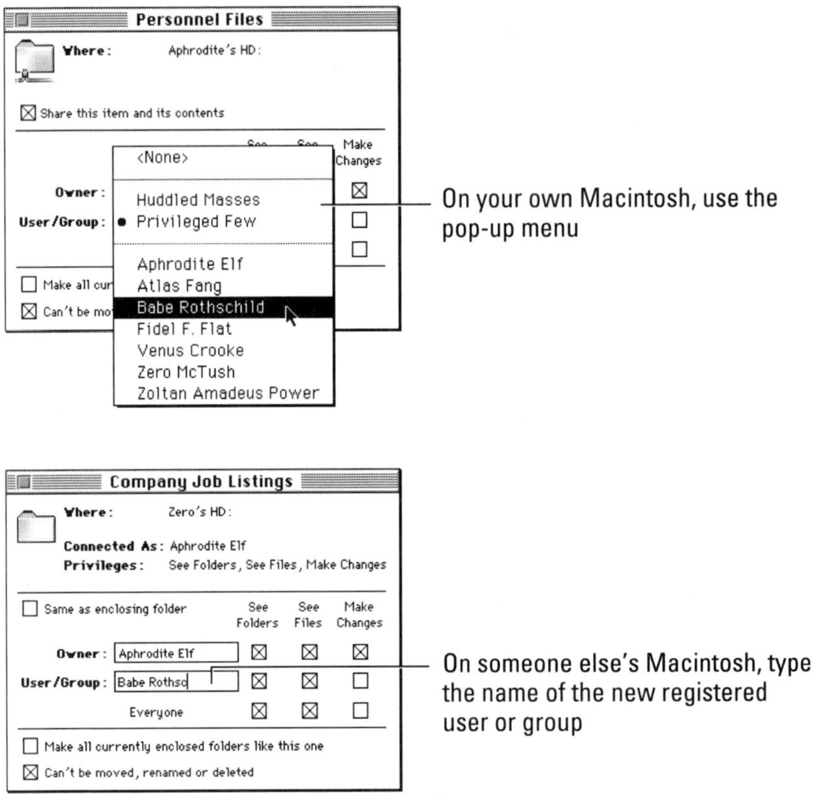

Figure 8-18
Changing an item's User/Group

accessing it from another computer on the network). In this case you must type the name of the registered user or group because the pop-up menu does not appear.

QUICK TIPS

It's important to remember to set Everyone's access privileges less than or the same as the designated user or group. Furthermore, you want to set the User/Group privileges below the Owner privileges. For example, granting broad access privileges to the User/Group category is useless if you don't also restrict access privileges of the Everyone category. Just remember, rank hath its privileges.

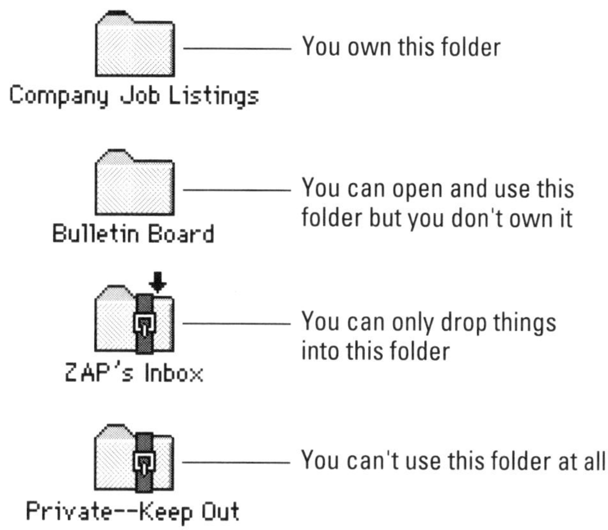

Figure 8-19
The four shared-folder icons

Icon indicators for access privileges

People who share your folders can easily see the privileges you have assigned to a folder by looking at its icon (Figure 8-19). A folder icon with a belt around it indicates that the user doesn't have access privileges. A belt-strapped folder icon with an accompanying down arrow acts like a mailbox; the user can drop items in the folder but cannot open it or use anything inside it. A tabbed folder icon tells the user he or she is the folder's owner. A plain folder icon means the user can open and use the folder.

Access privilege scenarios

Controlling who can do what with files in shared areas opens up new possibilities for working in groups. Using access privilege settings, you can keep folders private between two users or make them accessible to everyone on the network and lots of combinations between these extremes. The following sections explain setting access privileges for two interesting file sharing scenarios.

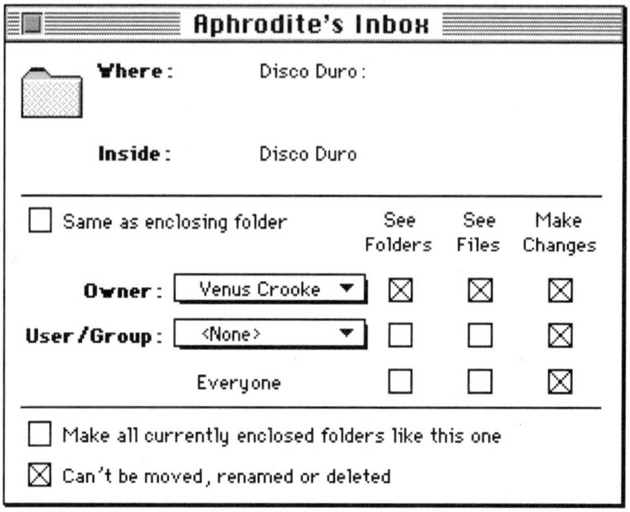

Figure 8-20
Access privileges for an inbox folder

Creating a private inbox folder

Setting up a folder to act as an inbox, or in basket, allows other network users to deposit documents, folders, and other items into it. This inbox is sometimes referred to as a drop folder, meaning other users can drop in items, but only you can take them out.

You prevent all other people from seeing, removing, or changing your folder's contents by denying the User/Group and Everyone access privileges to see folders and files (Figure 8-20). Anyone connecting to your Macintosh sees a strapped folder accompanied by a down arrow, indicating that they can only add folders and documents to the folder.

Creating a user or group bulletin board

Another useful configuration of access privileges is to set up a folder to act as a bulletin board, allowing other users to open and read documents, but preventing them from adding or changing documents. To establish a bulletin board folder, create and name an empty folder. Select the folder and choose Sharing from the File menu. If you don't want to share your bulletin folder with everyone, select the user or group you want to have access to the bulletin board folder and set their access privileges to see folders and files. Deny privileges to make changes for the User/Group

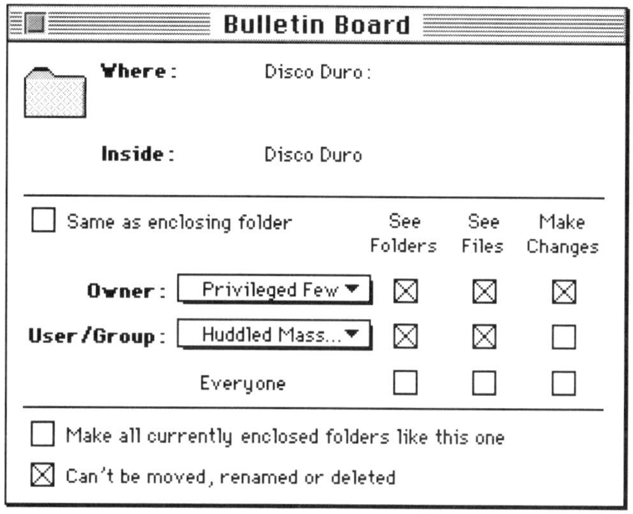

Figure 8-21
Access privileges for a bulletin board folder

and Everyone categories (Figure 8-21). If you only want a user or group to access your bulletin board folder, deny all privileges to the Everyone category.

Monitoring file sharing activity

When file sharing is on, you can view who is connected to your Macintosh and list which of your folders and disks you are sharing. To monitor file sharing activity, open the File Sharing Monitor control panel (Figure 8-22). A list of your shared folders and disks appears on the left side of the File Sharing Monitor control panel. Only the folders and disks you're sharing using the Sharing command are displayed; all the files and folders contained in them are also accessible although they aren't explicitly listed. A list of network computer users currently connected to your Macintosh appears on the right side of the control panel window. The File Sharing Activity indicator shows you how much of your Macintosh's total processing time is now being spent handling file sharing.

Temporarily disconnecting users

The File Sharing Monitor control panel also allows you to disconnect a user currently connected to your Macintosh. This disconnection doesn't

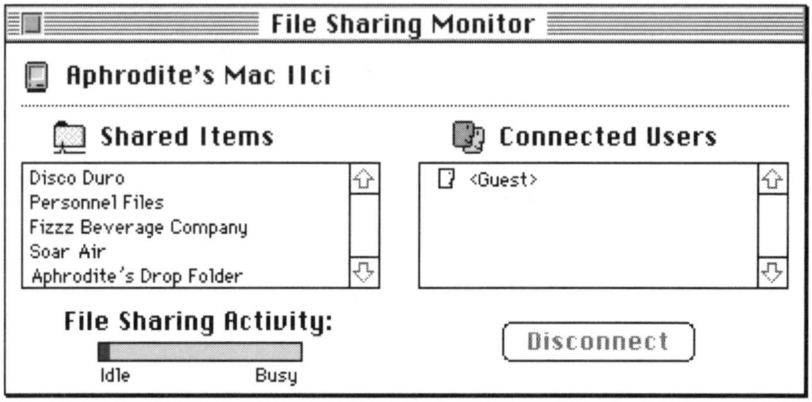

Figure 8-22
The File Sharing Monitor control panel

turn off file sharing, like the Sharing Setup control panel, but allows you to temporarily disconnect all, or selected users, from sharing items on your Macintosh.

To disconnect a user, select the user you want to disconnect from the list of connected users in the File Sharing Monitor control panel. To select more than one user, hold down the Shift key while clicking on the names of the users you want to disconnect. When you click the Disconnect button, the system asks you to specify the number of minutes you want to elapse before the disconnection occurs. It's good networking etiquette to give people enough time to save any changes they have made to the files before disconnecting them. To disconnect a user immediately, specify 0 minutes. Remember this only temporarily disconnects the user; he or she can still connect again and access your shared folders.

Sharing someone else's folders and disks

Until now, you've created and set access privileges for items you're sharing with other network users. Other users on the network who are sharing their items have performed similar tasks to make folders or disks available to you and other users. Before you can access another user's shared items as a guest, you need to know the name of the Macintosh you want to access. To access the shared items as a registered user, you must also know your registered name and password on the other computer. If your network has zones, you also need to find out the name of the zone the other Macintosh is in.

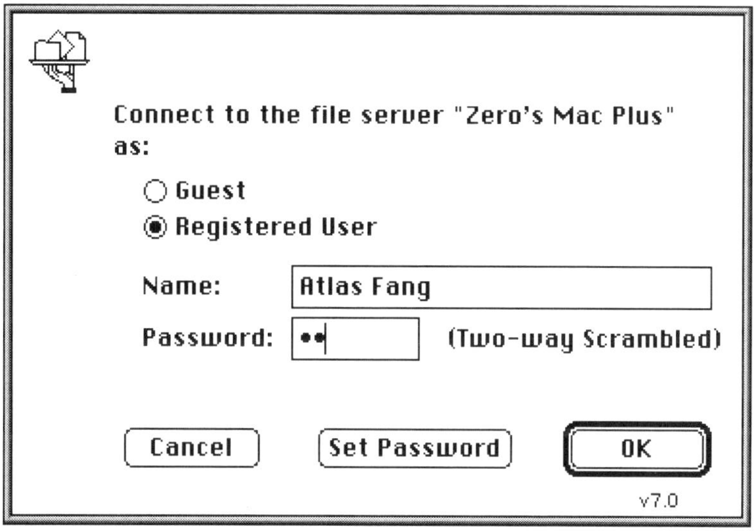

Figure 8-23
Identifying yourself to another computer

Connecting as a registered user or guest

To make the connection to another Macintosh, open the Chooser. Make sure that AppleTalk is active in order to connect to another Macintosh on the Network, and click the AppleShare icon. If your network contains zones, click the zone in which the other Macintosh you want to connect to resides. The Chooser then displays a list of computers whose folders and disks you can share. From the list, select the name of a Macintosh to which you want to connect and click the OK button. A dialog box appears in which you identify yourself as a registered user or guest (Figure 8-23).

To connect as a registered user, click the Registered User button and enter your registered name and password in the spaces provided. This name and password must have been previously assigned by the owner of the Macintosh you want to access. Type your password exactly as assigned, including uppercase and lowercase letters, and then click the OK button. If you're not a registered user and the Guest option isn't dimmed, you can access the other Macintosh as a guest. If the Guest option is dimmed, then guests are not permitted access to the selected Macintosh. If you're accessing your own Macintosh from another Macintosh, you enter your password (the owner password in the Sharing Setup control panel on your Macintosh). You can connect to another Macintosh on the network automatically by using aliases (see Chapter 6).

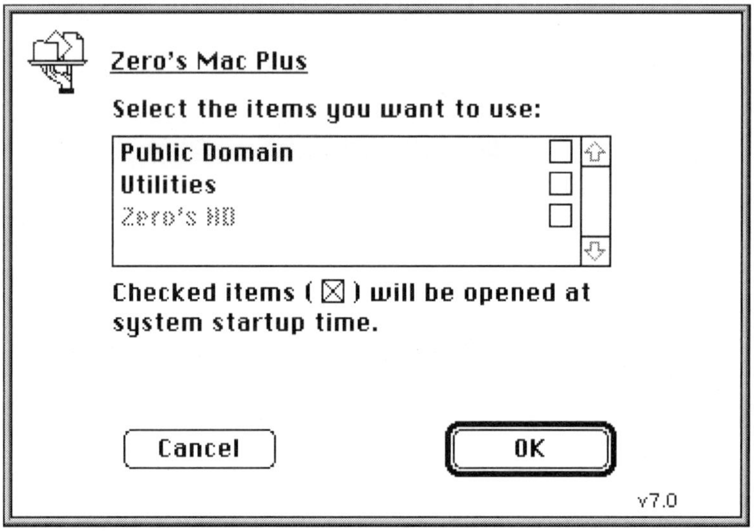

Figure 8-24
The Chooser's list of shareable items

You change your password by clicking the Set Password button. A dimmed Set Password button indicates the owner of the Macintosh which you want to connect to does not allow you to change your password.

Selecting shared disks and folders

After connecting as a registered user or guest, the Chooser displays a list of the items you can share (Figure 8-24). A dimmed name indicates either that you're already sharing that folder or disk, or that its user hasn't granted you access privileges to see it.

Select the name of the shared folders and disks you want to use. To select more than one, hold down the Shift key and click the names of the shared folders or disks you want. You can scroll through the list or type the first few letters of a shared item's name to find it. When you click OK to close the dialog box, a shared volume icon appears on your desktop (Figure 8-25). Your Macintosh treats a shared volume like a disk, no matter whether it's a folder or a disk on the owner's Macintosh.

Automatically sharing items from another Macintosh

You also use the Chooser's list of shareable items to designate which of them you want System 7 to open automatically at startup time. This

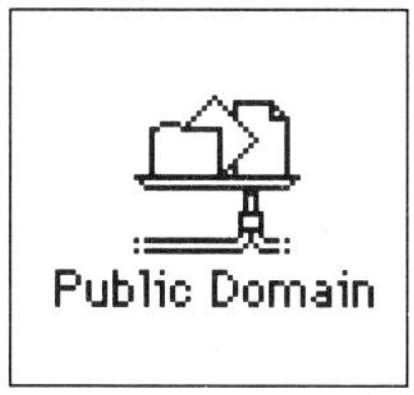

Figure 8-25
A shared volume's icon

feature is a real time-saver if you frequently use certain shared folders or disks. Designate the items you want automatically opened by marking the checkbox next to each one.

If you mark a check box and are a registered user, two options appear in the dialog box below the list. Select the "Save My Name Only" option if you want the system to ask for your password before opening the shared folder or disk during startup. Use this option to prevent unauthorized people from accessing the shared folder or disk from your Macintosh. If you select the "Save My Name and Password" option, your Macintosh automatically supplies your password when it opens the marked items. Table 8-2 shows the access privileges you need to perform common tasks with a shared item.

Table 8-2: Access privileges for common tasks

To do this with a shared folder or disk:	You need these privileges: See Folders	See Files	Make Changes
Open a file from		✓	
Save changes to a file in		✓	✓
Drag something to			✓
Copy a file from		✓	
Copy a folder from	✓		
Discard a file from		✓	✓
Discard a folder from	✓		✓
Create a new folder in	✓		✓

Working with items shared from another Macintosh

You use the items shared from another Macintosh in the same manner you use items on your own Macintosh. Of course, what you can do with a shared item depends on the access privileges its owner has granted you. To see your access privileges, select the shared item and choose Sharing from the File menu. For an item shared from another Macintosh, the Sharing info window tells where the item is, the name by which you're connected, and your access privileges for that item.

UNDOCUMENTED

When you open a shared document, the Finder searches your local disks for the program needed to open the document. If the program isn't found, the Finder tries to find it on the Macintosh you're sharing the file from and open it across the network. Running programs over a network is considerably slower than running a program on your Macintosh. Whenever you send or receive information across the network using System 7's file sharing, a double-arrow icon flashes in the upper-left corner of the menu bar.

If you access your own Macintosh remotely (or another Macintosh as its owner), you can see and use everything on that Macintosh. In other words, you have full access privileges to all items, whether they have been designated for sharing (using the Sharing command) or not. This is handy, for example, if you've forgotten an important file or if you need to refer to some information that you have on your Macintosh but you're no longer in your office. By connecting to your computer over the network, you can copy those files to the Macintosh you're working at and read, change, or print them.

Transferring items between computers

The most common use of sharing folders and disks is to transfer items from one Macintosh to another. For the most part, you transfer items between computers just as you would copy files to a floppy disk. If you try to move a folder or file to the desktop, a message asks whether you want to copy the item to your startup disk. If you click OK, the item will appear on your desktop.

Disconnecting from another Macintosh

There are three ways you can disconnect from another Macintosh. You can select the icons of all items you're sharing from it and choose Put Away from the File menu. You can also drag those file server icons to the Trash. If you're done working on your Macintosh, choose Shut Down command from the Finder's Special menu.

Summary

- System 7's built-in file sharing makes connecting Macintosh computers and sharing files, folders, and disks easier than ever before.
- Using LocalTalk or PhoneNet connectors to connect two or more Macintosh computers, anyone can create a ready-to-use AppleTalk network to share and transfer files.
- You use the Sharing Setup control panel to start and stop file sharing from your Macintosh.
- With the Users & Groups control panel, you create registered users and groups of users and assign general access privileges to each.
- You use the Finder's Sharing command to designate which of your disks and folders you want to share with others and what each item's access privileges are for three categories of users: the owner, one registered user or group, and everyone on the network.
- The File Sharing Monitor control panel tells you which items you are sharing with others and who is presently connected to your Macintosh.
- You get access to other computers and the folders and disks on them using the Chooser desk accessory. Once you have access to a shared item, your Macintosh treats it like a disk.

Chapter 9

Creating Living Documents

In This Chapter

- Creating publishers: saving live copies of material from your documents as edition files.
- Subscribing to editions: including live copies of material in your document from other documents.
- What happens when you change a publisher (or a subscriber).
- How to have publishers and subscribers updated automatically or manually.

The United States Constitution is often referred to as a "living document" because it has the ability to change with the times. Application programs supporting System 7's new publish and subscribe capabilities allow you to create your own living documents. The Create Publisher and Subscribe To commands allow you to dynamically share information between documents. Think of the Create Publisher and Subscribe To commands as live Copy and Paste commands. For example, you can copy a group of cells or a chart from a spreadsheet and paste it into a word processing report document. Any time the selected information in the spreadsheet is changed, the report is automatically updated. In this chapter you'll learn how to breathe life into your documents using the Create Publisher, Subscribe To, and other related commands.

About publishers, editions, and subscribers

System 7 borrows concepts and terminology from the publishing industry for its publish and subscribe technology. A selected area of a document becomes a publisher when you make a live copy of it available to other documents. The publisher can include any information you can select within a document. Publishing material from a document creates a live copy of the material in a separate file, which is called an edition (Figure 9-1). You include a copy of an edition in another document by

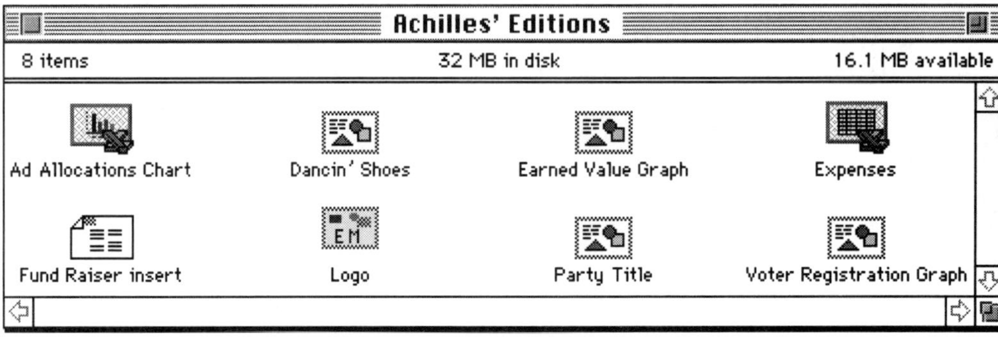

Figure 9-1
Some edition files

subscribing to the edition. The area of the document that contains a copy of an edition is called a subscriber. A document can contain any number and combination of publishers and subscribers.

Saving a document after changing a publisher in it can automatically update the publisher's edition (or you can update the edition manually). When an edition is updated, System 7 notifies all subscribers to that edition that a new edition is available. The subscriber can automatically reflect the latest information from the edition or you can update it manually. Documents containing subscribers do not have to be open for the subscribers to receive edition updates. System 7 stores notices of edition updates destined to closed subscribers and forwards each stored notice when you open the document that contains the subscriber. Information always flows from the publisher to an edition and then to the edition's subscribers (Figure 9-2).

UNDOCUMENTED

Publishing and subscribing work across a network just as well as they work locally on your Macintosh. You can subscribe and get updates to editions that are on any disk or folder you are sharing from someone else. Likewise other people can subscribe and get updates to editions on disks or folders those people are sharing from you. If you are not sharing a disk or folder when an edition on it is updated, System 7 stores the update notice and forwards it to the subscribers on your local disks the next time you share the disk or folder. (For more information on file sharing, see Chapter 8.)

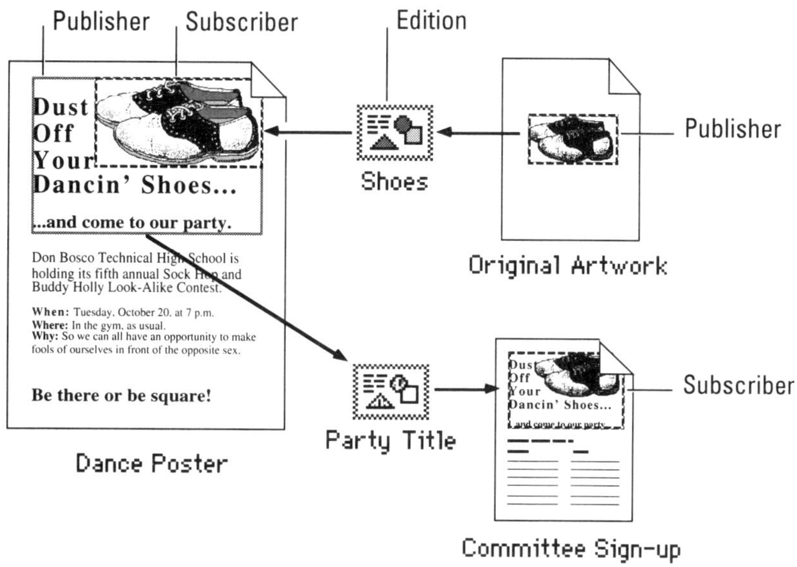

Figure 9-2
The relationship between publisher, edition, and subscriber

Publishing and subscribing doesn't work in programs that existed before System 7 first became available. You can't use System 7's publish and subscribe technology with a program that doesn't contain publishing commands in its Edit menu or in a submenu of its Edit menu. If you have a program that lacks those commands, check with the program's developer to see if an upgraded version is available.

Creating a publisher

You create a publisher by selecting the information that you want to share and choosing Create Publisher from the Edit menu of your program (Figure 9-3). Some programs, such as Claris's MacWrite Pro and Resolve, put the Create Publisher command in a Publishing submenu of the Edit menu. In most programs you need to select text or graphics in your document in order to create a publisher. If you haven't selected anything, the Create Publisher command appears dimmed. In a few programs, such as MacWrite Pro, you can publish an entire document by choosing Create Publisher without having selected anything.

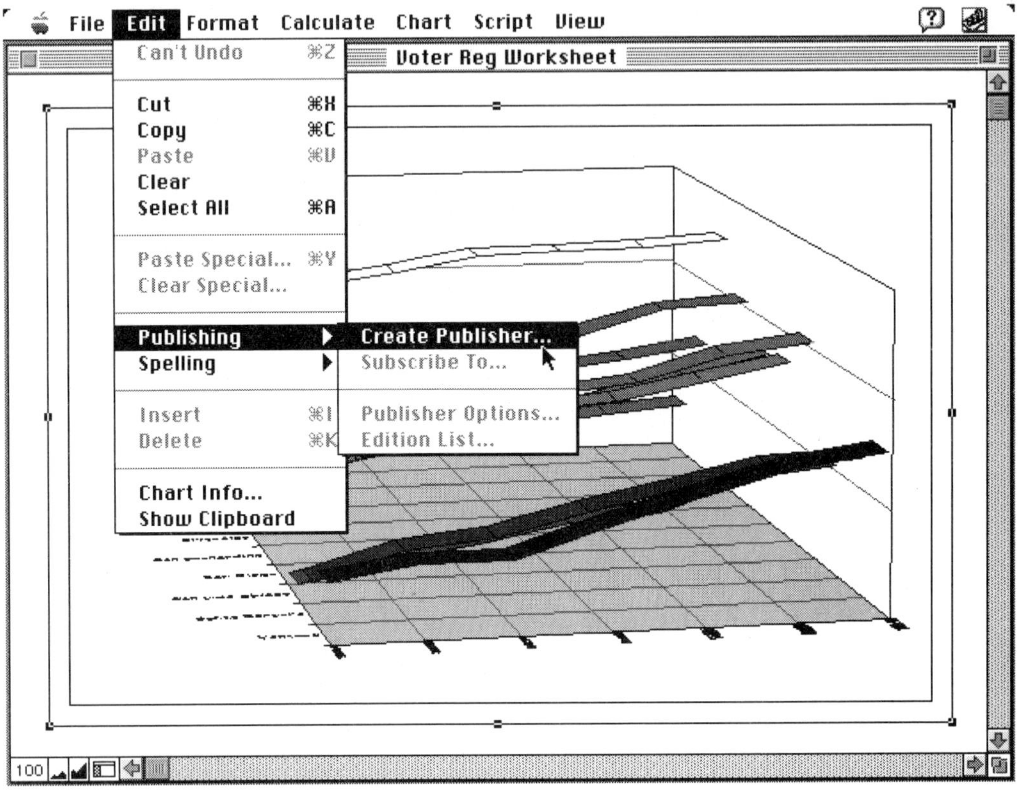

Figure 9-3
Creating a publisher

After choosing the Create Publisher command, the Publisher dialog box appears (Figure 9-4). A thumbnail view of the material you selected appears in the Preview area of the dialog box. Usually the folder in which you saved the last edition is already open. System 7 knows which folder to open because it keeps an alias of the most recently saved edition in the Preferences folder inside the System Folder. You can go to a different folder by using the same methods you would use with the Save As command. If you want to make the edition available to other users on your network, be sure to save the edition to a folder or disk you allow them to share.

WARNING

To keep a new publisher you must save the document that contains it. If you close the document without saving, all programs ask whether you want to save changes. Only a few advise that you lose the publisher if you decline to save.

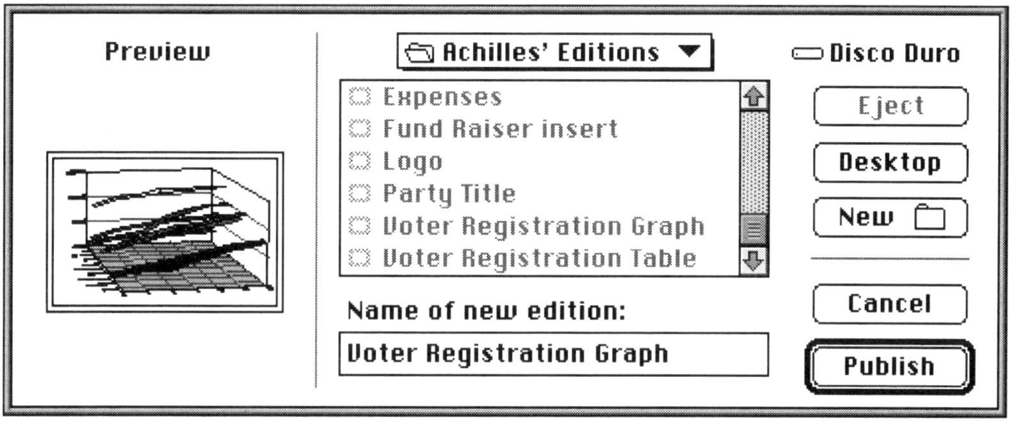

Figure 9-4
Saving an edition

You can create as many independent publishers in a document as you want. Some programs allow publishers to overlap partially or completely — one publisher can include all or part of the information contained in another publisher. Apple's guidelines suggest word processing programs permit nested publishers but not overlapping publishers. Spreadsheet programs and graphics programs should permit both nesting and overlapping publishers. A program that does not allow overlapped or nested publishers dims the Create Publisher command when you select any part of a document that is already part of an existing publisher.

A Publisher's format — plain text, styled text, paint-type picture, object-type graphic, and so on — is determined by the program that created the document containing the publisher. Some programs save information in several formats in an edition file. When you subscribe to a multi-format edition, the program that created the subscribing document uses the most appropriate format. Microsoft Excel, for example, saves spreadsheet cells as a picture, as a text table, and as a range of formatted Excel cells. A graphics document subscribing to an Excel edition would use the picture format; a word processor would probably use the text table (though some might use the picture); and another Excel worksheet would use the formatted cells.

Subscribing to an edition

You subscribe to an edition to incorporate live information from another document into the document you're currently working on. To

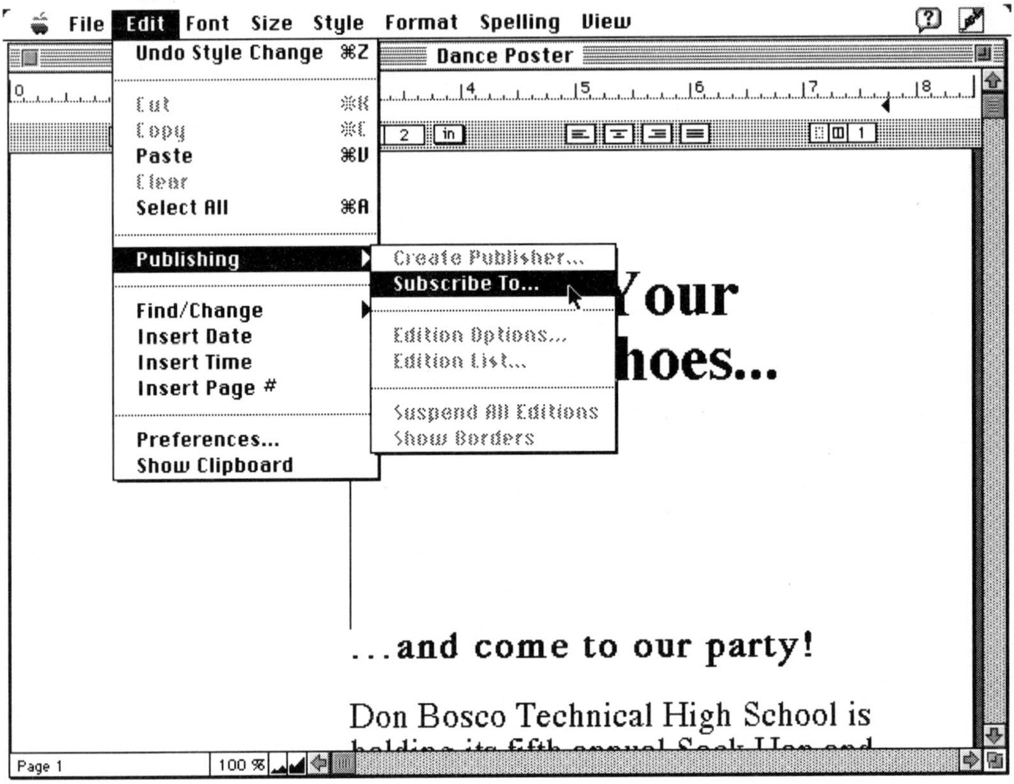

Figure 9-5
Subscribing to an edition

subscribe to an edition, select a place in your document for the edition and choose Subscribe To from the Edit menu (Figure 9-5). Some programs put the Subscribe To command in a Publishing submenu of the Edit menu. The place you select for the edition depends on the type of document that's subscribing to it. In a word processing document, you click an insertion point. In a spreadsheet document, you select a cell or range of cells. You do not have to select a place in most graphics documents.

Choosing Subscribe To from the Edit menu displays the Subscribe To dialog box (Figure 9-6). The dialog box displays the highlighted name of the last edition you published or subscribed to, and you can select a different edition as if you were using an Open command. When you

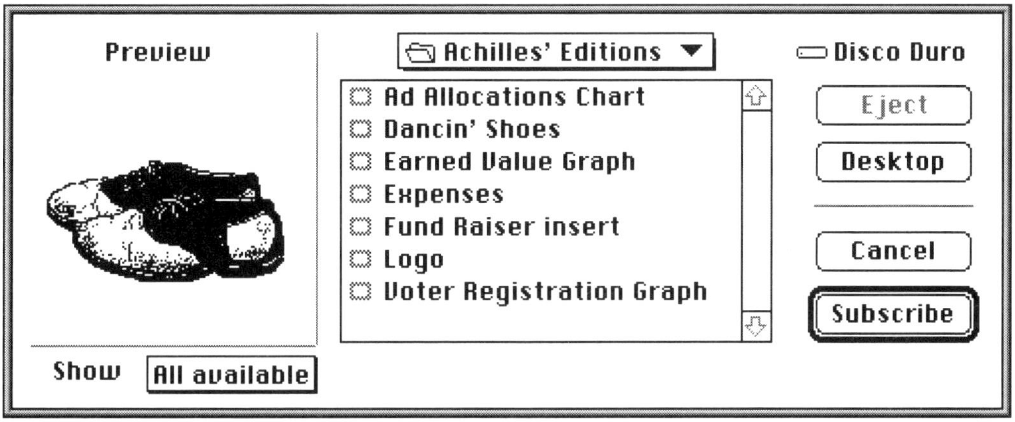

Figure 9-6
Selecting an edition to subscribe to

select an edition, a thumbnail view of its contents appear in the Preview area of the dialog box. Clicking the Subscribe button places a copy of the selected edition into your document.

You can subscribe to as many editions in a document as you want. The editions can be on a disk directly connected to your Macintosh or on a disk or folder you're sharing from another Macintosh on the same network.

Publisher and subscriber borders

Most programs display a gray border around a publisher or subscriber when you click or select something inside one. The border also appears if you select part of a document that contains a publisher or subscriber (Figure 9-7). The standard border lines are 3-pixels thick and are medium gray (50% gray) for publishers and dark gray (75% gray) for subscribers. Clicking outside the publisher or subscriber makes the border disappear.

An optional Edit menu command, Show Borders, displays borders around all publishers and subscribers in the active document. After choosing the Show Borders command, it becomes the Hide borders command, which (surprise!) hides all borders except the one for the subscriber or publisher you have clicked. Some programs have different methods for showing and hiding all borders. In Claris Resolve, for example, you choose Show from the View menu and turn the Edition Borders option on or off.

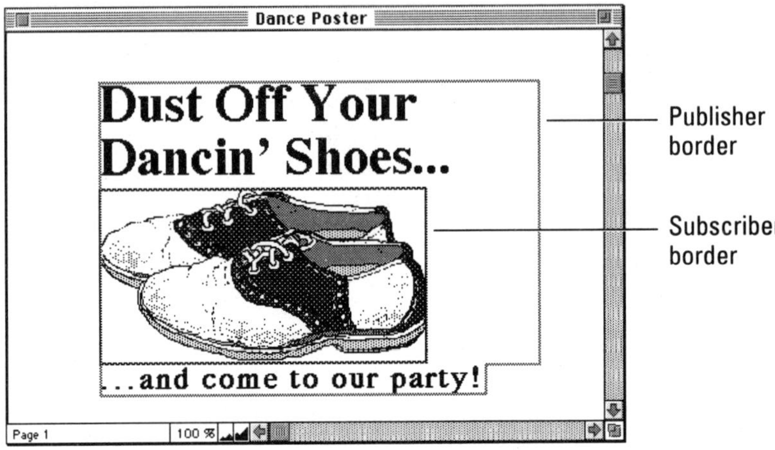

Figure 9-7
Borders around publishers and subscribers

Some programs, including Microsoft Excel 3.0, don't show publisher or subscriber borders. Excel's Links command can select a publisher's range of cells (but not a chart or other type of publisher nor a subscriber). You select the publisher you want by name from a list of publishers in the document and click a Select button. Then Excel selects the range of cells and scrolls the document window so you can see it.

Publisher and subscriber options

System 7 provides you with several options for working with publishers and subscribers. You can adorn a subscriber (change its formatting), locate and open a subscriber's publisher, control edition updates, and cancel or suspend a publisher or subscriber.

Not all application programs use the same methods to perform these publisher and subscriber options. Apple's guidelines are quite specific: The Edit menu should contain a Publisher Options command when a publisher is selected in the active window, or a Subscriber Options command when a subscriber is selected. Choosing one of those commands brings up a dialog box in which you set the publisher or subscriber options (Figures 9-8 and 9-9).

Some programs follow Apple's guidelines for the Publisher Options and Subscriber Options commands. Others, such as MacWrite Pro and Claris Resolve, come close by putting the commands in a Publishing

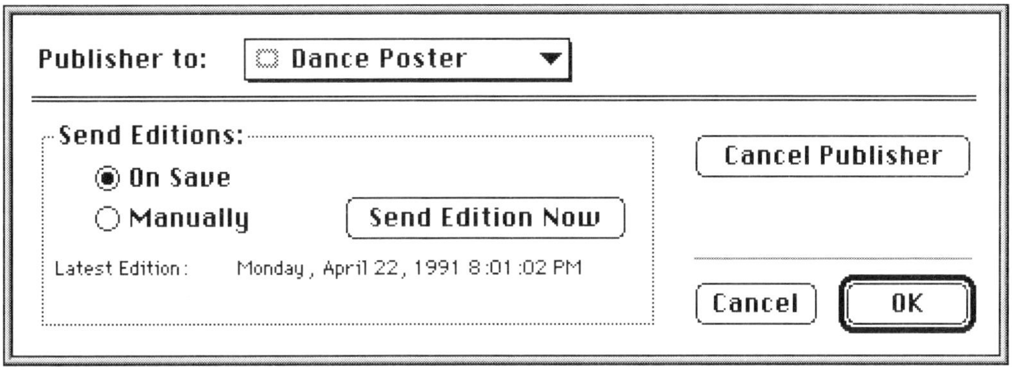

Figure 9-8
A Publisher Options dialog box

submenu of the Edit menu. Then there's Microsoft Excel, which has its own eccentric methods. In Excel, you choose the Links command from the File menu to see the Links dialog box. In it you choose Publisher or Subscriber from the Link Type pop-up menu to see a list of the publishers or subscribers that are in the document. Then you select the one whose options you want to see and click an Options button. As a shortcut, you can double-click any part of a publisher or subscriber on a worksheet. (The double-click trick doesn't work for chart publishers.)

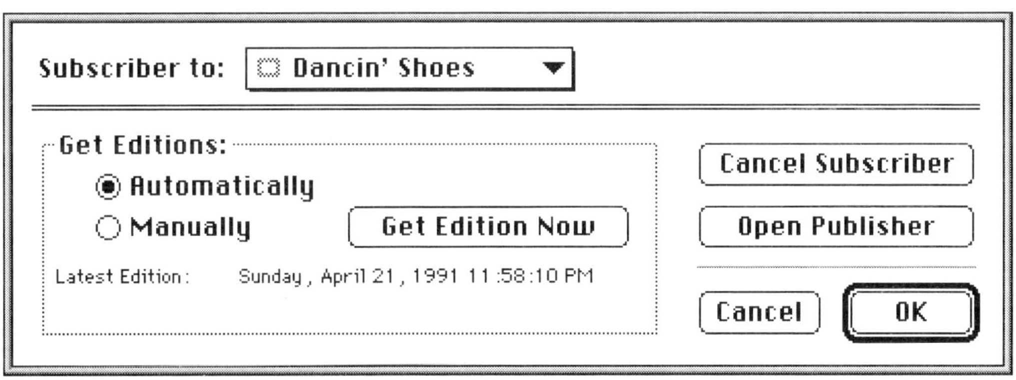

Figure 9-9
A Subscriber Options dialog box

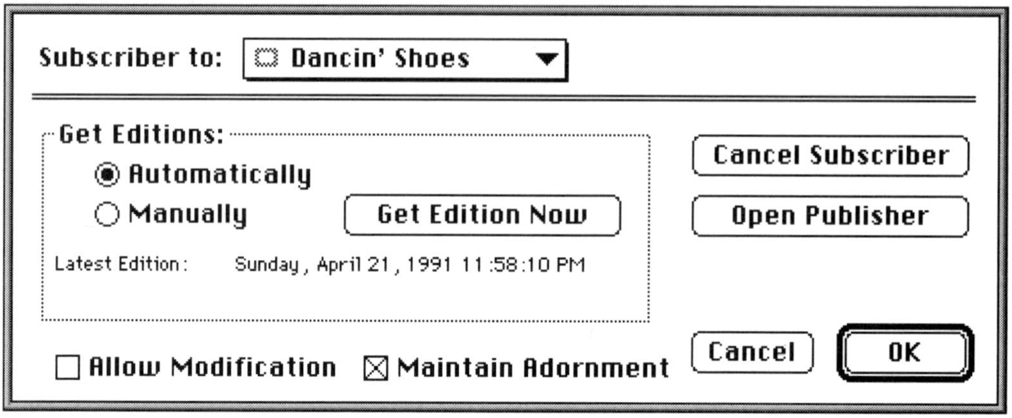

Figure 9-10
The Maintain Adornment option

Adorning a subscriber

Most programs do not allow you to change the contents of a subscriber directly, because your changes would disappear the next time the subscriber was updated. However, many programs do let you adorn a subscriber in ways that the program can reapply to a new edition. For example, you may be able to resize or crop an entire subscriber as you would resize or crop a graphic in a word processing document. You may be able to change all the text in a subscriber to a different font, style, or size. Some programs provide a Maintain Adornment option in the Subscriber Options dialog box (Figure 9-10). Turning on this option allows you to maintain any formatting applied to the entire subscriber when the edition is updated.

In programs such as MacWrite Pro that do let you modify a subscriber, you should suspend or cancel automatic edition updating before you begin editing a subscriber, as explained later in "Updating Editions." This preserves your changes until you update the subscriber manually by clicking the Get Edition Now button in the Subscriber Options dialog box. If you don't turn off automatic updating for a subscriber, the program may warn you and do it for you, but not all programs do.

Opening a subscriber's publisher

Generally you make changes to a subscriber by opening its publisher and changing the publisher. To help you open a publisher, the Subscriber Options dialog box includes an Open Publisher button. Clicking it opens

Figure 9-11
An Edition window

the document that contains the subscriber's publisher (and the program that created the publisher's document, if it's not already open), scrolls the publisher into view, and selects the publisher. Some programs also allow you to open a publisher by pressing the Option key while double-clicking a subscriber.

You can also open a publisher by opening its edition icon in the Finder. When you do, an Edition window appears (Figure 9-11). The window contains a miniature view of the publisher and an Open Publisher button. Clicking it opens the publisher's original document, just like the Open Publisher button in the Subscriber Options dialog box.

You can always see the last edition you used by opening the Preferences folder in the System folder. Opening the alias named Last Edition Used gets you the edition window of the last edition that was saved.

Making changes to a publisher

You can modify a publisher within a document just like any other part of a document. You can add material to a publisher or delete material from it, making the publisher get larger or smaller. You can cut an entire publisher and paste it at a different place in the document. However, it's not a good idea to copy-and-paste or otherwise duplicate a publisher. If you do, all duplicates of the publisher share one edition, making the contents of subscribers to that edition seem unpredictable. (The edition reflects the contents of the most recently updated duplicate publisher.)

Each time you save a document containing a revised publisher, the application program automatically updates the publisher's edition. You can turn off automatic updating and only update manually, as described in the next section.

Updating editions

The Subscriber and Publisher Options dialog boxes allow you to control whether edition updates are sent or received automatically or manually. Various programs label these dialog box options differently. You can set update options individually for each publisher and subscriber. For example, you may want one subscriber in a document, such as a logo, to be updated on request and another subscriber, such as daily sales figures, updated automatically.

A publisher's Publisher Options dialog box controls when new editions of the publisher are sent. With the standard setting, On Save, the program automatically sends a new edition the next time you save the document (if you have modified the publisher). Setting the Manually option suspends sending new editions of the publisher until you click the Send Edition Now button in the Publishers Options dialog box.

The subscriber can receive new editions automatically or manually. If the Automatically option is set in the subscriber's Subscriber Options dialog box, the subscriber gets updated as soon as the program receives a new edition. You can suspend automatic subscriber updating by setting the Manually option in the subscriber's Subscriber Options dialog box. To get a manual update, you click the Get Edition Now button in the Subscriber Options dialog box.

You can cancel a publisher or subscriber by clicking the Cancel Subscriber or Cancel Publisher button in its Publisher or Subscriber Options dialog box. Canceling a publisher or subscriber permanently breaks the link between the publisher and the subscriber.

Some programs allow you to temporarily suspend all updating activity by providing a Stop All Editions command in the Edit menu. When this command is on, a check mark appears next to it in the menu and the program blocks all publishers from sending new editions and all subscribers from receiving new editions. Turning off the command removes the check mark from the menu and updates with any new editions all subscribers that are set to receive new editions automatically. The Stop All Editions command only affects publishers and subscribers in documents created by the program in which you use the command.

Summary

- The Create Publisher command saves a live copy of material you have selected to an edition file, and the Subscribe To command puts a copy of an edition into the document you're currently working on.
- You can publish editions to your shared folders and disks and subscribe to editions from folders and disks you're sharing from other computers on your network.
- In most programs, you can recognize publishers and subscribers by their gray borders.
- Although you can't usually change a subscriber directly, you can usually adorn it. To change the content of a subscriber, you open its publisher by clicking the Open Publisher button in the Subscriber Options dialog or the Edition window.
- The Publisher Options and Subscriber Options dialog boxes let you control whether an individual publisher or subscriber is updated automatically or manually.
- Publishing and subscribing methods differ somewhat from one program to the next.

Chapter 10

Advanced Capabilities

In This Chapter

- What program linking means to you: compound documents, mix 'n' match program modules, and system-wide user scripting.
- A look at a real-world example of program linking using Claris's MacProject II v2.5 and Resolve.
- Accessing database management systems using one menu command in some programs.
- Using query documents to access data from a database management system.

You upgrade to System 7 not only for the new capabilities it gives your Macintosh immediately, but also for its possibilities. Two of System 7's most advanced capabilities, program linking and data access, pave the way for future improvements in Macintosh programs.

Program linking

Underlying the live copy-paste technology described in the previous chapter is a language and basic vocabulary that lets your documents share information dynamically. This same language and additional vocabulary also allows programs to link with other programs and share services.

For example, a word processing program could get spell-checking services from a second program, thesaurus services from a third program, outlining services from a fourth, indexing services from a fifth, and so on. You could combine program modules a la carte instead of settling for a packaged TV dinner. You might pick an elaborate outlining module, a thesaurus, and no drawing module whereas the next person might want an elaborate drawing module, no thesaurus, and basic outlining. Not only would you get a word processor you really like, you could also use the same spelling checker (and the same spelling dictionary) with other programs.

Before System 7, program linking like this was pure speculation. When System 7 first became available, a few Macintosh programs took advantage of program linking. Claris's project management software, MacProject II v2.5, for example, has Claris's spreadsheet software, Resolve, prepare graphs and charts. As time goes by, more and more programs will know how to work together.

Understanding program linking

People have worked together for thousands of years but personal computer programs are just beginning to. Why? People have been talking (or otherwise communicating) but programs have not — at least not aside from the limited communications that the Copy and Paste commands provide. The technology behind programs working together, which Apple calls inter-application communication (IAC), was not implemented system-wide before System 7. The publish and subscribe capabilities described in Chapter 9 together with the Copy and Paste commands are one part of IAC. The other part of IAC enables programs to send messages to one another.

System 7's language for IAC, called AppleEvents, has a basic vocabulary of four messages, which Table 10-1 defines. Finder 7 uses these basic AppleEvents messages to open programs, open documents, print documents, and quit programs. When you double-click a program icon, the Finder sends the program an Open Application message. When you double-click a document, the Finder sends the program that created the document an Open Application message and an Open Documents message with the name of the document you double-clicked. When you select one or more documents and choose Print from the Finder's menu, the Finder sends the document an Open Application message, a Print Documents message with the names of the documents you selected, and a Quit Application message. When you choose the Shut Down or Restart commands, the Finder sends a Quit Application message to each open program. For programs that don't understand the basic AppleEvents, the Finder uses its traditional means of opening, printing, and quitting.

Beyond the four basic AppleEvents messages, Apple recommends that application programs understand another two dozen messages. They encompass actions and objects almost all programs have in common, such as close, save, undo, redo, cut, copy, and paste. Programs with related capabilities recognize additional sets of AppleEvents messages. For example, word processors understand messages about text manipulation and drawing programs understand messages about graphics manipulation.

Table 10-1: Basic AppleEvents messages

Message	Meaning
Open Application	Open the selected program
Open Documents	Open the selected documents
Print Documents	Print the selected documents without displaying them
Quit Application	Same as when you choose Quit from the program's File menu

Program developers can also define personal messages that only their own programs know.

System 7 provides the means of communicating AppleEvents messages between programs. The programs can be on the same computer or on different computers connected to the same network. A program doesn't have to be open or even accessible to receive its messages. System 7 stores messages and forwards them when the program becomes available.

To understand how the parts of IAC's program linking capabilities relate, think of them as a telephone system. System 7 software furnishes a telephone and answering machine for each program and the wires between them. For messages sent across a network, System 7 uses the built-in AppleTalk networking software and LocalTalk or other networking connectors and cables (as described in the first two sections of Chapter 8). Programs talk on the telephones and leave each other messages, speaking the AppleEvents language. Some programs have a basic four-"word" vocabulary and others understand more.

Using program linking

Program linking works automatically on your own Macintosh when you use programs that understand AppleEvents messages. The methods for linking with a program on someone else's Macintosh vary from one program to the next. You'll have to consult your program manual for detailed information.

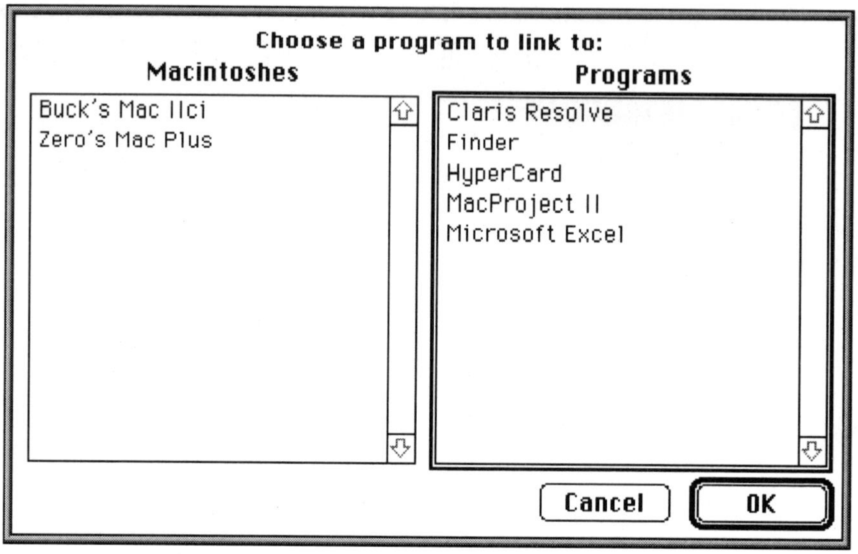

Figure 10-1
Computers and programs available for linking

In most cases you link with a remote program by choosing a menu item to display a dialog box that lists the computers with programs available for linking on your network (Figure 10-1). If your network has zones, the dialog box also lists them; you select the zone in which the Macintosh whose program you want to link to is located. After you select the computer whose program you want to link to, the dialog box displays a list of the programs available for sharing on that computer. You select the one you want and click the OK button.

Before others on your network can link to your programs, you must start, or activate, program linking on your Macintosh. Do that by clicking the Start button in the Program Linking section of the Sharing Setup control panel (Figure 10-2).

Soon after you click the Start button it changes to a Stop button. Pressing the Stop button prevents all other computers on your network from linking to your programs.

After starting program linking on your Macintosh, you must designate which application programs you want to share. To allow others to link to one of your programs, select the program and choose Sharing from the

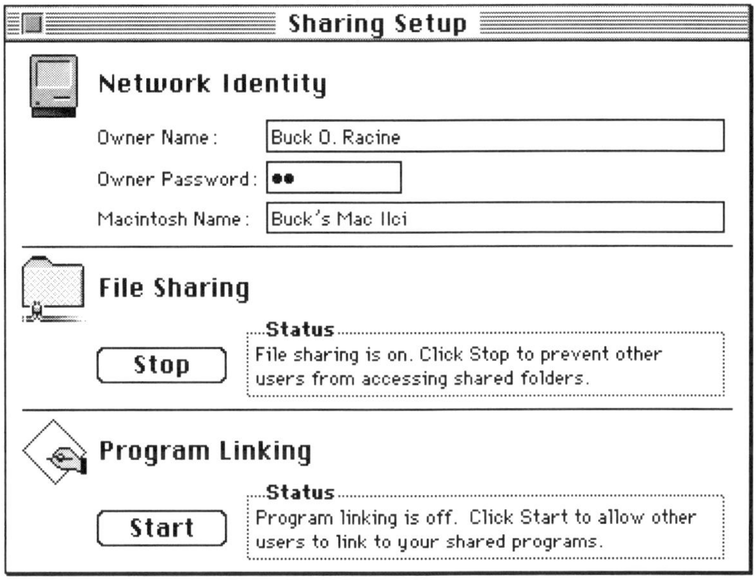

Figure 10-2
Starting program linking

Finder's File menu. The Finder displays a program linking info window (Figure 10-3). Turn on the "Allow remote program linking" option and close the window. Turning off that option prevents others from linking to the program. If the option is dim, then the program is open; you must quit a program before changing its program linking option.

Figure 10-3
A program linking info window

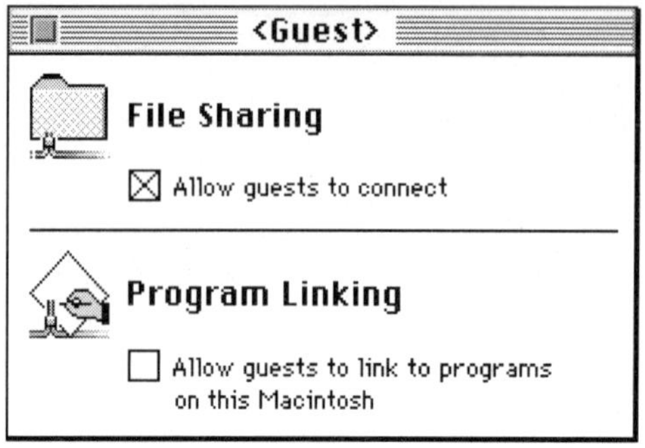

Figure 10-4
A Guest's access privileges

You also control who on your network can share your programs. You do this with the Users & Groups control panel.

To allow everyone on your network access to your programs, open the Guest icon in the Users & Groups control panel to display the Guest privileges window (Figure 10-4) and turn on the "Allow guests to link to programs on this Macintosh" option. Turning off that option prevents unwelcome users from sharing your programs.

If you don't allow guests program linking privileges, you need to designate which registered users in your Users & Groups control panel can share your programs. To allow a registered user to link his or her programs to yours, open that user's icon in your Users & Groups control panel to display the user's access privileges window (Figure 10-5). In that window turn on the "Allow user to link to programs on this Macintosh" option. (For information on registering users, see "Registered users" in Chapter 8.)

You can block any registered user from linking to your programs by turning off that user's "Allow user to link to programs on this Macintosh" option.

Program linking example

Two of the first programs to use System 7's program linking capabilities were Claris's MacProject II v2.5 and Resolve. MacProject II keeps lots of tables of project-related information but can't graph the tabular information. Resolve can graph tabular information and Resolve can be controlled

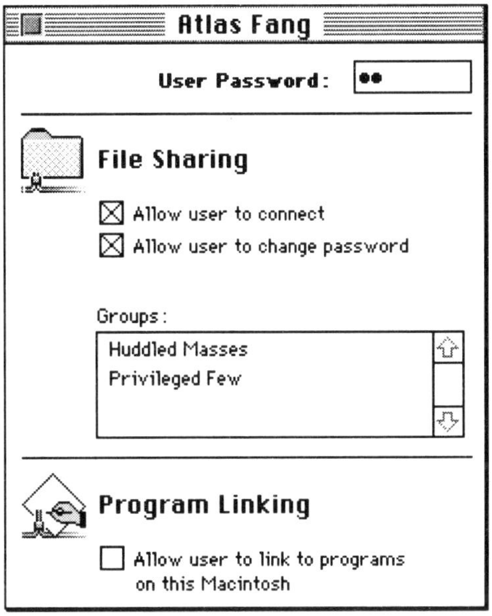

Figure 10-5
A registered user's access privileges

by scripts. Claris decided to write Resolve scripts that prepare graphs and summary tables in response to AppleEvents messages from MacProject II. Here's how it works:

1. Using MacProject II, you build a project schedule in the usual manner (Figure 10-6). As the project proceeds, you update it with actual start dates, completion dates, and costs.

2. Whenever you want a graph or summary table based on the current status of your project, you choose the type of graph or summary you want from the Exchange submenu of MacProject II's File menu (Figure 10-7).

3. MacProject II automatically exports its Cash Flow Table, Project Table, Task Cost Entry Table, Dependency Table, and Resource Table as needed for the item you chose. That is, it saves them on disk in a plain-text format that Resolve can understand.

4. MacProject II sends an AppleEvents message to open Resolve if it's not already open. You see Resolve open on your Macintosh (Figure 10-8).

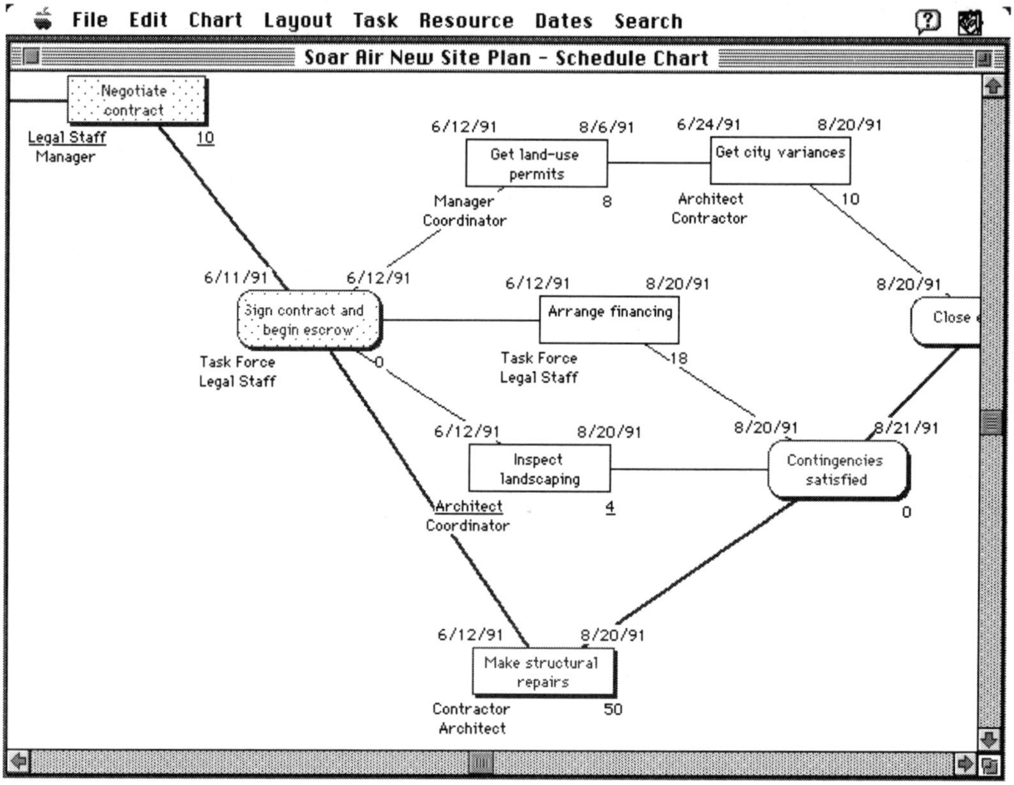

Figure 10-6
A MacProject II project schedule

5. MacProject II sends Resolve a message to open the document containing the script that creates the graph or summary table you requested. Resolve recognizes that the document contains a script and runs the script. You see Resolve constructing the spreadsheet on which the graph is based and then creating a graph (Figure 10-9).

6. The Resolve script asks whether you want to copy the graph to the Clipboard and then close the graph window without saving it. You can answer no if you want to change the graph's appearance. For example, you might want to change a resource allocation bar chart to a pie chart. (You would then use Resolve's Copy command to put a copy of the revised graph on the Clipboard.)

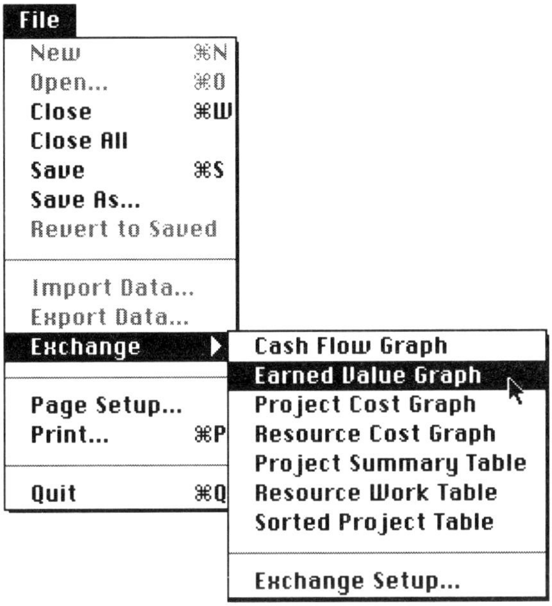

Figure 10-7
Choosing a MacProject II graph or summary table

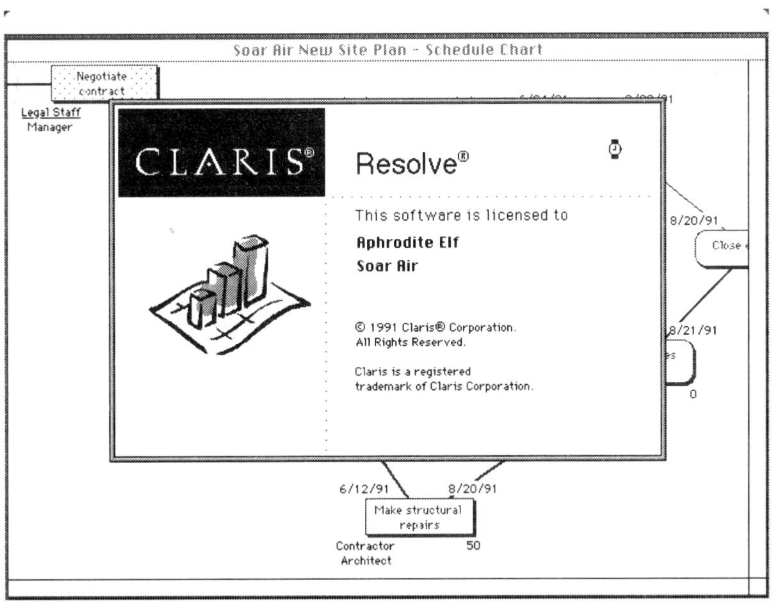

Figure 10-8
MacProject II opens Resolve

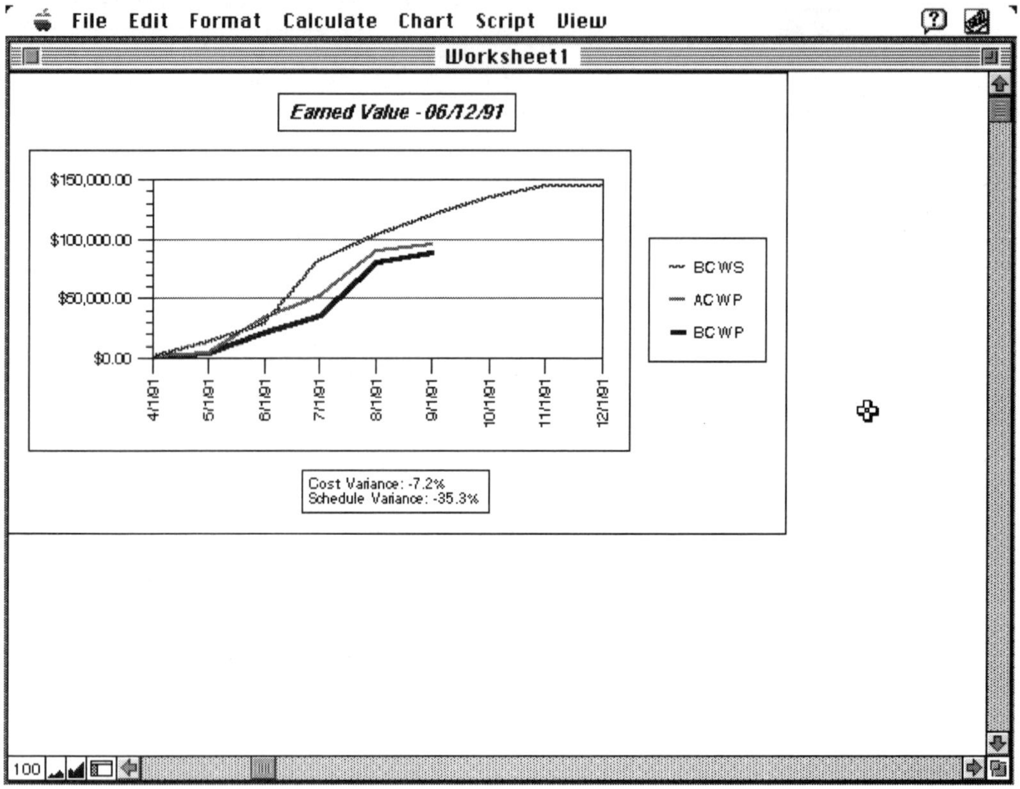

Figure 10-9
A Resolve script constructs a graph

7. You make MacProject II the active program by clicking one of its windows or by choosing it from the Application menu. Then you open the MacProject II window where you want to put the Resolve graph and choose Paste from the Edit menu, placing a copy of the graph as a graphic in that window (Figure 10-10). You can drag the pasted graph to a new place in the MacProject II window and you can resize the graph by dragging any of its handles.

You can add more items to MacProject II's Exchange menu by specifying the names and folder locations of additional Resolve scripts and for each script you add, specifying which MacProject II tables you want exported.

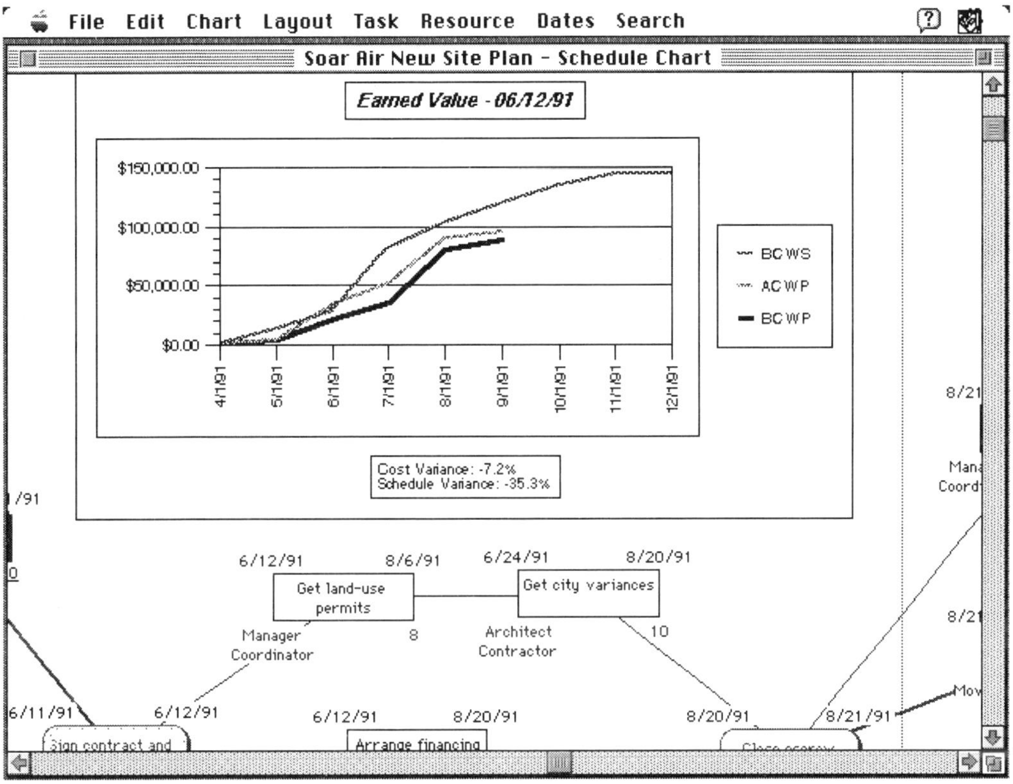

Figure 10-10
A Resolve graph in MacProject II's schedule window

The promise of AppleEvents

MacProject II's use of Resolve's graphing capabilities are just a beginning. When MacProject gets publish and subscribe capabilities, it will be able to have Resolve not only create graphs but keep them up-to-date as you make changes to a project in MacProject. The result is called a compound document. The MacProject document contains a type of information that it can't directly manipulate (a graph), but the foreign information is linked to its natural environment (Resolve).

Resolve and many other programs can be controlled by scripts you write. Program linking makes scripting like this possible system-wide. HyperCard, for example, can use the scripting language in HyperCard version 2.1 (distributed with System 7) to send AppleEvents messages to saavy programs such as Resolve. Imagine being able to write a script that causes your Macintosh to do with one mouse click (or at preset times) a routine procedure that otherwise involves much tedious manual work with many programs. A script can be your agent, knowing how to complete a task and report back to you when it finishes.

Mix 'n' match programs, compound documents on a large scale, and system-wide user scripting are all possibilities thanks to System 7's program linking capabilities. You'll realize the benefits of the possibilities when a scripting language becomes available and the programs you use all understand AppleEvents messages.

Data access

Program linking and file sharing give you access to Macintosh programs and to documents that your programs can open on other computers in your local network. Like many people, you may also need access to data kept in an external database management system (DBMS), whose files your programs can't open. Typically the DBMS is a corporate database on a large computer that is not part of your local network. System 7's data access management capabilities let you access an external database with one simple menu command. The same command can also provide simplified access to a database on your own Macintosh or on another computer on your local network. Macintosh program developers can easily add that command to their software products.

Using data access

You get data from a database management system by choosing a menu command (Figure 10-11). Apple suggests the data access command be named Open Query and be located in the File menu, but not all programs follow this suggestion. In Microsoft Excel, for example, you open the Data Access Macro, which adds four new commands to the Data menu and one to the Options menu. Then you choose Query Assistant from the Data menu and click the Open button. You'll have to consult your program manual to see if and how the program offers data access.

The Open Query command (or its equivalent) displays a directory dialog box in which you open a document that specifies what data you want from the database management system (Figure 10-12). The document contains a predefined sequence of commands, called a query, in a language the database management system understands. But you don't type the commands or even see them.

Figure 10-11
Choosing the data access command

When you open a query document, you see a dialog box that describes the data you'll get if you click the button that starts the query (Figure 10-13). The dialog box may also contain buttons, checkboxes, and text entry boxes that you use to narrow the scope of the query. If you opened

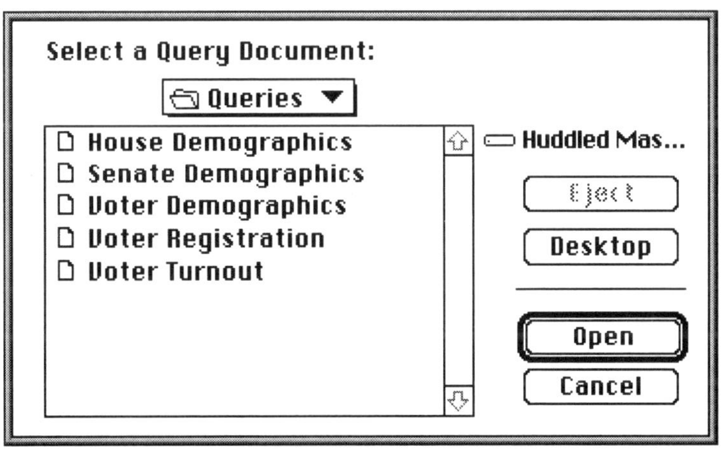

Figure 10-12
Opening a query document

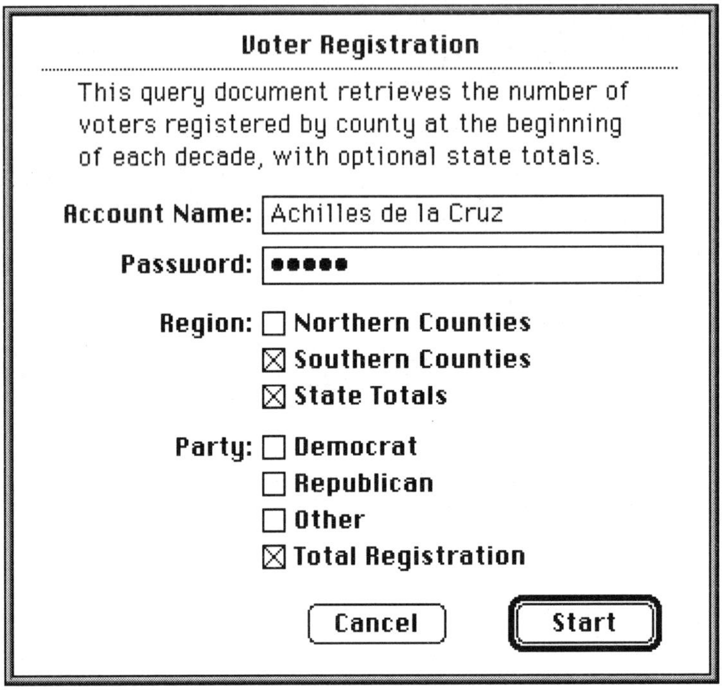

Figure 10-13
Specifying query document options

a query document to get voter registration data, for example, you might have to specify the political parties and counties for which you wanted data.

After you click the button that starts the query, System 7 sends the query to the database management system and periodically checks for a response. When the database management system supplies the requested data, System 7 puts it into a table. Each column of the table can be a different type of data, such as true/false, integer number, decimal number, date, time, money value, or general text. The program in which you opened the query document can take the table as is or can have System 7 convert it to plain text. Then the program either displays the table for you or puts it on the Clipboard so you can paste it into your document (Figure 10-14).

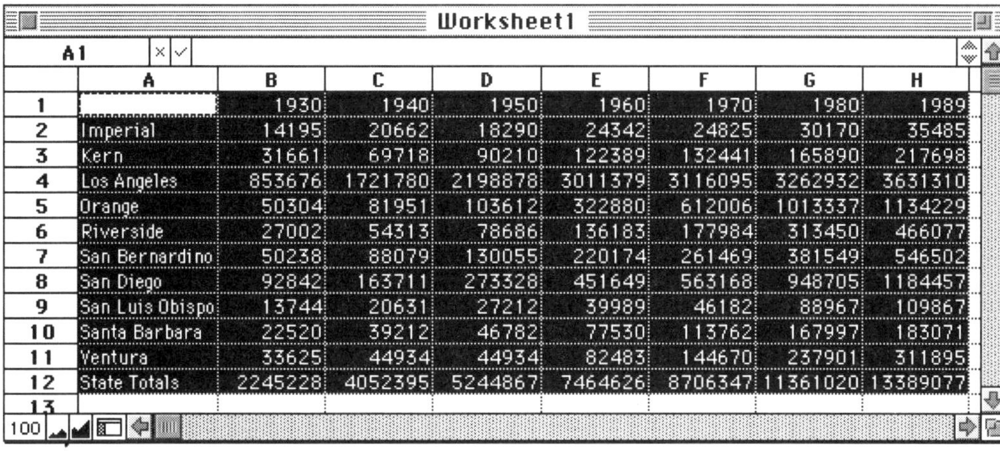

Worksheet1

	A	B	C	D	E	F	G	H
1		1930	1940	1950	1960	1970	1980	1989
2	Imperial	14195	20662	18290	24342	24825	30170	35485
3	Kern	31661	69718	90210	122389	132441	165890	217698
4	Los Angeles	853676	1721780	2198878	3011379	3116095	3262932	3631310
5	Orange	50304	81951	103612	322880	612006	1013337	1134229
6	Riverside	27002	54313	78686	136183	177984	313450	466077
7	San Bernardino	50238	88079	130055	220174	261469	381549	546502
8	San Diego	92842	163711	273328	451649	563168	948705	1184457
9	San Luis Obispo	13744	20631	27212	39989	46182	88967	109867
10	Santa Barbara	22520	39212	46782	77530	113762	167997	183071
11	Ventura	33625	44934	44934	82483	144670	237901	311895
12	State Totals	2245228	4052395	5244867	7464626	8706347	11361020	13389077

Figure 10-14
Retrieved data pasted into a spreadsheet

About query documents

Query documents work with the most popular database management systems, host computers, and networks. These include the Informix, Ingres, Rdb, Oracle, and Sybase database management systems on DEC VAX/VMS computers connected to your Macintosh via an Async or ADSP (AppleTalk Data Stream Protocol) network. Query documents also work with a DB2 database on an IBM MVS/TSO mainframe computer and an SQL/DS database on an IBM VM/CMS mainframe computer. Connecting your Macintosh to an IBM mainframe computer requires an internal network adapter card or an external network adapter.

Query documents send queries in one command language, called Data Access Language (DAL), regardless of the type of host computer, brand of database management system, or type of network. A DAL server program must be installed on the host computer to translate DAL commands to the language the particular database management system understands. Your Macintosh must have the DAL system extension in its Extensions folder, which is inside the System Folder.

UNDOCUMENTED

A single query document works with any program that has an Open Query command (or equivalent). Most people use predefined query documents and do not create their own. The person who creates a query document must know the database structure and usually needs a special program and an understanding of the database access language.

All these installation and setup details sound complicated but they're usually handled by a system administrator or MIS support person in your company. To get data, you just choose a menu command, select a query document, fill in its dialog box, wait, and paste.

Summary

- Program linking — which paves the way for modular programs, compound documents, and system-wide user scripting — relies on System 7's IAC technology.
- Programs link with each other and share services by sending messages using System 7's IAC language, AppleEvents. Some programs understand only the four basic AppleEvents messages but other programs understand two dozen or more.
- You control whether programs from other computers on your network can link to your programs using the Sharing Setup control panel, the Users & Groups control panel, and the Finder's Sharing command.
- Some programs let you access data from a database management system by opening a query document and selecting a few options in its dialog box. The query document contains a hidden sequence of database-access commands, which someone familiar with the database management system has prepared in advance.

Chapter 11
Tips and Secrets

In This Chapter

- Finder tips: icons, aliases, windows, folders, and the Trash.
- Directory dialog box, Apple menu, and Application menu shortcuts.
- Desk accessory, control panel, and file sharing tips.
- Memory use, performance, and troubleshooting tips.

Scattered throughout the first ten chapters of this book are scores of tips and secret methods for getting more out of System 7. For your convenience, this chapter contains a digest of the most useful six dozen.

Icons

In this section, you'll find ideas for saving time and effort while editing icon names, making and using aliases on the desktop, getting icons to look the way you want, and manipulating font icons.

Spotting a name selected for editing

For a visual cue that you have selected the name of an icon on a color or grayscale monitor, use the Colors control panel to set the text highlight color to something other than black and white. Then you know a name highlighted in color (or gray) is ready for editing, whereas a name highlighted in black and white is not (Figure 11-1).

Edit, don't open

If you have trouble editing icon names without opening the item, try setting a briefer Double-Click Speed with the Mouse control panel (Figure 11-2). You must wait the duration of a double-click interval — about 1.9 second, 1.3 second, or 0.9 second, as set in the Mouse control panel — after selecting an icon name before selecting an insertion point, a word, or a range of text. If you click again too soon, the Finder thinks you're double-clicking the icon and opens it.

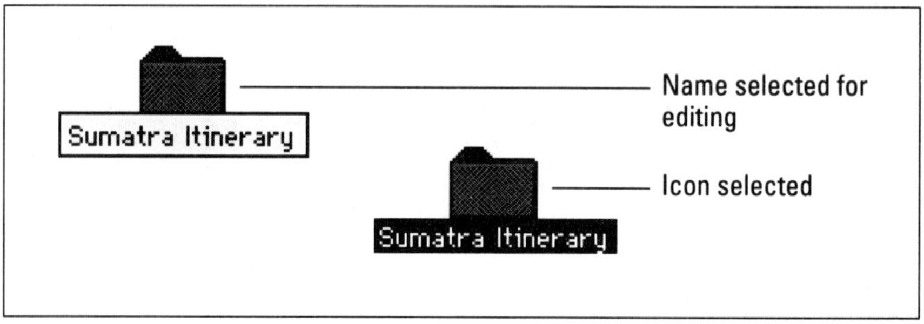

Figure 11-1
Ready for editing, or not

You don't have to wait if you move the insertion point by pressing the arrow keys. Pressing Up Arrow moves the insertion point to the beginning of the name, Down Arrow moves it to the end, Left Arrow moves it left, and Right arrow moves it right.

Undoing accidental name change

If you rename an icon by mistake, choose Undo from the Edit menu or press Command-Z to restore the original name. Another way to restore the icon's original name is to press the Backspace or Delete key until the name is empty, and then press Return or click outside the icon.

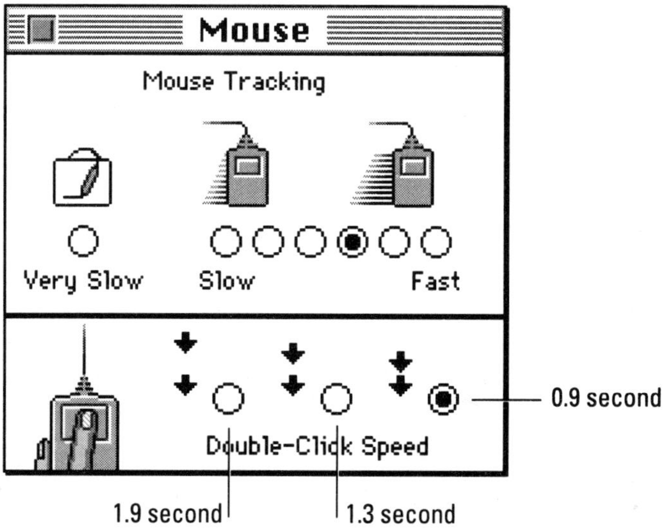

Figure 11-2
Wait this long before clicking again

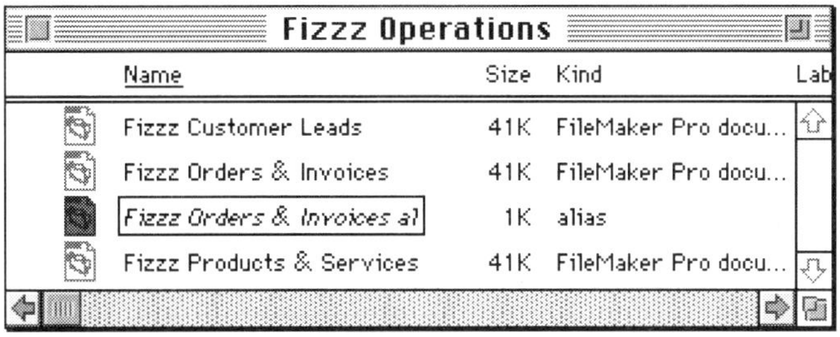

Figure 11-3
A long alias name

Copy/Paste icon names

While editing a name, you can use the Undo, Cut, Copy, Paste, and Select All commands in the Edit menu. You cannot undo your changes to a name after you finish editing it, only while it is still selected for editing. You can also copy the entire name of any item by selecting its icon (or its whole name) and using the Copy command (Paste menu). This capability comes in handy when you're copying a disk and want to name the copy the same as the original.

The name of a locked item can't be changed. (Unlock an item with the Get Info command, or if it's a disk, by sliding its locking tab.) However, you can copy its entire name as just described.

Removing "alias"

The name the Finder constructs for an alias can be so long you can't see it all in a list view (Figure 11-3). If you want to remove the word "alias" from the end, select the icon name for editing, press the Right Arrow or Down Arrow key to move the insertion point to the end of the name, and press Delete six times.

You can also drag the alias to the desktop or switch the view to By Icon or by Small Icon and edit the name in icon view. In icon view you can click the name once to select it for editing, pause briefly, double-click the last word of the name, and press the Delete key twice. If you double-click too quickly after selecting the name, the Finder opens the alias instead of selecting the last word of the name.

Figure 11-4
After opening an alias of an item on a floppy disk

Desktop aliases

Rather than drag frequently used programs, control panels, documents, and folders themselves into the desktop, make aliases of them and put the aliases on the desktop. You get quick access to the original items through their desktop aliases. Also, you can open several related items at the same time, even if the original items happen to be in different folders or on different disks, by opening aliases on the desktop. If your desktop becomes too cluttered with aliases, you can put related aliases together in a desktop folder.

Express access to CD ROM

Cut through the drudgery of wading through folders on a CD ROM by making aliases of items inside the CD ROM folders. Because CD ROMs are permanently locked, you must put the aliases on your hard disk (or a floppy disk). Opening an alias makes a beeline to the original item on the CD ROM.

Cataloging items on floppy disks

You can use aliases to keep track of and quickly open items on floppy disks — even floppies that aren't inserted in your Macintosh. Make aliases of the items on a floppy disk and copy the aliases to your startup disk. (You can then delete the aliases from the floppy disk.) When you need the item again, the Finder tells you the name of the disk to insert so it can open the alias's original item (Figure 11-4). If you change your mind or can't find the needed disk, click the Cancel button.

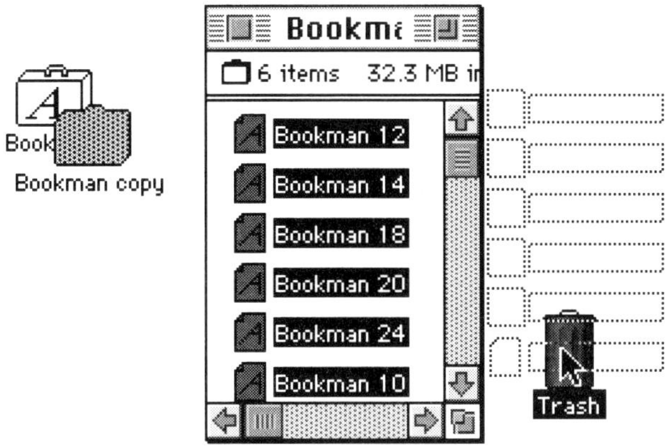

Figure 11-5
A new font suitcase

Making many aliases

To make aliases for several items in the same window at once, select them all and use the Make Alias command. An alias appears for every item you selected. All the new aliases are automatically selected so you can immediately drag them to another place without having to manually select them as a group.

Duplicating fonts

Because you can't rename fonts with the Finder, you can't duplicate them in the same folder. To duplicate a font, press Option and drag it to another folder or to the desktop. (Dragging to another disk automatically makes a copy of the font on the target disk.)

Making a font suitcase

You can create a new font suitcase file with System 7 by duplicating an existing font suitcase file, opening the duplicate, and dragging its contents to the Trash (Figure 11-5).

Stationery workaround

You can work around the Finder asking you to name and save a new document every time you open a particular stationery pad. Instead, make it an ordinary document, but lock it using the Finder's Get Info command. You might want to use this method with templates for printing single

Figure 11-6
Ready to update icons

envelopes and mailing labels, for example. Then you could open the locked template, type or paste the recipient's address, print, and close without saving.

Icon updating

When you install an updated program that includes redesigned icons on your disk, you will usually have to rebuild the disk's desktop to see the new icons for that program and its documents. To rebuild the desktop of any disk whose icon normally appears on the desktop after startup, press the Command and Option keys while starting your Macintosh. For each disk in turn, the Finder asks whether you want the disk's desktop rebuilt (Figure 11-6). To rebuild the desktop of a floppy disk or other removable disk whose icon is not on the desktop, press Command-Option while inserting the disk.

Revert to standard icon

You can revert to an item's standard icon after having replaced the icon with custom graphics. Just select the item, choose Get Info from the Finder's File menu, select the icon in the Get Info window, and choose Clear or Cut from the Edit menu.

Folders and windows

The tips in this section involve Finder windows and folders.

Finder power

The Finder has a great deal of hidden power, which you tap by pressing the Command and Option keys at the opportune moment. In addition, much of what you can do with the mouse you can also do with the keyboard alone. Tables 3-3, 3-4, 3-5, and 3-6 list power methods and keyboard equivalents for selecting items in windows or on the desktop; opening and closing items; expanding and collapsing outlines of folders in list views; and more. For the most part, these tables do not list keyboard equivalents for menu commands because you can review them on screen by pulling down the menus.

Special folder replacement

Should you happen to discard one of the special folders inside the System Folder, you can make a replacement using the Finder's New Folder command (File menu). After creating a new folder, change its name to be the same as the special folder you want: Apple Menu Items, Control Panels, Extensions, Preferences, or Startup Items. Wait a few seconds and you'll see its icon get the distinctive look of the special folder you're creating.

Special folder mistakes

The Finder sometimes makes mistakes when it puts items in the System Folder's special folders for you. It may put some items in the correct places and incorrectly leave others in the System Folder itself. For example, it may put a control panel in the Control Panels folder but leave that control panel's auxiliary folder in the System Folder. That control panel won't work right because it expects to find its auxiliary folder in the same folder as it is in. You must open the System Folder and drag the auxiliary folder to the Control Panels folder yourself.

Removing from the System Folder

Before you can remove an item from the System Folder, you must know which inner folder it is in. If you're not sure, use the Finder's Find command to locate the item (see "Fast file finding" in Chapter 3). Be sure to put items you drag from the special folders within the System Folder onto the desktop or into an ordinary folder. Many items you drag out of special folders are still effective if you merely drag them to the System Folder window.

Easy startup items

If you want an item opened at startup time, put an alias of it in the Startup Items folder. Don't put original items there, because returning them to their original locations when you no longer want them opened at startup time can be a drag. When you're done with an alias, you can just drag it to the Trash.

Seeing desktop items

If the windows of open programs obscure desktop icons, you can hide those windows by choosing Hide Others from the Application menu while the Finder is active. If Finder windows cover desktop icons, you can close all those windows at once by pressing Option while clicking the close box of any Finder window.

Narrow Finder windows

You can reduce the width of Finder windows to show just the item names in list views without laboriously dragging the size boxes of each window. Use the Views control panel to temporarily set all List View options off. Then shrink each window to fit the new format by clicking its zoom box. After shrinking all windows, you can turn on List View options in the Views control panel. You can scroll the contents of a narrow window to see columns that are out of view.

Viewing by size

Items in Finder windows viewed by size may be out of order right after you turn on the Calculate Folder Sizes option in the Views control panel. The Finder takes a while to calculate the sizes, and in the meantime it has already displayed the window contents. You can force the Finder to re-sort a window's contents according to size by clicking another column heading (such as Name) and then clicking the Size column heading again.

Find in next window

Sometimes the Finder's Find Next command gets you bogged down in a window that contains many matches to what you specified in the Find command, but you know the window doesn't contain the item you want. To cancel searching in the active window and skip to the next folder that contains a match, close the window by clicking the close box or pressing Command-W.

Drag to scroll

You can scroll a window in Finder 7 without using the scroll bars. Simply place the pointer in the window, press the mouse button, and drag toward the area you want to come into view. Drag the pointer up, down, left, or right past the window's active area and scrolling begins. Dragging past a window corner scrolls diagonally. To scroll slowly, drag just to the window's edge (and continue pressing the mouse button). Increase scrolling speed by dragging beyond the window's edge.

Trash

This section has tips on throwing stuff away and retrieving it from the Trash afterwards.

Skip the Trash warning

To skip the standard Trash warning the next time you empty the Trash, press the Option key while choosing the Empty Trash command. You can also reverse the Trash Warning setting by selecting the Trash, choosing Get Info and reversing the setting of the "Skip Trash Warnings" option. You can't use these techniques to get rid of locked items in the Trash, however.

Discarding locked items

Before you can remove a locked item that you have dragged to the Trash, you must use the Finder's Get Info command to unlock the item. If you use the Empty Trash command while the Trash contains locked items, the Finder reminds you it can't dispose of those items.

Trash retrieval

To put items currently in the Trash back where they came from, open the Trash, select the items, and choose Put Away from the Finder's File menu. The Finder returns each selected item to its previous folder, though not necessarily to the same place in the folder window.

Discarding items from one disk

To remove items from only one disk, you must open the Trash and drag the items from other disks to the desktop or to another folder. Then use the Empty Trash command.

Rescued items

Sometimes the Trash contains a folder named Rescued Items. It usually contains formerly invisible temporary files found when you started up your Macintosh. The Rescued Items folder may appear after a system crash and you may be able to recreate your work up to the time of the system crash from the contents of the Rescued Items folder.

Directory dialog boxes

You can save time and effort in the directory dialog boxes you get with the Open, Save As, and other disk-related commands by using the tips in this section.

Directory dialog keystrokes

The System 7 directory dialog boxes recognize more keyboard equivalents than older versions. Table 2-1 has the details.

Find an alias's original item

You can quickly go to an alias's original item in a directory dialog box by pressing the Option key while opening the alias (by double-clicking it, for example). Alias names appear in italics in directory dialog boxes, just as they do in Finder windows.

Folder switching

If you find yourself frequently going back and forth between two folders, just put an alias of each folder in the other. Whichever folder you are in, you can go to the other in one step.

Aliases for favorite folders

Putting aliases of your favorite folders on the desktop or inside disk windows allows you to quickly open a favorite folder from a directory dialog box. Instead of working your way down through one branch of your folder structure and then working your way up another branch to the folder you want, you zip to the desktop level or the disk level and there open the alias of the folder you want. It's as if you could jump from one branch of a tree to the root level and then jump to a spot on another branch without crawling up the trunk and along the other branch.

You can quickly get to aliases of favorite folders on the desktop by clicking the Desktop button. Get to aliases at the disk window level by choosing the disk from the directory dialog's pop-up menu.

Copy and Paste

You can copy-and-paste a document's name from the document to a Save or Save As dialog box (or vice versa). If the Cut, Copy, and Paste commands are not available from the Edit menu, you can use their keyboard equivalents, Command-X, Command-C, and Command-V. When pasting, only the first 31 characters are used; any additional are omitted.

Double-click sidestep

As usual you can open an item in the directory window by double-clicking it. If you double-click the wrong item and realize it before you release the mouse button, continue pressing and drag the pointer to the item you want to open. When you release the mouse button, the currently selected item opens.

Double-click cancel

To cancel a double click in a System 7 directory dialog box, hold down the mouse button on the second click and drag the pointer outside the dialog box before releasing the mouse button.

Desk accessories

You'll find ideas for getting more from the standard desk accessories that come with System 7 in this section.

Puzzle pictures

Puzzle 7.0 has two games, one with numbered tiles and another with a picture of the Apple logo. Choose Clear from the Edit menu to switch between them. You can replace the picture of the Apple logo. Just copy a picture in another program, switch to the Puzzle, and paste.

Scripted calculator

You can copy the text of a calculation — for example, 69.95+26.98+14.99*.0725 — and paste it into the standard Calculator desk accessory. Be sure to use the asterisk (*) symbol for multiplication and the slash (/) symbol for division.

Printed key caps

You might like to print the Key Caps desk accessory as a handy reference, but it has no Print command. To work around this, take a picture of the screen and print that as follows. Open Key Caps, choose the font you want it to show, and press any modifier keys (Shift, Option, Control, or Command) you want in effect. Move the pointer to an empty area of the menu bar, hold down the mouse button, temporarily release the modifier keys, press Command-Shift-3, again press the modifier keys you released temporarily, and finally release the mouse button. Your gyrations should be rewarded by the sound of a camera shutter as the system snaps a picture of the screen. Open your startup disk and look for a document named Picture 1. Print this document using TeachText or any graphics program. Cut out the Key Caps window with scissors after printing or crop it out with a graphics program before printing. If you take additional snapshots, they will be numbered sequentially.

Alternate scrapbooks

After extensive use, your Scrapbook may become cluttered with old clippings. If you can't bear to throw them out forever, make a copy of the

Scrapbook File in your System Folder (use the Finder's Duplicate command) before you start weeding. Later you can use the old copy you made by dragging the current Scrapbook File out of the System Folder, dragging the old copy in, and changing its name to Scrapbook File.

Control panels

This section has tips on using the standard control panels that come with System 7.

Revert to standard gray desktop

After changing the standard gray desktop pattern as described in Chapter 2, you can easily revert to the standard gray colors. Simply open the General Controls control panel and scroll through the available desktop patterns until you see the standard gray pattern. Clicking that pattern in the control panel makes it take over the desktop. Caution: your custom pattern is not saved anywhere.

Revert to standard labels

If you want to reset the Labels control panel to factory standard colors and names, use the settings in Table 3-2.

Easy Access shortcuts

Instead of using the Easy Access control panel to turn Mouse Keys or Sticky Keys on and off, you can use the keyboard. To turn on Mouse Keys, press Command-Shift-Clear. To turn it off press Clear. To turn on Sticky Keys, press the Shift key five times in succession. Turn it off by pressing Shift five times again or by pressing any two modifier keys simultaneously.

Big map

You can enlarge the world map in the Map control panel by pressing the Option key while opening the control panel. To magnify more, press Shift-Option while opening.

Color map

If your Map control panel displays a black-and-white world map on your color or grayscale monitor, you can colorize the map. First look through your Scrapbook for a color version of the world map used in the Map control panel. If you find one, copy it, open the Map control panel, and paste.

If you can't find a color version of the world map, you can colorize the black-and-white version using a color painting program such as SuperPaint, Studio/8, or Photoshop. To begin, open the Map control panel and use the Copy command to put a copy of the map on the Clipboard. Next open a new document in the color painting program and paste the map there. Color it. Then copy the color map, return to the Map control panel, and paste.

Apple and Application menus

Use the tips in this section to get more from the Apple menu and the Application menu.

Hiding windows while switching

To hide the active program's windows as you switch to a particular program, press the Option key while choosing the other program from the Application menu. Or press Option while clicking another program's window. You hide windows and switch to the Finder by pressing Option while clicking the desktop or a Finder icon.

Hide windows to boost performance

With several programs open, you can spend lots of your time waiting while inactive programs redraw portions of their windows as dialog boxes come and go. This delay is particularly protracted when using virtual memory, because the window redrawing may require disk access. Eliminate all the delay by choosing Hide Others from the Application menu. Hidden windows don't require updating.

Apple menu organization

You can make an item appear at the top of the Apple menu by prefixing its name (in the Apple Menu Items folder inside the System Folder) with a blank space. Alternatively, you can prefix the name with an Apple logo or solid diamond ♦ symbol. You do that by setting the Key Caps desk accessory to the Chicago font, typing Control-T for the Apple logo or Control-S for the solid diamond, copying the symbol, and pasting it at the beginning of the item name. These special symbols look like boxes in the Apple Menu Items window because they're not part of the Geneva font, which the Finder uses for text in windows unless you specify another font with the Views control panel. They look right in the Apple menu, which uses the Chicago font.

To make items appear at the bottom of the Apple menu, prefix with a hollow diamond (◊) or a bullet (•). Type Shift-Option-V for the hollow diamond or Option-8 for the bullet.

Fast Apple menu changes

To quickly add or remove items to the Apple menu, list the Apple Menu Items folder on the Apple menu. How? Make an alias of the Apple Menu Items folder and put that alias in that folder.

Too-full Apple menu

If your Apple menu becomes so crowded that it takes too long to find items in it, consider moving the least-used items from the Apple Menu Items folder into other folders within the Apple Menu Items folder.

File sharing

Get more out of System 7's file sharing by using the tips in this section.

Reducing network cabling cost

For a less expensive network, use Farallon's PhoneNet connectors (or equivalent) and ordinary telephone cables instead of Apple's LocalTalk connectors and cables. Not only does PhoneNet cost less, it also allows greater cable lengths than LocalTalk.

Picking a secure password

Pick a password that is easy to remember but difficult for others to guess. For better security mix letters with numbers; try replacing the letters I and O with the numbers 1 and 0.

Allow saving, not trashing

You can allow others to save changes to a file you're sharing but prevent them from throwing the file away. Simply share an alias to the file and put the original item in a folder that isn't shared (or that only you have privileges for making changes). If someone discards the alias, then the original item isn't affected.

Share disks or outer folders

Once you share a folder, System 7 won't let you share the folder or disk that contains it (Figure 11-7). You have to drag the shared folder to another place or unshare it before you can share the outer folder or disk. To avoid this situation, share from the highest level of your disk and folder structure.

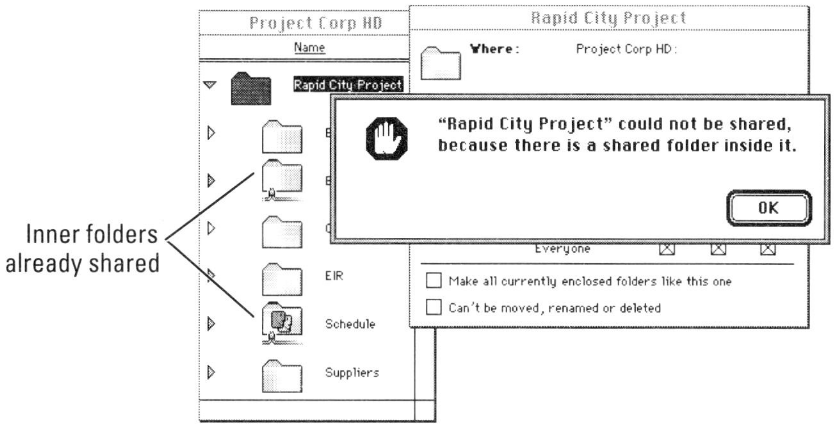

Figure 11-7
Can't share outer folder

Improving file sharing performance

For best performance of your Macintosh, share as few of your folders as possible. The more items others access on your Macintosh, the greater the demands on your Macintosh's performance. Sharing too many folders can slow your system to a crawl. In situations where you need to share numerous files or share folders simultaneously with several users, consider setting up a dedicated Macintosh to act as a centralized file server for the shared information.

Cutting file sharing red tape

Getting access to shared items involves wading through a fair amount of bureaucracy. Aliases cut through the red tape. Here's how: You access a shared disk or folder once using the Chooser desk accessory, as described in Chapter 8. Next you select the shared item or any folder or file in it and choose Make Alias from the File menu. Finally, you copy the alias to your desktop or hard disk. An alias keeps track of its original item even if the original item is on another networked Macintosh.

Once you have made an alias of a shared item, you can access the shared item by opening the alias either from the Finder or from an Open command's directory dialog box. Dragging something to the alias of a shared disk or folder also automatically accesses that shared item. You still must enter a password unless you initially accessed the original item as a guest. If the shared item is not available — for example because the Macintosh where it resides is turned off — a message tells you that.

Office on a disk

Aliases can give you nearly automatic access to your Macintosh's hard disks using a floppy disk in any other Macintosh on the same network. To easily access your disks from another Macintosh open the Sharing Setup control panel and check the File Sharing status. If it is off, click the start button and wait until it is on (the Start button becomes a Stop button).

Next select all your hard disk icons and choose Sharing from the File menu to open a Sharing info window for each disk. In each window turn on the "Share this item and its contents" option and turn off the See Folders, See Files, and Make Changes options for the User/Group and Everyone categories. These settings restrict access to your disks so that only you can make changes or see files or folders. Make an alias of each disk and copy the aliases to a floppy disk.

As long as file sharing is active on your Macintosh, you use that floppy disk to access your hard disk from any Macintosh on your network. You simply insert the disk, open the alias for the disk you want to use, and enter your password when asked. Correctly entering your password allows you access to all applications, folders, and documents on your disk from any remote Macintosh. You don't have to bother with opening the Chooser, selecting AppleShare, selecting your computer, and typing your name as the registered user.

The latest shared document

To make sure others who share your documents have the latest version, share an alias of the original and keep the original in an inaccessible folder. Other users can copy the alias to their disks and use the alias to open the original document. If you later replace the original document with a version having the same name, the aliases people already copied will open the new version. People who share the alias always get the newest version of the original item it represents, even if the original frequently changes.

What people have trashed

Items from your shared disk or folder that someone has dragged to the Trash — but has not yet permanently removed — on another Macintosh don't appear in your Trash. System 7 puts those items in folders whose names begin Trash Can #. You can use the Finder's Find command to search for those names. To see which disk the items come from, select the Trash Can # icon and use the Finder's Get Info command, or open the Trash Can # folder and press Command while clicking the title of its window.

Memory and performance

The tips in this section help you make the most of your computer's memory and increase its performance.

Disk Cache performance boost

If you have a Macintosh IIsi and you set the number of colors or grays for its built-in video to 4 or more, you can improve system performance by setting the Disk Cache to 768K in the Memory control panel. Then the Disk Cache and the built-in video together use up all the memory that's soldered to the main circuit board. This forces the system software and your programs into the part of memory in the four SIMM sockets. Programs may work much slower if they are located in the soldered-on memory along with the built-in video.

The same trick works in a Macintosh IIci with 5MB, 9MB or 17MB of RAM. To get the performance boost, the 256K SIMMs must be installed in the four sockets nearest the disk drive. Realizing a performance increase on a IIci with other RAM capacities isn't feasible because you would have to set the Disk Cache so high as to waste a large amount of memory.

Finder out of memory

Finder 7 is supposed to manage its memory size automatically (by borrowing from the system area of memory as the need arises). If you get a message that there wasn't enough memory to use a control panel or open a window right now, try quitting an application program or desk accessory. If quitting programs doesn't help, you must restart your Macintosh.

If you get out-of-memory messages often, you may want to try increasing the Finder's memory size. However, Finder 7 won't let you set its memory size. You can work around this situation by restarting your Macintosh using a version of system software older than 7.0. Then open the System Folder on your System 7 startup hard disk, select the Finder, and choose Get Info from the File menu (Figure 11-8). In the info window that appears, set the Application Memory Size to 550K or so.

Quitting startup programs

If you have several programs opened during startup, you may later have to quit some of them to free up memory for opening another. Naturally you'll want to quit the programs least important to you. You'll

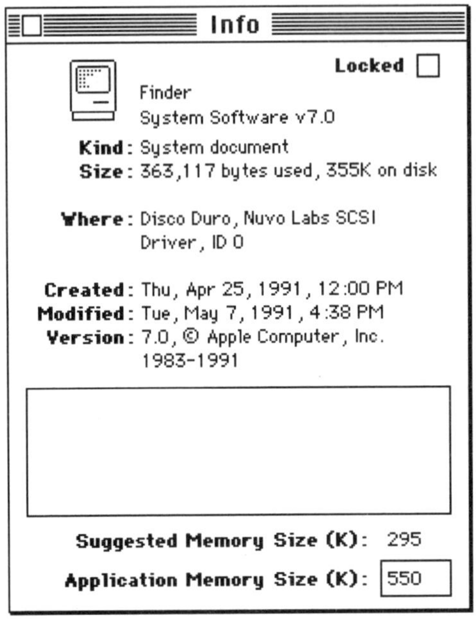

Figure 11-8
Using Finder 6 to change Finder 7's memory size

get maximum benefit from quitting them if they were the last items opened during startup. To make that happen, rename the items in your Startup Items folder so the most important comes first alphabetically, the next-most important comes second, and so on. You can avoid renaming original items by putting aliases in the Startup Items folder.

Paring memory to the bone

If your Macintosh has just the minimum 2MB of RAM required to use System 7, you should pare program memory sizes to the bone. For example, giving your favorite word processing program the full amount of memory available after the system software takes its chunk leaves you no room to use the Chooser to select a printer or share someone's files. (Though you can work around the file sharing limitation by making aliases of the items you most often share, as described in Chapter 8.) Also, there wouldn't be any memory left for background printing.

Fragmented memory

To check for fragmented memory, add up the memory sizes of all the open programs and the system software as listed in the About This

Macintosh window. If you have a monitor connected to the built-in video on a Macintosh IIsi or IIci, add another 320K (or less if you have limited the number of colors to less than 256 as described in "Monitor" in Chapter 5). If the total exceeds the Largest Unused Block amount by more than 50K or so, then the unused memory is fragmented into two or more chunks.

To consolidate fragmented memory, quit all open programs and then open them again. Restarting your Macintosh also fixes fragmentation and may reduce the amount of memory used by system software as well.

You can avoid memory fragmentation by planning the order in which you open and quit programs. First open the programs you're least likely to quit first, and last open the programs you're most likely to quit last. When you need more memory to open another program, quit the most recently opened program. If that doesn't free enough memory, quit the next most recently opened program, and so on. This method frees up a contiguous chunk of memory. Quitting programs helter-skelter leads to memory fragmentation.

Troubleshooting

If you're having trouble with System 7, check out the tips in this section.

Printed font doesn't match display

If you have both fixed-size and TrueType fonts installed, text may not look quite the same on screen as it does on paper. Character shapes may be different. More importantly, spacing of words on the line may not match. When this happens, the system software has used a fixed-size font for display (at 72 dots per inch) and a TrueType font for printing (at a higher resolution). You can fix the problem by removing the fixed-size font from your System file. Some programs may also allow you to set an option that causes fixed-size fonts to be ignored.

Can't put away hard disk icon

The Finder won't let you remove a hard disk icon from the desktop while file sharing is turned on. If you drag the disk icon to the Trash or use the Put Away command, you get a message about items being in use (Figure 11-9). You'll have to stop file sharing using the Sharing Setup control panel, put away the disk, and then start file sharing again.

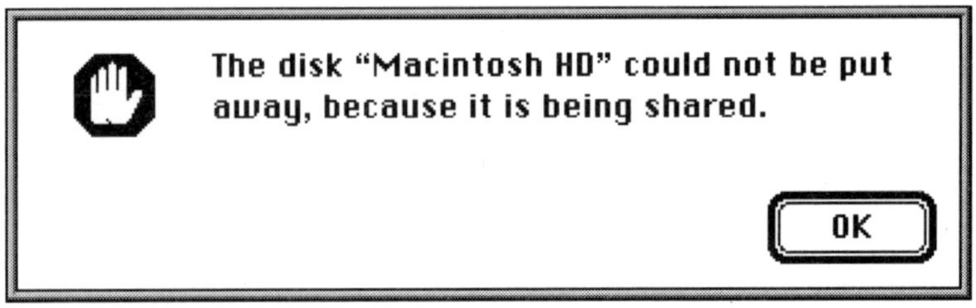

Figure 11-9
Can't put away with file sharing on

Can't switch cartridges

If you have file sharing turned on in the Sharing Setup control panel, the Finder may not let you switch cartridges in a removable hard disk drive, CD ROM drive, or other removable-media storage device. You must stop file sharing, put away the disk icon, and then start sharing again. Now you'll be able to switch cartridges at will, but you won't be able to share them with others (but see the next tip).

Can't share a disk

To use the Finder's Sharing command with a disk or any folder in the disk, the disk must be mounted (it's icon must be on the desktop) when you start file sharing using the Sharing Setup control panel (Figure 11-10). Also, the disk capacity must be at least 2 MB to be shareable. If you start file sharing with no cartridge inserted in a removable hard disk drive or CD ROM drive, for example, you won't be able to share a cartridge you insert later until you stop file sharing and then start it again while the disk icon is on the desktop.

Blank icons

Blank icons are a sign of a corrupt desktop database. Restarting your Macintosh may eliminate the blank icons. If not, rebuilding the desktop usually does the trick. To rebuild the desktop, simply press the Command and Option keys while starting up, and wait for the Finder to inquire whether you indeed wish to rebuild the desktop on your hard disk. If you have multiple hard disks, the Finder asks about rebuilding each one in turn. To rebuild the desktop on a floppy disk, hold down Command and Option while inserting the floppy.

Rebuilding the desktop erases all comments you have entered in Get Info windows for items on the disks involved.

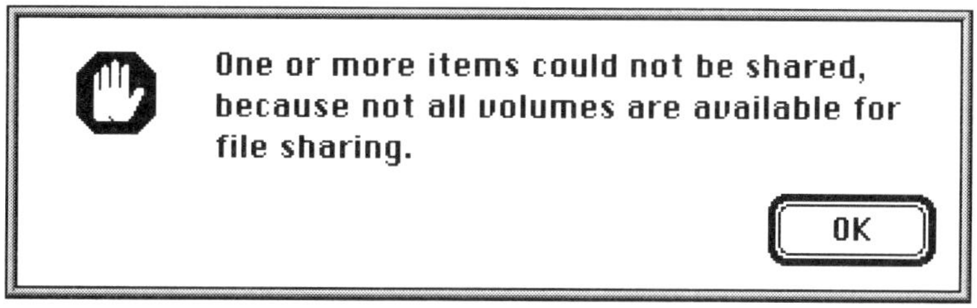

Figure 11-10
Disk was unmounted when file sharing started

Can't open a document

If the Finder advises it can't open a document you have double-clicked but it used to be able to do so, then the desktop database may be corrupt. Try the fixes described in the previous tip. If they don't work, the program that created the document you're trying to open may be missing. Use the Finder's Find command to search for it.

Bomb message causes

Apple hasn't yet managed to eliminate system errors and their dread bomb alert boxes. Table 2-2 lists the error messages that can appear in a system error alert box and their likely causes.

Emergency quit

Sometimes you can recover from a system error — or the related problem of a hung or frozen system — without restarting your Macintosh. Pressing Command-Option-Escape may bring up a dialog box asking whether you want to force the Finder (or some other program) to quit (Figure 11-11). If so, click the Force Quit button and cross your fingers. If you get to the Finder, immediately save all open documents and restart the computer.

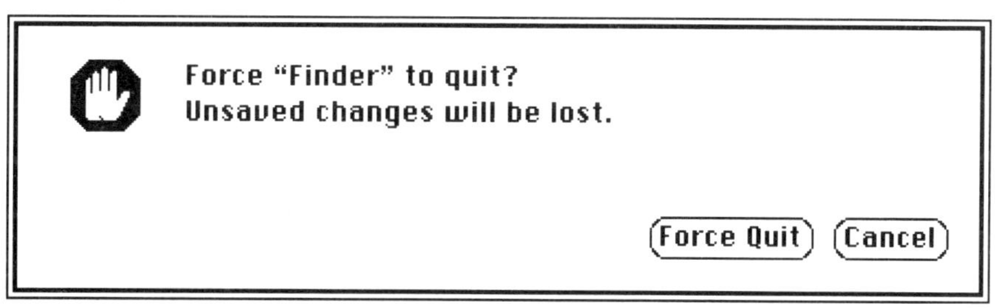

Figure 11-11
Forcing a program to quit

Figure 11-12
Secret passage to the Finder

Bomb recovery

If that trick doesn't work and the plastic programmer's switch is installed on your Macintosh, try pressing the Interrupt part of the switch (not the Restart part). On most Macintosh models, the Interrupt part is labeled with a tiny circle and the Restart part is labeled with a tiny arrow. (The Mac LC and IIsi have no programmer's switch.) With luck, you'll see a dialog box containing a greater-than symbol in its upper-left corner (Figure 11-12). Type G FINDER and press Return. If you get to the Finder, immediately save all open documents and restart the computer.

System extension conflicts

If items you add to the System Folder, Extensions folder, or Control Panels folder don't work, or if your Macintosh refuses to start up, then some of the system extensions in those places may be in conflict during startup. Sometimes changing the order in which the Macintosh installs system extensions resolves the conflict.

To have control panels whose names begin with blank spaces installed first during startup, put them in the Extensions folder. To have control panels whose names start with tildes or diamonds installed last during startup, put them in the System Folder. For convenient access to the control panels you move out of the Control Panels folder, make aliases of them and put the aliases in the Control Panels folder.

To have system extensions whose names begin with tildes and diamonds installed last during startup, drag them from the Extensions folder to the System Folder. Leave system extensions whose names begin with blank spaces in the Extensions folder so they will be installed first during startup.

Fixing other conflicts between system extensions and control panels involves experimenting. Start by removing all the items you have added to the System Folder and its inner folders since the trouble began. Then add them back one at a time, restarting your Macintosh each time. When you find an item that causes a conflict, try renaming it so it comes before or after other system extensions in the same folder. By experimenting with names you may find a startup sequence that works.

As a last resort, remove all system extensions and control panels to the desktop. Then put them in the System Folder (not the Extensions or Control Panels folder) one at a time, from most important to least. Restart your Macintosh each time you add another item to the System Folder. When you find an item that causes a conflict, discard it and try the next item you previously moved to the desktop. You may be able to resume using the items you discarded when they are next upgraded.

(If a conflict prevents starting up from your hard disk, start from a floppy disk with any version of system software. Make a change to the System Folder on the hard disk and try restarting from it.)

Summary

- To avoid opening an item when editing an icon's name, set a briefer Double-Click Speed with the Mouse control panel.
- You can quickly access programs, control panels, documents, and folders themselves by making aliases of them and putting the aliases on the desktop.
- Aliases can be used to keep track of and quickly open items on floppy disks that aren't inserted in your Macintosh.
- If you want an item opened at startup time, put an alias of it in the Startup Items folder. Don't put original items there, because returning them to their original locations when you no longer want them opened at startup time can be a drag.
- If the windows of open programs obscure desktop items, you can hide those windows by choosing Hide Others from the Application menu while the Finder is active.
- Sometimes the Trash contains a folder named Rescued Items that contains formerly invisible temporary files found when the Mac is started up. It only appears after a system crash, possibly allowing a user to recreate completed work up to the time of the crash.
- To avoid going back and forth between two folders, put an alias of each folder in the other.
- Memory fragmentation is best avoided by planning the order in which programs are opened and quit. Open programs you're least likely to quit first, then open programs you're most likely to quit last.

Chapter 12

Moving to System 7

In This Chapter

- Equipping your Macintosh to use System 7.
- Picking the best system software version for you.
- Using System 7 in a network where others use older system software.
- System compatibility information products.
- Where to get System 7.

If you're not already using System 7, should you? If you are already using it, would an older version of system software work better for you? These are the questions this chapter addresses.

Equipment requirements

All Macintosh models except the three oldest can use System 7. Only the original Mac 128K, the Mac 512K, and the Mac XL lack the necessary software in their ROMs (read-only memory). All other models can use System 7 if they have sufficient RAM (random-access memory) and disk space.

Memory requirements

QUICK TIPS

System 7 requires at least 2MB of RAM. You can tell how much RAM your Macintosh has by choosing About the Finder from the Finder's Apple menu. In the dialog box that appears (Figure 12-1), the Total Memory is the amount of RAM installed, reported in K instead of MB. To convert to MB, divide the number of K by 1024 (for example, 2048K ÷ 1024 = 2MB).

QUICK TIPS

You'll need more than the minimum 2MB if you use large or complex application programs or if you want to open several programs at once. As a rule of thumb, figure you'll need 1MB more than you need with older system software. You'll enjoy System 7 more if your Macintosh has at least 4MB of RAM.

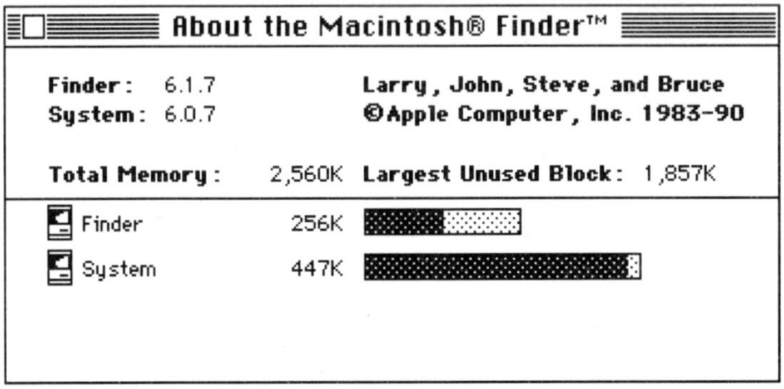

Figure 12-1
Checking installed memory

UNDOCUMENTED

Each Macintosh model has specific memory configuration rules. You can only install RAM modules, called SIMMs (single inline memory modules) in certain combinations on each model. Table 12-1 has the basic rules; dealers and companies that sell SIMMs have complete details.

If your Mac needs more RAM, you can have it upgraded by a trained technician or you can upgrade it yourself. Upgrading involves opening the Macintosh (tricky on a Plus, SE, SE/30, Classic), removing some small

Table 12-1: Macintosh memory configurations

Model	Built-in Ram (MB)	SIMM Slots	SIMM sizes	Total RAM
Plus, SE	0	4	256K, 1MB	1, 2, 2.5, 4
Classic	1	*	256K, 1MB	1, 2, 2.5, 4
LC	2	2	512K, 1MB, 2MB, 4MB	2, 3, 4, 6, 10
SE/30, II, IIx, IIcx	0	8	256K, 512K, 1MB, 4MB	1, 2, 4, 5, 8, 16†, 17†, 20†, 32†
IIsi	1	4	256K, 512K, 1MB, 2MB, 4MB, 16MB	2, 3, 5, 9, 17, 65
IIci	0	8	256K, 512K, 1MB, 2MB, 4MB, 16MB	1, 2, 3, 4, 5, 6, 8, 9, 10, 12, 16, 17, 18, 20, 24, 32, 64, 65, 66, 68, 80, 128
IIfx	0	8	1MB, 4MB, 8MB, 16MB	4, 8, 16, 20, 32, 48, 64, 68, 80, 96, 128

*The Classic uses a special memory expansion card that has 2 SIMM slots.
†The SE/30, II, IIx, and IIcx cannot use 32-bit addressing and require Connectix Corp.'s MODE 32 software to make use of more than 8MB total RAM for opening programs.

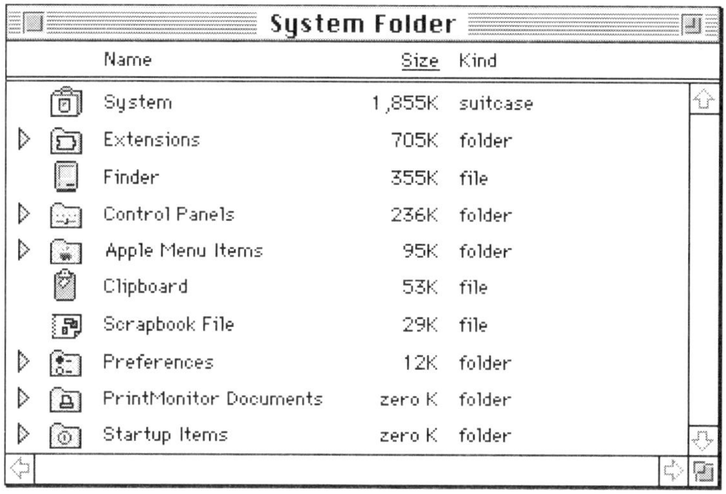

Figure 12-2
A typical System Folder after installation

circuit boards called SIMMs, and snapping in other SIMMs. You must also clip a resistor on a Mac Plus or older SE and move a jumper on a newer SE. Complete instructions come with the SIMMs, which you can order by mail from a plethora of companies who advertise in *Macworld*, *Mac User*, and *MacWeek* magazines. If you don't want to do the upgrade yourself and you live in a metropolitan area, use the Yellow Pages to shop for the best deal. Memory prices are highly competitive.

Disk requirements

Not only do you need plenty of memory, you also need a hard disk to make practical use of System 7. A standard installation of System 7 with software and fonts for LaserWriter printing takes up 3.2MB of disk space (Figure 12-2). Additional control panels, desk accessories, fonts, sounds, and extensions increase the size.

QUICK TIPS

You can install a stripped-down System 7 on a 1.4MB high-density floppy disk, but you can't do much with it. Worse, System 7 on a floppy disk is pokey.

A hard disk is easy for anyone to plug into the back of a Macintosh. Like memory prices, hard disk prices are competitive. You can buy a good-quality new 40MB hard disk from someone other than Apple for less than the cost of an Apple external floppy disk drive.

The best system software for you

For Macintosh users whose machines have enough RAM and a hard disk, System 7 is the best version of system software. Nonetheless, some people cling to their older system software. Don't let these three myths discourage you from using it:

Myth: System 7 is too slow for a Mac Plus, SE, or Classic.
Fact: System 7 performs adequately on those models.

Myth: System 7 is too complex.
Fact: Most of System 7's complexity is hidden — easy to get at when you want its power, but not in your face all the time.

Myth: System 7 uses too much RAM.
Fact: The 2MB that System 7 requires is roughly equivalent to having 1MB with System 6.0.5 and MultiFinder.

There are only three reasons why you might want to continue using older system software:

1. Your Macintosh doesn't have enough memory for System 7 and the programs you now use routinely. That can only be the case if all of the following are true: you have a Plus, SE, Classic, LC, or Portable and therefore can't use virtual memory; you can't install any more memory in your computer (it won't hold any more or you can't afford more); and you don't use MultiFinder with your older system software.

2. Someone else in your company has decided you may not move up to System 7 yet.

3. Programs you use regularly are incompatible with System 7 and new versions aren't available or you can't get them. (For more information on compatibility, see "Compatibility" later in this chapter.)

In case one of these reasons applies to you, Table 12-2 recommends an alternate version of system software for each Macintosh model and identifies versions that are OK to use.

Mixing systems

Like many Macintosh users, you may have access to more than one Macintosh. Or your Macintosh may be connected to a network with others. In either scenario, some computers may use System 7 while others use older system software, such as System 6.

Table 12-2: Recommended system software versions

System Software	7.0	6.0.7	6.0.5	6.0.4	6.0.3	6.0.2	5.0	2.0.1	2.0	1.1	1.0	n/a
System	7.0	6.0.7	6.0.5	6.0.4	6.0.3	6.0.2	4.2	4.1	4.1	3.2	3.2	2.0
Finder	7.0	6.1.7	6.1.5	6.1	6.1	6.1	6.0	5.5	5.5	5.3	5.3	4.1
128												★
XL										★	☆	
512K										★	☆	
512KE								★	☆	☆	☆	
Plus	★	☆	★	☆	☆	☆	☆	☆	☆	☆	☆	
SE	★	☆	★	☆	☆	☆	☆	☆	☆			
II	★	☆	★	☆	☆	☆	☆	☆	☆			
IIx	★	☆	★	☆	☆							
SE/30	★	☆	★	☆	☆							
IIcx	★	☆	★	☆	☆							
IIci	★	☆	★	☆								
IIfx	★	☆	★									
Portable	★	☆	★	☆								
Portable (backlit)	★	★										
Classic	★	★										
LC	★	★										
IIsi	★	★										

Legend:
★ Recommended
☆ OK to use

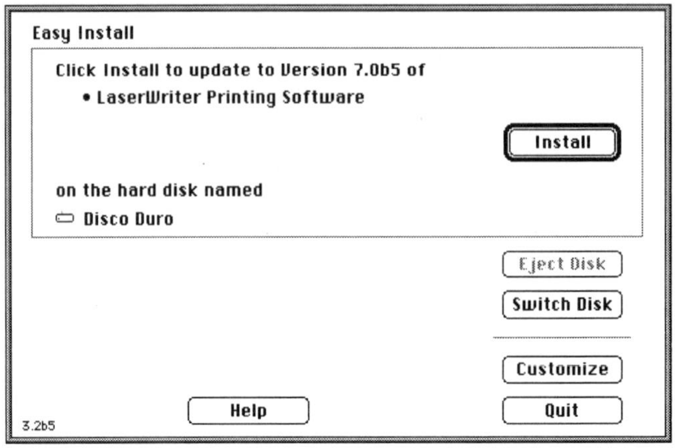

Figure 12-3
Installing LaserWriter software

Mixed networks

All computers on a network must use the same version of LaserWriter software. Otherwise the printer must be reinitialized whenever someone uses it with a version of LaserWriter software different than the previous user's version. In the past, this situation meant all computers on a network had to upgrade to a new version of system software at the same time. Not so with System 7.

System 7 and System 6 can coexist on the same network if all System 6 users install the LaserWriter software that comes with System 7. They must install it using the Installer program on the *Printing* disk (Figure 12-3); dragging the LaserWriter icon from that disk to their System Folders will not work.

Extra folders and missing items

When using disks with System 6 after using them with System 7, you may think icons that were on the desktop have mysteriously vanished. But they're only moved to the Desktop Folder. In System 7, the Desktop Folder is always open and its contents are displayed on the desktop, but the folder itself is invisible. In System 6, the Desktop Folder becomes visible but its contents are concealed inside it instead of being on the desktop. The Trash folder also becomes visible when you use older system software. It contains items you dragged to the Trash and left there (by virtue of not using the Empty Trash command) in System 7.

Desk accessories and fonts

Older system software sees individual desk accessories and fonts as meaningless documents with blank icons. To use fonts and desk accessories with older system software, they must be in suitcase files. Then you must install the suitcase files using the Font/DA Mover program or utility software such as Suitcase II or Master Juggler.

Automatic Rebuilding

When you restart your Macintosh with System 7 after using an earlier version of system software, the Finder may automatically rebuild its desktop database on the startup hard disk. You lose all info window comments in the process.

Compatibility

Moving to System 7 is as much a lifestyle change for your programs as it is for you. Most of the programs you already have will work with System 7. Many will have minor cosmetic flaws that won't affect their operation. Some will lose minor capabilities but still be able to function. A number of programs won't work with 32-Bit Addressing turned on or with virtual memory active. Several important System 7 capabilities — balloon help, publish and subscribe, program linking, and data access — don't work in a program until it's developer updates it to take advantage of them. Lesser improvements such as separate large and small icon designs, color icons, and the New Folder button in the Save As dialog box may also require software revision.

Where to get System 7

During Summer 1991 Apple began shipping System 7 with all new Macintosh models except those few with less than 2MB of RAM and no hard disk. If you already own a Macintosh and want to upgrade it, you can obtain System 7 from a variety of sources:

❖ Buy the System 7 package from an authorized Apple dealer, VAR (value-added reseller), or other reseller. The $99 price includes the installation disks, the complete set of Apple manuals and training disks, and 90 days of phone support direct from Apple. A $349 group upgrade kit includes the software on CD ROM, a set of user manuals, and a special upgrade book for group support personnel. Individuals in the group can upgrade over the network from the CD ROM.

- ❖ Buy a set of installation disks from a user group that has a license to distribute system software. These usually cost $30 to $40 per set. Try BMUG at 415/549-2684 or BCS•Mac at 617/625-7080. Or contact the Apple user group clearinghouse at 800/538-9696 for the name and number of the user group nearest you.

- ❖ Copy the System 7 installation disks from a person, group, or business. Unless your source has a license from Apple to distribute system software, such copying is technically illegal. Apple has not yet sued anyone for copying system software, however.

QUICK TIPS

You can pay for direct phone support from Apple ($2 per minute) even if you didn't buy Apple's official upgrade kit. Call 900/535-2775. In addition, you can listen to prerecorded answers to frequently asked questions by calling 408/257-7700. You pay only for the call.

Summary

- ✔ To use System 7, your Macintosh needs at least 3.2MB of hard disk space and 2MB of RAM — probably more of both.
- ✔ System 7 is the best system software for all Macintosh models from the Plus up, but some circumstances may dictate using System 6.0.7 or 6.0.5.
- ✔ You can use the same disks with System 7 and older system software. Also, computers on a network can use both System 7 and System 6 as long as they all use the LaserWriter software that comes with System 7.
- ✔ Most of the programs you already have work fine with System 7, but you'll probably want to upgrade them with versions that take advantage of System 7's balloon help, publish and subscribe, program linking, and data access capabilities.

Appendix A

To see how compatible with System 7 your programs and hardware products are, check their version numbers against Appendix A. (You can usually find a program's version number in its info window; use the Finder's Get Info command.) If your version number is greater than the version listed in the OK column, then you don't have to upgrade before using the product with System 7. The Best column lists the lowest version number that's fully compatible with System 7 (or if none is planned, the best version to use). For more information on any product, contact the company listed in the Source column. The information in this Appendix is based partly on information in the compatability checker software and was reported by developers and has not been independently verified. You can also check compatibility using the Compatibility Checker software that comes with System 7.

Product compatibility

Product	Version: OK	Version: Best	Notes	Source
1 Shot Opener	1.0.0	1.0.1		Baseline Publishing, 212 254-8235
1 Shot Worksheet	1.0	1.0.1		Baseline Publishing, 212 254-8235
3+File	1.7	1.7		3 COM, 408 492-1790
3+Mail CP	1.6	1.7	32	3 COM, 408 492-1790
3D Works	1.0	1.0		MacroMind, 415 442-0200
4D Calc	1.0.1	1.0.1		Acius, 408 252-4444
4D Compiler	1.0.1	1.0.1		Acius, 408 252-4444

Legend:
NO none available • **NI** no information • **CS** contact source for version info • **32** 32-Bit Addressing problem • **VM** virtual memory problem • **UG** get from user group, info system, or dealer • **$0** free upgrade • **NN** not needed with System 7 • **S7** comes with System 7 • **FS** file sharing problem • **!!** upgrade strongly recommended • **TT** can't set TrueType sizes above 127

Product compatibility *(cont'd)*

Product	Version OK	Version Best	Notes	Source
4D SQL Server	1.0	1.0		Acius, 408 252-4444
4D Write	1.0.1	1.0.1		Acius, 408 252-4444
4th DIMENSION	2.1.1	2.1.1		Acius, 408 252-4444
8•24 GC	7.0	7.0		Authorized Apple dealer, see local phone book
800k Eject INIT	NO	NO	NN	Apple Computer, 800 776-2333
A.M.E. INIT	NI	NI	CS	Casady & Greene, 408 484-9228
A/UX Startup	2.1	2.1		Authorized Apple dealer, see local phone book
Aapps DigiVideo	1.3	NI	32	Aaps, 408 735-8550
Aask	NO	NO		CE Software, 515 224-1953
Abaton Scanner Driver	2.0.2	2.0.2		Everex Systems, 415 498-4440
Accelerator	1.01	1.01		SuperMac Technology, 408 245-0646
Accelerator	3.0	3.0	UG	Radius, 408 434-1010
Accelerator	2.6	NI		RasterOps, 408 562-4200
Access PC	1.1	1.1		Insignia Solutions, 415 694-7600
ActaAdvantage	1.0	1.0		Symmetry, 602 998-9106
Address Book Plus	1.0	2.0	32	Power Up Software, 415 345-9381
AdminLAT	1.0	NI		DEC, 508 490-0450
AdminTCP	1.1	1.1		Authorized Apple dealer, see local phone book
Adobe Illustrator	3.0	NI		Adobe Systems, 415 961-0911
Adobe Photoshop	1.0	NI		Adobe Systems, 415 961-0911

Legend:
NO none available • **NI** no information • **CS** contact source for version info • **32** 32-Bit Addressing problem • **VM** virtual memory problem • **UG** get from user group, info system, or dealer • **$0** free upgrade • **NN** not needed with System 7 • **S7** comes with System 7 • **FS** file sharing problem • **!!** upgrade strongly recommended • **TT** can't set TrueType sizes above 127

Product compatibility *(cont'd)*

Product	Version OK	Version Best	Notes	Source
Adobe Separator	1.0	1.0		Adobe Systems, 415 961-0911
Adobe Streamline	1.0	NI		Adobe Systems, 415 961-0911
Adobe Type Manager	2.0	NI		Adobe Systems, 415 961-0911
Adobe Type Reunion	1.0	NI		Adobe Systems, 415 961-0911
Adobe TypeAlign	1.0	NI		Adobe Systems, 415 961-0911
AffiniFile	1.1	NI		Affinity Microsystems, 303 442-4840
After Dark	2.0t	2.0u		Berkeley Systems, 415 540-5535
Alarming Events	1.0.3	NI	CS	CE Software, 515 224-1953
AlarmsClock	2.0	3.0	UG	Now Software, 503 274-2800
Alchemy	2.23	NI		Passport Design, 415 726-0280
Aldus FreeHand	3.0	NI		Aldus, 206 628-2320
Algebra	1.0	NI		Wings for Learning, 800 321-7511
Algebra Shop	1.1.2	NI		Scholastic, 212 505-6006
Alisa	NO	NO	CS	Alisa Systems, 800 992-5472
Amazing Paint	1.0	1.0.1	32	CE Software, 515 224-1953
America Online	1.0	2.0	VM	Quantum Computer, 800 227-6364
American Discovery	2.3	3.0		GreatWave Software, 408 438-1990
AntiToxin	1.4	1.4		Mainstay, 818 991-6540
AntiToxin INIT	1.4	1.4		Mainstay, 818 991-6540
APIDriver	2.0	2.0		Tri-Data Systems, 408 727-3270
APIPrinter	1.0	1.0		Tri-Data Systems, 408 727-3270
Apple CD-ROM	3.0	3.1	UG	Authorized Apple dealer, see local phone book
Apple File Exchange	7.0	7.0	S7	Apple Computer, 800 776-2333
Apple HD SC Setup	2.0.4	2.0.4	S7	Apple Computer, 800 776-2333

Product compatibility *(cont'd)*

Product	Version OK	Version Best	Notes	Source
Apple-Digital	1.0	NI		DEC, 508 490-0450
AppleFax	NI	NI		Authorized Apple dealer, see local phone book
AppleLink	5.1.1	6.0.2	!!	Apple Computer, 408 974-3309
AppleScan	1.0	1.0.2		Authorized Apple dealer, see local phone book
AppleTalk Tuner	NI	NI		Solana Electronics, 619 490-5050
Archive	1.1.1	2.0		Software Architects, 206 487-0122
Art Importer	2.0	2.0		Altsys, 214 680-2093
Astrix	1.01	NI	CS	Microseeds Publishing, 813 882-8635
AT Driver	5.3	5.3		Pacer Software, 508 898-3300
AtOnce!	1.0	1.0		Symmetry, 602 998-9106
Audiomedia	2.02	NI	VM	Digidesign, 415 327-0777
Audiotrax	1.0	NI		Passport Design, 415 726-0280
AutoSave II	2.0	2.0		Magic Software, 800 342-6243
AutoStart	2.2	2.2		Fifth Generation Systems, 800 873-4384
Avatar Control Panel	3.33	3.4		Avatar, 508 435-3000
BackFAX	1.1.2	1.1.2		Solutions, 802 865-9220
Backmatic	2.0	2.0		Magic Software, 800 342-6243
BigThesaurus	1.0d	2.0	CS	Deneba Software, 305 594-6965
Blockers and Finders	1.0	2.0		Wings for Learning, 800 321-7511

Legend:
NO none available • **NI** no information • **CS** contact source for version info • **32** 32-Bit Addressing problem • **VM** virtual memory problem • **UG** get from user group, info system, or dealer • **$0** free upgrade • **NN** not needed with System 7 • **S7** comes with System 7 • **FS** file sharing problem • **!!** upgrade strongly recommended • **TT** can't set TrueType sizes above 127

Product compatibility *(cont'd)*

Product	Version OK	Version Best	Notes	Source
C•A•T III	1.0	1.0		Chang Laboratories, 408 727-8096
C-Server	NI	NI		Solana Electronics, 619 490-5050
C-Server Manager	NI	NI		Solana Electronics, 619 490-5050
CA Cricket Presents	2.0.1	2.1		Computer Associates Intl., 800 531-5236
Calendar Creator	1.0	NI	32	Power Up Software, 415 345-9381
CalendarMaker	3.0	3.0.1	32	CE Software, 515 224-1953
CannonMO INIT	1.0	1.0		Software Architects, 206 487-0122
Canvas	1.0	3.0		Deneba Software, 305 594-6965
Capture	4.0	4.0		Mainstay, 818 991-6540
Carbon Copy	2.0	NI	CS	Microcom Software, 919 490-1277
CEToolbox	1.6	1.6	$0	CE Software, 515 224-1953
Cheque	1.0.0	1.0.0		Baseline Publishing, 212 254-8235
Claris CAD	2.0v2	2.0v3		Claris, 408 727-8227
Claris CGT	1.0v1	1.1v1	$0	Claris, 408 727-8227
Claris Resolve	1.0v1	1.0v1		Claris, 408 727-8227
Classic/SE Display	3.8	4.0	UG	Radius, 408 434-1012
ClearVue/Classic	1.1	NI		RasterOps, 800 729-2656
ClearVue/SE	1.0	NI		RasterOps, 800 729-2656
ClickChange	1.0.5	1.0.5		Dubl-Click, 818 700-9525
ClickPaste	2.0.2	2.0.2		Mainstay, 818 991-6540
Clicktracks	2.1	NI		Passport Design, 415 726-0280
Clinic	2.0.6	3.0		Peter Norton Computing, 800 441-7234

Legend:
NO none available • **NI** no information • **CS** contact source for version info • **32** 32-Bit Addressing problem • **VM** virtual memory problem • **UG** get from user group, info system, or dealer • **$0** free upgrade • **NN** not needed with System 7 • **S7** comes with System 7 • **FS** file sharing problem • **!!** upgrade strongly recommended • **TT** can't set TrueType sizes above 127

Product compatibility *(cont'd)*

Product	Version OK	Version Best	Notes	Source
Coach Pro	4.0	4.0	CS	Deneba Software, 305 594-6965
Coax Gateway Server	3.33	3.4	32	Avatar, 508 435-3000
Color MacCheese	1.0.5	2.0.8		Baseline Publishing, 212 254-8235
Color Pivot Resolutions	1.0	1.0		Radius, 408 434-1012
Color◊Space	NO	NO		Mass Microsystems, 408 522-1200
ColorBoard 364 F.G.	3.2	3.2		RasterOps, 800 729-2656
ColorDesk	1.0	1.0		Microseeds Publishing, 813 882-8635
Colorizer	1.14	2.0		Palomar Software, 619 721-7000
ColorSnap 32+	1.1	1.1		Computer Friends, 503 626-2291
ColorStudio	1.11	1.5		Letraset USA, 201 845-6100
Comic Strip Factory	1.6	1.6		Foundation Publishing, 612 445-8860
Comment	NI	NI	CS	Deneba Software, 305 594-6965
CommGATE	1.0	1.0		Solutions, 802 865-9220
CompleteUndelete	1.0	1.0		Microcom Software, 919 490-1277
CompleteUndelete	2.0	2.0		Microcom Software, 919 490-1277
ConcertWare	4.0.5	4.0.5		GreatWave Software, 408 438-1990
CONNECT	1.04	1.5		Connect, 408 973-0110
Connect	1.1	1.1		Pixar, 415 236-4000
ConnectivityLoader	2.0.6	2.0.6		Tri-Data Systems, 408 727-3270
ConnectivityManager	2.0.7	2.0.7		Tri-Data Systems, 408 727-3270
Control-1	NO	NO	NN	CE Software, 515 224-1953
Cricket Draw	1.1.1	1.1.1		Computer Associates Intl., 800 531-5236

Legend:
NO none available • **NI** no information • **CS** contact source for version info • **32** 32-Bit Addressing problem • **VM** virtual memory problem • **UG** get from user group, info system, or dealer • **$0** free upgrade • **NN** not needed with System 7 • **S7** comes with System 7 • **FS** file sharing problem • **!!** upgrade strongly recommended • **TT** can't set TrueType sizes above 127

Product compatibility *(cont'd)*

Product	Version OK	Version Best	Notes	Source
CricketGraph	1.3.2	NI	32	Computer Associates Intl., 800 531-5236
CS-1	1.0	NI	VM	Digidesign, 415 327-0777
Curator	NO	NO		Solutions, 802 865-9220
Customizer	NI	NI		Now Software, 503 274-2800
CUT Driver	3.34	3.4	32	Avatar, 508 435-3000
DART	1.4	1.4		Apple Computer, 800 776-2333
DATa	2.0	NI	VM	Digidesign, 415 327-0777
DAtabase Builder	1.5.0	2.0.0		Baseline Publishing, 212 254-8235
DAtabase Converter	1.5.0	2.0.0		Baseline Publishing, 212 254-8235
DAtabase Personalizer	1.5.0	2.0.0		Baseline Publishing, 212 254-8235
DAtabase Upgrader	1.5.0	2.0.0		Baseline Publishing, 212 254-8235
Data Models	1.0	1.0		Sunburst, 800-628-8897
DataPak	2.7	2.7		Mass Microsystems, 408 522-1200
DataPak M.O.	1.0	1.0		Mass Microsystems, 408 522-1200
DataPrism	1.1	1.7		Brio, 415 961-4110
DataStream	NO	NO		SuperMac Technology, 408 245-0646
_DATE	1.0	1.0		T/Maker Co., 415 962-0195
DaynaFile	2.8	3.0		Dayna Communication, 801 972-2000
Dbase Mac	1.0.1	NI	32	New Era Software, 305 255-5586
DECK	1.03	NI	VM	Digidesign, 415 327-0777
DECnet Control	1.0	NI		DEC, 508 490-0450
DECnet/Mac	1.0	NI		DEC, 508 490-0450

Legend:
NO none available • **NI** no information • **CS** contact source for version info • **32** 32-Bit Addressing problem • **VM** virtual memory problem • **UG** get from user group, info system, or dealer • **$0** free upgrade • **NN** not needed with System 7 • **S7** comes with System 7 • **FS** file sharing problem • **!!** upgrade strongly recommended • **TT** can't set TrueType sizes above 127

Product compatibility *(cont'd)*

Product	Version OK	Version Best	Notes	Source
DeltaGraph	1.5	NI	32	Deltapoint, 408 648-4000
DesignStudio	2.0	2.0		Letraset USA, 201 845-6100
DeskPicture	2.0	3.0		Now Software, 503 274-2800
DFT Driver	3.34	3.4	32	Avatar, 508 435-3000
DigiSystem INIT	1.0	NI	VM	Digidesign, 415 327-0777
Digital Darkroom	2.0	2.01		Silicon Beach Software, 619 695-6956
DigiVideo Color App	1.05	NI	32	Aaps, 408 735-8550
Dimmer	1.0	1.0		Microseeds Publishing, 813 882-8635
Direct Mail Application	1.0.1	1.0.3		Baseline Publishing, 212 254-8235
Disinfectant	2.4	2.4	UG	Northwestern University, no phone
Disinfectant INIT	2.4	2.4	UG	Northwestern University, no phone
Disk Copy	4.1	4.2		Apple Computer, 800 776-2333
Disk First Aid	1.5	1.5	S7	Apple Computer, 800 776-2333
DiskDoubler App	1.0	1.0		Salient Software, 415 321-5375
DiskDoubler INIT	3.7	3.7		Salient Software, 415 321-5375
DiskDup+	1.5.2	1.5.2		LACie Limited, 503 691-0771
DiskExpress I	None	None		Alsoft, 713 353-1510
DiskExpress II	2.07	2.07		Alsoft, 713 353-1510
DiskFit	1.5.1	2.7		SuperMac Software, 408 773-4489
DiskLock	2.01	2.1	$0	Fifth Generation Systems, 800 873-4384
DiskPaper Reader	1.0	1.0		Farallon Computing, 415 596-9000
DiskTop	4.01	NI		CE Software, 515 224-1953

Legend:
NO none available • **NI** no information • **CS** contact source for version info • **32** 32-Bit Addressing problem • **VM** virtual memory problem • **UG** get from user group, info system, or dealer • **$0** free upgrade • **NN** not needed with System 7 • **S7** comes with System 7 • **FS** file sharing problem • **!!** upgrade strongly recommended • **TT** can't set TrueType sizes above 127

Product compatibility *(cont'd)*

Product	Version OK	Version Best	Notes	Source
DiskTop.Extras	1.0	1.0	32	CE Software, 515 224-1953
Dollars and $ense	5.0	5.0		Software Toolworks, 415 883-5157
DOS Mounter	2.0	2.03		Dayna Communication, 801 972-2000
Double Helix	3.0.6	3.5.0		Odesta, 708 498-5615
Double Helix Client	3.0.6	3.5.0		Odesta, 708 498-5615
Double Helix Engine	3.0.6	3.5.0		Odesta, 708 498-5615
Double Helix Server	3.0.6	3.5.0		Odesta, 708 498-5615
Double Helix Utility	3.0.6	3.5.0		Odesta, 708 498-5615
DoubleTalk	1.0.0	2.0.0		Baseline Publishing, 212 254-8235
DrawOver	1.0	1.0		Adobe Systems, 415 961-0911
Dreams	1.0	1.1	32	Innovative Data Design, 415 680-6818
DriveManager	7.0	7.0		GCC, 617 890-0880
Dynodex	1.21a	2.0		Portfolio Systems, 914 876-7744
DynoPage	1.0	1.0		Portfolio Systems, 914 876-7744
Easy Color Paint	2.0	2.0		Creative Software, 201 665-9361
EasyShare INIT	1.2	1.2		Symmetry, 602 998-9106
E-Machines	3.0	3.2		E-Machines, 503 646-6699
Empower II	4.0.7	4.0.7	FS	Magna, 408 433-5467
Encore	2.0	NI		Passport Design, 415 726-0280
EtherGate	3.6	3.6	$0	Shiva, 617 252-6400
EtherPort	4.0	NI	VM	Shiva, 617 252-6400
EtherPort SE	3.0	3.0	$0	Shiva, 617 252-6400

Legend:
NO none available • **NI** no information • **CS** contact source for version info • **32** 32-Bit Addressing problem • **VM** virtual memory problem • **UG** get from user group, info system, or dealer • **$0** free upgrade • **NN** not needed with System 7 • **S7** comes with System 7 • **FS** file sharing problem • **!!** upgrade strongly recommended • **TT** can't set TrueType sizes above 127

Product compatibility *(cont'd)*

Product	Version OK	Version Best	Notes	Source
eXodus	2.1	3.0		White Pine Software, 603 886-9050
Explorer	1.0	NI		Wings for Learning, 800 321-7511
Exposure Pro	1.0.2	1.0.2		Baseline Publishing, 212 254-8235
Exposure Pro Customizer	1.0.0	1.0.1		Baseline Publishing, 212 254-8235
Exposure Pro Personalizer	1.0.0	1.0.1		Baseline Publishing, 212 254-8235
ExpressTape	4.0.1	4.0.2		Baseline Publishing, 212 254-8235
Extension Manager	1.0.1	1.0.1	32	CE Software, 515 224-1953
EZ-Menu	1.1	1.1	32	CE Software, 515 224-1953
EZVision	1.0	NI	VM	Opcode Systems, 415 369-8131
F2MO INIT	1.0	1.0		Software Architects, 206 487-0122
F2RC INIT	1.0	1.0		Software Architects, 206 487-0122
Family Builder	3.2	3.2	$0	Altsys, 214 680-2093
Fast Forms	1.2.1	2.0		Power Up Software, 415 345-9381
Fast Forms Filler	2.0	2.0		Power Up Software, 415 345-9381
Fastback II	2.5	NI		Fifth Generation Systems, 800 873-4384
FastPath Manager II	5.2.2	5.2.2	$0	Shiva, 617 252-6400
FAXGATE	1.5.1	1.5.1		Solutions, 802 865-9220
File Director	NO	NO		Fifth Generation Systems, 800 873-4384
FileForce	1.1.1	1.1.1		Acius, 408 252-4444
FileGuard	2.5.3	2.5.3		ASD Software, 714 624-2594
FileMaker	NI	NI	CS	Claris, 408 727-8227
FileMaker II	1.1	NI	!!	Claris, 408 727-8227

Legend:
NO none available • **NI** no information • **CS** contact source for version info • **32** 32-Bit Addressing problem • **VM** virtual memory problem • **UG** get from user group, info system, or dealer • **$0** free upgrade • **NN** not needed with System 7 • **S7** comes with System 7 • **FS** file sharing problem • **!!** upgrade strongly recommended • **TT** can't set TrueType sizes above 127

Product compatibility *(cont'd)*

Product	Version OK	Version Best	Notes	Source
FileMaker Plus	NI	NI	CS	Claris, 408 727-8227
FileMaker Pro	1.0v1	1.0v2	$0	Claris, 408 727-8227
FileSaver	1.1	1.1		Peter Norton Computing, 800 441-7234
Finder Sounds	NO	NO		Greg Smith, no phone
FinderKeys	NI	NI		Now Software, 503 274-2800
Findswell	NI	NI		Working Software, 408 423-5696
First Aid HFS	1.0	NI	CS	Microcom Software, 919 490-1277
FlashTalk INIT	NI	NI	CS	Sitka, 800 848-8677
Flowfazer	1.0	NI		Utopia Software, 415 331-0714
FolderBolt	1.01	1.02	CS	Kent◊Marsh Ltd., 713 623-4950
FolderBolt Admin.	1.01	1.02		Kent◊Marsh Ltd., 713 623-4950
FolderLock	2.01	NI		Fifth Generation Systems, 800 873-4384
FolderShare	1.1	1.1	32	CE Software, 515 224-1953
Font Harmony	1.28	1.28		Fifth Generation Systems, 800 873-4384
~Font Porter	1.0	NI		Adobe Systems, 415 961-0911
Font/DA Juggler	NO	NO		Alsoft, 713 353-1510
Font/DA Mover	4.1	4.1	NN	Apple Computer, 800 776-2333
Fontastic Plus	2.0.2	2.0.3		Altsys, 214 680-2093
Fontographer	3.05	3.2		Altsys, 214 680-2093
FontStudio	2.0	2.0		Letraset USA, 201 845-6100
FormatterFive	1.0	1.2		Software Architects, 206 487-0122
FormatterFive INIT	1.0	1.0		Software Architects, 206 487-0122

Legend:
NO none available • **NI** no information • **CS** contact source for version info • **32** 32-Bit Addressing problem • **VM** virtual memory problem • **UG** get from user group, info system, or dealer • **$0** free upgrade • **NN** not needed with System 7 • **S7** comes with System 7 • **FS** file sharing problem • **!!** upgrade strongly recommended • **TT** can't set TrueType sizes above 127

Product compatibility *(cont'd)*

Product	Version OK	Version Best	Notes	Source
FormatterOne	3.29	3.40		Software Architects, 206 487-0122
FormatterTwo	3.29	3.40		Software Architects, 206 487-0122
Forms Designer	NO	NO		Softview Inc., 800 622-6829
Forum	1.0	1.0		Pacer Software, 508 898-3300
FoxBASE+	2.00	2.01	$0	Fox Software, 419 874-0162
FrameGrabber 324	2.1	2.1		RasterOps, 800 729-2656
FrameMaker	2.1	2.1.1		Frame, 408 433-3311
Full Impact	2.0	NI	32	Ashton-Tate, 800 227-4866
FullWrite Professional	1.5	1.6		Ashton-Tate, 805 375-1467
Galaxy	1.0	1.1	VM	Opcode Systems, 415 369-8131
Gateway Client Driver	3.33	3.4		Avatar, 508 435-3000
GatorBoxTFTP	1.0	1.0		Cayman Systems, 617 494-1999
GatorInstaller	1.0	1.0		Cayman Systems, 617 494-1999
GatorKeeper	1.5.0	1.5.0		Cayman Systems, 617 494-1999
Genetics Model	1.0	NI		Wings for Learning, 800 321-7511
Geometric Supposer Quad.	1.0	1.0		Sunburst, 800-628-8897
Geometric Supposer Tria.	1.0	1.0		Sunburst, 800-628-8897
Globe	1.0	1.0		Microseeds Publishing, 813 882-8635
GOfer	2.1	NI		Microlytics, 716 248-9150
Grammatik Mac	2.0	NI	32	Reference Software, 415 541-0222
Graph 3D	1.0.2	1.0.2		Acius, 408 252-4444
Gravity Model	1.0	NI		Wings for Learning, 800 321-7511

Legend:
NO none available • **NI** no information • **CS** contact source for version info • **32** 32-Bit Addressing problem • **VM** virtual memory problem • **UG** get from user group, info system, or dealer • **$0** free upgrade • **NN** not needed with System 7 • **S7** comes with System 7 • **FS** file sharing problem • **!!** upgrade strongly recommended • **TT** can't set TrueType sizes above 127

Product compatibility *(cont'd)*

Product	Version OK	Version Best	Notes	Source
GROUPwriter	1.0	1.0		Sunburst, 800-628-8897
GuardCard Configure	1.0	1.0		Kent◊Marsh Ltd., 713 623-4950
Hammer Install	1.3	1.3		FWB, 415 474-8055
HAND-Off	2.2.0	2.2.0		Connectix, 415 324-0727
Hard disk Deadbolt	1.0	1.0		FWB, 415 474-8055
Hard Disk Installer	3.28	3.29	VM	Mitek Systems, 800 367-5660
HayesConnect	2.1A	2.1A		Hayes Microcomputer, 404 441-1617
HayesConnect Server	2.1A	2.1A		Hayes Microcomputer, 404 441-1617
HDBackup	NO	NO		Apple Computer, 800 776-2333
HDP	3.02	3.02		FWB, 415 474-8055
HeapFixer	NO	NO	NN	CE Software, 515 224-1953
heirDA	3.0	3.0		Now Software, 503 274-2800
HostPrint	2.0	2.0		IDEAssociates, 800 257-5027
Hot Dog Stand	1.0	1.0		Sunburst, 800-628-8897
HPMO INIT	3.0	3.0		Software Architects, 206 487-0122
HyperCard	2.0v2	2.1	S7	Claris, 408 727-8227
HyperSound & Toolkit	2.0.3	NI		Farallon Computing, 415 596-9000
Icon-It!	2.1	NI		Tactic, 305 378-4110
IconMover	3.0	3.0	32	CE Software, 515 224-1953
IDEAcomm Mac	1.2	2.0		IDEAssociates, 800 257-5027
IDEAcomm Printer	1.2	1.2		IDEAssociates, 800 257-5027
IDEAcomm Utilities	1.2	2.0		IDEAssociates, 800 257-5027

Legend:
NO none available • **NI** no information • **CS** contact source for version info • **32** 32-Bit Addressing problem • **VM** virtual memory problem • **UG** get from user group, info system, or dealer • **$0** free upgrade • **NN** not needed with System 7 • **S7** comes with System 7 • **FS** file sharing problem • **!!** upgrade strongly recommended • **TT** can't set TrueType sizes above 127

Product compatibility *(cont'd)*

Product	Version OK	Version Best	Notes	Source
IDEAlink	2.0	2.0		IDEAssociates, 800 257-5027
ifXFS	1.0	1.0		Softview Inc., 800 622-6829
ImageStudio	1.62	1.7		Letraset USA, 201 845-6100
ImageWorks	1.0	1.0		MacroMind, 415 442-0200
ImpressIT	1.0	1.0	UG	Radius, 408 434-1012
In-Box	3.0	NI		Sitka, 800 848-8677
In-Box cdev	3.0	NI		Sitka, 800 848-8677
In-Box INIT	3.0	NI		Sitka, 800 848-8677
InBox+ Admin	3.0	NI		Sitka, 800 848-8677
InBox Setup	3.0	NI		Sitka, 800 848-8677
In/Out	1.0.1	NI	32	CE Software, 515 224-1953
In/Out Server	NO	NO		CE Software, 515 224-1953
Infini-D	1.0	1.0		Specular International, 413 549-7600
INIT Analyzer	1.0.0	1.1.0		Baseline Publishing, 212 254-8235
INIT Manager	1.1.0	1.1.0		Baseline Publishing, 212 254-8235
INITPicker	2.01	3.0		Microseeds Publishing, 813 882-8635
Installer	3.2	3.2	NN	Apple Computer, 800 776-2333
Install FlashTalk	NI	NI	CS	Sitka, 800 848-8677
Inter•Poll	1.0	1.0.1		Authorized Apple dealer, see local phone book
InterBase	NI	NI		Sitka, 800 848-8677
InterBridge Manager	2.0A	2.0B		Hayes Microcomputer, 404 441-1617

Legend:
NO none available • **NI** no information • **CS** contact source for version info • **32** 32-Bit Addressing problem • **VM** virtual memory problem • **UG** get from user group, info system, or dealer • **$0** free upgrade • **NN** not needed with System 7 • **S7** comes with System 7 • **FS** file sharing problem • **!!** upgrade strongly recommended • **TT** can't set TrueType sizes above 127

Product compatibility *(cont'd)*

Product	Version OK	Version Best	Notes	Source
Internet Manager	1.8	1.8	$0	Shiva, 617 252-6400
JetLink Express	2.1	2.2		GDT Softworks, 604 291-9121
Jukebox	NI	NI	CS	Farallon Computing, 415 596-9000
KeyPlan	1.0	1.0		Symmetry, 602 998-9106
KidsMath	1.1	1.1		GreatWave Software, 408 438-1990
KidsTime	1.2	1.3		GreatWave Software, 408 438-1990
KiwiEnvelopes	3.1.1	NI		Kiwi, 805 685-4031
KiwiFinder Extender	1.0.2	NI		Kiwi, 805 685-4031
LapLink INIT	3.2	3.2		Traveling Software, 206 483-8088
LASER Award Maker	1.0	1.0		Baudville, 616 698-0888
LaserFrame INIT	4.1	4.1		SuperMac Technology, 408 245-0646
LaserWriter Font Utility	6.0	7.0	S7	Apple Computer, 800 776-2333
LAT	1.0	NI		DEC, 508 490-0450
Layout Mover	1.0.1	1.0.3		Baseline Publishing, 212 254-8235
LCINIT	1.0	1.0		SuperMac Technology, 408 245-0646
LetraStudio	1.5	2.0		Letraset USA, 201 845-6100
LEXIS/NEXIS	1.40	1.40		Mead Data Central, 408 543-6862
Live List	2.0	NI	VM	Digidesign, 415 327-0777
LookUp	2.2	NI	CS	Working Software, 408 423-5696
LWStatus	1.01	NI		Farallon Computing, 415 596-9000
Mac II Video Card Util.	NO	NO		Apple Computer, 800 776-2333
Mac Daisy Link	1.1.6	2.0		GDT Softworks, 604 291-9121
Mac240	3.1	3.1		White Pine Software, 603 886-9050

Product compatibility *(cont'd)*

Product	Version OK	Version Best	Notes	Source
MacBanner	1.0	1.0	32	CE Software, 515 224-1953
MacBILLBOARD	4.1	4.1		CE Software, 515 224-1953
MacDFT Config	NO	NO		Authorized Apple dealer, see local phone book
MacDraft	2.0	2.0		Innovative Data Design, 415 680-6818
MacDraw	NI	NI	CS	Claris, 408 727-8227
MacDraw II	1.0v4	1.1v2	VM	Claris, 408 727-8227
MacDraw Pro	1.0v1	1.0v1		Claris, 408 727-8227
MacFlow	3.5.3	3.5.3		Mainstay, 818 991-6540
MacInTax	1.4	1.4		Softview Inc., 800 622-6829
MacInteriors	1.0	1.11	VM	Microspot Ltd., 408 253-2000
Macintosh Common Lisp	1.3.2	2.0b1	VM	APDA, 800 282-2732
Macintosh Common Lisp	2.0b1	2.0b1		APDA, 800 282-2732
Macintosh Workstation	3.1	3.1		APDA, 800 282-2732
MacIRMA API	1.3.0	1.3.1	32	DCA, 404 740-0300
MacIRMA CUT	2.0.0	2.0.0		DCA, 404 740-0300
MacIRMA DAL	1.0.0	1.1.0	32	DCA, 404 740-0300
MacIRMA Entry Emulator	1.2.2	1.2.6	32	DCA, 404 740-0300
MacIRMA Graphics Inst.	2.0.0	2.0.0		DCA, 404 740-0300
MacIRMA Graphics Workstation	2.0.0	2.0.0		DCA, 404 740-0300
MacIRMA PCLK Graphics	1.0.2	NI		DCA, 404 740-0300

Legend:
NO none available • **NI** no information • **CS** contact source for version info • **32** 32-Bit Addressing problem • **VM** virtual memory problem • **UG** get from user group, info system, or dealer • **$0** free upgrade • **NN** not needed with System 7 • **S7** comes with System 7 • **FS** file sharing problem • **!!** upgrade strongly recommended • **TT** can't set TrueType sizes above 127

Product compatibility *(cont'd)*

Product	Version OK	Version Best	Notes	Source
MacIRMA PrDriver	1.1.2	2.0.0		DCA, 404 740-0300
MacIRMA SNA	1.1.2	2.0.0	32	DCA, 404 740-0300
MacIRMA Workstation	1.1.2	2.0.0		DCA, 404 740-0300
MacIRMATalk	1.1.2	2.0.0		DCA, 404 740-0300
MacIRMAtrac	2.0.0	2.0.0		DCA, 404 740-0300
MacIRMAtrac Diagnostics	2.0.0	2.0.0		DCA, 404 740-0300
MacLink Plus/Translators	4.5	5.0		DataViz, 203 268-0030
MacLink Plus/Wang OIS	4.5	5.0		DataViz, 203 268-0030
MacLink Plus/Wang VS	4.5	5.0		DataViz, 203 268-0030
MacLinkPlus/PC	4.5	5.0		DataViz, 203 268-0030
MacMainFrame 3287	3.34	3.4		Avatar, 508 435-3000
MacMainFrame Checker	3.34	3.4		Avatar, 508 435-3000
MacMainFrame Client	3.33	3.4		Avatar, 508 435-3000
MacMainFrame Graphics	3.34	3.4		Avatar, 508 435-3000
MacMainFrame Work.	3.34	3.4		Avatar, 508 435-3000
MacMoney	3.02	3.51		Survivor Software Ltd., 213 410-9527
MacNetway 3270	8.2	8.2.3		Tri-Data Systems, 408 727-3270
MacNetway 3287	8.2.2	8.2.2		Tri-Data Systems, 408 727-3270
MacPaint	2.0	NI		Claris, 408 727-8227
MacPassword	3.8.7	3.8.8		Evergreen Software, 206 483-6576
MacPassword Customizer	3.8.7	3.8.8		Evergreen Software, 206 483-6576

Legend:
NO none available • **NI** no information • **CS** contact source for version info • **32** 32-Bit Addressing problem • **VM** virtual memory problem • **UG** get from user group, info system, or dealer • **$0** free upgrade • **NN** not needed with System 7 • **S7** comes with System 7 • **FS** file sharing problem • **!!** upgrade strongly recommended • **TT** can't set TrueType sizes above 127

Product compatibility *(cont'd)*

Product	Version OK	Version Best	Notes	Source
MacPlot Configure	3.6.2	3.7.2	VM	Microspot Ltd., 408 253-2000
MacProject	NI	2.5v1	CS	Claris, 408 727-8227
MacProject II	2.1v2	NI		Claris, 408 727-8227
MacProteus Batteries	1.0	NI	VM	Digidesign, 415 327-0777
MacProteus Front Panel	1.0F2	NI	VM	Digidesign, 415 327-0777
MacRecorder Driver	1.0	1.0.1	VM	Farallon Computing, 415 596-9000
MacroMaker	NO	NO		Apple Computer, 800 776-2333
MacroMind Accelerator	2.0.1	2.0.1		MacroMind, 415 442-0200
MacroMind Director	2.0	2.01	32	MacroMind, 415 442-0200
MacroMind Player	2.0	2.0		MacroMind, 415 442-0200
MacSafe	2.0	2.01	$0	Kent◊Marsh Ltd., 713 623-4950
MacSafe II Administrator	2.0	2.01	$0	Kent◊Marsh Ltd., 713 623-4950
MacsBug	2.0	2.0		APDA, 800 282-2732
MacSchedule	2.5.5	2.5.5		Mainstay, 818 991-6540
MacSchedulePLUS	1.0.5	1.0.5		Mainstay, 818 991-6540
MacSnoop	1.5.5	1.5.5		Evergreen Software, 206 483-6576
MacSpin	3.0	3.01	32	Abacus Concepts, 415 540-1949
MacTCP	1.1	1.1		Authorized Apple dealer, see local phone book
MacTerminal	3.0	3.0		Authorized Apple dealer, see local phone book
Mac-to-Mac	1.1.0	1.1.1		Caravelle Networks, 613 596-2802

Legend:
NO none available • **NI** no information • **CS** contact source for version info • **32** 32-Bit Addressing problem • **VM** virtual memory problem • **UG** get from user group, info system, or dealer • **$0** free upgrade • **NN** not needed with System 7 • **S7** comes with System 7 • **FS** file sharing problem • **!!** upgrade strongly recommended • **TT** can't set TrueType sizes above 127

Product compatibility *(cont'd)*

Product	Version OK	Version Best	Notes	Source
MacTools Backup	2.0	2.1		Central Point Software, 503 690-8090
MacTools Mirror	2.1.1	NI	CS	Central Point Software, 503 690-8090
MacTools Optimizer	2.0.1	NI	CS	Central Point Software, 503 690-8090
MacTools Partition INIT	1.0	NI	CS	Central Point Software, 503 690-8090
MacTools Rescue	1.1.1	NI	CS	Central Point Software, 503 690-8090
MacTOPS Filing	NI	NI		Sitka, 800 848-8677
MacVision Image Processing	4.0	4.1		Koala Technologies, 408 287-6311
MacWrite	NI	NI	CS	Claris, 408 727-8227
MacWrite II	1.0v2	1.1v2	TT	Claris, 408 727-8227
MacWrite Pro	1.0v1	1.0v1		Claris, 408 727-8227
MacX	1.1	1.1.7		Authorized Apple dealer, see local phone book
Magic Typist	1.1.3	NI		Tactic, 305 378-4110
Mail Backup Utility	3.0	3.0		Microsoft, 800 426-9400
Mail Dial-In Host	3.0	3.0		Microsoft, 800 426-9400
Mail for Macintosh	1.0	NI		DEC, 508 490-0450
Mail Network Administrator	2.0.1	3.0		Microsoft, 800 426-9400
Mail Tools	1.9.9	3.0		Microsoft, 800 426-9400
MailMaker	1.1.2	1.1.2		Solutions, 802 865-9220
Manager	4.1	NI	VM	SuperMac Technology, 408 245-0646
Manager 3.26	3.26	NI	VM	SuperMac Technology, 408 245-0646
Manager CDEV	4.1	4.1		SuperMac Technology, 408 245-0646

Legend:
NO none available • **NI** no information • **CS** contact source for version info • **32** 32-Bit Addressing problem • **VM** virtual memory problem • **UG** get from user group, info system, or dealer • **$0** free upgrade • **NN** not needed with System 7 • **S7** comes with System 7 • **FS** file sharing problem • **!!** upgrade strongly recommended • **TT** can't set TrueType sizes above 127

Product compatibility *(cont'd)*

Product	Version OK	Version Best	Notes	Source
Managing Your Money	4.0	4.0		MECA Software, 203 222-9150
MARATHON COMM	2.0	2.0	$0	Dove Computer, 919 763-7918
MarcoPolo	1.02	1.02		Mainstay, 818 991-6540
Mariah	1.0	1.0		Symmetry, 602 998-9106
MarkUp	2.0	2.0		Mainstay, 818 991-6540
Master List	2.01	NI	VM	Digidesign, 415 327-0777
MasterColor	1.0.0	1.0.1		Baseline Publishing, 212 254-8235
MasterFinder	1.1	NI		Tactic, 305 378-4110
MasterJuggler	None	None		Alsoft, 713 353-1510
MasterPaint	1.0.0	1.0.1		Baseline Publishing, 212 254-8235
Master Tracks Pro 4	4.1.4	NI		Passport Design, 415 726-0280
Math Shop	1.1.2	NI		Scholastic, 212 505-6006
Math Shop Jr.	1.1.2	NI		Scholastic, 212 505-6006
Math Shop Spotlight :F&D	1.1.2	NI		Scholastic, 212 505-6006
Mathematica	1.2.2	1.2.2	$0	Wolfram Research, 217 398-0700
Mavis Beacon Teaches Typing	1.3	1.3		Software Toolworks, 415 883-5157
Maxima	2.0.0	2.0.0		Connectix, 415 324-0727
MaxNotes	1.1	1.1		Alisa Systems, 800 992-5472
MediaGrabber	1.0	NI		RasterOps, 800 729-2656
MediaMaker	1.0	1.0		MacroMind, 415 442-0200
MediaTracks	1.0.1	1.0.1		Farallon Computing, 415 596-9000
Meeting Maker Startup	1.0	1.0		ON Technology, 617 876-5122

Legend:
NO none available • **NI** no information • **CS** contact source for version info • **32** 32-Bit Addressing problem • **VM** virtual memory problem • **UG** get from user group, info system, or dealer • **$0** free upgrade • **NN** not needed with System 7 • **S7** comes with System 7 • **FS** file sharing problem • **!!** upgrade strongly recommended • **TT** can't set TrueType sizes above 127

Product compatibility *(cont'd)*

Product	Version OK	Version Best	Notes	Source
Memory Manager INIT	NO	NO		Apple Computer, 800 776-2333
MenuFonts	4.0	4.0		Dubl-Click, 818 700-9525
Metamorphosis	1.5	2.0	$0	Altsys, 214 680-2093
Metro CD INIT	1.3.0	1.3.0		Everex Systems, 415 498-4440
MicroPhone II	3.0	4.0		Software Ventures, 800 336-6477
Microsoft BASIC	NO	NO		Microsoft, 800 426-9400
Microsoft Excel	2.2	3.0	32	Microsoft, 800 426-9400
MS Excel Dialog Editor	2.2	3.0		Microsoft, 800 426-9400
Microsoft Excel Setup	3.0	3.0		Microsoft, 800 426-9400
Microsoft File	2.0	2.0		Microsoft, 800 426-9400
MS Flight Simulator	NO	NO		Microsoft, 800 426-9400
Microsoft Word	4.0	4.0	TT	Microsoft, 800 426-9400
Microsoft Works	2.00b	2.00b	32	Microsoft, 800 426-9400
Microsoft Write	NI	NI	CS	Microsoft, 800 426-9400
MIDI Manager	2.0	2.0.1		APDA, 800 282-2732
MIDI Port Fix	1.0	NI	VM	Digidesign, 415 327-0777
MindWrite	2.1	2.1		Deltapoint, 408 648-4000
MitekSQ INIT	3.06	3.06		Mitek Systems, 800 367-5660
Mobius	4.5	4.6		MOBIUS Technologies, 415 654-0556
Mobius CDEV	1.0	1.0		MOBIUS Technologies, 415 654-0556
MockTerminal Utility	NO	NO		CE Software, 515 224-1953
ModelShop	2.0	2.0		Paracomp, 415 956-4091

Legend:
NO none available • **NI** no information • **CS** contact source for version info • **32** 32-Bit Addressing problem • **VM** virtual memory problem • **UG** get from user group, info system, or dealer • **$0** free upgrade • **NN** not needed with System 7 • **S7** comes with System 7 • **FS** file sharing problem • **!!** upgrade strongly recommended • **TT** can't set TrueType sizes above 127

Product compatibility *(cont'd)*

Product	Version OK	Version Best	Notes	Source
Modern Artist	NO	NO		Computer Friends, 503 626-2291
Money Building Blocks	1.0	1.0.2	FS	Sunburst, 800-628-8897
MORE	2.0.1	3.0	!!	Symantec, 800 441-7234
MPW	3.2	3.2		APDA, 800 282-2732
MS Mail Gateway Driver	3.0a	3.0a		Microsoft, 800 426-9400
MS Mail Server	3.0	3.0		Microsoft, 800 426-9400
MS Mail Workstation	3.0	3.0		Microsoft, 800 426-9400
MS Mail Workstation Driver	3.0	3.0		Microsoft, 800 426-9400
Mth Shop Spotlight: W&M	1.1.2	NI		Scholastic, 212 505-6006
MultiClip	3.0	NI		Oldovai, 305 665-4665
MultiDisk	1.27	1.27		Alsoft, 713 353-1510
Multi-Driver	1.3.8	1.3.8		Insignia Solutions, 415 694-7600
MultiMaster	3.0	3.0		Now Software, 503 274-2800
NameServer	2.2.3h	NI	32	CE Software, 515 224-1953
NCP	1.0	NI		DEC, 508 490-0450
NCP	2.0	2.0		Alisa Systems, 800 992-5472
Net Control	2.0.2	2.0.2		Alisa Systems, 800 992-5472
NetAtlas	1.0	1.0		Farallon Computing, 415 596-9000
NetCopy	1.0	NI		DEC, 508 490-0450
NetCopy	2.0.2	2.0.2		Alisa Systems, 800 992-5472
NetMail	2.0.2	2.0.2		Alisa Systems, 800 992-5472
NetModem	3.6	3.6	$0	Shiva, 617 252-6400

Legend:
NO none available • **NI** no information • **CS** contact source for version info • **32** 32-Bit Addressing problem • **VM** virtual memory problem • **UG** get from user group, info system, or dealer • **$0** free upgrade • **NN** not needed with System 7 • **S7** comes with System 7 • **FS** file sharing problem • **!!** upgrade strongly recommended • **TT** can't set TrueType sizes above 127

Product compatibility *(cont'd)*

Product	Version OK	Version Best	Notes	Source
NetSerial	3.6	3.6	$0	Shiva, 617 252-6400
NetSwitch	NO	NO		3 COM, 408 492-1790
Netutil	1.1.2	1.1.2		DCA, 404 740-0300
Netway 3270A	1.0	1.0		Tri-Data Systems, 408 727-3270
Netway 3270A/G	1.0	1.0		Tri-Data Systems, 408 727-3270
Netway1000	8.1	NI		Tri-Data Systems, 408 727-3270
Network DiskFit	1.5.1	2.7		SuperMac Software, 408 773-4489
NightWatch Administrator	1.03	1.03	CS	Kent◊Marsh Ltd., 713 623-4950
NightWatch Professor	NO	NO	CS	Kent◊Marsh Ltd., 713 623-4950
NightWatch ShutDown	1.03	1.03	UG	Kent◊Marsh Ltd., 713 623-4950
Nisus	3.06	3.06		Paragon Concepts, 619 481-1477
NodeHint	1.0.1	1.02		Farallon Computing, 415 596-9000
Norton Utilities	1.1	1.1		Peter Norton Computing, 800 441-7234
Notewriter II	2.69	NI		Passport Design, 415 726-0280
Notification Toolbox	1.0.3	NI	32	CE Software, 515 224-1953
NowMenus	3.0	3.0		Now Software, 503 274-2800
Number Munchers	1.0	1.0		MECC, 612 481-3569
NumberMaze Decimals & Fractions	1.0	1.0		GreatWave Software, 408 438-1990
NumberMaze	1.0	1.0		GreatWave Software, 408 438-1990
ODMS Client	3.5.0	3.5.1		Odesta, 708 498-5615
ODMS Design Station	3.5.0	3.5.1		Odesta, 708 498-5615

Legend:
NO none available • **NI** no information • **CS** contact source for version info • **32** 32-Bit Addressing problem • **VM** virtual memory problem • **UG** get from user group, info system, or dealer • **$0** free upgrade • **NN** not needed with System 7 • **S7** comes with System 7 • **FS** file sharing problem • **!!** upgrade strongly recommended • **TT** can't set TrueType sizes above 127

Product compatibility *(cont'd)*

Product	Version OK	Version Best	Notes	Source
ODMS Server	3.5.0	3.5.1		Odesta, 708 498-5615
Okyto	1.0	1.0		The FreeSoft Co., 412 846-2700
OL Startup	NI	NI		ON Technology, 617 876-5122
OmniPage	2.12	2.14		Caere, 408 395-7000
Omnis	5.0v1.2	5.0v1.21		Blythe Software, 415 571-0222
On Cue	NI	NI	CS	ICOM Simulations, 708 520-4440
ON Location	1.0.2	NI		ON Technology, 617 876-5122
OPTIMA/32	1.0.1	1.0.1		Connectix, 415 324-0727
Oracle	1.0.1	1.0.1		Oracle, 800 672-2531
ORACLE Settings	2.0.1	2.0.1		Oracle, 800 672-2531
~OracleInit	1.0.1.9	1.0.1.9		Oracle, 800 672-2531
OutNumbered!	1.0	1.0		Learning Company, 415 792-2101
PacerLink	5.3a	5.3a		Pacer Software, 508 898-3300
PackIt III	1.3	1.3		Harry Chesley, no phone
PageMaker	4.0	NI		Aldus, 206 628-2320
Pantone Color Toolkit	1.1	1.1	UG	Radius, 408 434-1010
Partner	None	None		Salient Software, 415 321-5375
PassProof	1.0	1.1		Kensington Microware Ltd., 415 572-2700
PassProof cdev	1.0	1.1		Kensington Microware Ltd., 415 572-2700
PassProof Startup	1.0	1.1		Kensington Microware Ltd., 415 572-2700

Legend:
NO none available • **NI** no information • **CS** contact source for version info • **32** 32-Bit Addressing problem • **VM** virtual memory problem • **UG** get from user group, info system, or dealer • **$0** free upgrade • **NN** not needed with System 7 • **S7** comes with System 7 • **FS** file sharing problem • **!!** upgrade strongly recommended • **TT** can't set TrueType sizes above 127

Product compatibility *(cont'd)*

Product	Version OK	Version Best	Notes	Source
PassProof User Log	1.0	1.1		Kensington Microware Ltd., 415 572-2700
PatchBay	2.0	2.0		APDA, 800 282-2732
PCSession Prep	NO	NO		Authorized Apple dealer, see local phone book
Personal Press	1.01	1.01		Silicon Beach Software, 619 695-6956
Personal*STATUS	1.0	1.0		Pharos Technologies, 800 548-8871
Personality!	1.0.0	1.0.2		Baseline Publishing, 212 254-8235
Persuasion	2.0	NI		Aldus, 206 628-2320
PhoneNET CheckNET	1.11	NI		Farallon Computing, 415 596-9000
PhoneNET Liaison	3.0.2	3.0.2	VM	Farallon Computing, 415 596-9000
PhotoMac	1.52	NI		Data Translation, 508 485-3322
PhotoRMan	1.1	1.1	CS	Pixar, 415 236-4000
PictureBase	1.1	1.2		Symmetry, 602 998-9106
PixelPaint	2.1	2.1		SuperMac Software, 408 773-4489
PixelPaint Professional	1.0.1	2.0		SuperMac Software, 408 773-4489
PLICDR	1.27	1.27		PLI, 415 657-2211
Plus Display	2.5	2.6	UG	Radius, 408 434-1012
Point of View	1.1	2.0		Scholastic, 212 505-6006
Port Control	1.2	1.2	$0	Dove Computer, 919 763-7918
Portable Profiler	1.0	1.1		Pharos Technologies, 800 548-8871
POWERicons	1.1	1.11		Magic Software, 800 342-6243

Legend:
NO none available • **NI** no information • **CS** contact source for version info • **32** 32-Bit Addressing problem • **VM** virtual memory problem • **UG** get from user group, info system, or dealer • **$0** free upgrade • **NN** not needed with System 7 • **S7** comes with System 7 • **FS** file sharing problem • **!!** upgrade strongly recommended • **TT** can't set TrueType sizes above 127

Product compatibility *(cont'd)*

Product	Version OK	Version Best	Notes	Source
PowerPoint	2.01	2.01E		Microsoft, 800 426-9400
Precision Color	2.0	2.0	UG	Radius, 408 434-1012
PrePrint	1.0	NI		Aldus, 206 628-2320
PrintLink Collection	4.0.1	4.1		GDT Softworks, 604 291-9121
Prism	1.8	1.9		Analytical Vision, 919 851-8111
Prodigy	1.0	1.5		SuperMac Technology, 408 245-0646
Profiler	2.0	3.0		Now Software, 503 274-2800
Programmer's Key	1.0	1.0	UG	P. Mercer, no phone
Public Folder	1.0.1	NI	FS	Claris, 408 727-8227
PV INITSQ	1.0	1.0		Peripherial Vision, 215 232-9800
PV Installer	3.0	3.4	VM	Peripherial Vision, 215 232-9800
PVINIT SMO	1.0	1.0		Peripherial Vision, 215 232-9800
Pyro!	4.0	4.0		Fifth Generation Systems, 800 873-4384
Q-Sheet A/V	2.01	NI	VM	Digidesign, 415 327-0777
QM Administrator	2.5	NI	CS	CE Software, 515 224-1953
QM Forms	2.2.3	NI	CS,32	CE Software, 515 224-1953
QM Menu	2.2.3	NI	CS,32	CE Software, 515 224-1953
QM Remote	2.2.3h	NI	CS	CE Software, 515 224-1953
QM Server	NI	NI	CS	CE Software, 515 224-1953
QUED-M	2.1	2.1		Paragon Concepts, 619 481-1477
Queue INIT	2.0	2.0		Palomar Software, 619 721-7000
Queue Monitor	1.04	2.0		Palomar Software, 619 721-7000

Legend:
NO none available • **NI** no information • **CS** contact source for version info • **32** 32-Bit Addressing problem • **VM** virtual memory problem • **UG** get from user group, info system, or dealer • **$0** free upgrade • **NN** not needed with System 7 • **S7** comes with System 7 • **FS** file sharing problem • **!!** upgrade strongly recommended • **TT** can't set TrueType sizes above 127

Product compatibility *(cont'd)*

Product	Version OK	Version Best	Notes	Source
QueueWatcher	1.0	2.0		Palomar Software, 619 721-7000
Quick Mount	1.0.7	NI	UG	Apple Computer, 800 776-2333
QuickCAD	2.0	2.1	UG	Radius, 408 434-1012
QuickColor	1.7	1.7	UG	Radius, 408 434-1012
QuickDex	1.4d	2.0		Casady & Greene, 408 484-9228
Quicken	1.5	1.5		Intuit, 415 322-2800
QuicKeys	NI	NI	CS	CE Software, 515 224-1953
QuicKeys 2	2.1	2.1	CS	CE Software, 515 224-1953
QuickImage24	1.0	1.5		Mass Microsystems, 408 522-1200
Quickletter	1.1.4	2.0	32	Working Software, 408 423-5696
QuickLock	2.0	2.0		Kent◊Marsh Ltd., 713 623-4950
QuickMail INIT	2.2.3	2.5	32	CE Software, 515 224-1953
QuickView Studio	1.0	2.0		E-Machines, 503 646-6699
Radius Grabber	1.3	1.3	UG	Radius, 408 434-1012
Radius Theatrics	1.3	1.3	UG	Radius, 408 434-1012
Radius/GX	1.2	1.2	UG	Radius, 408 434-1012
RadiusMath	1.4	1.5	UG	Radius, 408 434-1012
RadiusWare	1.8	2.0	UG	Radius, 408 434-1012
RasterOps Monitors	1.53	NI		RasterOps, 800 729-2656
READ-IT! O.C.R.	2.0	2.1		Oldovai, 305 665-4665
Reading Maze	1.0	1.0		GreatWave Software, 408 438-1990
Ready Set Go!	4.5a	4.5a		Letraset USA, 201 845-6100

Legend:
NO none available • **NI** no information • **CS** contact source for version info • **32** 32-Bit Addressing problem • **VM** virtual memory problem • **UG** get from user group, info system, or dealer • **$0** free upgrade • **NN** not needed with System 7 • **S7** comes with System 7 • **FS** file sharing problem • **!!** upgrade strongly recommended • **TT** can't set TrueType sizes above 127

Product compatibility *(cont'd)*

Product	Version OK	Version Best	Notes	Source
RecvInit	3.1	3.1		PLI, 415 657-2211
Redirector	5.3	5.3		Pacer Software, 508 898-3300
Redux	2.0	2.0	CS	Microseeds Publishing, 813 882-8635
Reggie	2.0	2.0		White Pine Software, 603 886-9050
RenderApp	1.1	1.1	CS	Pixar, 415 236-4000
RenderWorks	1.0	1.0		MacroMind, 415 442-0200
ResEdit	2.0b2	2.1		APDA, 800 282-2732
Retro.SCSI	1.2	1.2		Dantz Development, 415 849-0293
Retrospect	1.2	1.3		Dantz Development, 415 849-0293
RetrospectINIT	1.2	1.3		Dantz Development, 415 849-0293
RicohCart INIT	3.0	3.0		Software Architects, 206 487-0122
RicohMO INIT	3.0	3.0		Software Architects, 206 487-0122
Rival	1.1.5	1.1.5		Microseeds Publishing, 813 882-8635
!RManINIT	1.1	1.1		Pixar, 415 236-4000
RocketWare	1.2	1.2	UG	Radius, 408 434-1012
Runtime Converter	3.0.6	3.5.0		Odesta, 708 498-5615
Sade	1.3	1.3		APDA, 800 282-2732
SAM Intercept	2.0.6	NI	FS	Symantec, 800 441-7234
SAM Intercept Jr	3.0	NI	FS	Symantec, 800 441-7234
SAM Virus Clinic	2.0.6	3.0		Symantec, 800 441-7234
SampleCell Editor	1.2	NI	VM	Digidesign, 415 327-0777
Sans Faute	2.0	2.0		Acius, 408 252-4444

Legend:
NO none available • **NI** no information • **CS** contact source for version info • **32** 32-Bit Addressing problem • **VM** virtual memory problem • **UG** get from user group, info system, or dealer • **$0** free upgrade • **NN** not needed with System 7 • **S7** comes with System 7 • **FS** file sharing problem • **!!** upgrade strongly recommended • **TT** can't set TrueType sizes above 127

Product compatibility *(cont'd)*

Product	Version OK	Version Best	Notes	Source
SaveGuard	3.0	3.0		Now Software, 503 274-2800
Scanner	1.0	1.0.1		Authorized Apple dealer, see local phone book
Schedule+	1.0	1.0		Microsoft, 800 426-9400
ScreenGems	1.1	NI		Microseeds Publishing, 813 882-8635
Screen Locker	2.0	3.0		Now Software, 503 274-2800
ScreenRecorder	2.0.1	2.0.1		Farallon Computing, 415 596-9000
Screenshot	1.2.0	1.2.0		Baseline Publishing, 212 254-8235
SCSIInUse	1.0	1.0		Sam Barone, no phone
SCSIProbe	2.01	2.01		Robert Polic, no phone
SDLC Driver	3.34	3.4	32	Avatar, 508 435-3000
SDLC Gateway Server	3.33	3.4	32	Avatar, 508 435-3000
SecondSight	2.0	2.0		The FreeSoft Co., 412 846-2700
Sentinel	2.2	2.2		SuperMac Software, 408 773-4489
Server Control	3.33	3.4		Avatar, 508 435-3000
Shiva Config	3.6	3.6	$0	Shiva, 617 252-6400
Shiva Modems	3.6	3.6	$0	Shiva, 617 252-6400
Shortcut	1.5	NI		Alladin Systems, 408 685-9175
ShowPlace	NI	NI		Pixar, 415 236-4000
Silhouette	2.0.2	2.0.2		Everex Systems, 415 498-4440
Silver INIT	5.28	5.30		LACie Limited, 503 691-0771
Silverlining	5.28	5.30		LACie Limited, 503 691-0771

Legend:
NO none available • **NI** no information • **CS** contact source for version info • **32** 32-Bit Addressing problem • **VM** virtual memory problem • **UG** get from user group, info system, or dealer • **$0** free upgrade • **NN** not needed with System 7 • **S7** comes with System 7 • **FS** file sharing problem • **!!** upgrade strongly recommended • **TT** can't set TrueType sizes above 127

Product compatibility *(cont'd)*

Product	Version OK	Version Best	Notes	Source
SILVERRUN-DFD	1.1.5	2.0.5		CSA Research Ltd., 418 687-5764
SILVERRUN-ERM	1.3.2	NI		CSA Research Ltd., 418 687-5764
SILVERRUN-ERX	2.0.5	2.0.5		CSA Research Ltd., 418 687-5764
SILVERRUN-ERX->RDM	2.0.5	2.0.5		CSA Research Ltd., 418 687-5764
SILVERRUN-LDM	1.1.4	NI		CSA Research Ltd., 418 687-5764
SILVERRUN-RDM	2.0.5	2.0.5		CSA Research Ltd., 418 687-5764
SILVERRUN-SRL	1.2.2	NI		CSA Research Ltd., 418 687-5764
Silverscan	1.3	1.3		LACie Limited, 503 691-0771
SILVERUN-DFD	1.1.5	2.0.5		CSA Research Ltd., 418 687-5764
Slimeline INIT	3.0	3.4	VM	Control Concepts, 703 876-6444
SmartAlarms	3.0.7	NI		JAM, 415 442-0795
Smartcom	1.0a	1.0a		Hayes Microcomputer, 404 441-1617
Smartcom II	3.0a	3.2a		Hayes Microcomputer, 404 441-1617
SmartForm Assistant	1.1v2	1.1v2		Claris, 408 727-8227
SmartForm Designer	1.1v2	1.1v2		Claris, 408 727-8227
SmartFormat	3.0	3.4		MacLand, 800 333-3353
SmartFormat Syquest	3.0	3.4		MacLand, 800 333-3353
SmartImage	1.1.1	2.0		MacLand, 800 333-3353
SmartRestore	1.1.1	2.0		MacLand, 800 333-3353
SmartScrap & The Clipper	1.2	NI		Solutions, 802 865-9220
SnapJot	3.01	NI		Wildflower, 708 916-9360
SNA.3278	7.5.6	7.5.6		Tri-Data Systems, 408 727-3270

Legend:
NO none available • **NI** no information • **CS** contact source for version info • **32** 32-Bit Addressing problem • **VM** virtual memory problem • **UG** get from user group, info system, or dealer • **$0** free upgrade • **NN** not needed with System 7 • **S7** comes with System 7 • **FS** file sharing problem • **!!** upgrade strongly recommended • **TT** can't set TrueType sizes above 127

Product compatibility *(cont'd)*

Product	Version OK	Version Best	Notes	Source
Soft Pivot	1.2	1.2	UG	Radius, 408 434-1012
SoftPC	1.3	1.3		Insignia Solutions, 415 694-7600
SoftPC EGA/AT	1.4	1.4		Insignia Solutions, 415 694-7600
SoftTalk	NI	NI		Sitka, 800 848-8677
Sony MO INIT	3.0	3.0		Software Architects, 206 487-0122
Sound Accelerator	1.0	NI	VM	Digidesign, 415 327-0777
Sound Designer II	2.02	NI	VM	Digidesign, 415 327-0777
Sound Designer II SC	2.02	NI	VM	Digidesign, 415 327-0777
SoundEdit	2.04	2.0.4		Farallon Computing, 415 596-9000
SoundMaster	1.5	1.5		Bruce Tomlin, no phone
Speed Beep	1.0	2.0.5	UG	L Products, no phone
SpeedCard	NO	NO		SuperMac Technology, 408 245-0646
Spellswell	2.2j	2.2k	$0	Working Software, 408 423-5696
Spool	NI	NI		Sitka, 800 848-8677
StarCommand	2.1.1	2.2.1	UG	Farallon Computing, 415 596-9000
Start TOPS	NI	NI		Sitka, 800 848-8677
StartUp Manager	2.0.3	3.0		Now Software, 503 274-2800
Statistics Workshop	1.0	1.0		Sunburst, 800-628-8897
STATUS*Installer	1.0	1.0		Pharos Technologies, 800 548-8871
STATUS*Mac	1.0	1.1		Pharos Technologies, 800 548-8871
STATUS* Mac	2.0	2.0		Pharos Technologies, 800 548-8871
STATUS*Profiler	1.0	1.0		Pharos Technologies, 800 548-8871

Legend:
NO none available • **NI** no information • **CS** contact source for version info • **32** 32-Bit Addressing problem • **VM** virtual memory problem • **UG** get from user group, info system, or dealer • **$0** free upgrade • **NN** not needed with System 7 • **S7** comes with System 7 • **FS** file sharing problem • **!!** upgrade strongly recommended • **TT** can't set TrueType sizes above 127

Product compatibility *(cont'd)*

Product	Version OK	Version Best	Notes	Source
StatView II	1.03	1.03		Abacus Concepts, 415 540-1949
StatViewSE+Graphics	1.03	1.03		Abacus Concepts, 415 540-1949
Stepping Out II	2.02	NI		Berkeley Systems, 415 540-5535
StrataFlight	1.0	1.0		Strata, 801 628-9751
StrataVision 3d	1.0	1.0		Strata, 801 628-9751
Studio Vision	1.0	1.3	VM	Opcode Systems, 415 369-8131
Studio/1	1.0	NI	VM	Electronic Arts, 415 572-2787
Studio/8	2.0	NI	VM	Electronic Arts, 415 572-2787
Studio/32	1.1	NI	VM	Electronic Arts, 415 572-2787
Stuffit Classic	1.6	NI		Alladin Systems, 408 685-9175
StuffIt Deluxe	2.01	3.0		Alladin Systems, 408 685-9175
Success with Writing	2.0	NI		Scholastic, 212 505-6006
Suitcase II	1.29	1.29	$0	Fifth Generation Systems, 800 873-4384
SUM Partition INIT	2.1	2.1		Symantec, 800 441-7234
SUM Shield INIT	2.1	2.1		Symantec, 800 441-7234
SUM Tools	2.1	2.1		Symantec, 800 441-7234
Sumo INIT	3.2	4.0.3		Sumo Systems, 408 453-5744
Super Boomerang	2.0.3	3.0		Now Software, 503 274-2800
Super3D	2.1	2.5		Silicon Beach Software, 619 695-6956
SuperANOVA	1.1	1.11		Abacus Concepts, 415 540-1949
SuperCard	1.5	1.51	32	Silicon Beach Software, 619 695-6956

Legend:
NO none available • **NI** no information • **CS** contact source for version info • **32** 32-Bit Addressing problem • **VM** virtual memory problem • **UG** get from user group, info system, or dealer • **$0** free upgrade • **NN** not needed with System 7 • **S7** comes with System 7 • **FS** file sharing problem • **!!** upgrade strongly recommended • **TT** can't set TrueType sizes above 127

Product compatibility (cont'd)

Product	Version OK	Version Best	Notes	Source
SuperClock!	3.8	3.8	UG	Steve Christensen, no phone
SuperGlue	2.01	NI		Solutions, 802 865-9220
SuperLaserSpool	2.03	3.0		Fifth Generation Systems, 800 873-4384
SuperMatch INIT	1.0	1.0		SuperMac Technology, 408 245-0646
SuperPaint	2.0	2.0a		Silicon Beach Software, 619 695-6956
SuperVideo	NI	NI	CS	SuperMac Technology, 408 245-0646
SuperView	2.2	NI	CS	SuperMac Technology, 408 245-0646
SuperView II	1.02	NI	CS	SuperMac Technology, 408 245-0646
Swivel 3D	1.2	1.5		Paracomp, 415 956-4091
Syquest INIT	1.0	1.0		MacLand, 800 333-3353
SyQuest INIT	3.0	3.0		Software Architects, 206 487-0122
TAA	2.0.7	NI		CE Software, 515 224-1953
TahitiMO INIT	3.0	3.0		Software Architects, 206 487-0122
Talking Moose	3.1.0	3.1.0		Baseline Publishing, 212 254-8235
Talking Reader Rabbit	3.0	3.0		Learning Company, 415 792-2101
Tangent.INIT	2.0.1	NI		CE Software, 515 224-1953
Tape Backup 40SC	NO	NO		Authorized Apple dealer, see local phone book
Tape Disk	NO	NO		Authorized Apple dealer, see local phone book
TapeDriver	NO	NO		SuperMac Technology, 408 245-0646
TCPort	1.11	NI	VM	Novell, 800 733-9673
TeachText	1.2	7.0	S7	Apple Computer, 800 776-2333

Legend:
NO none available • **NI** no information • **CS** contact source for version info • **32** 32-Bit Addressing problem • **VM** virtual memory problem • **UG** get from user group, info system, or dealer • **$0** free upgrade • **NN** not needed with System 7 • **S7** comes with System 7 • **FS** file sharing problem • **!!** upgrade strongly recommended • **TT** can't set TrueType sizes above 127

Product compatibility *(cont'd)*

Product	Version OK	Version Best	Notes	Source
TeleBridge	3.6	3.6	$0	Shiva, 617 252-6400
Teleport	1.0	1.06		Global Village, 800 736-4821
TELNET Driver	5.3	5.3		Pacer Software, 508 898-3300
Template Printer	2.0	2.0.1	32	CE Software, 515 224-1953
Tempo II	None	None		Affinity Microsystems, 303 442-4840
Tempo II PLUS	2.1.0	2.1.0		Affinity Microsystems, 303 442-4840
The Bank Street Writer	1.0	NI		Scholastic, 212 505-6006
The Connection	1.0	1.0	UG	Kent◊Marsh Ltd., 713 623-4950
The Namer	2.1	2.1	UG	Apple Computer, 800 776-2333
The Oregon Trail	1.0	1.0		MECC, 612 481-3569
THINK C	4.0.4	NI	VM	Symantec, 800 441-7234
THINK Pascal	3.0.1p4	NI	VM	Symantec, 800 441-7234
ThinkTank	NO	NO		Symantec, 800 441-7234
Thunder 7	1.0.7	1.0.4	32	Baseline Publishing, 212 254-8235
Thunder 7 Utility	2.0.2	2.0.4		Baseline Publishing, 212 254-8235
Timbuktu	3.1.2	4.0	CS	Farallon Computing, 415 596-9000
Timbuktu/Remote	2.0.1	NI	CS	Farallon Computing, 415 596-9000
Time Drive	1.0	1.0		LACie Limited, 503 691-0771
TMON	3.0	3.0		ICOM Simulations, 708 520-4440
Token Ring Driver	3.34	3.4		Avatar, 508 435-3000
Token Ring Gateway Serv.	3.33	3.4	32	Avatar, 508 435-3000

Legend:
NO none available • **NI** no information • **CS** contact source for version info • **32** 32-Bit Addressing problem • **VM** virtual memory problem • **UG** get from user group, info system, or dealer • **$0** free upgrade • **NN** not needed with System 7 • **S7** comes with System 7 • **FS** file sharing problem • **!!** upgrade strongly recommended • **TT** can't set TrueType sizes above 127

Product compatibility *(cont'd)*

Product	Version OK	Version Best	Notes	Source
TOPS	NI	NI		Sitka, 800 848-8677
Tops	NI	NI		Sitka, 800 848-8677
Tops DA	NI	NI		Sitka, 800 848-8677
Tops InBox Server	3.0	NI		Sitka, 800 848-8677
TPD INIT	1.1	NI	CS	SuperMac Technology, 408 245-0646
tpdrvr	1.1	1.1		Caere, 408 395-7000
TrafficWatch	1.0.8	1.0.8		Farallon Computing, 415 596-9000
TraficWatch II	1.0	NI	32	Farallon Computing, 415 596-9000
Trapeze	2.1	2.1	32	Deltapoint, 408 648-4000
TRAX	2.1	NI		Passport Design, 415 726-0280
Tri-Data API	NO	NO		Tri-Data Systems, 408 727-3270
TrueForm Fill Out	1.0	NI		Adobe Systems, 415 961-0911
TrueForm Setup	1.0	NI		Adobe Systems, 415 961-0911
TrueType INIT	1.0	1.0	NN	Apple Computer, 800 776-2333
TSSNet	2.0.2	NI	CS	Alisa Systems, 800 992-5472
TurboMouse	1.0	1.0		Kensington Microware Ltd., 415 572-2700
Turbosynth	2.0	NI	VM	Digidesign, 415 327-0777
TYPIST	1.0	1.1		Caere, 408 395-7000
TYPISTINIT	1.1	1.1		Caere, 408 395-7000
UltraPaint	1.0	2.0		Deneba Software, 305 594-6965

Legend:
NO none available • **NI** no information • **CS** contact source for version info • **32** 32-Bit Addressing problem • **VM** virtual memory problem • **UG** get from user group, info system, or dealer • **$0** free upgrade • **NN** not needed with System 7 • **S7** comes with System 7 • **FS** file sharing problem • **!!** upgrade strongly recommended • **TT** can't set TrueType sizes above 127

Product compatibility *(cont'd)*

Product	Version OK	Version Best	Notes	Source
Update Collection	3.5.0	3.0.6		Odesta, 708 498-5615
V.I.P	2.51	2.51		Mainstay, 818 991-6540
Vaccine	1.0	1.0.1	32	CE Software, 515 224-1953
Vantage External	1.5.0	1.6		Baseline Publishing, 212 254-8235
Vantage Opener	1.5.0	1.6		Baseline Publishing, 212 254-8235
VDISK driver	5.3	5.3		Pacer Software, 508 898-3300
VectRMan	1.1	1.1		Pixar, 415 236-4000
Ventura Publisher	3.0.1	3.0.1		Ventura Software, 800 822-8221
VersaCAD 3D	1.0	1.0		Versacad, 617 275-1800
VersacadII	3.0	3.0		Versacad, 617 275-1800
VideoSync	1.0	1.0		APDA, 800 282-2732
Virex	1.0	1.0		Microcom Software, 919 490-1277
Virex INIT	3.5	NI	CS	Microcom Software, 919 490-1277
Virtual	3.0.0	3.0.0		Connectix, 415 324-0727
Vision	1.0	1.3	VM	Opcode Systems, 415 369-8131
VTXpress	1.0	1.0		White Pine Software, 603 886-9050
Wagon train 1848	1.0	1.0		MECC, 612 481-3569
Watch	1.6	1.6		Cayman Systems, 617 494-1999
White Knight	11.0	11.0		The FreeSoft Co., 412 846-2700
Widgets	3.0.4	NI	32	CE Software, 515 224-1953
Wingz	1.0	1.1a		Informix, 800 331-1763
Word Finder	2.1	NI		Microlytics, 716 248-9150

Legend:
NO none available • **NI** no information • **CS** contact source for version info • **32** 32-Bit Addressing problem • **VM** virtual memory problem • **UG** get from user group, info system, or dealer • **$0** free upgrade • **NN** not needed with System 7 • **S7** comes with System 7 • **FS** file sharing problem • **!!** upgrade strongly recommended • **TT** can't set TrueType sizes above 127

Product compatibility *(cont'd)*

Product	Version OK	Version Best	Notes	Source
Word Munchers	1.0	1.1		MECC, 612 481-3569
WordPerfect	1.0.5	2.0		WordPerfect, 801 225-5000
WriteNow	2.0	NI	VM	T/Maker Co., 415 962-0195
WYSIWYG Menus	2.0	3.0		Now Software, 503 274-2800
XP60+B	1.05	1.05		SuperMac Technology, 408 245-0646

Legend:
NO none available • **NI** no information • **CS** contact source for version info • **32** 32-Bit Addressing problem • **VM** virtual memory problem • **UG** get from user group, info system, or dealer • **$0** free upgrade • **NN** not needed with System 7 • **S7** comes with System 7 • **FS** file sharing problem • **!!** upgrade strongly recommended • **TT** can't set TrueType sizes above 127

Appendix B: Glossary

32-Bit Addressing A System 7 capability that increases the amount of RAM that some Macintosh models can use.

active window The frontmost (topmost) window on the desktop in which you view, create or edit a document. Only the active window has visible scroll bars and stripes in its title bar.

alert box A dialog box, often accompanied by the system alert sound, that notifies you of an error message or provides you with a warning.

Apple File Exchange A utility program for converting documents from one format to another, for example from MS-DOS to Macintosh.

Apple menu Lists the items contained in the Apple Menu Items folder, which is in the System Folder. Choosing an item from the Apple menu opens the item.

AppleEvents Systems 7's language for IAC. Programs can send messages to one another.

AppleShare Apple's file sharing software designed specifically for dedicated file sharing on larger networks. AppleShare is compatible with System 7's file sharing capabilities.

AppleTalk The networking software built into every Macintosh and most LaserWriters.

Application menu The menu located at the far right end of the menu bar that lists which programs are open and provides commands for hiding them.

application program Software developed for a specific purpose such as word processing or number crunching.

auto scroll To scroll without using the scroll bars by dragging the pointer from inside a window past the window's edge.

background copying Finder 7's ability to copy or duplicate items in the background while you work with other programs.

bitmap A graphic image composed of black dots and white dots.

bitmapped font See **fixed-size fonts.**

cache See **Disk Cache.**

cdev Acronym for Control Panel Device; see **control panels.**

checkbox A small box that you use to turn an option in a dialog box or window on or off. When an "x" appears in a checkbox, the option is on; when a checkbox is empty, the option is off.

Chooser A desk accessory that lets you choose among different devices, such as printers and shared disks on a network.

Clipboard A storage place for whatever you last cut or copied. Pasting puts a copy of the Clipboard into a document or other area you're editing.

control panels Small programs that let you change various Macintosh settings such as mouse options, date and time, and Finder window format. Control panels are located in the Control Panels folder inside the System Folder.

DAL Acronym for Data Access Language, which is built into System 7 and simplifies retrieving data from a database management system.

DBMS Acronym for database management system. A program which manages large amounts of structured data.

deselect To cancel the currently selected item, usually by selecting something else.

desktop database Information the Finder keeps in an invisible file about items on the desktop, in folders, and disks. This information includes info window comments, icon graphics, folder locations, and more.

desktop The location of the Trash icon, disk icons, and optionally other icons.

dialog box A window that contains a message, requests information from you, or allows you to change settings.

dimmed Appearing grayed out; indicates an icon, menu item, or other item is unavailable or in use.

directory dialog box The dialog box you get when you use an Open, Save As, or other disk-related command, in which you locate files and change disks from within an application program.

Disk Cache That portion of the Macintosh main memory which is set aside to store frequently used information from disk. You adjust the size of the disk cache using the Memory control panel.

drag select To select text, graphics, icons, or other items by dragging the cursor across them.

driver Software that controls the operation of a peripheral device, such as a printer or disk drive. Some drivers are represented by icons in the Preferences folder, which is inside the System Folder.

Easy Access A control panel that assists people who have difficulty typing on the keyboard or manipulating the mouse.

edition A file that contains a live copy of a publisher. When the publisher changes, the edition is updated. Subscribers contain copies of editions. See also **publisher** and **subscriber.**

EtherTalk An AppleTalk network connected by Ethernet cables.

expansion card A removable circuit board that plugs into a slot inside some Macintosh models. An expansion card enables the computer to use a special device or to perform an additional function.

file A document, program, or other named body of information stored on a disk.

file server A computer that contains files shared by other computers on a network.

Finder The part of the Macintosh system software that creates the desktop environment and keeps track of your files, folders, and disks.

fixed-size font A font made up of bitmapped characters. Each fixed-size font looks good in only one size.

Font/DA Mover A utility program for adding and removing fonts and desk accessories from older system software.

grayscale monitor A video monitor that displays shades of gray (not just black and white).

IAC An acronym for interapplication communication. IAC allows programs to communicate with each other.

INIT An old name for a system extension.

insertion point The place in a document where something will be added; marked in text by a flashing vertical line. You move the insertion point by clicking at another spot with the mouse.

kilobyte An amount of memory or disk space equal to 1024 bytes.

LocalTalk Apple's cabling system for connecting computers, printers, and other devices to make an AppleTalk network. LocalTalk uses the built-in printer ports of Macintosh computers and the LocalTalk ports of many LaserWriter printers.

megabyte An amount of memory or disk space equal to 1024 kilobytes or 1,048,576 bytes.

memory The part of the computer hardware that stores information for fastest retrieval.

mouse tracking The relationship between how fast you move the mouse and how fast the pointer moves on the screen.

MultiFinder A part of Macintosh system software older than System 7 that lets you open multiple programs simultaneously.

nested folder A folder you have put inside another folder in the process of organizing your disks.

network A collection of interconnected, individually controlled computers, printers, and other devices together with the hardware and software used to connect them. A network lets users share data and devices such as a printer.

parent folder The folder that contains a nested folder.

PhoneNet An inexpensive cabling system for connecting computers, printers, and other devices to make an AppleTalk network. Uses the built-in printer ports of Macintosh computers and the LocalTalk ports of many LaserWriter printers.

PICT A standard format for Macintosh graphics on disk and on the Clipboard.

pixel Short for picture element. The smallest dot that the computer and monitor can display.

PMMU Acronym for paged memory management unit. The part of the computer hardware that makes virtual memory possible.

PostScript font A text font designed for use with Adobe System's page description language, PostScript.

printer port The socket on the computer's back panel marked with a printer icon. You can attach a printer or a LocalTalk connector to it.

program An application program, desk accessory, or other software. Consists of a set of instructions that tell the computer how to perform a task.

publisher Part of a document, a copy of which has been saved as an edition for other documents to subscribe to. See also **subscriber** and **edition.**

RAM An acronym for random-access memory. Holds open programs, documents, and parts of the system software that have been copied from disk. The contents of RAM are lost when the computer is turned off.

ROM Acronym for read-only memory. Holds much of the system software. The contents of ROM are set permanently during manufacturing and are not lost when the computer is turned off.

shared item A folder or disk you are using from another computer on your network, or a folder or disk of yours that someone else on the network is using.

SIMM An acronym for Single Inline Memory Module. A circuit board that contains RAM chips and snaps into a socket inside the computer.

start-up disk A disk with the Finder and System files in its System Folder, which allows the computer to begin operation.

stationery A document which acts as a template and has set graphic or text elements which you created. Each time you open a stationery pad the original remains unchanged and you get a copy.

subscriber A copy of an edition that has been placed in a document and can be updated automatically when the edition is updated by its publisher. See also **publisher** and **edition.**

System extensions Software that expands the capabilities of system software. System extensions are normally stored in the Extensions folder of the System Folder.

System file A file containing fonts, sounds, keyboard layouts, language scripts, and system software. A System file must be in the System Folder for the Macintosh to start up.

System Folder The folder that contains the System file and Finder.

system software Software that supports application programs by managing memory and by communicating with input and output devices. Also known as the operating system.

TeachText A utility program on the Systems Tools disk with limited word-processing capabilities. It can also display and print graphics documents saved in the PICT format.

title bar The top part of some Macintosh windows that contains the name of the window. You drag a window by its title bar.

Token-Ring network A type of network commonly used by IBM computers.

TokenTalk Optional software included with System 7 that allows a Macintosh equipped with an extra-cost adaptor to connect to a Token-Ring network.

TrueType A font technology built into System 7 for displaying and printing text smoothly at any size and any resolution.

utility program Software that handles specialized tasks such as installing software, keeping track of appointments, blanking the screen, and so on.

virtual memory A System 7 capability that allows some Macintosh computers to increase the amount of memory available for opening programs and documents by using hard disk space as if it were RAM.

volume A disk, part of a disk, or other storage device that looks and works like a disk on the computer. Each volume has its own icon on the desktop. Hard disk and file servers are the most often referred to volumes.

Index

— A —

— D —

— E —

— F —

— N —

— T —

— U —

Protect Your Investment

2 FREE *Macworld Guide to System 7 Updates*

Protect your investment in this book! Complete and return the form below and we'll send you two valuable *Macworld Guide to System 7 Updates* absolutely free. You'll get inside information on the latest news about System 7, software and hardware compatibility and much more!

Yes! Send me 2 FREE updates to the *Macworld Guide to System 7*:

Name ______________________________

Company Name ______________________________

Address ______________________________

City/State/Zip ______________________________

When did you buy this book? ______________________________

Where did you buy this book?

Bookstore: Name ______________________________
Electronics/Software Store: Name ______________________________
Advertisement: If magazine, which? ______________________________
Mail order: Name of catalog/mail house ______________________________
Other: ______________________________

Please give us any additional comments.

____
____
____

IDG BOOKS

Fold Here

Place
Stamp
Here

IDG Books Worldwide
155 Bovet Road, Suite 730
San Mateo, CA 94402

Attn: Macworld Guide to System 7 Updates

IDG Books Worldwide Registration Card

MACWORLD
GUIDE TO SYSTEM 7

Fill this out—and hear about updates to this book & other IDG Books Worldwide products!

Name ______________________________

Company/Title ______________________________

Address ______________________________

City/State/Zip ______________________________

What is the single most important reason you bought this book? ______________________________

____

Where did you buy this book?

- ❐ Bookstore (Name ______________________________)
- ❐ Electronics/Software Store (Name ______________________________)
- ❐ Advertisement (If magazine, which?______________________________)
- ❐ Mail Order (Name of catalog/mail order house______________________________)
- ❐ Other: ______________________________

How did you hear about this book?

- ❐ Book review in: ______________
- ❐ Advertisement in: ______________
- ❐ Catalog
- ❐ Found in store
- ❐ Other: ______________

How many computer books do you purchase a year?

- ❐ 1
- ❐ 6-10
- ❐ 2-5
- ❐ More than 10

What is your favorite computer book? ______________________________

How would you rate the overall content of this book?

- ❐ Very good
- ❐ Satisfactory
- ❐ Good
- ❐ Poor

Why? ______________________________

What chapters did you find most valuable? ______________________________

What did you find least useful? ______________________________

What kind of chapter or topic would you add to future editions of this book?______________________________

____

Please give us any additional comments. ______________________________

____

❐ I liked this book! By checking this box, I give you permission to use my name and quote me in future IDG Books Worldwide promotional materials.

❐ FREE! Send me a copy of your computer book and book/disk catalog.

Thank you!

Fold Here

Place
stamp
here

IDG Books Worldwide, Inc.
155 Bovet Road
Suite 730
San Mateo, CA 94402

Attn: Reader Response

Tape or staple bottom here.